The Art and Practice of
Argumentation and Debate

The Art and Practice of Argumentation and Debate

Bill Hill
Richard W. Leeman
University of North Carolina, Charlotte

 MAYFIELD PUBLISHING COMPANY
MOUNTAIN VIEW, CALIFORNIA
LONDON • TORONTO

Library of Congress Cataloging-in-Publication Data

Hill, Bill.
    The art and practice of argumentation and debate / Bill Hill,
Richard W. Leeman.
        p.   cm.
    Includes bibliographical references and index.
    ISBN 1-55934-448-2
    1. Debates and debating.   I. Leeman, Richard W.   II. Title.
PN4181.H55   1996
808.53—dc20   96-28745
                                                                                CIP

Manufactured in the United States of America
10   9   8   7   6   5   4   3   2

Mayfield Publishing Company
1280 Villa Street
Mountain View, California 94041

Sponsoring editor, Holly J. Allen; production editor, Carla L. White; text designer, Adriane Bosworth; cover designer, Terri Wright; art manager, Jean Mailander; manufacturing manager, Randy Hurst. The text was set in Adobe Garamond by TBH Typecast, Inc. and printed on 50# Butte des Morts by Banta Company. Cover image: Images © 1996 PhotoDisc, Inc.

 This book is printed on recycled paper.

Acknowledgement

Page 16 Definition of "ethics." Copyright © 1981 by Houghton Mifflin Company. Adapted and reproduced by permission from *The American Heritage Dictionary of the English Language.*

We lovingly dedicate our work on this project to our children,
Brian and Jenna Hill and Christopher and Gregory Leeman,
who—at very early ages—have demonstrated their own unique interests in
and approaches to the subject matter of this book.

BRIEF CONTENTS

CONTENTS

Illustrations

PREFACE

Most people participate in some form of argumentation on a daily basis. Whether formal or informal, emotionally charged or dispassionate, focused on a major issue or seemingly trivial, argumentation is engaging. Many students use the debate process to develop and sharpen their argumentation skills. In so doing, they quickly find that preparing for and participating in a formal debate —whether in a classroom or in a tournament setting—can be an exceptionally exciting experience. *The Art and Practice of Argumentation and Debate* introduces students to the fundamental concepts, principles, and theories of argumentation and debate in an engaging and exciting manner.

This textbook covers topics from both theoretical and practical perspectives, offering students a well-rounded view of argumentation and debate. Basic concepts as well as more advanced applications are explained in an easy to understand manner, making this text useful to both beginning and experienced students. The book provides thorough coverage of both policy and nonpolicy applications, thus equipping students to understand and successfully practice virtually every type of argumentation and debate they might encounter. In addition, the emphasis on ethics and fundamental principles of communication makes *The Art and Practice of Argumentation and Debate* a socially and pedagogically responsible textbook. Extensive chapters on evidence and reasoning provide students with thorough treatments of those fundamental argumentative building blocks. The book provides students with a basic introduction to the key analytical models and paradigms in debate and clearly illustrate how students can use them. In addition, this text provides extensive coverage of new theoretical and practical applications in debate, including using the narrative paradigm, developing criteria, and employing the holistic model of presumption.

Chapter One provides an overview of the nature of argumentation and the debate process. Students will explore why and how argumentation occurs, the multifaceted nature of debate, and the similarities and differences between policy and nonpolicy issues in argumentation and debate. Chapter Two focuses on ethically responsible argumentation and debate. In that chapter, we examine the importance of ethics in argumentation and debate and some major frameworks for developing appropriate ethical standards. Chapters Three, Four, Five, and Six focus on the building blocks of argumentation. In these chapters, students learn to identify and analyze the key components of an argument, to select and assess evidence for arguments, to productively use various modes of reasoning in the construction of their arguments, to support their position, and to challenge their opponent's position by constructing effective refutation. The concepts and principles discussed in these four chapters are applicable to virtually every episode of argumentation a student may observe or participate in. Moreover, an understanding of the concepts in these chapters will enhance students' critical thinking and advocacy skills.

With a firm grounding in the basics of argumentation, students are ready to use their argumentative skills in a debate. Chapter Seven explores the functions and characteristics of a formal debate proposition and teaches how to properly classify and distinguish between policy and nonpolicy propositions. Chapters Eight and Nine introduce students to the logical constructs upon which every debate is based as well as the various analytical models and paradigms used to formulate and assess arguments in a debate. These chapters examine key principles such as the Burden of Proof and Presumption and their roles in a debate setting. Students will discover what issues are, how issues emerge in a debate, and how issues might be assessed according to five prominent analytical models and paradigms. In Chapter Ten we present principles and skills every debater must understand, such as the debate format and basic speaker responsibilities, as well as how to select and use evidence, how to enter refutation into a debate, and how to take notes during a debate.

Chapter Eleven explores the fundamentals of constructing an affirmative case, including developing case components, defining terms, and developing major claims to include in a case. In Chapter Twelve, students examine distinctive elements of an affirmative case for nonpolicy propositions, including how to define nonpolicy terms, develop criteria, and integrate criteria and major claims. Chapter Thirteen explores the distinctive elements of an affirmative case for a policy proposition, including how to define policy terms, how to construct a plan of action, and how to justify adoption of the plan. Chapter Fourteen prepares students to debate the negative side of either a policy or nonpolicy proposition. In that chapter, students are introduced to general principles applicable to all negative argument and to various approaches that negatives may use to refute definitions and major claims. Students also explore approaches that negative debaters use when debating a nonpolicy proposition, including value objections, countercontentions, and counterexamples, in addition to useful approaches for debating a policy proposition, including solvency arguments, disadvantages, and counterplans.

Chapter Fifteen, the final chapter in *The Art and Practice of Argumentation and Debate,* reinforces the fundamental idea that students must be effective communicators in order to be successful in either argumentation or debate. In this chapter, students are shown how basic principles of effective communication such as audience analysis, credibility, listening, and cross-examination affect argumentation and debate as well as ways to successfully apply those principles to their argumentation and debate.

We have written *The Art and Practice of Argumentation and Debate* to be a useful and useable text for students of argumentation and debate alike. Virtually every student can benefit in some important way from the material and examples discussed in this book. Argumentation and debate know no sociological, professional, or demographic bounds; they are universal and, we believe, universally engaging and exciting. We hope that the students who read this book will come to fully understand and appreciate this sentiment.

We gratefully acknowledge the support and input of those who reviewed this book: Nicholas F. Burnett, California State University, Sacramento; Sara L. Cornette, University of Richmond; Carrie Crenshaw, University of Alabama; Arthur F. Dauria, SUNY, College at Oneonta; Ann M. Gill, Colorado State University; Steven B. Hunt, Lewis and Clark College; John T. Morello, Mary Washington College; Clark D. Olson, Arizona State University; C. Thomas Preston, Jr., University of Missouri, St. Louis; Rachelle C. Prioleau, University of South Carolina, Spartanburg; Glenda J. Treadaway, Appalachian State University, and Dianna Wynn, Prince George's Community College.

ARGUMENTATION AND DEBATE:
Setting the Stage

*A*rgumentation is a fact of life. No matter who you are, where you live, what your professional goals are, what your religious beliefs are, how old you are, or how shy you are, you likely engage in argumentation on a daily basis. Consider the following scenarios.

You are a member of a group assigned to work on a class project. To complete the assignment successfully, the group must develop the procedures it will follow throughout the project. While discussing possible procedures, one group member suggests that the group assign individual members specific tasks, let those persons complete the tasks on their own, and then reassemble as a group when all individual assignments are finished. Although you understand that following such a procedure might be more efficient, you believe that having group members work together on each stage of the task will enable the group to produce a better final product. You openly state your position and the group member who suggested individual assignments challenges it. You defend your position against the attack.

During casual conversation at a family reunion, you and your cousin talk about "the state of the world," and that conversation quickly focuses on politicians in general and then specifically on candidates for president. Your cousin is an outspoken conservative whereas you hold more moderate views. Your cousin believes that the only "right" choice for president is the most conservative of the Republican candidates; you believe that the moderate Democrat would be the best choice for our nation now. Your cousin bombards you with "facts" about the conservative candidate and you take exception to your cousin's interpretation of that candidate's record and potential to be a good president.

Although different in subject matter, duration, and intensity, each interaction illustrates an argumentative encounter. Imagine those scenarios recast to portray interactions engaged in on a daily basis by your friends; teachers; local, state, and national leaders; business leaders; scientists; doctors; corporate executives; and world leaders. This exercise should help you begin to understand and appreciate the first words of the chapter: argumentation is a fact of life.

In this chapter, we discuss some of the fundamental characteristics of both argumentation and debate. First, we discuss the essential characteristics that must be present for argumentation to occur. Second, we examine four key characteristics you should understand about academic debate. Finally, we briefly explain the focus of the book and distinguish between policy and nonpolicy debate.

Argumentation: The Basics

In its most basic sense, argumentation is the communicative process in which individuals present and test reasons supporting opposing points of view. Argumentation occurs when two or more people express differing points of view, have sufficient motivation to engage in an argumentative interaction, construct reasons to support their particular point of view, and test the reasons offered by each other. In each of the above scenarios, for example, you were engaged in argumentation because you and another person held and expressed differing points of view, you were motivated to explain and support your held beliefs, and you each tested the support the other offered while simultaneously defending the point of view and reasons you offered. In this section, we discuss each of these characteristics more fully.

Differing Points of View

For argumentation to occur, individuals must hold *differing points of view*. This situation occurs when some individuals subscribe to beliefs, attitudes, or actions that appear to be incompatible with those of others. Without differing points of view, argumentation would not occur. Consider the following scenario.

> Jon and Lisa are discussing government regulation of sexually explicit material. Jon believes that any government regulation of material based solely on sexual imagery violates the First Amendment and should not be allowed. Lisa also believes that the government should not violate the First Amendment and that regulation of sexually explicit material is such a violation. Jon says to Lisa, "The federal government should not ban sexually explicit material because that is a violation of the First Amendment." Lisa replies, "Jon, I couldn't agree more—they just should not do it."

Obviously, Jon and Lisa do not hold differing points of view. In the scenario, what would probably happen next is that Jon and Lisa would acknowledge the wisdom of their shared beliefs and move their discussion to another topic. There would be no need for argumentation because there are no differing points of view to resolve. The following scenario, however, depicts quite a different situation and illustrates how differing points of view provide a foundation for argumentation to occur.

> You and a friend see a movie; afterward, you discuss its merits and discover that you have very different points of view. You believe the movie is not at all well done whereas your friend believes that the movie is exceptionally provocative and entertaining. You contemplate your friend's position but cannot understand how she could possibly reach that judgment. At the same time, your friend is frankly amazed that you do not like the movie.

It is important to understand the role that perception plays in determining the discrepancy between one person's point of view and that held by another. Differences of opinion need not be "real" for argumentation to occur; they need only to be *perceived* as real. Sometimes, people who engage in argumentation do not actually have substantive differences of opinion; they simply perceive that they do. Each person determines whether there are sufficient differences between positions to warrant argumentation, and as long an individual believes there is some substantive difference, that may be sufficient grounds for him or her to consider engaging in argumentation.

Motivation to Engage

For argumentation to occur, individuals must be motivated to engage in the interaction. Argumentation is a highly active process and individuals must make a conscious decision to participate in it. Consider a slight modification to the previous scenario.

> Jon and Lisa are discussing government regulation of sexually explicit material. Jon believes that any government regulation of material based solely on sexual imagery violates the First Amendment and should not be allowed. Lisa believes that the government should not violate the First Amendment but that sexually explicit material is not protected by the First Amendment. Jon says to Lisa, "The federal government should not ban sexually explicit material because that is a violation of the First Amendment." Lisa replies, "Jon, I disagree. The framers of the Constitution never intended to protect sexually explicit material under the First Amendment." To that statement, Jon replies: "I have heard others suggest the same thing. I guess its just

a matter of what each person wants to believe. Say, did you see the latest poll about the presidential election?"

The scenario presents the possibility for argumentation because Jon and Lisa hold different points of view. Jon believes regulation of sexually explicit material is a violation of the First Amendment whereas Lisa believes the First Amendment was never intended to protect such forms of expression. However, argumentation does not occur because Jon chooses not to attempt to resolve the difference. In fact, after the difference is revealed, Jon explicitly tries to discourage argumentation by acknowledging that the difference is simply a "matter of what each person wants to believe," and then he changes the subject. As you can see from this example, even when a clear difference of opinion exists, argumentation can occur only if the parties are motivated to resolve their differences.

People who engage in argumentation must be motivated to do so, and there can be just as many *different* motivations—or reasons—for engaging in argumentation as there are people who hold different points of view. Every person has her or his own reasons for engaging in argumentation: some may desire to determine the "truth," others may desire to "win," and others may simply enjoy the intellectual challenge of robust argumentation. There is no necessarily "right" reason for engaging in argumentation in every situation; but whatever the reason, it must be sufficiently powerful or it will not motivate the person to argue.

Constructing Reasons

Although the perception of a discrepancy between points of view and the corresponding presence of sufficient motivation make argumentation possible, argumentation is actually *initiated* when individuals *offer reasons to support their respective points of view*. We call such reasons an argument. Arguments are the substance of argumentation; they are the focus of the argumentative interaction. Arguments can be expressed in many different forms: some are complex, others are less involved, some are passionately held, others are casually accepted. Regardless of their individual stylistic differences, every argument is composed of similar components.

First, there is a claim that is the formal expression of a held belief. In the previous example, Jon expressed his held belief with the following claim: "The federal government should not ban sexually explicit material." Second, some *data* are offered to support the claim. The data constitute the reason the claim should be accepted and are thus a critical part of any argumentation. To support his claim that "The federal government should not ban sexually explicit material," Jon offered as data the observation that doing so ". . . is a violation of the First Amendment." Third, there is a stated or implied warrant that links the data to the claim. The warrant functions as a connecting bridge that enables one to move from acceptance of the data to acceptance of the claim. In the previous example, the warrant that connects Jon's data ("that is a violation of the First Amendment") to his claim ("The federal government should not ban sexually explicit material") is implied and might be expressed as follows: "the government should not be allowed to take any action that directly violates the Constitution." Consider another example.

> Tom and Sally hold very strong but incompatible beliefs about abortion. Sally believes that abortion under any circumstance other than rape is wrong while Tom believes strongly in pro choice. Sally asserts to Tom: "Abortion is just like murder"; Tom asserts to Sally: "Abortion is not murder." To Tom, Sally responds even more forcefully than before: "I told you abortion is nothing more than murder." To which Tom aggressively responds, "It is not murder."

In this example, Tom and Sally are engaged in an intense interaction and each is offering a claim with which the other disagrees. However, neither is offering reasons—data or warrants—to support their claim. They are not, therefore, engaged in argumentation.

Arguments might also contain other components such as backing, qualifiers, and rebuttal, and we discuss each of those components in Chapter 3. In that chapter, we also discuss more fully the primary components—claim, data, and warrant—of an argument. We introduced those basic components here because it is important for you to understand from the outset that an argument consists of more than simple contradiction of claims. In addition, it is also necessary for you to begin to understand the relationship between arguments and argumentation. Argumentation is the process: it describes an interaction between two or more people. Arguments, on the other hand, are the claims and reasons that are presented and tested in the process.

Testing Arguments

Argumentation proceeds when individuals *test the arguments*. Whereas arguments are the focal point of argumentation, testing arguments is the purpose of the process. When individuals test arguments, they analyze the soundness and acceptability of the various components of the argument. They may question the data, the warrant connecting the data to the claim, the claim itself, or any of the other possible components. Ultimately, the purpose of testing the various components of any argument is to determine whether that argument provides sufficient reason to accept it. In Chapters 4 and 5 we discuss ways to test arguments and reasoning.

When students first enroll in a course in argumentation, it is common to hear some proudly proclaim that they are "good arguers." No doubt many probably are! However, the experiences most have in mind when they talk about "being good arguers" are not actually examples of argumentation. Consider the following example.

> Sally and Tom continue their discussion of abortion and Sally asserts that "abortion is murder because the fetus is a human being." To that claim, Tom responds, "Women should make their own decisions because they are fully responsible human beings." Sally, becoming even more agitated retorts, "The fetus is a human being, so abortion must be murder." Tom responds with equal fervor that "women should be allowed to make their own decisions."

Sound familiar? It should, because such situations are common. The scenario began with the possibility for argumentation because Tom and Sally held different and apparently incompatible points of view. However, the prospect for argumentation broke down when Sally and Tom expressed those points of view. Each offered a claim and a reason to support the claim; however, neither seriously tested the reasons offered by the other. In short, they neither analyzed the opposing point of view nor actually defended their own point of view.

Both Sally and Tom asserted their point of view, but then the interaction degenerated into little more than repetition of their claims. What neither Sally nor Tom did was attempt to **clash** with the other. Clash is an indispensable part of testing reasons, and unless advocates analyze the reasons presented to support claims, they are not engaged in argumentation. Rather, when advocates simply assert and reassert claims without testing reasons, they are actually engaged in a quarrel.

As you can tell, testing arguments is a critical function of argumentation. It is this very function that defines the primary purpose of the process and helps distinguish argumentation from other types of communicative interactions. To be successful in argumentation, one must be able to evaluate the soundness of an argument.

The Debate Process

Most people have seen or even participated in some form of debate. Debates occur in many different contexts. Candidates for public office debate about the critical issues of the campaign, leaders of groups debate about social issues with those who oppose their point of view, scholars debate about the meaning and implications of research findings, legislators debate about public policy actions, and corporate executives debate about the goals of their organization. Although the nature of the debate varies considerably from setting to setting, the debates that occur within all these contexts share a common purpose: they are argumentative interactions designed to allow competing advocates to present and test arguments.

Many students study the debate process in college and university courses, and many colleges and universities sponsor competitive debate teams. Debates that occur in the academic setting, such as in the classroom or at the competitive tournament, are among the most formal types of argumentation a student will experience. Such debates typically follow a structured format, are governed by explicit and implicit codes of conduct, and usually produce a declared "winner."

For students to prepare to debate effectively, they must first understand the basic characteristics of the debate process. In this section, we discuss each of four critical characteristics of academic debate. Students should reflect on these characteristics when they are trying to understand how to fulfill the role of debater-advocate. We begin our discussion by explaining how students can use academic debate to develop their argumentation skills.

Debate as an Educational Activity

Much debate occurs in academic settings, and it is in the academy that students such as you have the opportunity to develop and refine their debate skills. Academic debate provides an excellent forum that students can use to learn and refine their argumentation skills. Many scholars and educators term academic debate a *laboratory* for testing and developing approaches to argumentation. Students who participate in academic debate, whether in the classroom or on the tournament circuit, are expected to meet rigorous standards of argumentation. Precisely because of the rigor of the debate process, students who participate in academic debate have the opportunity to develop four important types of skills.

First, students can develop *analytical skills* as they learn to identify the components of an argument, critically assess the strength of evidence, and pinpoint assumptions and weaknesses in an opponent's position. Developing analytical skills is critical for any student who wants to be successful in either academic debate or argumentation outside the debate setting. We focus on these types of skills in Chapters 3, 4, 5, and 6 when we discuss components of argument, evidence, reasoning, and refutation.

Second, students can develop *compositional skills* as they learn how to construct claims, formulate a position from a series of claims, or develop an attack against an opponent's argument. Successful debaters and successful students of argumentation must know how to construct their position in the clearest, most strategically sound manner possible. Much of the force of an argument can be eroded if it is poorly constructed. We address these types of skills in Chapters 11, 12, 13, and 14 in which we explain how to construct and defend affirmative and negative positions.

Third, students can also develop a variety of *interactional skills* as they learn to work with others, ask and answer questions, formulate arguments for a variety of audiences, and directly engage their opponents in argumentation. Successful debaters as well as successful students of argumentation must not only know the fundamentals of analysis and composition but must also understand the psychology of interacting directly with others. Moreover, they must learn how to interact with others in ethically responsible ways. We discuss how to be an ethically responsible advocate in Chapter 2. We explore other interactional aspects of argumentation and debate in Chapter 15 when we discuss approaches to cross-examination and how to improve listening skills, and when we discuss how to adapt arguments to different types of audiences.

Finally, students can develop *process skills* as they learn to analyze, compose, and interact in ways that are basic to the core assumptions of the process, ways that reflect the student's understanding of the burdens, responsibilities, and procedural expectations imposed on debaters. We discuss these burdens and responsibilities fully in Chapter 8, where we describe and explain the fundamental logical constructs of the debate process, and in Chapter 9, where we explain and illustrate the issues and analytical models that undergird the decision-making process in academic debate. In Chapter 10, we discuss the procedural expectations of the debate process, including the format, speaking order, time limits, and note-taking requirements.

One issue that deserves special attention is the relationship between academic debate as an *educational* activity and academic debate as a *competitive* activity. Academic debate, whether in a classroom or tournament setting, is by nature also a competitive activity. In most academic debates there will be a declared "winner." On the tournament circuit, national rankings are determined by "wins." Even in the classroom setting, opponents vie against one another, each hoping to best the other's arguments. Some observers argue that because it motivates students to perform, competition enhances attainment of educational goals. Others have claimed—as early as 1915—that the competitive nature of academic debate produces a win-at-any-cost mentality that mitigates against the educational value of the activity.

Whether competition will have a positive or negative effect on the educational value of academic debate will depend largely on the motivations of the individual debaters. In a study that assessed college debater's motivations for being involved in academic tournament debate, Hill found that educational needs, such as improving communication skills, analytical skills, and research skills, were more powerful motivators than competition for many students who participate in academic debate (77–88). Hill's findings were largely confirmed in a more recent study by Stephen Wood and Pamela A. Rowland-Morin. They, too, found that educational needs seem to exert more influence than a sense of competitiveness on students' choice to participate in academic debate. Their conclusion is important.

> The tension between winning and pedagogy in academic debate identified in 1915 continues to exist. The results of this study, however, reinforce the role of debate in the speech communication field and as a fundamental part of the larger educational mission of colleges and universities. Administrators, speech colleagues, coaches and students should be aware that students who debate attribute their motivation for debating first and foremost to educational objectives. (Wood and Rowland-Morin 95).

Debaters at all levels—in the classroom and on the tournament circuit—must keep a clear perspective on the role of competition in the debate process. All debate, like all argumentation, is competitive to some degree. However, competition is not and should not be the ultimate outcome of the debate process. The purpose of participating in academic debate is to learn; it is not simply to compete. "Winning" in academic debate means much more than being declared the victor in a particular debate or amassing the most sweepstakes points in the national rankings. Ultimately, the true winners in academic debate are those students who develop and refine their skills in argumentation.

Debate as a Communicative Interaction

Debate is a communicative interaction. Regardless of the context in which it occurs, every human communicative encounter has a **source, receiver,** and **message.** When a debater advances a claim or series of claims about either the proposition or some claim or series of claims her opponent has advanced, she is the primary source in the interaction and the claim she advances is the message. The debater, judge, or auditor who processes the message is the receiver in the interaction. Thus, you should remember that debaters are primarily sources and receivers of messages and that a debate or argumentative encounter is a communicative interaction.

To be meaningful, every communicative interaction needs to be as clear as possible. To enhance the quality of the interaction, debaters need to make certain their messages are clearly formulated. Their claims should be precisely worded and complete. Evidence should be carefully selected, presented properly, and well explained. Speeches should be appropriately organized and debaters should use organizational markers such as signposts and transitions in their speeches. Words should be selected for their precision and clarity. Where necessary, thorough explanations should be provided to clarify claims, evidence, and warrants. Refutation should be applied directly to your opponent's arguments, and the significance of your responses should be explained.

In addition to having a clearly formulated message, debaters must make certain their message is presented effectively. Delivery is important in any communicative interaction, and this is true of debate. Although some argue that debate is not primarily designed to promote development of delivery skills, it is nonsensical to assume that delivery does not affect a debate interaction. Claims and evidence are surely the substance of the debate, but unless they are presented so they can be understood, little productive argument can take place. Remember one cardinal principle of the debate process: the strength of your arguments and refutation will be directly related to how well they are understood by the receivers.

Debaters should attempt to develop and exhibit suitable communicative behaviors—behaviors that treat presentation of the message as an important contribution to the meaningfulness of the entire interaction. All speeches should be presented at a comprehensible rate of speed, and where appropriate, should incorporate internal summaries, restatement, or repetition. Debaters must remember that their opponents as well as the judge need to be able both to understand and to record their message in order for the communicative interaction to be productive. Receivers must attempt to understand the message, but sources have the ultimate responsibility of presenting the message in understandable ways.

Debate as a Prepared Argument

Debaters should view debate as a prepared argument. Although they do engage in a significant amount of spontaneous argumentation during a debate, much of the substance of the debate—the affirmative **case,** negative claims, **disadvantages**—are or can be prepared prior to the interaction. Prepared arguments should be more complete, carefully developed, and convincing than arguments constructed spontaneously. Arguments designed to refute or counter claims presented by an opponent are likely to be more powerful and compelling if they have been carefully prepared rather than constructed spontaneously.

This does not mean that debaters cannot construct powerful and compelling arguments spontaneously; certainly, they do, and training in debate helps promote the development of that very important skill. We believe, however, that as a general rule, the more time a debater has to formulate an argument, the clearer and more complete that argument is likely to be.

Viewing debate as a prepared argumentative encounter imposes on all debaters the responsibility to anticipate the arguments their opponent will present. Debaters caught off guard by their opponent's arguments will have a difficult time responding to those arguments. To defend their case effectively, debaters must attempt to anticipate possible responses their opponents might make, and they should develop a complete set of alternative responses to those arguments. Debaters should carefully assess the various arguments they construct and ascertain how their opponent will probably respond to those arguments.

We are not suggesting that debaters should rely exclusively on prepared arguments for their debates. Certainly, debaters must adapt the arguments they have prepared to the context and applications of the specific debate. However, debaters will be in a better position to present well-developed arguments and the entire argumentative level of the debate will be enhanced if debaters prepare portions of their arguments ahead of time by trying to anticipate what their opponents might argue.

Debate as a Team Activity

Debaters are members of a team. Many debates follow a team format—the debate takes place between two opposing teams. Students learn very quickly that being a member of a debate team requires a high degree of interaction with and dependence on another person. Debate partners must be exactly that—they must share the responsibilities and decision making with another person. Neither member of the team can or should attempt to "carry" the other. Both debaters must make a direct and significant contribution to the team effort, and both must understand that what each does individually will have a direct and significant effect on the overall performance of the team.

Some debates follow a Lincoln–Douglas format, which pits one debater against another. Even when following this format, every debater is still part of a team. Every person in your class or on your debate team shares a common bond: you are all students of argumentation. You work together directly and indirectly to develop your analytical, compositional, interactional, and process skills. You have a responsibility to help each other learn by being as good a role model as possible. Even when competing against another person, you and the other person are still a team trying to learn. How each of you models your argumentation skills will directly affect what the other learns.

There are some very important practical implications if you are to function well as a team. Partners must be clear in how they will delegate responsibilities, and they should assume equal responsibility in all phases of preparation including research, case development, and strategy planning. Prior to the debate, partners need to provide constructive feedback to help the other improve her or his performance, and both debaters must develop the ability to process constructive feedback in a productive manner. During a debate, both team members must be involved in the decision-making process about which arguments and approaches to use. Moreover, during the debate, team members must be prepared and willing to help their partner, and they must keep an open line of communication with their partner without attempting to "direct" or "supervise" the partner's performance. The only way debaters can be successful and truly enjoy the debate experience is to work together cooperatively with their partners.

Policy and Nonpolicy Debate

All academic debate begins with a debate proposition—a formally stated claim that identifies both the general subject matter for the debate and the general responsibilities of the debaters. For example, the proposition, "Resolved: that the United States should significantly increase the development of the earth's ocean resources," indicates that ocean resource policy is the general subject for the debate. At the same time, it establishes the broad claim that is to be tested during the debate: "the United States should/should not significantly increase development of the earth's ocean resources."

We mention propositions now because we use examples of both **policy** and **nonpolicy** debate propositions in this book. A policy debate is one that focuses on a formal decision to implement a specified policy. For example, the proposition, "Resolved: that the United States should adopt a policy to substantially reduce consumption of marine resources," is a policy proposition. The proposition in the previous paragraph is also a policy proposition.

A nonpolicy proposition requires confirmation of a judgment that something is or is not the case, or confirmation of an evaluation about a designated entity. Theorists typically consider this type as being a proposition of either fact or value. The proposition, "Resolved: that the United States has developed a comprehensive program to control energy development," is an example of a nonpolicy proposition of fact; the proposition, "Resolved: that implementing a comprehensive program to control energy development in the United States would be desirable," is an example of a nonpolicy proposition of value. We discuss the components, characteristics, and functions of policy and nonpolicy propositions fully in Chapter 7.

Although we distinguish between policy and nonpolicy debate propositions, it is important to acknowledge that policy and nonpolicy *issues* are often intimately related. In most circumstances, addressing one will invariably call into question the other. A policy issue cannot be resolved without resolution first of issues of fact and value; similarly, when an issue of value is resolved, policy implications will also emerge. That policy and nonpolicy issues are related, however, does not mean that policy and nonpolicy propositions are debated in the same way.

We make the distinction between policy and nonpolicy propositions because the type of proposition can greatly affect the nature of the debate. The primary way the type of proposition affects the debate process is by defining the stock issues and analytical models that can be used in the debate. **Stock issues,** a term with which you should become very familiar, refers to the recurring issues that must be addressed if the debaters are to reach a complete and defensible conclusion about a given debate proposition. Stock issues operationally define what a debater has to prove to "win" a debate. They also provide a framework debaters can use to research and construct their case.

Policy propositions have been used in academic debate for many years and theorists have well-developed stock issues and analytical models to describe how policy propositions can and should be debated. Conversely, nonpolicy propositions have not been used in academic debate as long as policy propositions, and the issues and analytical models used in debates about nonpolicy propositions are less clearly defined. There are, however, clear differences in the issues and models debaters will use when debating policy propositions and when debating nonpolicy propositions. We discuss the issues and analytical models for both policy and nonpolicy propositions in Chapter 9.

We believe that debaters need to know how to debate both policy and non-policy propositions. If academic debate is to be a truly meaningful laboratory for developing and refining argumentation skills, students should learn skills they can apply in all types of argumentative and debate settings. Argumentation and debate in the political, corporate, and social arenas focus on both policy and nonpolicy propositions. As our examples at the beginning of this chapter illustrated, advocates across all types of settings engage in argumentation and debate about a variety of policy and nonpolicy questions. As a student of argumentation and debate, you should understand how to debate different types of propositions effectively.

Conclusion

Argumentation and debate are pervasive activities. Individuals engage in argumentation on a daily basis about any number of issues, and many people have seen or participated in some sort of formal or informal debate. For argumentation to occur, individuals must hold seemingly different points of view, be motivated to engage in discussion of those differences, construct reasons to support their point of view, and test the reasons presented by the other person. Academic debate is a fertile training laboratory for students of argumentation. The debate process, however, should always be viewed as an educational activity, a communicative interaction, as a prepared argument, and as a team activity. When participating in academic debate, students may be assigned to debate a policy or a nonpolicy proposition. Because nonpolicy propositions have policy implications, and policy propositions demand evaluations of facts and values, all debaters should learn how to debate both kinds of propositions.

Selected Bibliography

Hill, Bill. "Intercollegiate Debate: Why Do Students Bother?" *The Southern Speech Communication Journal* 48 (1982): 77–88.

Jones, Kevin T. "Cerebral Gymnastics 101: Why Do Debaters Debate?" *CEDA Year Book* 15 (1994): 65–75.

Rowland, Robert. "The Practical Pedagogical Function of Academic Debate." *Contemporary Argumentation and Debate* 16 (1995): 98–108.

Terris, Walter. "The Classification of Argumentative Propositions." *Readings in Argumentation*. Ed. Jerry Anderson and Paul Dovre. New York: Harper & Row, 1963.

Wood, Stephen C., and Pamela A. Rowland-Morin, "Motivational Tension: Winning vs. Pedagogy in Academic Debate." *National Forensic Journal* 7 (1989) 81–98.

Discussion Questions

1. How might one's motivation affect the intensity of argumentation?
2. How might argumentation be used to help individuals reconcile different perspectives about the compatibility of their beliefs?
3. How might improving your skills in argumentation and debate help you achieve success in your chosen profession?

ETHICS

*C*onsider the following scenarios. Scenario 1: a debater knowingly alters a quotation in order to make it a much stronger endorsement of his position than it had been originally. Scenario 2: a debater intentionally humiliates her opponent, knowing that he is relatively inexperienced and will become distracted and confused by the attacks. Scenario 3: in cross-examination, a debater admits that her opponent's argument has some merit, but argues that her refutation outweighs the merits of her opponent's position.

As we described each of these situations, you probably made an ethical judgment about the debater's behavior. Even though you might have tried to resist doing so—knowing from the title that our focus in this chapter is on ethics—you probably found it impossible to keep from saying "that behavior would be wrong," "that behavior was admirable," or "that wouldn't have been an acceptable way of doing it for me." The point we hope to have made with these descriptions is simple: the act of making ethical judgments is virtually inseparable from the use of communication generally and, more specifically, from the act of arguing and debating. As experienced communicators (which, as human beings, we all are), we routinely evaluate the ethics of our own communication and that of others. When argumentation is involved—a communicative act designed to *persuade* others—ethical judgments are even harder to avoid.

Ethical judgments are integrally related not only to our acts of communication and argumentation, however. They are also, and as we shall argue in this chapter should be, important considerations for any debater. In this chapter, we look first at the relationship between debate and ethics. We then briefly examine several possible approaches for developing a perspective about communication ethics. Finally, we develop two specific approaches for evaluating ethical argumentation, both of which we endorse. Our main purpose in this chapter, however, is to alert you to the kinds of ethical issues that potentially reside in any debating situation and to help you in your development of an intelligent and informed ethic of debate.

Debate and Ethics

As noted in our opening discussion, the relationship between ethics and communication generally—and by implication between ethics and argumentation/debate specifically—is an integral one. Ethics can be defined as the "study of the general nature of morals and of the specific moral choices to be made by the individual in his [or her] relationship with others" ("Ethics" 450). Because debate is a particular kind of "relationship with others"—a relationship in which one individual attempts to change the beliefs or actions of another—the question of ethics is central to it. As we attempt to persuade another person, whether an opponent or a judge, which choices will be the moral ones? Which choices will not be moral?

Within academic debate, there are several broad areas of ethical concerns. A first category of concern involves *evidentiary issues*. For example, evidence must always be used "out of context," as no debate can be stopped long enough for the judge and debaters to read entire articles or books; but when is evidence being taken "out of context" *unethically?* In *editing* the evidence for use in a debate, two concerns typically arise. First, is the evidence true to its context or has the act of editing changed the meaning of the quotation? Second, is the quotation accurate or have words been added or deleted so as to alter the original meaning of the quotation?

Ethical concerns can also arise in the *reporting* of the evidence. Has the source and date of the evidence been accurately reported? Has the quotation itself been accurately read? Has the evidence been read or reported in ways that make it accessible to the opponents and the judge? Has it been read clearly enough to be understood? Do the listeners know where the quoted evidence ends and the debater's opinion begins? Has the evidence been overclaimed, that is, has the debater drawn a stronger conclusion than the evidence warrants? Evidentiary questions revolve around two major concerns: (1) *comprehension,* whether the opponents and the judge have heard the evidence accurately or *comprehended* the meaning of evidence, and (2) *accuracy,* whether the evidence accurately reflects the meaning intended in the original.

A second broad area of concern in any debate involves *argumentative issues.* As with evidence, the two major argumentative issues are *comprehension* and *accuracy.* Comprehension questions that may arise in a debate include these: Has the debater tried to make the meaning of the argument clear? Has the meaning been purposely obscured so the arguer can gain argumentative advantage? Is it ethical to be purposely ambiguous, waiting to hear the opponent's response before taking a definitive position of one's own? Is it ethical to so muddy an argument that disentangling the meaning consumes an inordinate amount of the opponent's time? Is it ethical to allow an opponent to misinterpret an argument throughout the constructive speeches, waiting until rebuttals to clarify it —too late to allow the opponent to formulate any relevant refutation?

Accuracy issues raise another set of questions: Is the debater accurate in describing his or her own argument and the opponent's arguments? Has there been intentional misstatement about one's own arguments or the opponent's? Has the debater taken advantage of the oral nature of debate to mislead the opponent or the judge regarding an earlier argument?

A third area of ethical concern may be termed *interpersonal.* In the course of a debate, a relationship evolves between opposing debaters and between the debater and the judge. What kind of a relationship is it? How does the process of debate enhance or retard that relationship? Because we are "attacking" our opponent's ideas, it is easy for the communication within a debate to have a negative effect on the relationship between ourselves and our opponent. Are there ways of preventing that from happening? Should we even try to prevent it from happening? Should we be ethically concerned about whether we have developed as full and meaningful a relationship as possible between ourselves and our opponent? Between ourselves and our judge?

An additional area of interpersonal ethics enters when we debate as a two-person team. What constitutes ethical behavior for us vis-à-vis our partner? Debate partnerships are typically intense interpersonal relationships. Even in a classroom setting, the need to research, prepare, and argue together can either create strong bonds between partners or test the best of friendships. Our communication within that relationship has tremendous potential to foster or inhibit our partner's growth as a person and/or as a debater. Also, how well we assume our individual responsibilities within the team has the potential to affect our debate partner in beneficial or detrimental ways. In our relationships with the judge, our opponents, and our partner, then, interpersonal issues that have ethical dimensions will invariably arise.

A fourth area concerns *competitive issues.* Academic debate is, in many senses, a game. Like any game, it has formal and informal rules that govern the sportsmanship and sportswomanship of the participants. As with many other sports and game activities, a major ethical concern is the degree to which we must abide by or fulfill the rules. Some hold that certain rules may be bent in the pursuit of winning; others argue for the strictest interpretation of those rules.

Part of the problem, of course, arises from the model of professional sports. There, winning is often paramount and breaking rules is "acceptable" as long as the umpire or referee doesn't catch you. Gaylord Perry is a baseball legend because of his use of the illegal spitball. Defensive linemen are expected to step on an opponent's hands or gouge his eyes while buried in the pile-up after a tackle. Even high school and college basketball has become increasingly physical, with many elbows thrown and jabbed the closer one gets to the basket. Two of the most famous sports sayings in American history are Leo Durocher's "Nice guys finish last" and Vince Lombardi's "Winning isn't everything; it's the only thing." With sports as our model for competition, it's small wonder that a similar emphasis on winning often arises in academic debate. And with that emphasis comes a host of ethical questions and concerns.

Another reason that debate's competitive nature provides some important ethical questions is that many of the "rules" are informal. That is, the "rule book" for debate—even for the most rigorously policed organizations—is a short one. Among the questions not usually answered in any formal code of rules are these: What language is appropriate in a debate round? Are some arguments so divorced from reality that, ethically, they should not be used? Can my teammate help me answer a question in cross-examination? Is it permissible for me to be a little noisy in my preparations so that I disrupt my opponent's train of thought while he or she is speaking? Can I make little "asides"—comments before or during the round that may "psych out" my opponent—to give myself a competitive edge?

Ethical questions about how to compete fairly are important. In fact, the element of competition is what gives rise to the ethical questions generated in all four areas of concern. Without the desire to win, there is no reason to misrepresent one's evidence or arguments, or to treat one's opponent so badly that it poisons relations between you. It is, however, useful to think of our ethical questions as falling into four categories: Have I used my evidence ethically? Have I used my arguments ethically? Have I developed an ethical relationship with my judge, my opponent, and my partner? Have I played the game ethically? In the next section, we outline several approaches for answering those questions.

Developing a Code of Ethics

In developing a code of ethic for communication, there are three basic approaches one can take. First, one can have an existing code of ethics, one external to the study of communication, which can then be applied to the particular act of communication (in this case, debate). Second, in a formalized arena of discourse—such as academic debate—a code of ethics specifically developed by the practitioners of that discourse can be adopted. Third, individuals can develop their own philosophies of ethics that they can then use to evaluate specific situations and reach conclusions about what constitutes ethical behavior in that situation.

Obviously, most generalized ethical codes can have some important things to say about what is "proper" and what is "improper" in the debate situation. The Mosaic command, "Thou shalt not lie," for example, is directly applicable to the questions of accuracy raised above. The Golden Rule of treating others as you would like to be treated has a bearing on all four of the areas cited but is especially relevant to interpersonal issues.

For several reasons, we will not detail the generalized codes of ethics available or the application of them to debate. For one, you probably have a pretty well-developed general code of ethics already in place. If so, you should be able, as you study argumentation and debate, to see the ways in which that code applies to specific situations. Also, the discussion of such generalized codes is best left to other forums, such as philosophy, religion, or ethics classes. A proper discussion of ethics codes would be too time-consuming for what we can attempt here.

There are, however, specialized codes of ethical behavior specifically designed for certain recurring, structured kinds of discourse. These are often found in professional settings, such as the National Association of Broadcasters' Television Code, first adopted in the 1950s. Specialized codes of behavior have also been developed for debate; they have been frequently discussed and sometimes adopted by the various debate organizations. An example of one such code is the American Forensic Association's (AFA) "Code of Ethics." Although much of this code concerns the administration of tournaments and the determination of who qualifies as a "competitor," it includes some ethical commandments for the individual debater to follow. For example, the AFA Code requires that "Forensics competitors shall not use fabricated or distorted evidence," which it defines as material that misrepresents

the actual or implied content of factual or opinion evidence. Distorted evidence is so defined without reference to whether or not the debater or speaker using it was the person responsible for distorting it. Distortions shall be judged by comparing the challenged evidence against the material as it appears in the original source. Distortion[s] include, but are not limited to:
1. quoting out of context.
2. misinterpreting the evidence so as to alter its meaning.
3. omitting salient information from quotations or paraphrases. . . .
4. adding words to a quotation which were not present in the original source of the evidence without identifying such an addition.

> 5. failure to provide complete documentation of the evidence (name of the author(s), source of publication, full date, page numbers and author(s) credentials where available in the original) when challenged. . . . (American Forensic Association 12)

The AFA Code is representative of both the advantages and disadvantages of using a specific code, or legal model, of ethics. The problem is that it is easy to construct situations that violate the code yet still seem ethical or that abide by the code yet still seem unethical. A couple of examples can illustrate this point.

Suppose we were quoting Jonathan Crane's study of horror films, *Terror and Everyday Life,* and added the bracketed words without indicating that they were additions:

> Anyone with even the slightest familiarity with today's horror films knows that the most popular monsters at [the] present [time] are those who never die and star in multiple sequels. Sequels are made not only because the audience for a horror film is preconstituted, the product presold; they are also made because that which returns again and again provides the audience with the greatest pleasure. (10)

The addition of "the" and "time" would not seem to constitute a major or even minor ethical breach of conduct, yet they violate rule #4 of the code. Anyone who failed to bracket the added material would probably be deemed foolish—for leaving himself or herself open to charges of unethical behavior—but would not seriously be termed *unethical.*

Or consider the case in which a person adds words that provide meaningful and important context for a quotation but fails to identify the added words. Again, from Crane's work:

> [According to negative critics,] [h]orror wakes us to the fact that, beyond all the good objects with which a subject seeks to identify, there is a vacuum. This vacuum is expressed in the unwavering commitment the masses have made to the production of horror. (33)

In this instance, the added phrase lets us know that Crane is characterizing the position held by a certain group of critics. Without this phrase, the quotation would violate rule #1 above: it would lead the reader to believe this position were Crane's own. If, however, the brackets were left out of the added material, it would violate rule #4. Even so, most observers would consider the perpetrator of the deleted brackets foolish but not unethical.

Finally, consider a scenario in which a debater, arguing in support of majoring in the humanities and social sciences, read the following quotation from William Bennett: "In a survey done at ATT it was found that, in the top four managerial levels, 43% had majored in the humanities and social sciences, while 32% had been business majors and only 23% were engineers." Suppose that in the next speech, it became clear that the debater's opponent had interpreted these data to include graduate degrees as well as undergraduate degrees. Nothing the first debater said had misled the opponent; in fact, such misinterpretations are common. The second debater's assumption that the data included graduate degrees (1) is not warranted by the quotation, (2) is probably wrong— one would suspect that many of the humanities, social science, and engineering majors had gone on for M.B.A.s (Master of *Business* Administration degrees)— and (3) is advantageous to the first debater as it makes the data broader than they actually are.

What if the first debater—the original presenter of the quotation—does nothing to clarify her opponent's misinterpretation? Technically, no rule of the AFA Code has been violated. The debater has not misinterpreted the data herself; she has simply allowed a misinterpretation to occur. Is this unethical? The win-at-all-cost approach would say no, but many debate coaches, debaters, and observers would say yes. They would argue that just as causing a misperception is unethical, so too is willfully allowing one to develop uncorrected.

Here, then, is the problem with adopting a formalized code of ethics: it is always possible for the spirit of the law to conflict with the letter of the law. There is, however, a third option for an ethical guide for debate: to develop a *philosophy* of what is ethical and then apply that philosophy to evaluating the ethics of our behavior. Specifically, we focus here on developing a communication-centered ethical approach that can then be applied to the situation of academic debate.

Most communication-centered approaches are **teleological** in nature. A teleological approach assumes (1) that there is a *telos*—an end or a purpose— contained within the activity itself; (2) that this telos can never be fully achieved but is instead something to be striven for; and (3) that ethical behavior helps move us toward the telos whereas unethical behavior prevents or retards our progress toward achieving the telos.

The telos of communication is generally conceptualized as building relationships. After all, inherent within any act of communication is the establishment of some kind of a "relationship"—economic, social, professional, romantic, familial, hostile, and so on. Had we no desire to *relate* to other people there would be no need for communication whatsoever. Communication is a vehicle, indeed, the prime vehicle, for the attainment of *community* with others.

It is not coincidental that the words community, communal, commune, communion, and communication all share the same Latin root word: *communis,* meaning "common" or "to share."

Of course, *total* community with one's fellow human beings is impossible. Complete and total communication of one's thoughts, or the establishment of a fully harmonic community, is possible only in science fiction stories. It is possible, however, to have *more* or *less* communication and to have *better* or *worse* communication, and as a result, to achieve a *greater* or *lesser* degree of community. The achievement of community, or the complete development of relationships among us all, is the *telos* of communication, impossible to attain completely but possible to be *striven toward.* Accordingly, most communication-centered approaches hold that ethical communication is discourse that helps build the "common"-ness or "shared"-ness between us; promotes the purpose of communication.

Sisela Bok's *On Lying: Moral Choice in Public and Private Lives,* provides an example of one such teleological, communication-centered code of ethics. Examining lying, Bok notes that for communication to succeed on a routine basis, we must assume that the person communicating with us is telling the truth (to the best of his or her knowledge). Bok illustrates her point by posing this question: What would happen if we assumed that *everyone was usually lying to us?* Communication would, of course, cease to function in any useful manner. The communication process can work only so long as we assume that, on a regular basis, people are telling us the truth.

Based on this assumption, Bok argues that ethical communication always entails truth-telling unless there is a compelling reason for lying; this reason would have to be one that directly compensates for the resulting diminution of communication's utility. For example, lying to an armed lunatic in order to save a life is justifiable. Death diminishes communication far more than does a lie, and with an armed lunatic, there is a very small chance of productive communication anyway.[1] Similar justifications might be made when national security is at risk; another instance could involve a very young child whose psychological well-being could be harmed by the truth. Bok notes, however, that although such lying is ethical, it still diminishes our confidence in the truth-telling of others and thus diminishes the power and utility of communication. Lying may be justifiable, but it never comes without cost.

Bok, then, provides an example of a communication-centered ethic in regard to lying. It is possible, however, to sketch out a broader set of ethics, also communication centered, that is generally applicable to communicative acts. Two such sets of ethics, similar although not identical, have been developed: a democratic ethic of communication and a dialogical ethic of communication. Both are especially relevant to the question of ethical debate.

Two Approaches: Democratic and Dialogical

In this section, we elaborate on two approaches to developing a communication ethic that are applicable to the debate setting. Both are teleological in their construction, and although they are grounded in different purposes or *telos,* both reach fairly similar conclusions about what constitutes ethical argumentation.

A Democratic Ethic

A democratic ethic is grounded in two beliefs. First, the ethic holds that democracy is the best, most ethical form of government. We won't attempt to defend that assumption here but will note later the appropriateness of that belief, given the assumptions about debate that we detailed in Chapter 1. The second belief that grounds a democratic ethic is that within any democratic system, communication plays a central role. Thus, participatory government becomes a meaningless form if the participants are ignorant of the decisions that must be made or of the ramifications of those decisions. Thomas Nilsen, writing in "Free Speech, Persuasion, and the Democratic Process," summarizes communication's role succinctly:

> If democracy is to function, ideas need to be expressed, the ideas need to be critically examined, the best ideas need to be found, and these ideas need to be accepted by the people if they are to be effectively translated into policies. . . . If freedom of choice is to have meaning there must be adequate information upon which to base the choice, and if self-determination is to have meaning there must be significant alternatives whose implications are known among which to choose. (236, 240)

According to Nilsen and others, any truly democratic system of government seeks an informed citizenry, a citizenry that cannot be achieved unless certain kinds of communication occur.

Most of these authors argue that such democratic communication will be grounded in certain fundamental values. Karl Wallace, for example, in "An Ethical Basis of Communication," outlined four values, or assumptions, that democratic communication contains: (1) a belief in the worth and dignity of each individual; (2) a profound faith in equality of opportunity; (3) a belief in freedom, "that each individual must be given as wide a field to roam in as he wishes"; and (4) the conviction that every person is capable of understanding the nature of democracy." Nilsen's list of values is similar: "a belief in the intrinsic worth of the human personality; a belief in reason as an instrument of individual and social development; self-determination as the means to individual fulfillment; man's fulfillment of his potentialities as a positive good" (236).

If, ethically speaking, our communication ought to embody these values, then we can judge ourselves as ethical when it does and as unethical when it does not. Nilsen, examining political campaign discourse, argued that oversimplifying issues, emphasizing the contest over the content, relying primarily on negative appeals and attack, and eliminating meaningful debate wherever possible all constituted *unethical* communication. Each of those acts, he held, betrayed one or more of the values listed above. They demeaned human worth and development while preventing self-determination and the achievement of the citizen's full potential (236–39). For many writers, the techniques of propaganda—those persuasive devices that are overtly manipulative—are undemocratic and thus unethical. The most famous of these "devices" are the seven outlined by the Institute for Propaganda Analysis in the late 1930s:

1. *Name-calling:* condemn an idea or a person by attaching a negative label to it or the individual.
2. *Glittering generality:* associate an idea or a person with a "virtue word" and thus encourage unquestioned acceptance.
3. *Transfer:* associate an idea or a person with some*thing*—a program, an agency, an event—that is admired or hated and thus gain unquestioned acceptance or rejection.
4. *Testimonial:* associate an idea or a person with some*one* who is admired or hated and thus gain unquestioned acceptance or rejection.
5. *Plain folks:* associate oneself or one's ideas with "the common person" and thus gain positive approval.
6. *Card stacking:* be selective in which facts or arguments one uses and thus give the audience a slanted view of the issue.
7. *Bandwagon appeal:* make it seem as if "everyone" agrees with you or the proposed action and so make the proposed action desirable because it is "popular." (Minnick 134)

We discuss many of these devices again as "fallacies of reasoning" in Chapter 5, but here it is important to note simply that, for several decades, this list and lists like it have been used to condemn certain communicative acts as "undemocratic." Although such lists of techniques may be simplistic—and we will argue in Chapter 5 that they are—they are useful illustrations of the kinds of lists often generated when using a democratic approach to ethics.

Even if such generalized lists are simplistic, however, they do not negate the potential utility of a democratic ethic. Instead of memorizing a list of "democratic practices," it may be far more useful to remember the *values* implied by a commitment to democratic communication and to apply those values *to the specific situation* one confronts. Rather than generating some preapproved list of do's and don'ts, a democratic approach to ethical communication can tell us what ethical communication *does* (such as promote intelligent, informed decision making) and we can decide which communicative behaviors will help us, or prevent us, from achieving those ends.

In a chapter entitled "Democratic Rhetoric," Leeman proposed three defining "attitudes" or "goals" that a democratic speaker would exhibit or seek (91–118). First, the ethical speaker (or debater) would display *respect for the other.* Being intolerant of, belittling, or attempting to "psych out" the opponent would all be signs that the speaker did *not* respect the other. Allowing opponents to answer questions fully in cross-examination and listening attentively to the opponent would be examples of behaviors that demonstrated respect for the other. Second, the ethical speaker would seek *a fully informed other.* The democratic debater would correct an opponent's misperception, work to clarify meanings of arguments and evidence, and explain arguments and evidence as fully and completely as possible. Third, the ethical speaker would be *intellectually honest.* Intellectual honesty means being truthful in the *spirit* of being honest. Intellectual honesty for a debater means that weak arguments be admitted as such, qualifiers to claims be honestly and openly advanced, and that evidence not be over- or underclaimed.

No matter which variation of a democratic approach to ethics is favored, the justification for using such a philosophy in ethical debating should be obvious. Almost every resolution used in academic debate is drawn from some issue that is actively being argued in our nation's political discourse. Further, academic debate is often viewed as a tool for learning and exhibiting *reasoned decision making*—as an educational program that prepares students for participating productively in a democracy, among other things. For these reasons, many observers have argued that debaters should adopt a democratic philosophy of ethics.

A Dialogical Ethic

In some significant respects, a dialogical approach to ethics resembles Sisela Bok's ethical defense of honesty. Where the democratic approach to ethics is grounded in a philosophy of government, a dialogical approach is grounded in a philosophy of the cultivation of healthy interpersonal relationships. Just as Bok asks, "How would we be able to relate to one another if we presumed everyone was lying?" so the dialogical approach sees within the act of communication an implied relationship: "How should I communicate with another person whom I consider an 'authentic other'?" That is, because communication is the "defining act" of being human—what other living being that we know of communicates as we do?—the act of communicating implicitly confers human status on those we communicate with. Moreover, dialogical ethicists usually argue, we need others to communicate with us in order to ascertain our own humanity.

However, the only way we can affirm each other's humanity is, in our discourse, to treat each other as unique, fully human individuals. "In a dialogic relation," writes Richard L. Johannesen, "each person . . . is accepted for what he is as a unique individual" (375). Johannesen describes a monologic approach to communication, an approach that is the opposite of a dialogic approach.

> The purpose of monologue is to get audience consensus with the speaker's view, to get others to do what he wants, and to impose his truth on someone else. The speaker has the superior attitude that he must tell people what they ought to know; he gives his answer to other people's questions. Monologue lacks mutual trust and plays a defensive spirit of self-justification. Monologue is seen, then, as unilateral persuasion aiming at the gaining of power of one person over the other. (377–78)

The problem is that competitive debate would, on the surface, appear to embrace the monologic approach. The point of the "game" is to get audience consensus (the win) to agree with the speaker's (debater's) view, to get what the debater wants, and to impose the debater's view of the proposition on the other debaters and the judge. The debater has been *assigned* a "superior attitude" because the sides have been assigned (for example, you must argue that the affirmative point of view is best). There may be mutual trust, although often there isn't, but it is almost unavoidable that there be a "defensive spirit of self-justification" (my side of the proposition is right) and there will certainly be "unilateral persuasion"—few opposing debaters will willingly help argue your case!

That being said, however, it is worthwhile to take a closer look at the competitive debate situation. True, the element of *competition* encourages the adoption of the monologic approach while the dialogic approach is usually more closely identified with an attitude of *cooperation*. But we might ask ourselves this question: Competition to achieve what? Do we competitively debate simply to win? To get the victory? Or do we competitively debate for other reasons? Here we might recall the discussion in Chapter 1 regarding the purposes for debate. We debate in order to learn how to reason better about issues that affect our world and how to formulate and present those arguments most effectively for an audience. *None* of these reasons suggest that debating is designed simply for the sense of self-gratification that accompanies winning a debate.

If our purpose for debating competitively is to improve our grasp of the art of argumentation, why not learn this art as we wish to practice it in "real life," outside the arena of academic debate? Although competitive debate *is* necessarily artificial in that the debater is assigned a particular point of view (affirmative or negative), why must that artificiality extend to our ethical stance toward argumentation? If a dialogical approach to ethical argumentation is attractive outside competitive debate, why not adopt it *within* competitive debate as well? In that way, we can use it to perfect the argumentation we wish to use in the future. A look at the specific elements of a dialogical approach may help to illustrate this compatibility.

In "Some Ethical Issues in Human Communication," Johannesen proposed eight elements that would constitute a dialogical approach to communication. These elements are shown in the following list, and from them, we can construct a comprehensive picture of dialogic communication. First, dialogical communication would pursue "self-discovery, social knowledge, or public action more than personal ambition" (#1). In academic debate, this means that enlarging the understanding of our opponents and our judge would be of higher priority than winning. It does *not* mean that we would not wish to or try to win; it does mean that we would not adopt a win-at-all-costs mentality. Trying to present our arguments and rationale clearly, and helping our opponents to present their case well, would be of greater importance to us than muddying the arguments in order to procure the "win." We would "be reflexive" (#3), that is, we would look at our own communication objectively, analyzing its strengths as well as its limitations. Being reflexive would mean that we would be *intellectually honest* about the strengths and weaknesses of our evidence. We would avoid overclaiming our evidence and shading the meaning of quoted materials.

Johannesen's Eight Characteristics of Dialogic Communication

1. Serve the ends of self-discovery, social knowledge, or public action more than ambition.
2. Avoid intolerance and acknowledge the audience's freedom of choice and freedom of assent.
3. Be reflexive; include self-scrutiny of one's evidence, reasoning, and motives.
4. Use accurate, complete, and relevant evidence and reasoning.
5. Be bilateral, including mutuality of personal and intellectual risk.
6. Be self-perpetuating. Disagreement on a subject leaves open deliberation on other matters and later discussion on the disputed subject.
7. Adopt an attitude of reasonableness, including tolerance of presentations by others, respect for the intrinsic worth of the other, and avoidance of personalizing the controversy.

8. Support values by the logic of good reasons. ("Issue Editor's Introduction" 147–48)

As we pursued "social knowledge" and prepared ourselves for being reflexive, we would also attempt to use our evidence and reasoning as accurately and completely as possible (#4). Only such complete and accurate use of evidence and reasoning will yield conclusions that we can have some degree of confidence in. Finally, as with our evidence and reasoning, in the interest of mutual self-discovery and the pursuit of social knowledge, even our values would be discussed and established as fully and completely as possible. Johannesen, referring to what is known as the School of Good Reasons, argues that our values should be upheld through the logic of good reasons.[2] What that means is that we should not hold blindly to our values but should instead test them and construct them through argumentation, as we do any question regarding human endeavor. If in the course of arguing values we are forced to make some leaps of faith, we can make those leaps explicit and as limited as possible by constructing a full rationale for those values.[3]

In addition to pursuing social knowledge, dialogic communication would engage the other communicator as an authentic person by avoiding intolerance. This includes acknowledging the audience's freedom of choice and freedom of assent (#2) and the display of an attitude of reasonableness (#7). Surely it is possible to adopt and display these attitudes within a debate: that we treat our opponents with respect and tolerance, that we acknowledge their freedom of choice and assent, *that we treat their arguments with respect even as we disagree with them.*

As we treat our opponents and their arguments with respect, we should search for commonalities, points of agreement on which to build bridges that span our disagreements (#6). Of Johannesen's eight elements of dialogic communication, this is the least applicable to academic debate because the rules of the game do not permit us to walk away from our disagreements in search of agreement. Searching for common ground is always an effective strategy of argumentation, but the competitive debate situation does not allow us to abandon our points of disagreement for very long. Indeed, the purpose of competitive debate is to force those points of disagreement and to highlight them, as it is the *differences* that allow a judge to select one side over the other as the winner. We should bear in mind, however, that competitive debate is designed to educate us toward better argumentation *outside* the world of academic debate. Perhaps the points of common ground we can foster in academic debate are those regarding purpose and ethics. Despite the specific "disagreements" about the resolution that are forced on us, we can find agreement within the educational value of debate and the pursuit of that value through ethical debating.

Finally, as dialogic communication embraces the tolerance of the other and pursues social knowledge, there is an element of risk that is embodied within it. I can only acknowledge the worth, reasonableness, and humanity of someone I am arguing with if I open my own arguments to *the possibility of being wrong*. This attitude, also called bilaterality (#5), is undoubtedly the most difficult of the eight elements to achieve, but it is arguably the heart of the dialogic approach. The dogmatist, the person who is certain of his or her correctness, typically finds it difficult to tolerate dissent, to prefer the fullness of argument over the successful conclusion of winning the argument, or to be reflexive about the weaknesses of one's own arguments or evidence. In academic debate there is a large temptation to present every argument and every piece of quoted evidence as a certainty: it *is* this way and cannot possibly be considered in any other fashion. The dialogic approach does not insist that we "give the game away" by wavering in our arguments or our commitment to the side of the resolution we are assigned. It does mean that we put ourselves at risk, however, as it insists that we be open with our evidence and arguments and that we treat our opponents and their arguments with respect. Although that may be a very difficult state to achieve fully, it certainly seems to be an ethical standard worth striving for.

The democratic and dialogic ethics, although not identical, share many common assumptions and lead to many similar conclusions about what is and what is not ethical communication. Both are communication-centered, teleological approaches. Both place a high value on all the participants in a communicative act and on the role communication plays in our lives. As a result, both approaches set high standards for ethical behavior: respect for one's opponents (and one's judge), fairness of argument, and perhaps most demanding of all, intellectual honesty. If, however, your purposes for learning and practicing competitive debate mirror those we enumerated in Chapter 1, it may be that the most arduous ethical path may also be the most effective road for achieving your educational goals.

Conclusion

Our primary purpose here has *not* been to espouse either the democratic or dialogical philosophy of ethics. We took an argumentative stance in our discussion of ethics because we believe that ethics is worth arguing about. To a large extent, we are what we communicate. Through communication, we shape our vision of the world, the world's vision of us, and in fact, our vision of ourselves. The same is true of ethics. It, too, plays a major role in shaping who we are in this world. The importance of which ethical standard of communication we choose for ourselves can hardly be understated. In this chapter, to help you develop and choose your own ethical standard, we have illustrated the central role ethical questions play in the debate situation, outlined three different approaches to developing ethical standards, and looked closely at two philosophies of ethical communication. As you begin the difficult task of studying and learning the art of debate, we hope you will always keep the questions of ethics—and some answers to those questions—close at hand.

Notes

1. Bok is particularly concerned with medical questions, such as when it is permissible for a doctor or the family to lie to the patient. Her answer here, too, is that to protect and promote good communication, the preferable course is against bad communication behaviors such as lying.
2. We discuss the logic of good reasons in more detail in Chapter 8.
3. Johannesen specifically references Walter R. Fisher's "Toward a Logic of Good Reasons," *Quarterly Journal of Speech* 64 (1978): 376–84 and "Rationality and the Logic of Good Reasons," *Philosophy and Rhetoric* 13 (1980): 121–30. A longer but invaluable (and highly readable) discussion of good reasons and values can be found in Wayne C. Booth's *Modern Dogma and the Rhetoric of Assent* (Chicago: U of Chicago P, 1974).

Selected Bibliography

American Forensic Association. *AFA Newsletter* 4 (June 1982): 12–14.

Bok, Sisela. *Lying: On Moral Choice in Public and Private Life.* New York: Pantheon, 1978.

Booth, Wayne C. *Modern Dogma and the Rhetoric of Assent.* Chicago: U of Chicago P, 1974.

Crane, Jonathan. *Terror in Everyday Life.* Thousand Oaks, CA: Sage, 1994.

Day, Dennis G. "The Ethics of Democratic Debate." *Central States Speech Journal* 17 (1966): 5–14.

"Ethics." *The American Heritage Dictionary of the English Language,* 1971.

Fisher, Walter R. "Rationality and the Logic of Good Reasons." *Philosophy and Rhetoric* 13 (1980): 121–130.

———. "Toward a Logic of Good Reasons." *Quarterly Journal of Speech* 64 (1978): 376–84.

Haiman, Franklyn S. "A Re-Examination of the Ethics of Persuasion." *Central States Speech Journal* 3 (1952): 4–9.

Johannesen, Richard L. "Issue Editor's Introduction: Some Ethical Questions in Human Communication." *Communication* 6 (1981): 145–57.

———. "The Emerging Concept of Communication as a Dialogue." *Quarterly Journal of Speech* 57 (1971): 373–82.

Keller, Paul W. "Interpersonal Dissent and the Ethics of Dialogue." *Communication* 6 (1981): 287–03.

Keller, Paul W., and Charles T. Brown. "An Interpersonal Ethic for Communication." *Journal of Communication* 18 (1968): 73–81.

Leeman, Richard W. *The Rhetoric of Terrorism and Counterterrorism.* Westport, CT: Greenwood, 1991.

Minnick, Wayne C. "The Ethics of Persuasion." *Ethics and Persuasion.* Ed. Richard Johannesen. New York: Random House, 1967.

Nilsen, Thomas R. "Free Speech, Persuasion, and the Democratic Process." *Quarterly Journal of Speech* 44 (1958): 235–43.

———. "Persuasion and Human Rights." *Western Speech Communication Journal* 24 (1960): 201–205.

Wallace, Karl R. "An Ethical Basis of Communication." *Speech Teacher* 4 (1955): 1–9.

Discussion Questions

1. What is a generalized code of ethics? How could one be applied to the practice of debate?
2. What is a specialized code of ethics? Can you think of any specialized codes that you have read or heard about?
3. What constitutes a communication-centered ethical approach? Why are most communication-centered approaches teleological?
4. How does one take a democratic approach to making ethical judgments?
5. In the dialogic approach, what does it mean to be reflexive?

THE COMPONENTS OF ARGUMENT

*T*he word *argument* has two, very distinct meanings. One definition is *a dispute.* For this meaning, two people verbally disagreeing with one another are said to be *arguing.* Arguments of this sort can range from the "Yes you are"/"No I'm not" of children to legal disputes argued before the Supreme Court. The second definition of argument is *the reasoning that supports a stated proposition.* The legal brief developed in support of a claim, a newspaper editorial explaining why we should support one candidate over another, and the reasons you chose the major that you did all constitute arguments of the second type.

Although these two kinds of arguments often develop simultaneously, they do not always occur together in our everyday behavior. Some arguments of the first sort contain no arguments of the second sort; that is, in some verbal arguments each disputant simply contradicts what the other says, with neither offering reasoning or arguments of the second sort in support of his or her position. In the same way, arguments of the second kind often occur separately from arguments of the first kind, as we develop reasons either to convince ourselves of a proposition or to preempt others from raising arguments of the first kind. In this chapter, we first examine the basic components that comprise reasoning that supports a proposition. We then look at how a clear understanding of the argument process can help us construct our own arguments and refute the arguments of others.

Toulmin's Model of Argumentation

There are many models of argument, some of which are discussed in Chapter 9 on paradigms, but many debaters and argumentation theorists have found Stephen Toulmin's model of argumentation to be especially useful. We should realize at the outset that his is a mechanistic model; that is, it labels the various parts of an argument in the same way we would label the parts of a machine. Consequently, it may oversimplify some of the complexities of the argument process, and it certainly makes the assumption that human beings argue rationally. Still, many have found it useful to identify these basic components of reasoned argument, and because the activity of debate is itself usually grounded in a rational theory of argument, the model may be especially workable for our purposes.

Toulmin developed his model in the late 1950s because he was unsatisfied with the prevailing model of logical argument, a model that had dominated argumentation theory for twenty-four centuries: the syllogism. In its basic form, a syllogism has three parts: the major premise, the minor premise, and the conclusion. The major premise establishes a generalization, such as "All people are mortal." The minor premise establishes a specific situation, such as "Socrates is a person." From the major and minor premises emerges an inescapable conclusion: in this case, that Socrates is mortal.

Syllogisms can be found in all types of discourse, and when the premises are accepted, the conclusion is logically inescapable. Henry Highland Garnet, in his famous 1843 "Appeal to the Slaves," used a syllogism to convince his audience to reject a commonplace argument that had supported acquiescence by slaves to the institution of slavery. According to this argument for acceptance, because slavery inherently forced slaves to endure evil meekly, the experience itself guaranteed them a place in heaven. Garnet countered: "If the ignorance of slavery is a passport to heaven, then it is a blessing, and no curse, and you should rather desire its perpetuity than its abolition" (Garnet 407). Garnet's syllogism could be modeled this way:

MAJOR PREMISE:	We should desire the perpetuity of anything that ensures us of a passport to heaven.
MINOR PREMISE:	Anyone who endures slavery has a passport to heaven.
CONCLUSION:	We should desire the perpetuity of slavery.

No slave, of course, and none of the free African-Americans attending the convention that Garnet was addressing would have agreed with the Conclusion of the syllogism. However, most if not all would agree with the major premise. The only way to hold those two beliefs is to reject the minor premise—the argument Garnet was attacking.

Today, syllogisms are called "symbolic" or "deductive" logic, and typically make up the subject matter for courses entitled Logic, Deductive Logic, or Symbolic Logic, usually taught in departments of philosophy. Toulmin, himself a philosopher, was dissatisfied with the syllogism because of its shortcomings in accounting for two elements he thought critical for understanding argument:

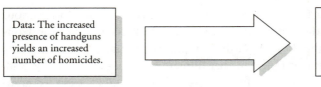

FIGURE 3.1 **Partial Toulmin Model of Argumentation**

the concept of probability and the establishment of the major premise. Thus, he designed what has come to be called "Toulmin's Model of Argument" (Toulmin 94–145).

Toulmin's model begins with the component called **Data,** or what in the syllogism is called a minor premise. The Data (or Grounds) for an argument consist of the facts or evidence on which the conclusion rests. Toulmin felt that, in everyday argumentation, people generally start with the observation of facts (or perceived facts) rather than with some generalization or major premise. "Socrates is a person" is one such example of what we would call a "fact." Another can be found in Figure 3.1 "The increased presence of handguns yields an increased number of homicides."

From these Data, Toulmin said, we derive a **Claim.** For the syllogism given above, the Claim is that "Socrates is mortal." In Figure 3.1, the Claim is that "Government action that reduced the presence of handguns would be desirable." At this point, Toulmin held, we might well have a "complete" argument as it appears in our day-to-day disputes or observations. "Well, Socrates was only a man, so he had to die someday," the statement might go. Or, "Look, the more handguns we have, the more people die from murder; so the government needs to do something to reduce the number of handguns." Neither argument presents the "major premise," yet both are easily understood as logical, rational claims (even if incorrect or disputable).[1]

On a strictly logical plane, however, the Data by itself can never yield the Claim. An inference is being made here in our logic; there is a gap that requires the presence of a *bridge* or a *connector* that allows us to come to the claim based on the data we see. That bridge is called a **Warrant.** Like the major premise, the Warrant is a generalization that, combined with the Data, allows us to arrive at the Claim. Without understanding that "All people are mortal," we cannot conclude that simply because Socrates is a person he is therefore mortal. Similarly, without believing that "Government action that reduces the incidence of homicides is desirable," it is illogical to conclude that the government should act to reduce the number of handguns simply because the presence of handguns increases the number of homicides (Figure 3.2). Toulmin argues that although

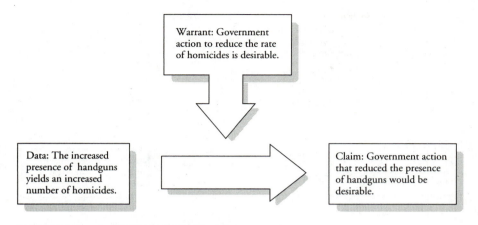

FIGURE 3.2   Partial Toulmin Model of Argumentation

the Warrant is often implied, a speaker, when pressed to do so, will be able to supply this generalization needed to link the Claim with the Data.

To this point, Toulmin's model has reordered the syllogism but has not altered or refined it. Toulmin noted, however, that human beings talk in terms of probabilities. We argue that things probably are, usually might be, almost certainly can be, or almost never are. Thus, we might hold that "Government action to reduce the presence of handguns would *probably* be desirable" (Figure 3). Whenever we admit an element of uncertainty, we are qualifying, or limiting, our commitment to the claim, and so the next component is called the **Qualifier.** Moreover, Toulmin noted that even when we do not explicitly qualify our Claims, they are often implicitly qualified.

Qualifiers are not arbitrary, however; they result from what may be called the **Rebuttal.** Note that in this model, the Rebuttal is *not* an argument made by an opponent (although an opponent might later make the same argument that the Rebuttal does). Nor does the Rebuttal mean that the Data-Warrant-Claim reasoning is illogical or fallacious. The Rebuttal is instead the recognition that there may be elements in the situation that would negate the Claim if they are in fact present or arise in the future. Think of the Rebuttal as an "unless" statement; it says that "the claim will be true *unless* XYZ occurs." For example, in Figure 3.3 we have supplied one rebuttal: "unless there are competing demands on government actions that take greater priority." Because the arguer feels reasonably certain that no such demands will be put forth, the Claim has been qualified as "probably" true. If the arguer felt that such demands would be likely, the qualifier would be that "maybe" the government should reduce the number of handguns, or even that it should "probably not" do so.

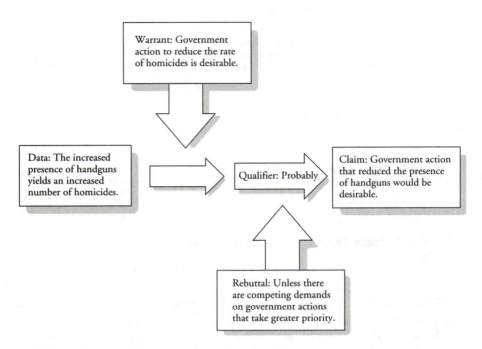

FIGURE 3.3   Partial Toulmin Model of Argumentation

Note also that there may be several rebuttals. For example, with Figure 3.3 we could easily have added several more Rebuttals: "unless the government can take no effective action for reducing the number of handguns," "unless any government action reducing handguns would in fact cause a further increase of homicides," and "unless the government is prevented by legal constraints from taking any action." Generally, the more Rebuttals there are, the stronger the Qualifier (or limitation) is and the weaker the resulting Claim will be. Even with a single Rebuttal, the stronger or more likely it is that the Rebuttal is true, the stronger the Qualifier and the weaker the Claim.

In addition to wanting to incorporate the concept of probability into his model of argument, Toulmin, like many other theorists through the centuries, wanted to account for how humans arrive at the generalizations that make up our Warrants. For many theorists, major premises are simply a priori assumptions; that is, they are assumptions made *prior* to the act of reasoning or the construction of argument. While Toulmin would probably agree that some major premises are indeed a priori, he also felt that in everyday argumentation, we can often defend our Warrants when they are questioned. This kind of defense Toulmin termed the **Backing** for our Warrants. Backing can be thought of as the data for the Warrant. In justifying the Warrant, the Backing explains

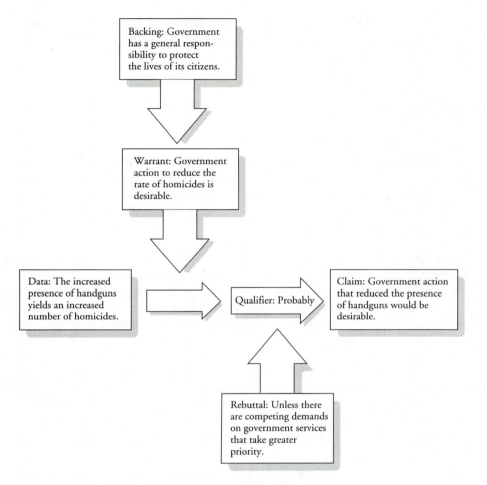

FIGURE 3.4   Complete Toulmin Model of Argumentation

why the Warrant is legitimate and offers grounds on which the warrant should be accepted. In Figure 3.4, the Backing might be that "Government has a responsibility to improve the quality of life in society, whereas fear of being a homicide victim decreases our quality of life," and that "Government has a general responsibility to protect the lives of its citizens." On two counts, then, we might conclude that "The government should reduce the rate of homicides."

Initially, identifying the components of an argument using Toulmin's model may be difficult. Figures introduced later in the chapter provide additional examples of the model, but the surest method for learning it is to model out several arguments for yourself. Once you understand the six components clearly, you will find that the model is useful for identifying the strengths and weaknesses of your own arguments or those of others. The examples discussed next should illustrate this point.

Analyzing Arguments

Applying Toulmin's model can be useful in three ways. First, we can use it to identify positions implicit in an argument. Second, it can help us assess the relative strengths and weaknesses in an argument. Third, it can help us discover and analyze potential counterarguments.

Identifying Implicit Positions

Toulmin's model is most often used for identifying the positions and beliefs implicit in one's argument because identifying assumptions is critical to understanding and analyzing arguments—whether another's or our own. Although any of the six elements may be omitted from the initial statement of one's argument, the most common components implicit in an argument are the Warrant and its Backing, and the Qualifier and its Rebuttal. In everyday argument, we will often ask "What are the hidden assumptions?" By this, we are usually questioning the Warrant and its Backing. For example, if I accept the Data showing that my department gives out a disproportionate number of A's and B's, must I agree with the claim that my colleagues are "easy graders"? The hidden assumption, or Warrant, is that "Giving out a large number of A's and B's indicates a lack of toughness in grading." What if, however, the Warrant really should be that "Good grades are indicators of good teaching"? Under this Warrant, it is the department on campus awarding a disproportionate number of D's and F's that becomes suspect—because the failing grades indicate "poor quality teaching" rather than "toughness of standards."

The meaning and proper interpretation of evidence, the principles of governing, the moral imperatives of "shoulds" and "oughts" are all common materials for Warrants in debate arguments. Examples of such Warrants would be that "government should protect its citizens from intrusive searches and seizures"; "government must preserve national security"; "the First Amendment rights of free and unrestricted expression provide the cornerstone of our democracy"; and "that which affects all of us is of greater importance to society than that which affects one of us." Depending on the argument, these various Warrants could stand in opposition to each other. If such Warrants are hidden and taken for granted, arguers may overlook potential issues and points of conflict.

Qualifiers and Rebuttals, too, are often hidden away in the initial statement of an argument. This is especially true in a debate, where arguers typically make categorical—that is, unqualified—claims. Categorical statements are those that implicitly or explicitly make all or nothing declarations. "Pens write with blue ink," "surveys reflect people's opinions," and "First Amendment rights always take precedence over other constitutional rights" are all examples of categorical statements. Each of us understands, of course, that some pens write with black ink, others with red, and so on, so that the first statement would be more accurate if it were qualified: "*most* pens write with blue ink." The second statement's categorical claim may be less obvious but is in need of similar qualification, which could be accomplished in one of two ways: "surveys *attempt to* reflect people's opinions"; or, "*some* surveys reflect people's opinions." Lacking either qualification, the speaker of the statement is saying that we should accept all surveys equally, without regard to possible methodological problems, potential survey bias, or the inherent limitations of survey research—all of which we return to in the next chapter.

Finally, the third statement's lack of qualification is more debatable. That is, some people indeed believe that First Amendment rights are *always* paramount. The freedoms of speech, religion, press, and assembly, they argue, are always absolute. Most, however, including the Supreme Court, have held that even these four freedoms are not absolute; that is, they are not *unqualified* rights. There are situations in which these rights are abridged. For example, it is unlawful to engage in speech that presents a "clear and present danger" to others; for example, "you can't yell fire in a crowded theater." Or, in the interest of the "public good," communities may ban a pornographic work if (1) it is patently offensive; (2) it appeals to prurient interest; and (3) taken as a whole, the work lacks serious literary, artistic, political, or scientific value.

For each of the categorical statements above, there are implicit Rebuttal statements that justify the Qualifier. For example, surveys may reflect people's opinions "unless the questions are biased," or "unless the population sampled is not representative of the general population." Indeed, many other Rebuttal statements could be constructed for this example, demonstrating why the Qualifier is that *some* surveys may be accurate rather than that *most* or *almost all* are accurate. Indeed, some critics of survey research might well argue that *very few* surveys are accurate. Similarly, numerous situations can occur that justify an abridgement of our First Amendment rights despite an agreement by many that those rights are the keystone of our democratic system.

Any six of Toulmin's components may be left unsaid in the initial statement of an argument, whether your own or your opponent's. An awareness of or the discovery of these unspoken components may be of critical importance to the success of your defense or refutation. Throughout this text we stress that *understanding* an argument—whether yours or your opposition's—is the necessary first step toward effective argumentation. Toulmin's Model of Argument is one method of making explicit these unspoken components.

Weakest  Strongest

Middle

FIGURE 3.5 **Continuum of Strength of Argument**

Assessing Strengths and Weaknesses

Toulmin's model is also useful because it can help us assess the relative strengths and weaknesses of an argument. We should note, however, that in this section we are assessing strength solely on a logical basis. That is, we are *not* judging the persuasiveness of the argument or the strength that it would have for the receiver. To say that one component of an argument is strong does not mean that it is convincing or impregnable to attack. "Strength" simply means that, *all other things being equal,* the arguer will have an easier time convincing an audience that the component is true or defending that belief from attack. Similarly, to say that a particular component is "weak" only notes its vulnerability to attack and the potential difficulty involved in convincing an audience of its validity. Furthermore, our intent is not to classify arguments simply as "strong" or "weak." We should instead visualize a spectrum, or continuum, of "strength": some arguments are very strong, some are less so, some are weak, some are weaker, and some are in the center with moderate strength/weakness (see Figure 3.5).

By identifying clearly the components of an argument, we can more easily assess the points of logical strength and weakness in the argument. For example, consider the legal argument that because drug testing violates our privacy and because privacy violations are prohibited by law, drug testing is prohibited by law. Examining the argument as modeled in Figure 3.6, we see quickly that there are two major strengths to this argument. First, the Warrant can be easily backed by finding and documenting the numerous court cases that protect privacy. Second, the Rebuttal puts the burden on the opposition to prove a "compelling" interest that would outweigh the legal right of privacy.

The argument's potential weak points also become readily discernible in the model. First, the Data may be difficult to establish. "Privacy" may prove to be a difficult concept to define, which means that violations of privacy may also be difficult to pinpoint. Second, just as there are numerous cases establishing the right of privacy, there are numerous cases and many possible "compelling" interests that can legitimate violations of that right—hence the ambiguity of the Qualifier, "sometimes." Although the opposition will need to prove that one of these compelling interests is at work, there will be *many* such interests from which they may choose.

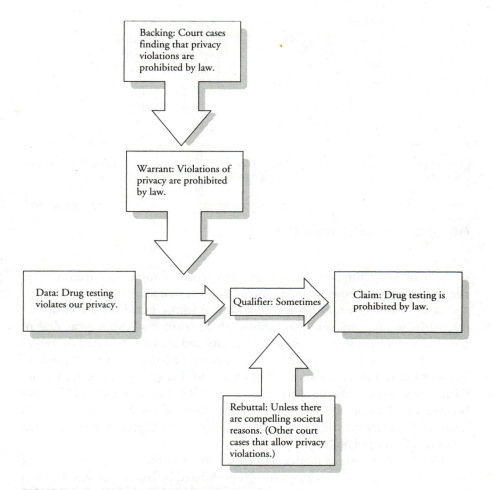

FIGURE 3.6 · **Toulmin Model of Drug Testing Argument**

Toulmin's model does not tell us *how* to construct a strong argument, defend a weak one, or make a weak argument stronger. It can, however, help us analyze the relative strengths and weaknesses of our argument by identifying the components of that argument.

Constructing Refutations

Toulmin's model can help us construct a refutation of our opponents' argument in two ways. First, we can use the model to identify the weakest link(s) in the opponents' argument chain. Second, the model can help us assess the relative

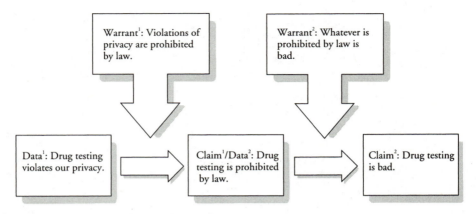

FIGURE 3.7   Extended Toulmin Model

strength of our refutation. Before exploring each of these opportunities, we need to look first at how Toulmin's model can be extended.

When we first introduced the Toulmin model, we noted the criticism that the model is simplistic and mechanistic. Both criticisms have a great deal of merit, but we can reduce the model's simplicity and increase its ability to "reflect reality" by extending it beyond the six components; that is, we can think of Toulmin's model as a "snapshot" of an argument. For example, one argument's Claim may become the next argument's Data. Or one argument's Data may become the Backing for another, with the Claim of the first argument then being the Warrant of the second. Or one argument's Claim may become the Rebuttal of a second argument.

Figure 3.7 provides a model of what we are describing. Here, the Claim of an earlier argument—that drug testing is prohibited by law—becomes the Data for the next step of the argument: that drug testing is bad. Modeled here is a typical argument in debate and everyday interactions, only the Claim[1]/Data[2] component, that "drug testing is prohibited by law," often goes unstated as well. (Superscripts refer to elements of Figure 3.7.) The argument typically runs like this: drug testing violates our privacy, and our privacy is protected by law. Therefore, drug testing is bad (Claim[2]).

Once the argument is outlined using an extended Toulmin model, identifying the weakest link in the opponents' argument chain becomes relatively easy. For Figure 3.7, note that to make Claim[2] based on Data[1] and Warrant[1], the arguer logically (even if only implicitly) needs Claim[1]/Data[2]. In turn, Warrant[2] is needed to imply Claim[2]; that is, the arguer is saying that anything prohibited by law is bad. Although such an assumption is common, it is also the weakest link in this argument chain, and Rebuttal statements are plentiful: (1) unless the law is a generally bad law; (2) unless the action prohibited is justified in that particular situation; (3) unless the law requires modification to meet current conditions. Slavery and the denial of suffrage to women are two common examples used to support Rebuttal 1. Speeding to get my injured child to the hospital emergency room illustrates the point of Rebuttal 2. In support of Rebuttal 3, we could note that a law prohibiting schools from counting students as absent during harvest season may have been appropriate once but would now be considered outmoded.

Toulmin did not require each arguer to fully conceptualize his or her argument, complete with all six components, for each individual "snapshot" argument contained within the larger argument structure. For Figure 3.7, the initial arguer may not realize that the key assumption is Warrant[2], nor do all disputants consciously identify the Backing, Qualifiers, or Rebuttals of their arguments. *If questioned carefully,* however, most arguers can articulate the various components of their argument.

Of course, whether the initial arguer can identify and defend the various components is in some sense beside the point here because refutation does not require the initial arguer to fully understand his or her argument.[2] Effective and efficient refutation does require *the respondent* to understand the opponent's argument, and extending Toulmin's model is one method for uncovering the hidden Warrants, Data, Qualifiers, and other elements that are typically honeycombed throughout our arguments.

There is a second way to extend Toulmin's model that can help us identify the strengths and weaknesses of our own refutative arguments. Instead of repeating terms across a series of steps in an argument, this method of extending the model is to sketch in potential points of refutation. In the next three figures, we model a common defense for increasing the fines levied against air pollution violators and three basic counterpositions to it: countering the Data, countering the Warrant, and providing Rebuttal scenarios.

Counterdata positions have varying levels of strength, depending on the degree to which the position questions, eliminates, or reverses the original Data. Suppose, for example, that the Data in this instance were based on several instances in which companies have continued to pollute the environment significantly, even after the passage of air pollution controls. According to this argument, these cases are representative of the industry as a whole. In response, we might argue, as in Counterdata 1, that other companies have not done so and that our group of companies is more representative of the industry as a whole (Figure 3.8). In this instance, the refutation can be termed relatively weak because it does not attack the argument itself. Our opponents' Data, Warrant, Backing, and Claim all remain in place, even if we prove that other companies are indeed not polluting. The effectiveness of our argument rests solely on our ability to persuade our audience that our case studies are more representative than our opponents'. This is not always a weak argument, but all other things

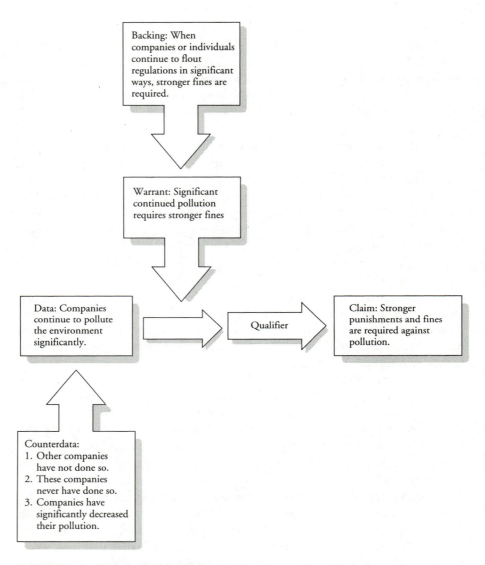

FIGURE 3.8   Toulmin Model with Counterdata

being equal, it is a less direct refutation of our opponents' argument than are other possible attacks.

Rather than simply questioning the interpretation of our opponents' Data, we can argue that their evidence is in fact wrong, as in Counterdata 2 (Figure 3.8). The companies they cite as continued polluters have, we argue, discontinued their pollution, or indeed have never significantly polluted at all. Without these Data, our opponents' argument falls because there is no evidence to justify the Claim. This Counterdata position is stronger than the first because it attacks our opponents' argument directly, but it is still weak in the sense that it leaves the basic structure of the argument standing. Even if our Counterdata statement is correct, we leave our opponents with the possibility of finding other cases of companies that have continued to pollute the environment significantly. If such Data are supplied, our opponents' argument is reestablished, even though we have won our initial argument.

All other things being equal, Counterdata 3, that the reverse of our opponents' Data is true, is the strongest Counterdata position we can take (Figure 3.8). Rather than simply questioning their Data or indicting their specific cases, we argue here that the opposite of their Data is true. Companies have not only *not* increased their pollution but they have actually *decreased* it. Because there is no significant continued pollution, harsher penalties are not warranted. Unlike Counterdata 1 and 2, if we carry this position, there is no response our opponents can give *within the original argumentative structure.* That is, perhaps our opponents might change the Warrant or modify the Claim, but the original position falls.

There are two Counterwarrant positions available for our refutation: (1) that the Warrant is not true, and (2) that the reverse of the Warrant is true (Figure 3.9). Either argument is relatively strong because both arguments threaten our opponents' basic argument. Removing the Warrant by proving that it is not true—that significant continued pollution does not require stronger fines—prevents our opponents from inferring the Claim from the Data. Here a persuader might argue that companies that do not respond to the fines already in place will not respond differently to increased fines. Thus the Counterwarrant here is that stronger fines are *never* the answer to the problem of continued pollution because the violating companies will never change their behavior simply because the monetary penalties for that behavior are increased.

Counterwarrant 1 is a strong argument in that, *if accepted,* it directly attacks the opponents' argument structure, but Counterwarrant 2 is even stronger in the sense that it justifies a Counterclaim exactly opposite the original Claim. For example, if our audience accepts our position that "significant continued pollution requires weaker fines," then our opponents' Data, combined with our Counterwarrant, yields the Counterclaim that "weaker fines are required in the area of pollution." We have not only refuted our opponents' position, but we have also established that precisely the opposite is true. Indeed, a similar argument has been made for reducing the severity of mandatory prison sentences. Juries are reluctant to find someone guilty of murdering a police officer, the argument goes, when the mandatory sentence for that crime is execution. It is better to provide a range of punishments so that juries will first find the person guilty and *then* turn to the matter of sentencing the criminal. A similar argument could be constructed on behalf of Counterwarrant 2.

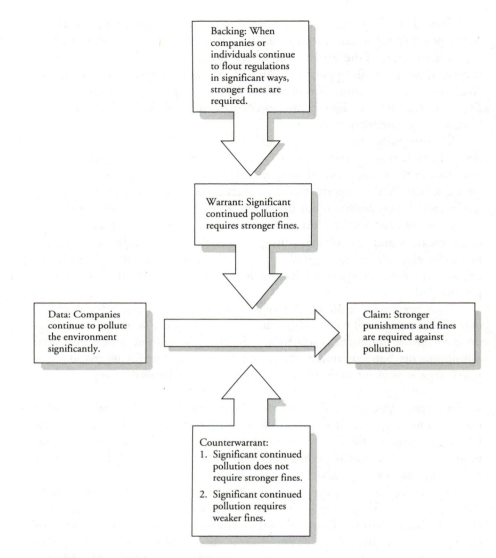

FIGURE 3.9   **Toulmin Model with Counterwarrants**

Our third group of counterpositions are the Rebuttals. Remember that in Toulmin's model, Rebuttals are *not* necessarily the arguments we bring up to refute the claim. Rebuttals are those situations in which the claim would be unjustified, but of course, we can always argue in refutation that such a situation *does* or *will soon* exist. However, Rebuttals (as Toulmin is using the term) always leave the opponents' basic argumentative structure standing because they simply say that in *this* situation, the claim is unjustified. Like Counterdata 1 and

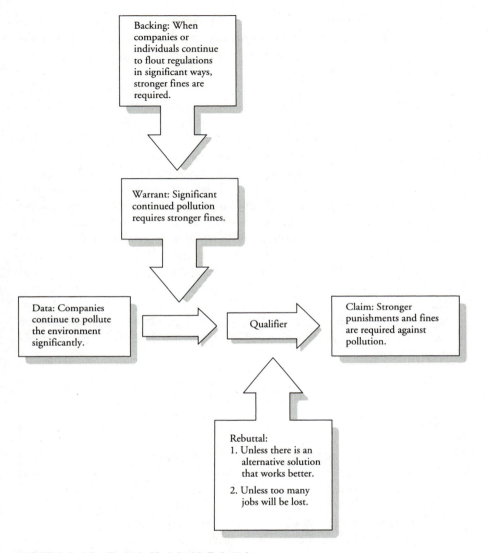

FIGURE 3.10   Toulmin Model with Rebuttals

2, the effectiveness of our Rebuttal depends on how well we can prove that the Rebuttal "situation" does in fact exist. In Figure 3.10, we have hypothesized two such situations. Rebuttal 1 argues that if there are alternative solutions, the Claim is unjustified. In this instance, an alternative solution might be increased government funding for research and development. Companies do not comply, the argument goes, because the technologies are not currently available in the quality or quantity needed. Increased fines will not increase compliance at this time, but increased availability of pollution control technology will. Providing tax breaks for improved compliance rather than punishment for continued non-compliance is a similar "alternative solution" argument that would favor the "carrot" over the "stick."

Rebuttal 2 is another common response to the type of argument modeled in Figure 10. Again, the Rebuttal is situation specific; it argues, in this particular instance, that the economic disadvantages of increasing the fines on companies outweighs the improved air quality that would result. Recent controversies over logging versus preservation of the spotted owl, tuna fishing versus preservation of dolphins, and strengthening controls on automobile emission standards are three examples of arguments similar to the one constructed here. In each case, the rebuttal does not hold that environmental protection is not desirable or that tougher standards are not justified; it says that because of current economics, such regulations are not justified in *this time* and *this place.*

We have looked at three types of counterpositions: Counterdata, Counter-warrants, and Rebuttals. Each refutes the original argument differently and thus offers different relevant strengths and weaknesses. Just as Toulmin's model enables us to conceptualize more clearly our own arguments and the arguments of others, it can help us identify potential points of refutation and the nature of the attack that each point of refutation would deliver on our opponents' argument.

Conclusion

There are two kinds of arguing: one is the act of contradicting what somebody else says; the other is the act of constructing a rationale that supports our own position. The second kind of argument can be more closely examined by using Toulmin's model of argumentation. Building on the three-part syllogism (major premise, minor premise, and conclusion), Toulmin identifies six basic components of argument: Data, Claim, Warrant, Backing, Qualifier, and Rebuttal. Although this model carries a risk of oversimplifying any particular argument, it can prove useful in analyzing arguments—our own or others'—for potential strengths and weaknesses. It can also be useful in identifying potential points of refutation and the varying strengths and weaknesses of those arguments.

Remember, however, that Toulmin's model identifies only *some* of the potential points of argument and *some* of the potential strengths or weaknesses of an argument. It does so in each case by locating particular parts of the argument chain and helping us understand how each part interacts with the others. Within those links are many different considerations the engaged disputant should examine. The validity and meaning of our evidence, the believability of our reasoning, and the acceptability of our arguments to the audience's prejudices, beliefs, and values will all be factors that influence the effectiveness of our argument. In the next chapter we examine the first of those factors: the validity and interpretation of evidence.

Notes

1. To call one's reasoning "logical" is only to say (1) that there are adequate premises for supporting one's conclusions, and (2) that none of the premises and conclusions contradict. Strictly speaking, the term *logical* does *not* denote the accuracy or validity of one's argument.
2. By "initial arguer" we mean the person being responded to in the refutation. It could be that we are refuting an attack on an argument we originated. Toulmin's model can be used to identify, understand, and analyze the components of argument no matter which stage of refutation we are engaged in.

Selected Bibliography

Burleson, Brant R. "On the Foundations of Rationality: Toulmin, Habermas, and the *a Priori* of Reason." *Argumentation and Advocacy* 16 (1979): 112–27.

Feezel, Jerry D. "A Qualified Certainty: Verbal Probability in Arguments." *Communication Monographs* 41 (1974): 348–56.

Garnet, Henry Highland. "Address to the Slaves of the United States of America." *The Black Abolitionist Papers*. Ed. Peter Ripley et al. Chapel Hill: U of North Carolina P, 1991.

Hample, Dale. "The Toulmin Model and the Syllogism." *Argumentation and Advocacy* 14 (1977): 1–9.

Leeman, Richard W., and Ralph Hamlett. "Calling a Counter-Warrant a Counter-Warrant: An Immodest Proposal." *CEDA Yearbook* 10 (1989): 54–66.

Lewis, Albert. "Stephen Toulmin: A Reappraisal." *Communication Studies* 23 (1972): 48–55.

Manicas, Peter T. "On Toulmin's Contribution to Logic and Argumentation." *Argumentation and Advocacy* 3 (1966): 83–94.

Toulmin, Stephen Edelston. *The Uses of Argument*. Cambridge: Cambridge UP, 1958.

Willard, Charles Arthur. "On the Utility of Descriptive Diagrams for the Analysis and Criticism of Arguments." *Communication Monographs* 43 (1976): 308–19.

Discussion Questions

1. How does Toulmin's Model of Argumentation add the ideas of probability and reasons for our assumptions to the syllogism?
2. In what sense can Toulmin's model be labeled "mechanistic"?
3. Construct your own example of Toulmin's Model of Argumentation.
4. Using the example you have constructed for #3, demonstrate how that model can be "extended" to other arguments.
5. Again using the example you constructed for #3, identify at least one example for each of the three types of counter positions discussed in this chapter.

EVIDENCE

*A*rguments—reasons in support of a stated proposition—can be built out of two kinds of materials: evidence and reasoning. It is often difficult to distinguish the two, but this distinction is a useful way to divide our discussion in the next two chapters. We can think of evidence as the data, or facts, on which we base our arguments.

Suppose a friend and I are arguing about whether the American League or the National League is better. Some of the evidence we introduce might be that the American League has won six of the last seven All-Star games, that National League teams have won five World Series championships over the same time period, or that the overall batting average for the American League was forty-seven points higher than the National League's batting average. Even if we agree on the accuracy of our figures, however, we may continue to disagree on the conclusions we should draw from them. My friend may feel that All-Star games are irrelevant as indicators of a league's talent; I may feel that the World Series compares only the two best teams from each league and does not reflect the overall quality of either. We may both agree that the American League's designated hitter rule makes a comparison of batting averages irrelevant. Each of the numbers is a point of evidence; what they *mean* is a point of interpretation or argument.

In this chapter, we are concerned with the first issue: What constitutes evidence? How do we find it? What makes evidence credible? Because the evidence we use to support an argument is only as good as its believability, we begin with the last question first: What makes data credible? Then we look at the different types of evidence and the various purposes they serve. Finally, we examine ways to find and prepare evidence.

Credibility of Evidence

In some disputes, the critical issue is "What does the evidence *mean?*" In the baseball example, for instance, my friend and I can probably agree pretty quickly about the accuracy of our data. We may argue all day, however, as to what the statistics mean in regard to the relative quality of the two leagues. In other disputes, however, the *accuracy* of the evidence will be the key issue. For example, did Hillary Clinton know or not know how the Whitewater files came to be in the White House living quarters? Was that area of the White House in fact accessible only to family and personal staff? Could, or did, an administrative staff member leave the notes there without either President Clinton or Mrs. Clinton being aware of that? The issue here is purely an evidentiary one and comes down to a single point: Who is telling the truth?

Of course, it isn't a simple point; many evidentiary controversies aren't. Did Franklin Roosevelt know in advance about the Japanese attack on Pearl Harbor? Do boot camps for youthful offenders prevent recidivism (repeated criminal behavior)? Would a national health care system save us money? Human motivations and behavior are complex—and so are the data that record our past, reflect our present, and predict our future. Complex data often lead to uncertain conclusions—or should—but even in the face of uncertainty we must make decisions. Which data are most believable? If we can answer that question thoughtfully, our decision making will not be infallible but it will be improved. Regardless of our own decision making, when we engage in argument, many in our audience will be trying to judge the credibility of *our* evidence. What are they looking for? What makes some data more believable than other data?

We will answer these questions by looking at six tests of evidence, but we should not think of these tests as absolute standards the data either pass or fail. As with the strength or weakness of an argument, the credibility of evidence rests on a continuum of *greater* or *lesser* believability. If our friend says the National League has won five All-Star games since 1989, we might find that evidence 99 percent believable. The numbers sound right to us and our friend is generally knowledgeable about baseball, but we also know that human fallibility being what it is, she might have read a sports report that contained an error, or she might be remembering it inaccurately. Conversely, a story in the *National Enquirer* about someone being kidnapped by aliens would probably strike us as unbelievable, although we would admit a very small possibility that it might be true. Other evidence—such as Hillary Rodham Clinton's story—we might place anywhere along our imaginary continuum, depending upon how believable we find it. Some might place it in the middle of the continuum, unable to decide whether to believe or not believe (see Figure 4.1). Others may be on either side of the middle—leaning toward believing the story or away from

Alien kidnapping   Clinton's story   All-star games

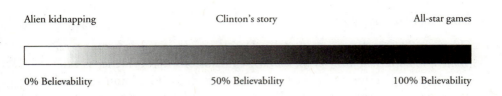

0% Believability   50% Believability   100% Believability

FIGURE 4.1   **Continuum of Believability of Evidence**

believing it, but still with a certain amount of uncertainty. Six tests of evidence —internal consistency, external consistency, source, timeliness, precision, and context—help us evaluate where on the believability continuum we will place any particular piece of data.

Internal Consistency

The test of **internal consistency** asks, *Does the evidence contradict itself?* From the standpoint of credibility, contradiction hurts evidence of any sort. If the evidence is contradictory, we find it less believable; if it is not contradictory, we find it more believable. Consider a witness who first claims that on the night in question, he was out of town, but in later testimony claims that he was in town. Not only is the witness's immediate claim now in doubt—was he or wasn't he in town?—but his entire testimony will become suspect for many people. Similarly, we become dubious if a report on polling data says in one paragraph that 787 people were polled on December 10, but in the chart reporting its findings says that 843 people were polled on November 24. There are possible explanations for the contradiction—typographical error, recording mistake, and so on —but for most of us, the contradiction would cause us to lose at least some faith in the accuracy of the poll results.

Internal consistency is unique among the six tests of evidence in that it is most easily used to *disqualify* data. If evidence is contradictory, we may decide to dismiss it as "unbelievable" without considering any of the other five tests of evidence. However, if the data are *not* contradictory we do not therefore find it *more* believable. Instead, we generally go on to the other five tests of evidence to determine our confidence in the data. Unless the data are extremely complex, so that the lack of contradiction becomes noteworthy in itself, internal consistency is a test most usually used *against*—and not *for*—the data's credibility. In this way, internal consistency is a *threshold* that we want our evidence to meet in order to be seriously considered within the decision-making process.

External Consistency

The test of **external consistency** asks, *Does the evidence contradict my experiences (that is, my understanding of the world)?* Conclusions that evidence is externally inconsistent are often embedded in reactions such as "Common sense tells me these facts are wrong" or "Well, *I've* never seen it happen that way." Just as all communication is filtered through our own experiences, so too is the evaluation of evidence. Election polls may be believable or unbelievable to us based on which candidate we intend to vote for. Testimony about the difficulties youth have finding summer jobs may be believable or unbelievable to us based on our own experiences looking for temporary employment. In fact, you may be reading these examples and saying to yourself, "No, I never do any of that stuff," and coming to the conclusion that we do not really use some mythical test of evidence called "external consistency." In that instance, of course, you are using the test of external consistency to reach the conclusion that there is no such test!

Because external consistency is based on individual perceptions, for us to know when it is being used by our listeners is often difficult. Depending on the particular situation, an analysis of how an audience will react may be able to identify precisely, only generalize, or perhaps miss altogether the kinds of experiences the audience will supply that will help or hinder their acceptance of our evidence. A further difficulty is that different members of the audience may use the test to reach very different conclusions. My experience may be that finding lucrative summer employment is extremely easy; yours may be that it is very difficult. From our different perspectives, we may read testimony from youths about the scarcity of summer jobs very differently. You find the youths' stories externally consistent; I think the young people "are just not looking hard enough" and conclude that the evidence is inaccurate.

Despite the difficulties of predicting when and how external consistency may be used, we must do so as well as we can if we wish to be successful persuaders because, psychologically, it is one of the strongest tests of evidence. Although we all realize intuitively that our experiences are limited, they are very real and very important *to us.* As a persuader, you cannot tell your audience that their experiences are wrong or that they have not really had those experiences.[1]

To overcome external inconsistency, we can employ two strategies. First, we may explain why our audience's experiences are atypical or not applicable *to this particular situation.* Summer work has been easy for me to find, you might tell me, because of my education and family background; *most* youth, you argue, do not have the advantages I have enjoyed and thus, for them, finding a job for the summer *is* difficult. In this scenario, what you have tried to do as a persuader is explain why I should not test this particular data with my own particular experiences. You have not said that my experiences are wrong, only that they are not applicable in this instance.

The second strategy for overcoming external inconsistency is to emphasize the other tests of evidence. If we want our audience to doubt the applicability of their own experience to the data in question, we must present the strongest evidence possible. Thus, we emphasize those points of the data that convincingly "pass" the other tests of evidence. Generally, of course, the artful persuader will use both strategies in concert.

Source

The third test of evidence, **source**, asks, *Who generated the evidence?* Who conducted the poll, the field study, the experiment, the data analysis? Who gave the testimony? Who told the story? Who reported the study?

Embedded in this question of "who" are a multitude of subsidiary questions. Is the person biased for or against a particular position? Does the person have the expertise needed to collect and interpret the data? Is the person in a position to know the data firsthand? Does the person have a credible track record that encourages confidence in the data? Of course, we can also substitute "what" for "who," as those responsible for generating evidence are often obscured behind organizational labels: NBC News, the *National Enquirer,* Mothers against Drunk Driving, the American Cancer Institute, a Gallup poll, or the Center for Disease Control. When we ask who said it or where it was reported, we are questioning the source of the information.

Source is typically an important test of evidence for two reasons. First, we know that humans are fallible, intentionally and unintentionally. Sometimes we lie and sometimes we make mistakes. The test of source asks whether either one of those is happening with the reporting of this particular evidence. Second, source is an easy test of evidence to identify, discuss, defend, and dispute. Whereas some of the other tests can be ambiguous, the credentials, experiences, biases, and track record of the source can often be clearly articulated. It is easy to argue that the *Washington Post* is a good source but *People Magazine* is not; or that a poll conducted by a political action committee is automatically suspect in a way that a poll conducted by the Roper organization is not. For both reasons, source is a popular test of evidence to use and dispute, and it is one that any advocate should be well prepared to debate. We return to specific questions about source in our discussion of testimony as evidence later in this chapter.

Timeliness

Where the test of source asks *who* generated the data, the test of **timeliness** asks *when was the evidence generated?* Sometimes this is called the test of recency, as some arguers hold that the more recent the evidence is, the better it is.[2] "Recency" is bad terminology, however, as the critical question is not how recently was the evidence generated but simply *when* was it generated? Considerations of timing help answer two larger questions: What events surrounded the generation of the data? Have conditions changed in ways that affect how the data should now be interpreted?

If the evidence needs to account for changing or current conditions, findings, or theories, then—all other things being equal—the more current it is, the more credible it is. If I am providing data about the economic prospects of Russia or Eastern Europe, I want the most recent evidence available because conditions there are changing almost daily. However, if the evidence is designed to demonstrate that certain truths are unchanging, then the older the evidence is, the more credible it is. For example, I may cite Aristotle's *Rhetoric,* circa 350 B.C.E., that people judge a speaker's ethos (credibility) by looking at good sense, good character, and goodwill. Some may find such appeals trite, but for others the fact that Aristotle's observations have "stood the test of time" for 2400 years enhances their credibility.

The test of timeliness can ask more than how new or how old the data are. What events surrounded the generation of the data? What had happened by that time? What had not happened? What has happened since the generation of the data?

Timeliness is an often misused test of evidence because it is simple to identify the when but it is difficult to sift through the importance of the data's timing. Which events are pertinent? Which aren't? It is very easy to oversimplify the matter of timing so that the issue of timeliness is argued with a lack of sophistication: "My evidence is from 1993 and yours is from 1992, so mine must be better." Such simplistic arguments about the timeliness of evidence should be avoided, but knowing when the evidence was generated can indeed help indicate the environment within which it was created, and thus help us better judge the accuracy of that evidence.

Context

Context as a test of evidence asks, *What was the context from which the evidence was drawn?* Generally, the more we know about the background from which the evidence was taken, the stronger our faith in that evidence will be. Suppose you read a movie advertisement with a quotation claiming it was "the year's best!" You might wonder what the rest of the sentence or paragraph was from which the quoted material was taken. Perhaps, you muse, the sentence originally read, "The year's best example of why we should outlaw sequels." Any doubts you have about the data because of this "wondering" results from the test of context. Or maybe you hear a television ad that says "nine out of ten doctors surveyed said they prefer Extra-Strength Bloxit pain reliever." Do you wonder which doctors were surveyed, or what exact question they were asked? After all, the only doctors "surveyed" may have been those who accept free samples from the Bloxit company, or the question was "Which pain reliever would you prefer for severe muscle strain: Regular strength aspirin or Extra-Strength Bloxit?" The doctors indeed "preferred" Bloxit, but only for a single type of pain relief and only when compared with regular strength aspirin. If you ask yourself questions like these, your doubts arise because you are using context as a measure of the data's credibility.

Like timeliness, contextual questions and issues may be very important but also very difficult to define. We suggest some standard questions of context in the next section of this chapter but realize that it is sometimes hard to know which questions to ask until you already know the answers. Similarly, it can be difficult at times for the persuader to know which questions about context an audience will *want* answered. Whether you are analyzing an argument or constructing one, only by researching the issue thoroughly and knowing as much about the generation of the data as possible can you be assured that you can ask and answer all the pertinent questions about context. It is generally true that thorough preparation is the key to successful arguing and that axiom is especially true for questions of context.

Precision

The test of **precision** asks, *How detailed is the evidence?* Broadly, the more details we know, the more confidence we have in the data.[3] For example, suppose I was arguing that you should invest in the MaikDoe mutual fund. I might tell you that MaikDoe has paid an average interest/dividend rate of 11.54 percent for the past ten years. Part of what makes my evidence believable is its precision. However, suppose I said instead that MaikDoe has paid about 11 percent interest for the last ten years? Do you start wondering how much or how little I've rounded the numbers off? Do you start wondering what the "about" hides? My evidence has become a little less believable simply because it is less precise.

Of all the tests of evidence, precision is probably the most abused because supplying details is so easy to do. Anyone can invent details—to stories, statistics, or testimony—which then enhance the data's credibility. The 1981 Pulitzer Prize-winning story about the life of "Jimmy," an "eight-year-old dope addict" was later discovered to be a complete fabrication. The detail with which the story had been told had made it compelling as well as believable. Even when parts of the data are not invented, it is easy to overload *questionable* evidence with an abundance of details that give that data an aura of "truth" that it does not deserve. Tainted surveys and interpretive statistical studies are two common examples of using precision as a persuasive strategy. Because the test of precision is so open to abuse, both the ethical persuader and the critical thinker will apply this test with some care.

In summary, we use six tests to determine how believable evidence is to us: internal consistency, external consistency, source, timeliness, context, and precision. Depending on the particular data and situation, we may prefer one or more of these tests over the others or we may weigh them all equally. Whenever we construct arguments, it is important that our data be *credible*. Understanding the tests of evidence can help us ensure that they are.

Types of Evidence

In addition to using credible evidence, it is important to use *appropriate* evidence. We can think of evidence as divided into three types: examples, statistics, and testimony. Each type can play a particular role as data in an argument, and each has certain strengths and weaknesses. In this section, we continue the discussion of credibility and begin a consideration of appropriateness.

Examples

The first type of evidence, examples, can best be thought of as stories. An example tells us *about* something and, like a story, helps us visualize how that something occurs. Typically, examples perform two argumentative functions. First, they can *demonstrate* to the audience that something has in fact happened. For example, the savings and loan crisis could demonstrate the fallibility of federal banking regulation. The experience of U.S. troop losses in Somalia might demonstrate the problematic nature of placing U.S. soldiers under United Nations command.

Second, examples can *illustrate* an argumentative point. John Hinckley's attempted assassination of Ronald Reagan illustrates the kind of crime that would not be prevented by a waiting period for gun purchases. Prior to the assassination attempt, Hinckley was never legally committed for treatment of his mental illness, and he purchased his weapon well in advance of the shooting. Examples may, of course, be used both to demonstrate and to illustrate.

Although most of the examples used in academic debate are actual examples, it is possible to employ hypothetical examples as well. Descriptions of the destruction that would be caused by a nuclear bomb dropped on a city or the effects of proposed tax regulations on the typical family of four would be two such hypothetical examples. Examples like these cannot be used to demonstrate that something *has* happened, of course, but they can be used to illustrate what *will* happen if the hypothetical situation becomes an actuality.

Several questions should be asked of either type of example when choosing one to support your argument.

1. Can the example be *verified?* Do you know that the example did in fact occur in the way you are portraying it? In his 1980 presidential campaign, Ronald Reagan routinely cited the example of the "welfare queen of Chicago," who was on the welfare rolls under twenty-seven names, drove a Cadillac, and wore fur coats. An investigation by reporters found that no such woman ever existed. Verification is relevant for hypothetical examples as well. Although you cannot ask whether a hypothetical example has happened, you do need to be prepared to verify that it *could* or *would* occur.

2. Is the example *representative?* Is it a typical example of the point you are demonstrating or illustrating? It need not be typical in every detail but it should be representative in all those regards that are pertinent to the point you are making. Ross Perot's campaign for president was interesting but it was not *typical* of presidential campaigns generally, nor (because of his wealth) was it typical of third party presidential campaigns. One might argue, however, that it did typify the media-oriented campaign of the future.

3. Is the example *valid?* Does it indeed demonstrate or illustrate your argument? In some instances, this can be an evidentiary question. Representative Dan Rostenkowski's legal problems do *not* demonstrate the legal problems of the Clinton administration, because, although both he and Clinton are Democrats, he is not part of the president's administration. In other cases, validity is a question of interpretation. Does the Gulf War illustrate the dangers of nuclear holocaust (as the type of regional war that could easily grow into a nuclear confrontation)? Or does the Gulf War illustrate our comparative safety (as the type of war that did not escalate into nuclear confrontation because of America's nuclear strength)? We return to the question of interpreting evidence in the next chapter.

4. Is the example *appropriately detailed?* It is not only important that the example be valid, but it is equally important that your audience understand and believe the example's validity. For that, you need to include sufficient and appropriate details. Like the story of your Spring Break vacation, the example is meant to illustrate a point. If you are relating your story to a friend, you include certain details and omit others. If you are telling it to your parents, you probably tell the story differently. In either case, you choose the details that illustrate your point (to your friends: "I had a wild and crazy time"; to your parents: "I was careful with the money you lent me"), and you omit those details that are irrelevant to your point. Also, you consider the time allowed for your story. A two-minute version will be different from the ten-minute version as you choose the details that best illustrate the point you are making. The same is true for examples used as evidence. You choose the best details for illustrating or demonstrating the point you are making, given the time you can allot to the example.

You might even use *undetailed* examples when there is little time to devote to the example and because the pertinent details are already known to your audience. An undetailed example is like telling your audience the title of the story but nothing of the plot ("Remember our spring break?" [wink, wink, nudge, nudge]). Undetailed examples can be powerful evidence because (1) you can pack many of them into the same time or space as a single detailed example, and (2) the audience supplies the pertinent details out of their own knowledge. The more involved an audience is in persuading themselves, the more successful and longer lasting the persuasion is likely to be. The challenge of undetailed examples is that when you use them you must try to be sure the audience will be able to answer each of the questions above positively: that the example is verified, representative, valid, and appropriately detailed.

Of the four questions above, the most problematic for the advocate is the second one: Is the example representative? It is very easy for an opponent to respond to any example by arguing that "It's just one example." There are four possible ways an advocate can demonstrate representativeness.

First, the advocate can use *enumeration*. With this persuasive tactic, the advocate enumerates a series of examples that all prove a common point. It is especially effective when the debater can leave the audience with the impression that these enumerated examples are just the "tip of the iceberg" and that "there are plenty more where they came from." From a logical standpoint, however, although the enumerated series of examples can be effective for showing that something has happened repeatedly or is likely to happen again, it is not necessarily logical proof that the examples are representative. Rarely do the enumerated examples make up a statistically significant sample that proves representativeness.

Second, the advocate can argue that certain elements of the example are *characteristic,* that certain features of the example are inherent in the situation and thus the example is representative. For instance, suppose I was arguing that the U.S. State Department's mishandling of the Bosnian situation is representative of that agency's poor foreign policy judgment. I might highlight three aspects of the situation to indicate that this example is representative. First, the Bosnian situation has engaged the department's attention at all levels; thus it is indicative of departmental decision making generally. Second, although the department has had multiple opportunities to correct its failed decisions, it has repeatedly continued its errors. Third, the situation has brought input from all the NATO countries, but even with intelligent advice, the department has not been able to set out a successful policy. On three counts, then, I could argue that this example is representative of U.S. State Department decision making generally.

Third, the advocate can *couple the example with statistical evidence* that demonstrates representativeness. If I were making the argument that many of those in poverty are hard-working victims of poor-paying economic jobs, I might begin with the example of Brian Deyo, who takes home $188.40 a week to his family of three, which includes a chronically ill two-year-old daughter. "Every day I'm making choices," he says; "do I pay the rent and risk having the power cut? Or do we take a chance on both and buy food?" (Horwitz A1). Despite his impossibly low pay, Deyo chooses to work rather than go on government assistance, which would include Medicaid for his child. I may then supplement that story with two statistics: (1) "almost 60% of poor families have at least one member working," and (2) "a full-time minimum wage worker grosses $8,840 a year—$2,300 under the poverty line for a family of three" (Horwitz A1). Not only does the statistical evidence suggest that the Deyos' case is indeed representative, but it identifies the approximate representativeness (60 percent).

Fourth, the advocate can use *authoritative* evidence that *testifies* to the example's representativeness. We consider the pros and cons of testimonial evidence later in this chapter, but we can mention one potential weakness here. If testimony is the only evidence used to show representativeness, the advocate is relying solely on the credibility of someone else's authority.[4]

Examples are useful, then, because they can document the occurrence of a particular situation and they can illustrate an advocate's point. To be used successfully, however, examples should be verifiable, representative, accurate, and appropriately detailed.

Statistics

Statistical evidence is information that contains numerical claims. Evidence using statistics appears in many forms that we see almost daily. Experimental and hypothetical studies, such as those conducted in medicine, psychology, and economics, routinely use numerical data to report their findings. Demographic studies—those like the census that report characteristics of the population—are statistical by nature. Business reports, driven by a concern with profits, rely heavily on numerical data. Polling data are also generally reported using numbers. So integral are statistical data to our everyday lives that we can hardly imagine life without the ability to count.

Psychologically, statistical evidence is impressive because it inherently utilizes the test of *precision*. When reported by a formidable sounding name—such as the Urban Institute for the Study of Metropolitan Foundations—precision combines with source to make the claims often seem infallible. Too few of us remember Mark Twain's admonition that there are three kinds of lies: lies, damn lies, and statistics. Or, as the other old adage goes, figures lie and liars figure.

What makes statistics so credible on the one hand yet so scorned on the other? Perhaps the key is to consider the nature of numbers themselves. Although statistics often take on a life of their own, it is important to remember that they are only conduits of meaning. By themselves, numbers have no meaning. Try this as an example: Is fifty thousand a lot or a little? If you answer, "It depends; fifty thousand *what?*" then you understand the point we are making here. Even if we say "fifty thousand dollars" we still don't know whether that should be evaluated as a lot or a little. Fifty thousand dollars added to my checking account is a lot; as a part of the federal budget, it's almost nothing. As Senator Everett Dirksen is reputed to have said, "A billion here, a billion there, and pretty soon you're talking about real money."

Numbers simply provide us with a rigorous way of holding ideas. We count up the money we make on one end of our budget and compare it to the amount we intend to spend on the other end. We count the number of people living in poverty in 1980, compare it to the number counted in 1990, and try to decide whether we have progressed or regressed. Because numbers operate as "conduits," two questions are always appropriate to ask about statistical data: (1) What counted as a "unit" going into the conduit? (2) How fairly have the numbers been interpreted coming out of the conduit? Let's look at each of these questions.

In gathering statistics, I first have to decide what is going to constitute a "unit" in my counting. When the census bureau counts those living in poverty, what constitutes a "poor family"? A family of four living on $10,000 a year? $11,000? $12,000? Where do I draw the line? Where do I draw it for families of one, two, three, five, or twelve? Even if I'm counting money, where a "dollar" is the unit, do I need to have a "standard dollar" so that my comparisons are fair? Inflation may cause a dollar to buy less now than it did a decade ago. In order to count "buying power," many economic reports will say something like "1.3 million *1977 dollars* were spent on the program in 1984, in comparison to 1.1 million *1977 dollars* in 1994." Thus, the program might have received more *real* dollars in 1994 than in 1984, but in terms of *buying power,* the program's funding has declined. Many questions can be asked on this "incoming" end of the conduit. A few of the more common ones are these:

1. How were the *units* (terms) *defined?* Numerous questions can be developed along this line of inquiry. Where was the poverty line drawn? What constituted a "dollar"? In a survey, what was the question asked? (There are many ways of skewing questions to make respondents appear to support something they really oppose.) In tabulating income, should benefits such as insurance or retirement be counted?

2. What was the *population* from which the numbers were drawn? In a poll, for example, who was surveyed? Was it a random sample, in which the respondents' demographic makeup does not necessarily mirror that of society? Was it a representative sample? Or was it neither random nor representative—for example, a mail-in survey connected with a fund-raising effort? Or in an experiment,

who were the subjects (whose responses were then "counted")? College students? Mostly male? Mostly white? Mostly middle class? These questions illustrate problems typical of many studies and experiments that use human subjects. However, the question of "population" does not always mean people. A study that rates the "best car" never considers *every* car on the market. The cars selected for the test—domestic mid-sized cars, for example—constitute the "population." Questions of population are always relevant when you are determining whether the advocate's end claim is justified. If I urge you to buy Import X because it was rated "best compact car," but the population surveyed was only import cars, a fair question for you would be, How does Import X compare with domestic compacts?

3. Were the data gathered and recorded *consistently?* In any experiment that requires the coding of data, a key concern is the reliability of the coders. Did the coders consistently assign numerical values to the same "units"? We can ask similar questions of other statistical data. Were the polling questions always asked in a similar manner? In demographic data, were occupations always recorded similarly? Were respondents of mixed race always recorded similarly? Depending on the claims made about the data, some of these questions may be irrelevant; some, however, may be very relevant.

On the other end of the conduit, we find that advocates are going to "interpret" the data as part of their argument. The sole question here is, Do the numbers justify the claim? Is a 10 percent increase "large" or "small"? Does it represent a problem or a continuation of status quo normalcy? We are constantly interpreting what the numbers "mean."

Polling data are good examples of how we interpret statistical data. Suppose you hear the claim, "According to the most recent Gallup poll, Americans rate violence as their number one domestic concern." Does that mean that violence should be the government's number one priority? We should look first at the polling method and then at what the specific numbers were. Was it an open-ended poll—"What do you think is the number one domestic concern?" What range of answers could respondents give that were then translated into the coded answer "violence"? Was it a close-ended poll—"Which of the following domestic issues is your number one concern?" Were respondents asked to rank the several issues or just pick their number one concern? In both instances, was the term *violence* defined at all? Could some of the respondents have been thinking about television violence while others were thinking of criminal violence while still others were thinking of domestic abuse? Is it fair to group those respondents together as having "similar concerns"?

What were the numbers? Fifty-five percent saying "violence" is far weaker than 95 percent saying it. How strongly did people feel about this number one concern? Those saying "violence" may have felt less committed to their choice than others who put "unemployment" first. If those answering "violence" had "unemployment" as their second choice, it might be fairer to say that unemployment is "Americans' number one concern."

A special case regarding the fairness of interpreting data is the use and abuse of the terms *average, median,* and *mode.* Strictly, the average is found by adding up the total number and dividing by the number of "participants." The median is the midway point in the numbers themselves. The mode is the most commonly occurring number in the group. Thus, for quiz scores of 10, 10, 9, 9, 6, 3, 2, 2, and 2, the average grade would be 5.88 (53 ÷ 9); the median grade would be 6; and the modal grade would be 2. The person who scored a 6 might seek consolation by saying that her score was "above average," but that hardly gives a good picture of her performance compared to the performance of other students. Similarly, those scoring a two could say they had "lots of company" because their grade was the "mode," yet they were outperformed by everyone else taking the quiz who scored higher than a two. Statistically, the term *average* is especially abused because it carries evaluative connotations: above average is typically considered "good" whereas "below average" is considered bad. Interpreting numbers often requires that we take a closer look at the numbers behind the average, median, and mode.

There are many questions to ask about statistical data, some of them general, some very technical. Indeed, there are too many technical questions for us to discuss them all here. However, because numbers hold little meaning for us by themselves, we should remember to ask whether the statistical data were fairly gathered and whether the numbers have been fairly interpreted. If we keep these two questions in mind, we can help ensure that we analyze thoughtfully any statistical data presented to us.

Testimony

In testimony, the advocate quotes the words of another person, which testify to the truth of a particular claim. For example, to support the claim that American schools lag behind Japanese schools, we might quote an American politician, an elementary schoolteacher, or perhaps a Japanese professor of education.

Broadly speaking, there are two types of testimony: primary and secondary. **Primary testimony** involves firsthand experience. The schoolteacher quoted above may have taught in America and in Japan and is thus providing primary testimony based on these comparative experiences. **Secondary testimony** involves expert opinion. With secondary testimony, we may quote from someone who, rather than having experienced an event firsthand, is an "expert" in the matter. With either kind of testimony, the advocate is using the experience or expertise of another to support the claim.

Testimony is inescapable because few of us are fully experienced or expert in the subject we are debating. Testimony can be used to (1) show that some event did in fact occur, (2) explain the reasons supporting a particular conclusion, or (3) interpret data. Authorities "interpret data" for us by testifying about historic or recent trends, the causes and effects of events, or the proper conclusions to be drawn from particular studies. Even if we as advocates have a great deal of experience or expertise in the matter being debated, it strengthens our credibility to demonstrate that other "experts" support our own observations.

Regardless of the type of testimony or the purpose for which it is used, there are five key questions that can be asked in analyzing the use of such evidence.

1. Does the source have *appropriate credentials?* No matter whether we are using primary or secondary testimony, the person quoted has certain credentials—a certain job, degree, or experience—that "qualifies" him or her to be a credible "authority" on the subject. For example, an American-trained accounting professor may not have the appropriate credentials to testify about Malaysian accounting practices because Malaysia follows British accounting practices and principles. The schoolteacher described above may be especially trained to teach science and mathematics. We may believe that those credentials provide adequate or inadequate preparation for comparing American and Japanese education generally. In either case, we are asking what the individual's "field of expertise" is that it qualifies him or her to make claims within that field.[5] It is especially important here not to be overawed by impressive-sounding credentials.

2. Is the source *biased?* Even if a source's credentials are impeccable and entirely appropriate, it is always useful to know something about the person's track record. Everyone is "biased" to some degree, but some of us are less objective than others. Does the source have a personal or professional motive to shade the truth? A philosophical bias that causes him or her to view events through ideological blinders? If the head of the American Nazi Party says, "America is declining morally, economically, and militarily," should we take that as an accurate assessment of the country's condition? Or is it fair to dismiss that testimony as (1) typical political exaggeration and/or (2) ideological tripe? Many of us would answer yes to both questions. In many instances, bias may not affect the accuracy of the data reported, but it will invariably affect how the source interprets that data.

3. What data or *experiences* did the source look at in arriving at his or her conclusions? Just as all authorities' credentials should be appropriate to their claims, their claims are stronger if the data they have drawn from are relevant.

What studies did the "expert" look at? What were his or her job experiences? An insurance executive's testimony about the effect of tort reform on the insurance industry generally would be less credible if her experience is solely in the area of automobile insurance. Why is her testimony believable regarding life, health, or homeowner's insurance? Similarly, the school teacher in our example above may have taught at atypical schools in America, Japan, or both, and thus not be "qualified" to testify about the two educational systems generally. In either case, we are asking, What is the "evidence" behind the evidence?

4. What is the authority's *reason* for making the stated claim? Some testimony employed in arguments can be called *conclusionary testimony*. By that, we mean that the advocate only quotes a source's evaluative conclusion without any of the accompanying reasons to justify the conclusion. The hypothetical example from the Nazi leader above would be conclusionary; no reasons are supplied for why the source reached that particular conclusion. When conclusionary testimony is used, it is important to realize that the advocate is placing the entire weight of the evidence on the authority's credibility. If the authority is very credible, conclusionary evidence may be effective. Whenever we are engaged in critical analysis and reasoned decision making, however, conclusionary evidence should be worth comparatively little. Overly broad and overly simplistic testimony frequently suffers from being conclusionary.

5. Has the testimony been *quoted accurately?* Although honest errors of transcription would fall within this question, problems of accuracy usually occur in one of two forms. First, has the testimony been taken out of context? Problems of this sort can range from outright deceit to somewhat shaded meanings. Sometimes, quoted material will sound stronger or weaker when it is read outside the larger text that surrounded it. The second, related problem is whether the quoted material has been edited fairly. For example, a reputable authority may be quoted as saying "UFOs have landed" when in fact she was only saying that some *other* people believed that unidentified flying objects (UFOs) had landed. There will be occasions when every advocate must delete words, phrases, sentences, or even entire paragraphs to fit the time frame available or to make the point more clearly understandable. The question to ask is whether the editorial form of the quotation has changed the original meaning. As advocates, we are obligated to quote our sources accurately and fairly. As critical consumers of argument, we need to be alert to the changes that can be wrought by a clever or unethical editor.

We have looked at what makes evidence believable and what the different types of evidence can do in support of our argument. We now turn to the final question: How do we find and prepare our evidence?

Preparing Evidence

There are two parts to the process of preparing evidence to use in academic debate or structured argumentation: researching and organizing. These parts overlap. We often begin organizing potential evidence even before we find it, and as we organize the evidence we have found, we almost inevitably find additional areas we wish to research.

To illustrate the research process, suppose we are preparing to support the proposition that "A major in liberal arts can be beneficial to most students." There are four steps to efficient preparation: identify potential sources, find source citations, read and record the useful information, and organize the records.

Identifying Potential Sources

Before sitting down at the first computer terminal available in your library, you must identify the potential sources for your research. Doing so is largely a matter of brainstorming, but it requires some familiarity with library resources to be fully effective. In our example, potential sources would include (1) books on education, (2) education articles, and (3) business articles describing the usefulness of liberal arts. Other sources of information might be uncovered along the way, but these seem to hold the most immediate promise.

For other topics, some potentially useful sources might be newspaper reports and editorials, political science and government articles, medical studies, legal review articles, government documents, *Statistical Abstracts of the U.S. Census Bureau,* and even general periodical articles. Most college libraries have good political science and government collections, an adequate number of microfilmed newspapers, and carry Statistical Abstracts. Many are also government repositories and will carry a large number of government documents, especially on microfilm. Some libraries may carry a few medical and legal journals, but universities with medical schools or law schools will have much better holdings. Many federal and some state courthouses have law libraries that are open to the public. In government documents, there are three general areas of useful resources: records of laws, congressional debates and hearings, and agency reports.

Finding Source Citations

Once we have ascertained the general sources from which we might obtain information, we can use the appropriate index or indexes for those sources. Finding the proper index is important. Indexes allow us to find source citations very quickly. However, they will provide citations only for those publications chosen for the index. You will not find *Time Magazine* articles indexed in the *Social Science Index;* nor will you find articles from *The Forensic of Pi Kappa Delta* in Infotrac. For our example of liberal arts, we consulted our library's computerized card catalogue, Infotrac (the expanded academic, newspaper, and business periodical index bases), the Business Periodical Index, ERIC (Educational Resources Information Center), the Educational Index, the New York Times Index, and the Washington Post Index. Infotrac and ERIC are both computerized; the others are in bound copies. Some indexes generally useful for debate research are contained in the list headed "Indexes" below. In addition to this material, you might also consult references in the list titled "Additional Beginning Sources" that follows the index list.

> **INDEXES**
> Infotrac
> Business Periodicals Index
> Education Index
> ERIC (Educational Resources Information Center)
> Public Affairs Information Service (An index to books and articles in political science)
> Social Science Index
> Humanities Index
> New York Times Index
> Washington Post Index
> Los Angeles Times Index
> Christian Science Monitor Index
> Wall Street Journal Index
> Index to Legal Periodicals
> Index to Nursing and Allied Health Periodicals
>
> **ADDITIONAL BEGINNING SOURCES**
> Editorials on File
> Facts on File
> Editorial Research Reports
> Black's Law Dictionary (for definitions)
> Corpus Juris Secundum (for definitions)
> Statistical Abstracts

After determining which indexes are appropriate, we must choose the *subject headings* relevant to our research. Most indexes include entries for author and title as well as subject, but the last will generally be more useful here. For book holdings, the Library of Congress issues a catalogue titled *Subject Headings* that is readily available at most libraries. In periodical or newspaper indexes, you may have to explore a bit to determine which subject heading is most useful for you. For our example, the subject headings most useful were "Education, humanistic," "Humanities," "Education, higher," and "College graduates—employment."

Under the subject headings you will find lists of books or articles. You will have to decide which look useful, but we offer one word of advice: it is far more profitable to spend some time exploring the indexes for the most promising books or articles than it is to run down the first few citations you find, discover that they are not quite what you need, and have to return to the indexes.

Reading and Recording the Evidence

Whether you take notes in the library or photocopy the chapters and articles for later study, the next step is to record the usable evidence. Here the major challenge is to separate the useful from the not-so-useful. You must be able to spot the example, statistic, or testimony that may be important later for supporting or countering an argument. The key is to know the arguments thoroughly. Some of that knowledge can be attained through general and specific researching. Some can come from brainstorming arguments and talking through the issues with others.

It is also important to realize that extended quotations will not be useful. You will need to discern the pertinent passages and/or be able to edit the material carefully and fairly. For example, the following is a single paragraph from the article "Why Hire Humanities Graduates," written by Robert W. Goddard and appearing in *Personnel Journal.* The person being quoted is Ian Rowland, chief executive officer (CEO) of Lincoln National Corporation.

> The emphasis on specialization and the early rewards pay for skills such as engineering, finance, and marketing had led to a de-emphasis on the humanities. Specialists function very well in the early years of their employment, but as they advance into management, unless they make a conscious effort to broaden themselves, their narrow view of the world has often proved to be a limiting factor in their development.

In this quotation Rowland is testifying to two claims: that an emphasis on specialization had led to a deemphasis of the humanities, and that specialization usually hurts the specialist's career as he or she advances in management. The first point is not terribly relevant to our argument unless we are somehow led into discussing why there is a deemphasis on the humanities. The point is also a bit circular: an increased emphasis on one approach led to a decreased emphasis on the other approach. Finally, the first sentence is ambiguous: an increased emphasis by whom? Employers? College students?

In contrast, the second point is directly relevant to our argument: if specializing as an undergraduate is potentially damaging to one's career, then the opposite approach of getting a general liberal arts should be helpful. Notice, too, how cleanly the quotation can now be used:

> IAN ROWLAND, CEO, Lincoln National Corporation.
> In Robert W. Goddard, "Why Hire Humanities Graduates?"
> *Personnel Journal* Feb. 1986: 22.
>
> "Specialists function very well in the early years of their employment, but as they advance into management, unless they make a conscious effort to broaden themselves, their narrow view of the world has often proved to be a limiting factor in their development."

The key here is to remember that each piece of quoted material should support only one idea/argument. For this reason, many academic debaters and even some speechwriters and other professional communicators record each piece of evidence on a separate notecard. Many other debaters prefer to organize their evidence into argumentative briefs, which we will discuss in the next section.[6] For either method, you must record the evidence in a fashion that will preserve the quoted material and bibliographic citation in a form usable to you at the next stage.

To record the information, you need to begin with the bibliographic citation. Article citations must include the person quoted (if different from the author), the author, the title of the article, the title of the periodical, the date, and the page number the quotation is taken from. Book citations must include the person quoted (if different from the author), the author, the book title, the publication date, and the page number the quotation is taken from. You may also choose to record information about the author's or expert's qualifications. Here are two examples of bibliographic citations:

> DANIEL M. LUNDBERG, section manager Computer Systems, Hewlett Packard.
> In Emanuel Sturman, "Do Corporations Really Want Liberal Arts Grads?"
> *Management Review* Sep. 1986: 57.
>
> ROY BOSTOCK, CEO, D'Arcy, Mascus, Benton & Bowles
> (undergraduate English major, Duke U., Harvard MBA)
> "Too Many Hummingbirds, Too Few Eagles," *Advertising Age* 28 Jan. 1991: 21.

Once you record the evidence, it is also useful to "label" it with the argument that it supports. In competitive debate this is often called using a "tag line." "Tagging" your evidence by writing the argument in a short sentence performs three functions. First, it ensures that you understand which argument you think the evidence supports. Putting the argument in writing often helps point out gaps in our logic, as we all frequently misinterpret evidence in our haste to support our position. Second, it makes sorting and organizing the evidence easier. Third, it makes using the evidence easier when you are debating or writing a speech, essay, or other form of structured argument. Here are two examples:

Specializing Hurts Career Advancement
IAN ROWLAND, CEO, Lincoln National Corporation.
In Robert W. Goddard, "Why Hire Humanities Graduates?"
Personnel Journal Feb. 1986: 22.

"Specialists function very well in the early years of their employment, but as they advance into management, unless they make a conscious effort to broaden themselves, their narrow view of the world has often proved to be a limiting factor in their development."

Liberal Arts Develops Critical Thinking/Perspective
ROY BOSTOCK, CEO, D'Arcy, Mascus, Benton & Bowles
(undergraduate English major, Duke U., Harvard MBA)
"Too Many Hummingbirds, Too Few Eagles," *Advertising Age* 28 Jan. 1991: 21.

"An undergraduate arts and sciences education develops the generalists. It gives them a perspective on the whole and helps them develop a facility to process and synthesize ideas and to put in proper perspective the concrete developments of specialization."

Organizing Your Records

No matter what medium of argument you are preparing for, it is critical that you organize your evidence. Organizing is a simple task, as you sort the evidence into categories of arguments. How narrowly you define those categories will depend on (1) how complex the argument is and (2) how voluminous your evidence is.

If you are using a notecard system, you need some file system for separating the notecards into their respective categories. Using argument briefs, the organization is done by argument. In both instances, your aim is to have the data accessible; organizing it along the lines of the argument it supports is the most efficient way of doing so. A sample argument brief will illustrate our point here.

Resolved: Majoring in the liberal arts is beneficial.
I. A liberal arts education teaches critical thinking.
 A. A liberal arts education provides a broad perspective.

1. ROY BOSTOCK, CEO, D'Arcy, Mascus, Benton & Bowles (undergraduate English major, Duke U., Harvard MBA) "Too Many Hummingbirds, Too Few Eagles," *Advertising Age* 28 Jan. 1991: 21.

   "An undergraduate arts and sciences education develops the generalists. It gives them a perspective on the whole and helps them develop a facility to process and synthesize ideas and to put in proper perspective the concrete developments of specialization."

B. A liberal arts education teaches valuable skills.

1. THOMAS VARGISH, prof., MIT Program for Senior Executives, "The Value of Humanities in Executive Development," *Sloan Management Review* Spring 1991: 84.

   "The essentially diffusive and personal quality of application gives the liberal arts course its extraordinary depth, flexibility, and power. And these qualities are precisely the ones that executives who take and evaluate such courses consistently appreciate."

II. Success in business requires the skills developed in a liberal arts education.

A. Business problems require managers with these analytical skills.

1. THOMAS WYMAN, Chairman, CBS. In "Business Again Looks to Liberal Arts Majors," *New York Times* 12 July 1986: 45.

   "Business problems today require creative and sometimes unorthodox approaches. This puts a premium on managers with the ability to be flexible, capable of continuous learning: managers with the skills to anticipate change. These are managers possessing the attributes we have come to associate with a liberal education."

2. BLUFORD H. PUTNAM, (chief economist, Kleinmort Benson, Ltd.) and EDWARD I. STEVENS (Professor of Management, Eckerd College), "Management as a Liberal Art," *Chronicle of Higher Education,* 24 July 1991: B2.

   "The practice of business today focuses on ideas, communication, and problem solving, not on learning a set of skills and applying them routinely. The better business schools have already shifted their curricula accordingly."

B. Businesses do look for and hire those with a good liberal education.

1. MINERVA REED, dir. of career services, Princeton. In Judith Waldrop, "The Resume," *American Demographics* June 1989: 6.

   "The pendulum is once again swinging back. For the past 15 or 20 years, the trend was for industry-specific graduates. Now those concentrations are seen as too limited. Liberal arts produces people who are able to think and move with the times—problem solvers."

2. DANIEL M. LUNDBERG, section manager Computer Systems, Hewlett Packard. In Emanuel Sturman, "Do Corporations Really Want Liberal Arts Grads?" *Management Review,* Sep. 1986: 57.

"We sell general purpose business computers, and liberal arts students are better able to relate to our customers. Above all else, customer satisfaction is what you need."

III. Liberal arts majors excel in business.

  A. Liberal Arts majors are promoted well.

     1. WILLIAM BENNETT, "Go Ahead, Major in the Liberal Arts," *Washington Post National Weekly* 28 Jan. 1985: 29.

       "In a survey done at ATT it was found that, in the top four managerial levels, 43% had majored in the humanities and social sciences, while 32% had been business majors and only 23% were engineers."

     2. JUDD ALEXANDER (VP, James River Corp.), "Liberal Learning," *Vital Speeches* 1 March 1986: 316. (Reporting on a *Pulp and Paper* survey)

       "In the last two years, the highest average salaries for paper people with ten years or more experience were reported by employees with four year liberal arts degrees, compared to those with educations in engineering, paper science, chemistry, business, or forestry."

If you were organizing notecards instead of a brief, you might put the evidence in section I into one category labeled "*Liberal Arts teaches valuable skills.*" The evidence from section II. A. might be filed in a category titled "*Business needs liberal arts skills.*" The evidence from section II. B. might be filed under "*Businesses hire liberal arts.*" Finally, the evidence from section III might be filed as "*Liberal arts majors succeed in business.*" You will, however, find that everybody's filing system is idiosyncratic to him or her. Whatever your system, you want to make sure that the evidence is (1) readily accessible and (2) that the argument each quotation supports is clearly understood. If you succeed in achieving those two goals, you will have an effective filing system, whether using notecards or briefs.

Conclusion

Arguments can be broken into two constituent parts: evidence and interpretation. Beginning one's research is a relatively easy process as long as the proper indexes and subject headings are used. Choosing which evidence to record is more difficult as the advocate must consider the evidence type and credibility. There are three types of evidence: examples, statistics, and testimony; each one has its particular uses. There are also questions specifically relevant to each type regarding its meaning and credibility. Six general tests of evidence can help us decide which evidence is most believable; the tests are of internal consistency, external consistency, source, timeliness, context, and precision. Finally, after the evidence has been chosen, it should be recorded in a form usable in argumentation, organized into arguments and with complete bibliographic citations.

With credible, appropriate, well-recorded and organized data at hand, the advocate has completed one of the most important tasks for undertaking any debate or argument. The next task is to decide what the evidence means and what positions can be reasonably constructed based on it.

Notes

1. We will return to a further discussion of audience members' use of their experiences to guide their evaluation of data and arguments when we examine psychological presumption in Chapter 7.
2. In academic debate, the argument is often phrased as "My evidence post-dates yours," meaning that my evidence is more recent than yours and therefore automatically more credible. As we will see, this is an extremely simplistic version of the test of timeliness.
3. Be careful not to confuse *precision* with *accuracy*. Data may be precise (very detailed) yet inaccurate (not true). They may also be accurate without being precise. We use all six tests of evidence to determine whether we believe data are accurate.
4. There is a fifth possible response, one that shifts the burden of proof back to the opposition. I could argue that because I have at least supplied *an* example, it should be *presumed* representative unless my opposition supplies one that demonstrates its unrepresentativeness. Such a response may be psychologically satisfying, but its logical weakness is twofold: (1) often the opposition can easily come up with one, two, or more counterexamples; and (2) the response does not use any pro-active arguments that defend the example's representativeness.
5. We return to the concept of fields of argument in Chapter 9.
6. Most debaters use a combination of the two methods, using briefs for their core arguments that are routinely argued, and notecards for those that are only occasionally used.

Selected Bibliography

Benson, James A. "The Use of Evidence in Intercollegiate Debate." *Argumentation and Advocacy* 7 (1970): 260–70.

Brownlee, Don. "The Consequences of Quantification." *CEDA Yearbook* 3 (1982): 29–31.

Horwitz, Tony. "The Working Poor." *Wall Street Journal* 12 Nov. 1993, A1.

Rieke, Richard D., and David H. Smith. "The Dilemma of Ethics and Advocacy in the Use of Evidence." *Western Journal of Speech Communication* 32 (1968): 223–33.

Newman, Robert P., and Dale R. Newman. *Evidence.* Boston: Houghton, Mifflin, 1969.

Spiker, Barry K., Tom D. Daniels, and Lawrence Bernabo. "The Quantitative Quandary in Forensics: The Use and Abuse of Statistical Evidence." *Argumentation and Advocacy* 19 (1982): 87–96.

Weiss, Robert O. "The Audience Standard." *CEDA Yearbook* 6 (1985): 43–49.

Discussion Questions

1. Choose an example of some evidence—such as a story, a survey, or an authoritative quotation—that you believe is perhaps true but that you are not certain about. Which tests of evidence could you use to support that evidence? Identify the tests of evidence you have used that support belief in that evidence and the ones that support disbelief. Remember that you may use the same test to support both belief and disbelief in the same evidence.

2. If you were arguing about a person's motivation for doing an act, which kinds of evidence would probably work best? Which kinds would probably be the hardest to use?

3. If you were arguing about global economic trends, which kinds of evidence would probably work best? Which kinds would probably be the hardest to use?

4. Why is conclusionary evidence considered the weakest kind of testimony?

REASONING

*D*efined broadly, reasoning is the process of inferring new ideas from already accepted data or premises. In some ways, we have already touched on reasoning in the previous two chapters. Toulmin's model indicates how we reason from data and warrants to new, though perhaps qualified, claims. The tests of evidence reveal how we reason toward seeing certain data as more or less credible. In this chapter, we examine two general types of reasoning: interpretive and causal. For each type of reasoning, we first look at the role it plays in policy and nonpolicy argument and then discuss the methods by which we reason. In the last section of the chapter, we examine common pitfalls in reasoning, traditionally known as fallacies of reasoning.

Interpretive Reasoning

As noted in the previous chapter, the world around us demands interpretation. If we see clouds and hear thunder, we decide that rain is on its way and head indoors. We may decide that a corporation's employee productivity is a better measure of success than its net profit. We may think that a fellow student's classroom contributions are intended only for the purpose of getting a better grade, or we may interpret those behaviors as genuinely motivated by a desire to learn. For each of these decisions, we draw our conclusions from a combination of past experiences and the phenomena that we (or others we trust) are currently observing. This process can be called **interpretive reasoning**.

Interpretive Reasoning and Argument

There are two reasons that interpretive reasoning is an integral part of any argument, including academic debate. First, the interpretation of phenomena is an inescapable part of being human; second, interpretations are inherently debatable.

Communication scholars have long recognized that *the interpretation of phenomena is an inescapable part of thought and language.* Meaning resides not in the words we use but in how we interpret them as individuals. This is true because we all process language through our own, unique perspective. For example, even a simple word/thought unit like "tea" carries hundreds of experiences and associations for us. We may think of our childhood, for instance, when our mother insisted that we drink hot tea when we were sick, and we may still experience nausea at the very mention of the word. Or we may think of iced tea, a Southern tradition that includes unlimited refills at a restaurant. Coupled with a hot summer's day, the mention of tea may evoke a rich, pleasant association even if we do not stop consciously to consider why. Someone else may think of herbal teas and have associations with health and nature.

For more complex ideas—such as the role of entitlement programs in a market economy or the principle of Mutually Assured Destruction as our nation's nuclear defense policy—the range of potential associations and interpretations multiplies tremendously. For example, how do we interpret entitlement programs such as Medicare and Social Security? Are they a sign of American decline, a disintegration of our culture's emphasis on individual risk and responsibility? Or should they be considered a "safety net" that keeps our nation from experiencing another Great Depression? Yet a third interpretation is that such entitlement programs are programs of "fairness" because "no one should go hungry in a country as rich as ours." Because we all have had different upbringings, teachers, and experiences; because we read different books, newspapers, and magazines; because we watch different television shows and movies, and listen to different music—because of all these differences and many, many more, it is inevitable that we will have different interpretations of phenomena. In any dispute, human beings bring these different interpretations to their reasoning and their arguments.

Second, individual interpretations are not only inescapable; *they are inherently debatable.* Everyone has an opinion, and each of those opinions is debatable. Indeed, the interpretation of phenomena is going to constitute much of the "stuff" of policy and nonpolicy argument. Does 5 percent unemployment really constitute "full employment"? Should we call 95 percent coverage on health insurance "full coverage"? Should capital punishment be considered as punishment designed to deter or as an act of societal retribution/justice? Is the

United Nations doing a good job? No matter how you answer any of these questions, your answer is debatable. Because none of us is omniscient, our opinions and beliefs are open to question. *We* may believe that our interpretations are The Truth, but as we should all have learned long ago, others may not be similarly convinced. Although it is *not* true that one person's opinion is as good as another's—*some people's opinions contain better reasoning*—it *is* true, as the old adage goes, that everyone has an opinion. And it is the combination of these two facts—that everyone has one and that some people's are better than others —that makes opinions—interpretive reasoning—inherently debatable.

Methods of Interpretive Reasoning

Many scholars of language, psychology, and argumentation have argued that *all* reasoning is "analogical." Even if such a sweeping claim is not entirely true, clearly much of it is. By analogical reasoning, these scholars mean that our reasoning (and language itself) is based on the process of **association** and **dissociation**; that is, reasoning occurs through the use of *comparing, contrasting,* and *categorizing.* To begin learning the word *chair,* for instance, a child begins to associate certain characteristics with that word: article of furniture, meant to be sat upon, usually with legs and a back, and so on. To fully understand how the word is used, we must simultaneously associate it with *and* dissociate it from other items of furniture: a chair is *like* other pieces of "furniture" in that it is part of the general category "furniture," but it is also *unlike* other pieces of furniture in that it is *not* a table, *not* a bed, and so on. In further developing our categories, we learn how to associate and dissociate rocking chairs and recliners, kitchen chairs and executive desk chairs; we come to grasp immediately and intuitively the ways in which they are similar to each other and the ways in which they are different.

Because reasoning is built from "language," it too requires the ability to associate and dissociate. For example, we may argue that achievement test scores are a good measure of how successful our educational system is, whereas SAT scores are not. That is, we *associate* achievement tests with the quality of education but *dissociate* SAT scores from it. Is that good and accurate reasoning? What educational outcomes or practices are measured by—that is, associated with—achievement test questions? In what ways are SAT tests and achievement tests different—that is, dissociated from each other? As we shall see throughout this chapter, our ability to reason well is based partly on our skill at discerning similarities (associations) and differences (dissociations), and partly on our skill at discerning which of these similarities and differences are *relevant.* We look first at the four types of interpretive reasoning—inductive, deductive, sign, and analogy.

Inductive Reasoning   One method of interpretive reasoning is called **inductive reasoning,** or reasoning by example. Inductive reasoning occurs when we draw a generalization from a series of examples. In our first few college classes, for example, we receive a course schedule called a syllabus. Before long, we conclude that college professors organize their courses around a syllabus and that we will receive one early in the semester. Or, we see president after president submit (and Congress after Congress approve) an imbalanced federal budget, and we conclude that the federal budget will continue to run a deficit for the foreseeable future. Inductive reasoning is often defined as reasoning from the specific to the general—that is, from examples to generalizations.

If we were debating that "U.S. membership in the United Nations is not beneficial," we might use inductive reasoning to support the argument that the United Nations fails to accomplish its goals. We might discuss several major examples of failed U.N. missions, and from those examples conclude that U.S. membership in a failed organization is not beneficial. Inductive reasoning could also be used to support the argument that "drug testing in the workplace carries risk of invasion of privacy." One or more examples in which a worker's privacy was violated by drug testing could yield the generalization that the risk of such damaging exposure is always present.

Association and dissociation are, of course, critical components of the inductive process. We must associate similar occurrences in similar situations in order to reach inductive generalizations. Additionally, to determine whether the induction is warranted, we must be able to discern any differences between these situations *or* similarities with situations that had dissimilar results. Was the United Nations solely responsible for each of the failed missions we enumerated? Are there other, more major or representative examples in which the United Nations succeeded in accomplishing its goals? Inductive reasoning is often difficult to sustain in an argument because there are simply too many examples to consider, discuss, and debate. It is, however, a psychologically satisfying method of reasoning. Human beings tend to generalize very quickly, often on the basis of very few examples or experiences. The importance to us of first impressions and the pervasiveness of racial and cultural stereotypes are two examples of the power of inductive reasoning. For both reasons—the potential for mistaken interpretations and the psychological appeal of such thinking—inductive reasoning should be considered (and argued) with some care.

Deductive Reasoning   **Deductive reasoning** is the opposite of inductive reasoning; instead of reasoning from the specific to the general, we reason from the general to the specific. From the induction about college syllabi above, we might develop a generalization that "All college courses begin with the distribution of a syllabus." We then predict that for the beginning of a particular course, "We will receive a syllabus." Or, we may argue that "The federal budget will not be balanced for the foreseeable future, so I do not expect to see a balanced budget for the year 1998." In each instance, we apply a generalization to a particular case, or reason from the general to the specific.

If we wished to use deduction to support the argument that "Drug testing in the workplace is not beneficial," we might argue that any employer practice that violates constitutional protections is not "beneficial." We might then argue that the removal of blood, urine, or hair from a person's body is an "unlawful search and seizure," as defined in the Fourth Amendment of the Constitution. Thus, we conclude, drug testing is not beneficial.

Again, the process of association is integral to deductive reasoning because one must be able to associate a generalized situation with a particular one. In what sense is the extraction of blood like the search of a person's house? Again, we must be able to recognize those dissimilarities that might prevent the generalization from applying to that particular case. For example, the Supreme Court has established a "reasonable expectation of privacy" test for deciding which searches are lawful. By this test, our homes are protected from unlawful searches (we may have a "reasonable expectation" of privacy there), but our automobiles are not (expectations of privacy there are "unreasonable"). Deductively, this test has been applied to employers testing for drugs, journalists scouring our trash, and principals searching children's lockers at school. In each case, the similarities and differences between the new case and the case on which the precedent was based have been debated and argued to determine whether the generalization applies to the specific instance.

Reasoning from Sign   Reasoning from sign occurs when we conclude that a certain situation exists because we see a "sign" that we associate with the occurrence of that situation. If we see the sign of smoke, we may interpret that to mean there is a fire, even though we do not see the fire itself. If you receive a poor grade in a subject, your parents may interpret that as a sign that you did not apply yourself well that semester. If the gross national product fails to grow as much as it was predicted to do, we may take that as a sign that the economy is stagnant or even declining.

Reasoning from sign is particularly important when we are interpreting evidence. What will we take as a sign, or measure, that the economy is healthy? That the streets are safer? That students are learning more in school? That the military is adequately prepared for any possible contingency? In each instance, we could look at a variety of measures, signs, or "indicators," any of which may operate more or less *accurately* as signs.[1]

When debating this kind of reasoning, we can easily fall into the "obviously" or "commonsense" trap. "Stock prices are down, so the economy is obviously doing poorly," someone might claim. But is that necessarily true? Do stock prices in fact accurately reflect economic performance, or do they reflect investors' perceptions of future economic performance? Consider a second example: If drop-out rates decline, are students really learning more in school, or are drop-out rates a sign that students are learning less? The reasoning for the second claim could be that the less-motivated students have been coerced into staying in school, thus detracting from the general learning environment. For any sign, it is important to consider (1) how consistent the occurrence of the sign is with the occurrence of the phenomenon it is a "sign" of, and (2) which characteristics of the phenomenon the sign is linked to.

By consistency, we are asking how often the phenomenon occurs without the resulting sign and how often the sign occurs without the occurrence of the phenomenon. How often is there fire without smoke, and how often is there smoke without fire? The fewer the exceptions, the more confident we can be about our use of that sign. Gross national product growth, unemployment rates, interest rates, and inventory levels are all considered good indicators of the nation's economic performance because they are consistently accurate. Conversely, stock prices, export/import levels, and dollar values are more debatable signs of the economy's health because their performance less consistently mirrors that of the economy.

In addition to consistency, we can also consider the relationship of the sign to the phenomenon. What characteristics of the phenomenon are linked to the sign? For example, if we look at dark clouds and say that they are a sign of rain, we are linking the presence and color of the clouds to their ability to create rain. For rain to occur, the water droplets must be large and they must be dense, thus creating a dark cloud. Thus, the link between the sign and the phenomenon we associate with it are relatively strong. However, if we return to the use of stock prices as a sign of economic performance, we see that the links between the two are weaker; that is, they are less direct and less consistent. Investors buy more or less stock because of their perceptions of how the economy—and the stock market itself—will perform *in the future*. Stock prices may also be linked to *future* economic performance in that falling or rising stock prices *may* affect the amount of capital companies have available for investment. Although stock prices have some relationship to future economic performance, they have a very weak link to current economic performance. Stock prices are, therefore, considered a poor indicator of how the economy is currently performing.

Reasoning from Analogy   We may broadly say that all reasoning is analogical, but there is a particular kind of interpretive reasoning that makes explicit use of comparisons. When we **reason from analogy,** we may do one of two things: (1) we might interpret an unknown situation based on a known situation, or (2) compare or contrast two known situations. You probably used the known to interpret the unknown when, as a freshman, you prepared for your college classes based on your high school experiences. Similarly, many observers look to

TABLE 5.1   Sample Analogies

Situation B		Situation A
College classes	*compared to*	High school classes
American national health care	*compared to*	Canadian national health care
American math & science education	*compared to*	Math and science education in other industrialized nations

the British and Canadian systems of national health care to estimate how well or how poorly an American national health care system would work.

As an example of the second type of analogy, we compare two known situations when we say that the United States ranks fourteenth among the industrialized nations in math and science scores. In this use of analogy, we are suggesting that (1) we are like the industrialized nations in our need for math and science, (2) because we rank fourteenth, we are not doing as good a job of educating our children in math and science as we should be, and (3) because the other nations are doing a better job, maybe we should learn something from *how* they are doing it.

For either use of reasoning from analogy, we can say that there is a situation B (unknown or known) that we are comparing to a situation A (always known). In Table 5.1 we illustrate how the comparisons in our previous examples could be formulated. Three questions are important to consider when reasoning from analogy: (1) How similar are the two situations? (2) How relevant are the similarities to the interpretation being made? (3) Do we really know what we think we know about situation A?

Because analogies make comparisons between two situations, it is important to ask how similar those two situations really are. Often, this question is considered numerically: How many points of similarity are there and how many points of difference? Canada and America share the same basic geography: that's a point of similarity. Both share a relatively similar history of development and culture, and our economic mix of agriculture, industry, and service sectors is generally similar. Although there are obvious differences between the two countries, most observers reasoning from analogy prefer using the Canadian system of health care to the British system because, of the two, Canada is perceived as being more similar to the United States. *The more similar the two situations are, the more confident we are that the interpretations drawn from the analogy are valid.*

It is not only important that the two situations be generally similar, however. Whether the similarities are relevant may be of much greater importance to the validity of the reasoning than the sheer number of similarities. For example, if we try to predict future costs of health care in the United States based on a comparison with Canada's health care system, there may be several important differences to consider. For example, will the quality of medical care be similar? If the United States plan allows the use of semiprivate rooms or the funding of multiple tests and the Canadian plan does not, then the cost of each plan will differ. If there are enough such relevant differences, we may conclude that the Canadian system does not offer a good comparison with the proposed U.S. plan. *The more relevant the similarities, the more confidence we have in the interpretations drawn from the analogy.*

Finally, it is also important to make sure that we really know what we think we know about Situation A—that is, the known situation we are reasoning *from*. It may seem obvious to say that we cannot make claims such as "We should pattern our health care plan after Canada's because the Canadian system works so well" if, upon investigation, it turns out that the Canadian system does not work well at all. It is an important point to remember, however, because far too often arguers focus on whether the situations are analogical—is Canada enough like the United States in ways that are relevant—rather than on whether the claims about Situation A are true. It is important to remember this critical point: *if our claims about the known situation are not accurate, our reasoning from analogy fails.*

Interpretive reasoning is important because it allows us to understand the past, take full measure of the present, and anticipate the future. In each instance, it can play an integral role in academic debate. Routinely, we use all four types of interpretive reasoning in such argument: inductive reasoning, deductive reasoning, reasoning from sign, and reasoning from analogy. We now turn to a related, but distinct, type of reasoning: causal reasoning.

Causal Reasoning

In **causal reasoning,** we are attempting to determine whether a cause-effect relationship exists between two phenomena. We say we have a cause-effect relationship when we believe that two entities have an interactive relationship in which one entity is producing (or is capable of producing) the other. We first examine the role of cause-effect claims in argument and then consider the two methods for determining that such a relationship does (or does not) exist.

Causal Reasoning and Argument

We may use many synonyms for the terms *cause* and *effect*—results in, forces us to, prevents us from, creates the effect of, and so on. Do poor vocabulary skills result in poor classroom performance? Would U.S. withdrawal from the United Nations prevent that organization from functioning effectively? Does pretrial publicity create a biased trial situation? However we phrase it, though, we are making the same claim: that a cause-effect relationship does (or does not) exist between two phenomena.

Cause-effect claims are part of almost any debate argument because such arguments usually discuss the *value* of an object or belief. Typically, we attach value to an object or belief because it *does* something, a "something" which, in turn, we find desirable, undesirable, beneficial, or unfortunate. For example, if we say that U.S. membership in the United Nations is beneficial, we would probably support that argument by saying that because of our membership, certain things happen. We might argue that U.S. membership *causes* the United Nations to be a stronger body, it *increases* the chances of peace, it *raises* our stature around the world, and it *increases* global stability through the many humanitarian programs our membership helps support. We have now made four cause-effect claims about U.S. membership in the United Nations. Each of these, we then argue, is of value to America, and therefore our membership in the United Nations is beneficial.

Whenever we argue that some belief or action is valuable because it has already or will in the future create certain desirable results, we are making a cause-effect claim. We are saying that X (a belief or action) will cause (or probably cause) Y (certain desirable results) to occur. Similarly, when we contend that some belief or action is *not* valuable because it will result in certain *undesirable* effects, we are advancing a cause-effect claim.

It is also important to remember that the same causal reasoning we employ to demonstrate the *presence* of a cause-effect relationship can also be employed to demonstrate the *absence* of one. To argue that belief X will *not* result in desired effect Y, or that belief X will *not* result in undesirable effect Y, we must again use causal reasoning. In any argument, it is usually just as important for us to show that our opponents' causal claims are not true as it is to show that our own causal claims are valid.

Methods of Establishing Cause and Effect

We can use two methods of causal reasoning: the associational method and the connectional method.[2] We will see that each method by itself is often incomplete and open to dispute, and that the strongest causal claims are those that can be supported using both methods.

The Associational Method   When we use the associational method, we are observing that Cause X and Effect Y occur together (or occur in association with each other) across situations. After making a "sufficient" number of such observations, we may conclude that X is indeed the cause of Y. Suppose, for example, you saw an advertisement for "Bigfish Pond" that promoted it as a place where the fish are big *and* biting. You go to Bigfish Pond, but the first time you go you catch no fish. The second and third times you go, you catch no fish again. Eventually, you'll probably conclude that Bigfish Pond had been falsely advertised and that, if you fished there again, it (fishing at the pond) would *cause* you to go home empty handed (you would catch no fish).

The experimental method, of course, is one use of the associational method. Based on John Stuart Mill's canons of causation, the experimental method makes two basic assumptions:

1. If the effect (Y) is present when the cause (X) is present; and the effect (Y) is not present when the cause (X) is not present, then a cause-effect relationship between X and Y exists.

2. If the effect (Y) is present when the cause (X) is *not* present; or the effect (Y) is not present when the cause (X) *is* present, then a cause-effect relationship between X and Y does *not* exist.

If we think of a few simple scientific claims—boiling water causes it to convert into steam, acidic solutions cause litmus paper to turn pink, hot air rises—we see the use of the associational method and canons of causation. In each instance, the cause (boiling, acidity, heat) *always and invariably* creates the effects (the water turns into steam, the litmus paper turns pink, the air rises). Three problems, however, prevent us from rigidly applying these canons of causation to *human* affairs, the usual subject of arguments in debate.

First is the problem of **absolute causality,** or the question of whether the cause invariably results in the effect. Traditionally, this has been a question of sufficiency—whether the cause is a **sufficient condition** in and of itself to result in the effect. In many situations, the "cause" by itself is *not* enough to result in the effect; that is, it will not *absolutely* cause the effect to happen. For example, we may believe that "poverty causes crime," but few of us would try to claim that poverty *always* causes crime. We know there are many times that a person lives in poverty (the cause is present) but that the person does not turn to crime (the effect is not present). Indeed, for some, poverty becomes a motivator that causes them to work harder so as to achieve legitimate economic success. Yet, we still may be comfortable with the claim that poverty causes some people to commit crimes. It is, we reason, at least a partial cause of the effect.

A second problem to using the canons of causation is **alternative causality,** or the question of whether other causes may have produced (or will produce) the effect. Here the question has traditionally been framed as one of necessity: Is the cause a **necessary condition** for the effect to take place? For many situations, there are many possible causes that can create the effect; that is, there are many *alternative* causes that may result in the effect's occurring. Returning to our example of poverty and crime, although we may believe that poverty causes crime, few of us would say that poverty is the *only* cause of crime. We know that some criminals are sociopaths, some people commit crimes while under the influence of drugs or alcohol, or that some commit crime purely out of greed. Put another way, we know that crime can occur (the effect can be present) even when the criminal is not poor (the cause is absent); there are other, alternative causes. It is not *necessary* for a person to be poor to commit a crime. Again, however, we may still be comfortable with the claim that "poverty causes crime," even though we know that poverty is not the only cause of crime.

A third problem confronting our use of the canons of causation is **measurability**, or whether occurrence of the cause and effect can be adequately observed and recorded. In order for the experimental method to work, we need to observe the cause and the effect in many different situations. Also, it is important to *control* for other factors that could influence the effect—that is, to try to remove them from the situation or to make sure they remain constant across the situations observed. How do we do that with humans, however? Experiments must usually conform to a strict code of ethics. But many experiments that would be necessary for a rigorous collection of data would be unethical to perform ("OK, let's subject this group of children to poverty and see how many of them commit crimes as compared to the control group"). Nor is it always possible to construct the experiments that would be necessary to *prove* a cause-effect relationship ("Let's start a nuclear war and see whether it *does* cause nuclear winter!"). Rather than being allowed to do experiments, with their rigor in controlling and collecting the data, we often have to draw our cause-effect reasoning from whatever data are available. Inevitably, the probability that a cause-effect relationship exists and the likelihood of the effect's occurring in a certain situation become critical considerations.

Despite these problems, the associational method is still an important one for causal reasoning. What we must realize is that we cannot hold strictly to the canons of causation but must use a looser version of them called the canon of correlation. This canon states that when a cause-effect relationship is present the following should occur: the more the cause (X) is present, the more the effect (Y) should be present; and the less the cause (X) is present, the less the effect (Y) should be present.

To return to the poverty and crime example, we may base our claim on two reasons. First, statistical studies of the past show that as poverty increases, so do crime rates—that is, as more of the suspected cause (poverty) is present, more of the effect (crime) is also present. Second, we may look at the demographic makeup of our prison populations and point to the statistics showing that a disproportionate number of the inmates come from poverty. Suppose, for example, that 15 percent of Americans live below the poverty level but that 60 percent of the prison population comes from that 15 percent. Because there is a higher chance of committing a crime if one is poor, we might conclude that poverty causes crime.

The argument for restricting handguns makes similar use of the canon of correlation. Typically, one argument is that if we reduce the number of handguns, the number of firearm deaths will also decrease. Part of the causal reasoning here is based on the associational method. About 66 percent of the firearms in America are long guns (rifles and shotguns); 33 percent are handguns. This 33 percent, however, accounts for 66 percent of firearm deaths and 90 percent of firearm injuries. If handguns did *not* cause firearm deaths and injuries, then the number of deaths and injuries should be *proportionate* to their overall numbers: 33 percent. The more handguns there are (cause is present), the more firearm deaths and injuries (effects) we see. Thus, the causal reasoning goes, decrease the handguns and you will decrease the deaths and injuries from guns.

The major argument used against causal reasoning supported by the associational method evokes the three problems discussed above: How do you know the cause *really* creates the effect? Isn't it just a correlation? Couldn't something else have caused it? Indeed, it is true that correlations may give false clues regarding the cause-and-effect relationship. For example, the disproportionate number of poor people in prison may occur *not* because they commit a disproportionate number of crimes but because they are disproportionately charged with crimes, disproportionately prosecuted for those crimes, and disproportionately found guilty of those crimes. Mock trials, for instance, have found that jurors are more likely to vote for a guilty verdict if the defendant *looks* poor and *talks* like a poor person. Thus, it may be that poverty does not cause crime but that it does cause people to be *convicted* of crime.

It is always possible to play the devil's advocate and ask, "But isn't that just a correlation?" Correlations, however, are usually the best we can do using the associational method, and they can still be useful for helping us to identify an effect's cause. Indeed, the mock trial evidence noted above *also* uses the associational method and is itself "*only a correlation*." Not all correlational claims are equal, however, and there are several ways by which we can strengthen our associational claims.

First, because the associational method looks at the presence of cause and effect across situations, *the more situations in which the correlation occurs, the greater will be our confidence in our causal claim.* Suppose we claimed that gun control laws reduce crime. If we showed that crime rates dropped in Los Angeles after the adoption of gun control laws, that would be correlational support for our point. If we could also show that it dropped in ten other cities after the adoption of gun control laws, we could advance our claim with greater certainty. The more often the pattern repeats itself—the more X, the more Y; the less X, the less Y—the more certain we can be that a cause-effect relationship does exist.

Second, a corollary point is that *the more diverse the situations across which the pattern holds true, the more confidence we have in our claim.* Suppose, for example, we can show that the adoption of gun control laws and the reduction of crime rates have occurred not only in eleven urban areas but also in eight suburban areas and fourteen rural areas where statistics are available. When the pattern of X and Y occurring together holds constant while other variables such as population density, ethnic background, and socioeconomic levels change, we have more confidence in our causal claim.

Third, *the more similar two situations are, where the only difference is that X is present in one of the situations but absent in the other, the more confident we can be in any causal claim that emerges.* For example, if we compared the strong gun control laws (the presence of X) of Washington, D.C., with the almost nonexistent gun control laws (the absence of X) of Idaho and saw higher crime rates in the former, we might have little confidence in any causal claim that emerges because the two situations—Washington, D.C., and Idaho—are too dissimilar. Conversely, if we could compare South Dakota with North Dakota, or Cleveland with Pittsburgh, where we saw X in one but not the other, our confidence would be stronger in any causal claim we made.

It is for this reason that many associational studies prefer "before and after" statistics, as in "New York before and after the adoption of gun control," or "Minnesota before and after the adoption of mandatory seat belt laws." Such before and after statistics are one way, though still not perfect, for "controlling" the similarities in the situations. They are not perfect because the situations will be similar but not identical; states, cities, and even individuals change from month to month and year to year. Only *identical* situations can yield claims for the canon of causation. *Similar* situations will still yield only correlational claims, but the more similar the situations are, the more confidence we can have in the conclusions we draw from them. A final way of strengthening a correlational claim is to use it with the connectional method, which we examine next.

The Connectional Method   Where the associational method relies on the observation that X and Y occur together, the connectional method discovers cause-effect relationships by considering what property of X causes Y to occur. Thus, whereas the associational method asks, "Do X and Y seem 'associated' in time and place?" the connectional method asks, "What is it about X that would cause Y to occur?"

In looking for the quality, characteristic, or property of X that results in Y, the term *inherent* can be useful. To say that a property is inherent in something is to say that it is an integral characteristic of that something. We might say that human beings are *inherently* land-dwelling creatures—we cannot exist naturally in the ocean. We might say that organizations are *inherently* bureaucratic, that dynamite is *inherently* dangerous, or that television is an *inherently* visual medium of communication. In each instance, by saying it is inherent, we are saying that a certain quality—bureaucratic, dangerous, or visual—is an integral and inseparable part of the phenomenon—organizations, dynamite, or television.

In the connectional method, as we ask "Why is it logical that X is the cause of Y?" we are typically asking, "What is *inherent* in X that causes Y to occur?" If we return to the causal claim that "if we reduce the number of handguns, the number of firearm deaths will also decrease," we see that part of the support is based on the connectional method.

Inherently, the difference between a handgun and a long gun is that the former is shorter than the latter. Because of this inherent property, handguns are easier to conceal and more portable. For both reasons, they lend themselves to being weapons of crime and weapons of self-defense whereas long guns are more frequently used for hunting and sporting purposes. As handguns are weapons whose purpose is often crime and self-defense, it is *logical* that we would see them involved in a disproportionate number of deaths and injuries.

Further, firearm safety rules routinely recommend that firearms be kept unloaded and locked up when not in use, with the ammunition stored and locked in a separate place. However, when kept as a weapon for self-defense, few people follow any of those rules. Stored in a "handy" place and kept continually loaded, handguns lend themselves to crimes of passion and to discovery by children and to unintended use.

Finally, the inherent quality of having a short barrel makes the handgun the weapon of choice for firearm suicides. Psychologically, most suicide victims are unwilling to maneuver the longer-barreled rifle or shotgun into a position to fatally shoot themselves. Handguns are far easier to use psychologically when one decides to use a firearm as the instrument of his or her own death.

We have seen, then, numerous connections between Cause X (handguns) and Effect Y (injuries and deaths), all stemming from one inherent quality of handguns—a short barrel.[3] If we return to the associational data once more, we can see one further illustration of the connectional method at work. Remember that handguns, as 33 percent of the total firearms owned in the United States, were used in 66 percent of firearm deaths and 90 percent of firearm injuries. A question we might ask is, "Why is the percentage of deaths lower than the percentage of injuries?" All else being equal, the percentages should be the same. The associational data tell us, however, that if we reduce the number of handguns, firearm deaths will decrease at a lower rate than will firearm injuries.

If we return to the connectional method of causal reasoning, we can ask, "What is there about X (handguns) that causes fewer deaths but more injuries?" The answer is that handguns typically fire lower caliber bullets and carry less powerful charges; the bullets are smaller and they travel at slower rates of speed. Thus, if a person is shot by a long gun, the bullet is more likely to do more damage to the body than is a bullet from a handgun; therefore, a wound from a long gun will more likely result in death than will a wound from a handgun. Conversely, one stands a better chance of having less damage done by a handgun bullet and therefore a better chance of surviving the shooting.

Traditionally, the skeptical response to the connectional method reasoning is to say, "Well, that's a good theory, but does it really happen in practice?" There are three ways of trying to show that the theory is in fact borne out by practice. First, examples and primary testimony can show that the inherent property does exist and/or is linked to the effect. For the handgun example, that means showing people who have used handguns in crimes of passion, or children who have found the weapon in Mom's purse, all loaded and ready to go. Second, expert or secondary testimony can show that the inherent property exists and/or is linked to the effect. A psychologist might testify that suicide victims find it psychologically easier to use handguns than long guns. Finally, we can use the connectional and the associational method in combination. The connectional method can show that the theory is good and that the data are more than just a "correlation," and the associational method can show that the phenomenon being examined "really does happen" in practice. Together, the two methods can establish strong causal reasoning for believing that X is the cause of Y.

Fallacies of Reasoning

In addition to learning how to support your reasoning with methods such as the ones just discussed, you also need to recognize methods of reasoning that are false—that is, reasoning that does not lead to valid conclusions. In this section, we examine several common fallacies of reasoning. Our purpose for doing so is twofold. First, there are certain common "traps" that arguers fall into or consciously abuse, and learning the signs of those traps or fallacies can be useful when we argue against them. Second, learning these fallacies of reasoning can sharpen our own thinking and reasoning. Not only can we learn what not to do, but studying the fallacies can also increase our understanding of how the reasoning process works and what therefore constitutes "good" reasoning.

As our discussion proceeds, it is important that we do not treat these fallacies as simple signs that indicate reasoning gone awry. Fallacies of reasoning occur *not* because we have followed the wrong "formula" of reasoning; indeed, these fallacies all grow out of the methods of reasoning discussed above. *Fallacies of reasoning occur when our reasoning is inappropriate for the particular situation.* This is a point we will underscore throughout this final section as we discuss thirteen common fallacies.

Composition

The **fallacy of composition** occurs when we believe that what is true of the part is necessarily true of the whole. Frequently called a **hasty generalization,** a fallacy of composition occurs when we have moved from the specific to the general too quickly in our inductive reasoning or our use of the associational method. Students frequently commit a fallacy of composition when they are first acquainted with Communication Studies courses, thinking that all the courses offered in that discipline will be variations of the Public Speaking class. Some of those courses are, such as Oral Interpretation or Advanced Public Speaking. Other communications classes, however, such as Interpersonal Communication or Organizational Communication, are very different. We commit a hasty generalization if we generalize to all communications classes based on our experience in Public Speaking.

Fallacies of composition are, unfortunately, common in debate argument, as we use one person's tragic experience or a couple of undesirable results and generalize to the entire population or experience. One person's privacy was violated by a drug test, so we conclude that many people's privacy is being violated on a daily basis. Two states passed stricter measures punishing criminals and crime rates dropped, so we argue that the same would occur if the other forty-eight states enacted stricter punishments also. In three crises, U.N. mediation failed to resolve the conflict peacefully, so we contend that U.N. mediation must always be useless. In each of these examples, we have made a fallacy of composition or hasty generalization.

The fallacy of composition does not mean that we should avoid inductive reasoning; it simply means that we must be careful in our inductions. We should avoid moving too quickly from the example to the generalization. We should ask if there is additional evidence to support our conclusion. We should avoid stereotypical thinking—about people, places, groups, or behaviors— because stereotyping is just another form of the fallacy of composition. Finally, when we ask whether our examples are representative of the whole or whether a statistical sampling was representative of the population, we are helping to prevent the fallacy of composition from occurring. Inductive thinking is an inescapable part of the reasoning process. Doing it well results in accurate generalizations that can help us negotiate the decisions of life; doing it poorly results in fallacious reasoning that can quickly mislead us.

Division

The **fallacy of division** occurs when we believe that what is true of the whole is necessarily true of the part. Misusing deductive reasoning, this fallacy applies an accurate generalization to a specific case in which the generalization is not true.

For example, it may be generally true that the federal government is bureaucratic, but that does not mean that every agency within the government is therefore bureaucratic. It may be generally true that handguns are weapons of self-defense rather than hunting or sporting, but that does not mean that every individual who buys a handgun does so for self-defense purposes. Similarly, it may be accurate to say that new weapons systems routinely incur large cost overruns, but that does not necessarily mean that a newly proposed system will do so as well.

Of course, like inductive reasoning, deductive reasoning is inescapable in debate argument. We have to generalize about things, and then we have to apply those generalizations to specific instances. However, we can avoid committing the fallacy of division by asking two questions about the application of a generalization to a specific instance. First, is there any evidence about or properties of the specific situation that suggest the generalization is applicable (or inapplicable) to it? For instance, if the proposed weapons system has been vaguely planned, the costs insufficiently detailed, and the contract awarded to a manufacturer who routinely runs over budget, I feel safer in applying my generalization that weapons systems typically incur large cost overruns and that this one will follow that pattern.

The second question I can ask is whether I have appropriately qualified my application of the generalization. Fallacies of division often occur when arguers make unqualified claims: it will, it always does, it will never happen. Appropriate qualifiers can help ensure that we are using the deductive process well. For example, if I have no additional data and reasoning about the newly proposed weapon system, I may qualify my claim by saying, "Because most weapon systems incur large cost overruns, this proposed system *probably* will, too." If my initial generalization can be defended well enough, I can even argue that with no reasons to believe the new system will *not* produce cost overruns, we should operate under the assumption that it will.

As with fallacies of composition, fallacies of division are common occurrences in all types of argumentation. However, we can help prevent our deductive reasoning from being fallacious if we remember to consider any additional data or reasons that support or deny our deductive conclusions and to qualify those conclusions appropriately when necessary.

Suppressed Major Premise

Another fallacy that concerns deductive reasoning occurs when we do not explicitly state a questionable generalization, which can also be called the major premise of the syllogism or the warrant of the argument (see Chapter 3). As we noted in our discussion of warrants in Chapter 3, they are often assumed and implied by an argument rather than developed explicitly. A fallacy of reasoning occurs when we assume that an incorrect generalization is true or when we avoid stating it explicitly because we know it is questionable.

One example of a suppressed major warrant is the argument that a two-year cap on recipients' welfare benefits will help turn "welfare into workfare." As many opponents have been quick to note, the **suppressed major premise** here is that people *want* to stay on welfare for as long as they possibly can, and without a two-year limit to force them off welfare, they will stay on it indefinitely. If that premise is not true, the two-year cap may not turn welfare into workfare but may instead turn welfare into a two-year resting spot on the way to permanent poverty.

Consider the argument that because the United Nations has failed to prevent numerous regional and internal wars from flaring up, it has failed in its peacekeeping mission. The suppressed major premise here is that the United Nations' peacekeeping mission is to prevent the outbreak of *any* kind of warfare. Most observers, however, would argue that such a goal is unrealistic in the extreme and that it is ahistorical. The purpose of the United Nations, they would argue, is to *contain* wars so that internal conflicts do not become regional wars, regional wars do not become international wars, and international wars do not become global superpower wars. Measured by its success in containing our wars, one might argue that the United Nations has been extremely effective.

While either claim about the United Nations is certainly debatable, the suppressed major premise in the first claim can prevent good reasoning about the question from taking place. We can help ourselves avoid committing this fallacy by stating our reasoning as explicitly and carefully as possible. We can help keep ourselves from being misled by others when we question their unstated premises, generalizations, and warrants.

False Dilemma

There was a popular bumper sticker during the Vietnam War that "protested" against the protest, saying "America: Love it or Leave it." For many antiwar protesters, this was a particularly maddening use of a **false dilemma.** Such a fallacy occurs when the arguer presents an artificially restricted choice of two options. The "dilemma" then is to decide between these two—often equally undesirable —choices. Many thought "Love it or Leave it" was such a fallacy because they believed many other options were justified: "Sort of like it but want to change it"; "Tolerate it and want to be left alone"; "Hate it as it is but it's mine as much as yours—You leave if you don't like me!"

The example of the bumper sticker is representative in that the false dilemma is a common tool of demagogues from all points of the political spectrum. Based on either-or thinking—*either* it's this way *or* it's that way—such bipolar reasoning is a natural part of the association/dissociation process and frequently occurs in arguments regarding policy and nonpolicy issues. Our first act of learning language is to associate some ideas with a word and to dissociate other ideas from that same word. Thus, we learn either-or thinking: either the object is a ball or it isn't; either the color is green or it isn't; either we can have the cookie or we can't. False dilemmas naturally appeal to this most basic level of reasoning and are often, like the bumper sticker, simplistically formulated.

False dilemmas do occur in more "thoughtful" argumentation as well, however, and can be more artfully constructed. In the debate about children's television, the broadcast industry has often argued that the violence portrayed in cartoons, the Three Stooges movies, or similar programming does not encourage violence in children. Their claim is that television cannot influence that type of behavior. In response, various consumer advocates have pointed out that the industry is quick to sell advertising for children's programs in the obvious belief that such advertising affects children's behavior. Television cannot have it both ways, these advocates argue in their dilemma: either television influences children's behavior or it does not.

This dilemma is inappropriate because it groups two *types* of actions into a single category of "behavior." It is possible, however, that the behavior of wanting a particular consumer product is a *qualitatively different kind of behavior* than is the behavior of committing violence. It may be that television can exercise some influence over the former but not over the latter. This speculation does not mean that the consumer advocates are wrong but simply that they are framing the argument with specious reasoning. The argument would contain better reasoning if phrased as an argument from analogy. The arguers should try to establish that the two kinds of behaviors are indeed similar and that the ability to influence one is partial proof that television can influence the other behavior as well. Phrased as a dilemma, the reasoning is oversimplified as the behaviors are assumed to be identical.

Of course, not all dilemmas are false ones. Sometimes we may indeed have only two options available to us; debate propositions are one such example! In another instance, one could argue that the use of urinalysis in drug testing is either invasive of one's privacy or susceptible to evasion. The only way to ensure that the urine sample is accurate—actually comes from the person being tested —is to be present when the person urinates, that is, to invade his or her privacy. There are, as far as we can see, no other alternatives. Some could argue that we may *reasonably* ensure both privacy and accuracy through several test-site and scheduling controls, but ultimately the dilemma for urinalysis remains the same: invade privacy or risk inaccuracy.

True dilemmas can be effective argumentation strategies as they outline the alternatives in clear, definitive choices. False dilemmas, however, result from simplistic thinking and may blind us to better, more reasonable alternatives. When you are confronting a dilemma in a debate, be sure to ask yourself whether the choices posed are indeed the only ones available. Before posing a dilemma, you should ask yourself the same question. Argumentatively, it is better to see the complexities of an argument than it is to try and squeeze your opponent into a false dilemma. Nothing destroys a false dilemma faster than the discovery of an alternative that the dilemma had not considered.

False Standards

Also known as the **fallacy of extension, false standards** arise when we use measurements that are apparently appropriate, but when carefully considered, are exposed as irrelevant. For example, propagandists for various nations have tried to use voter turnout as a standard for measuring how democratic a country is. "The Soviet Union's voter turnout is over 98 percent," Communist dictators used to boast, "whereas America's turnout is below 50 percent. Obviously, the U.S.S.R. is the more democratic country." The problem with this reasoning, of course, was that Soviet voters could vote for or against only the Communist slate of officers, that voting was not done by secret ballot, and that various rewards and sanctions were used to ensure artificially high turnouts.

This is not to say that voter turnout is a completely irrelevant standard for measuring the health of a democracy. Many scholars and observers of political life have argued that America's consistently low voter turnout is indeed the sign of an ailing democracy. What is a false standard in one situation—comparing the former U.S.S.R. to the United States—may be an appropriate standard in another situation.

To condemn Shakespeare's plays as being historically inaccurate uses the standard of historical accuracy inappropriately. Shakespeare's purpose was to entertain and enlighten through drama; history only provided the scenic backdrop. On the other hand, it is entirely appropriate to condemn *The Protocols of the Elders of Zion* for its historical inaccuracy. That booklet purported to be the record of a Jewish conspiracy to overthrow all the governments in Europe. Subsequent documentation proved, however, that the pamphlet was actually the work of the Okhrana, the Russian czar's secret police, who used it to justify its pogroms against the Jewish population. Because the writing was presented as historically accurate, the standard of historical accuracy is an appropriate criterion in this situation.

As we discuss in greater detail in Chapter 12, standards are exceptionally important components of nonpolicy argument.[4] Consider just a few questions about standards that we would encounter if we were arguing that "a national system of health care in the United States would be desirable": What constitutes improved health services? What level of medical costs are acceptable to us? What do we consider "good quality of life" as opposed to "poor quality of life"?

What standards can we use to determine when the quality of life becomes so poor that life itself becomes unjustifiable to us? No matter what proposition we may be arguing, the use of appropriate standards will be an important part of good reasoning.

As we will see again in Chapter 12, when we are deciding which standards to use, we should carefully consider the entire situation to determine whether a standard is appropriate *to that situation.* Often using multiple standards is the wisest choice so that no single standard—such as voter turnout—becomes our measure of quality.

False Consolation

A special kind of false standard is the **fallacy of false consolation,** which occurs when we use an inappropriate analogy as a standard of quality. Specifically, false consolation arises when we compare one situation (A) with another situation (B) or an average of situations (ABCD) and draw the conclusion that A is doing well because it is "better than B" or that it is doing badly because it is "below the average of ABCD." As we noted in the discussion of statistics in Chapter 4, the term *average* is often misused because a statistical average (the total number divided by number of units) is not the same as an evaluative average (something that is of "fair" worth). Two problems can arise in this confusion of terms: (1) we may be averaging situations that are qualitatively different, and (2) the statistical average may be completely unrelated to the evaluative average.

As an example of the first problem, consider the use of Scholastic Aptitude Test (SAT) scores as a standard for evaluating state educational systems. Typically, North Carolina ranks low among the fifty states on its average SAT scores, generally about forty-eighth. Does that mean that North Carolina's educational system is forty-eighth in the nation? Certainly the headline writers and editorialists frequently see it that way. However, in many states, few students take the SAT. Many may take the American College Test (ACT) instead; perhaps few students are planning to pursue further education so most of them take neither test. North Carolina is one of only a few states in which over 60 percent of high school seniors take the exam. Because the student populations taking the test vary so greatly, to use North Carolina's forty-eighth place ranking as an indication of how the state's school system compares to the school systems of other states is an inappropriate analogy.

In addition to possible problems of inappropriate averaging, rankings and averages may provide false consolation because the statistical average is unrelated to the evaluative average. To say that our school district is "above average" does not necessarily mean that it is good; the statistically "average" district may be doing an atrociously bad job of educating its children. It could be that even the top performers—the first- and second-ranked of the group—are also performing poorly. Conversely, perhaps *all* the school districts are doing a good job of educating their children; in this case, the statistically "below average" district is not "below average" in an evaluative sense.

As with false standards generally, the fallacy of false consolation does not mean that we can never use statistical averages as a method for evaluating quality or performance. For example, comparing North Carolina's dropout rate to the national average may be an appropriate measure of its educational performance. Again, what is important is that we (1) carefully qualify the claims we make about quality based on statistical averages or rankings and (2) use multiple standards and data whenever possible so that we have a better comprehension of the situation we are evaluating.

Is/Ought Fallacy

Another special kind of false standard is the **is/ought fallacy.** Sometimes called **de facto reasoning,** we commit this fallacy when we put a positive value on something solely because it exists or "is familiar" to us. If, for example, I argue that political reform is desirable because it makes us "more democratic," and being more democratic is good because "the United States is a democracy," I have committed the is/ought fallacy. I have evaluated the increase of democracy as desirable simply because the United States *is* a democracy. I have *not* established specific reasons for *why* democracy is a preferable form of government.

We frequently see the is/ought fallacy committed when cultural values and traditions are discussed. It is often difficult to get outside our culture so as to evaluate the *worth* of a traditional value or practice. We may place a positive value on monogamy, for instance, simply because it is the form of marriage practiced in our culture. Similarly, we may prefer the nuclear family—mother/father/children—over other social arrangements—the extended family, the tribe, or the commune—solely because it is the arrangement of social relations to which we are accustomed.

The is/ought fallacy is particularly prevalent in academic debate because of the central role "values" typically play in the discussion.[5] It is easy to fall into defending one's values with the argument "because that's the way it is" or "because that's the way it's *always* been." As we discuss in greater detail in Chapter 12, the reasoning that supports a value should be more substantial than that. We should have good reasons, directly related to the nature of the phenomenon we are evaluating, by which to justify the conclusion that this phenomenon is indeed of value to us.

Although you should be wary of using or accepting reasoning that employs the is/ought fallacy, in some situations it is appropriate to acknowledge that something has value simply because of its continued existence. This is particularly true when there are no other means for determining the preferable belief.

In common parlance, sometimes we're better off with the devil we know than with the one we don't. In academic debate, we usually hold that if there are no compelling reasons to change *or* to continue the status quo (the way things are), we will continue with the status quo. That is, we attach some value to the status quo simply because it *is* the status quo—the way things *are*. This use of is/ought reasoning is codified in academic debate through the concept of stipulated presumption, which we discuss in Chapter 8.

Despite this appropriate use of is/ought reasoning, by and large the equation of "is" with "ought" provides either a weak rationale or an outright fallacious one. Consequently, debaters should be extremely careful about using this reasoning in their arguments and should remember that the larger and more culturally accepted the "value," the greater are the chances that the fallacy is being committed.

Post Hoc Ergo Propter Hoc

Taken from Latin, **post hoc ergo propter hoc** means "after the fact, therefore because of the fact." **Post hoc fallacies** are improper applications of the associational method. In this reasoning, because event Y followed event X, we conclude that X is the cause of Y. The old elephant joke illustrates post hoc reasoning: A man sees a boy standing in his backyard flapping his arms. After being asked why he's doing that, the boy tells the man that he's scaring away the elephants. "But there are no elephants around here," the man responds. "See," replies the boy, "it's working." Common athletic superstitions such as wearing one's lucky socks for the big game (or worse, never washing one's "lucky socks") also illustrate the use of post hoc reasoning.

Although we may laugh at such unreasonable reasoning, post hoc fallacies are extremely common in our thinking about government and sociopolitical issues. Typically, we attribute our societal successes or failures to the politician in power or the just-passed legislation. Many studies indicate that Americans vote for presidents based on their personal economic well-being, even though a president may have very little control over the economy in general or an individual's economic success specifically. Similarly, we often attribute an improvement or decline in areas such as crime, education, environment, and so forth to the most recently passed legislation in those areas.

Again, the problem of post hoc reasoning does not mean that we must abandon the associational method of causal reasoning. The post hoc fallacy simply reminds us that we must examine the situations in which X precedes Y carefully, that we should examine the relationship of X to Y across as many situations as possible, and that it is always useful to use the associational method *in conjunction with* the connectional method.

Ad Novarrum

The **fallacy of ad novarrum** occurs when we use "newness" as a standard of quality. Ad novarrum is, of course, particularly abused in advertising. For example, an ad might claim that "Kleenup now has a new whitening formula" and the implicit claim is that because it's new, the formula is better. Another ad might claim that "Branedrane computer games contain the latest in computer technology," and the implicit claim is that because it's the "latest," the technology must also be the best. On reflection, however, most of us know that having the "latest" technology can be a mixed blessing; new technology is often less than perfect, and time is frequently required for a developer to work the kinks out of the "latest" system. Sometimes, buying technology that has been out for a year or two is much less frustrating than having the newest model or product.

Again, simplistic standards such as ad novarrum are common in academic debate because humans, when confronting complex subject matter, often like to find easy ways of making decisions. The latest banking reform, the newest alternative to imprisonment, the most recent suggestion for improving worker productivity—these are all touted as being desirable because they are the latest and the newest.

We confronted a variation of the ad novarrum fallacy in our discussion of timeliness in Chapter 4. Claiming that one's evidence is the "best" solely because it is newer than any other oversimplifies the reasoning needed for deciding which evidence is indeed the most believable. Newness may be an appropriate standard to consider but only if we have also considered what lies behind the simple fact of "newness" and have included that component of the situation in our reasoning as well.

Ad Verecundum

The reverse of ad novarrum, the **fallacy of ad verecundum** occurs when we use "oldness" as a standard of quality. Related in part to the is/ought fallacy, ad verecundum goes a step farther in equating the length of time something has existed to its measure of worth. "The good old days," "they don't make 'em like they used to," and any phrase containing the word "classic" are good candidates for the fallacy of ad verecundum.

Debate invites ad verecundum fallacies because our discussions of values often include appeals to the "old ways" as being tried and true. That a value, custom, or standard is "traditional" and has "been the norm for generations" is not only frequently heard but is often psychologically compelling as well. Venerating our elders and following ancient customs simply because they *are* ancient may be more prevalent in some cultures than others, but most humans attribute some value to doing things certain ways because "we've always done it that way." Recent appeals by politicians to "family values" are one such example of ad verecundum reasoning.

We should not, of course, dismiss the "tried and true" argument out of hand. What we need to do is ask, "What does that observation tell us?" In what situations has the custom or value been tried? How well did it work? How "true" was it? Are those situations analogous to the ones we are confronting today? Are they different?

Again, we should also ask, "Are there other standards that might better apply?" Classical music is worth listening to not because it has hung around a long time but because it is complex in its use of tones, musical themes, and instrumentation. Listening to classical music can enhance our musical appreciation in a way that a steady diet of three-chord pop songs does not. Considering the age of something may be a place to begin our examination of its value, but it should rarely be the stopping point of our reasoning process.

Ad Populum

Also known as the **bandwagon appeal,** the **ad populum fallacy** uses popularity as a standard of quality or as proof of truth. The argument that "everybody's doing it" as a justification that "it" is worth doing is an example of an ad populum standard of quality. The claim that "everyone knows" is an appeal to an ad populum proof of truth.

We all know people who have used such arguments, and we have probably resorted to them ourselves. Such uses of bandwagon appeals are employed every day in arguments that range from family disputes ("But Dad, everyone's wearing . . .") to nuclear nonproliferation ("everyone knows that country X has nuclear weaponry"), and they appear in policy and nonpolicy arguments as well. They are attractive arguments for several reasons. First, like false consolation, ad novarrum, and ad verecundum, ad populum appeals establish a single, simple basis for judgment. Such standards can greatly simplify arguments for us by narrowing the grounds we must construct and defend; of course, the danger is that they will *over*simplify the argument.

Second, ad populum arguments can be psychologically appealing because most of us desire social acceptance. Fitting in with the crowd often means valuing what they value and believing what they believe. Ad populum arguments can be *very* attractive if we think they have helped us discover what "people" believe so that we know what to believe, too. Remember, though, that ad populum appeals do not always make claims about what *everyone* thinks or does. When we make claims like "Everyone at Alma Mater U thinks that" or "Politically active people all know that," we have defined our bandwagon more narrowly than the mythic "everyone," but it is still a bandwagon.

Finally, ad populum appeals are often easy to advance with a minimum of evidence. Reasoning by induction is usually not followed very rigorously in this fallacy; a few examples become "proof" that "everyone" thinks or believes a certain way. Counterexamples are often dismissed by ambiguously qualifying the everyone into "most people," or "Well, the ones who *know* believe that . . ." Pressed to provide evidence of the claim, the ad populum arguer often proves to be slippery and elusive.

There is some value, of course, in examining and perhaps even accepting as true what most people believe to be true. Certainly, part of the theory of democracy is that government by the collective will is better than government by an autocracy or an oligarchy. When we discuss the concept of presumption in Chapter 8, we will see that some credibility is attached to beliefs and values that are commonly accepted. As with other standards we have discussed, this one can also be used, but it must be used with care. Is the opinion or value one that is *in fact* believed by most people? What does that fact tell us about the situation generally or about the opinion or value specifically? Knowing what most people believe may be helpful in deciding what we ourselves should believe, but we should avoid the attraction of following the crowd.

Ad Hominem

Meaning "against the man," the **ad hominem fallacy** occurs when we confuse the messenger with the message. If we dismiss the argument because we do not like the arguer, we have constructed no reasons—convincing or otherwise—as to why the *argument* is wrong. At most, all we have done is shown why our audience should not like our opponent.

A political example may illustrate the point here. In the 1990 campaign for U.S. senator in North Carolina, the incumbent Jesse Helms ran a television ad attacking his opponent, Harvey Gantt, for unethical behavior. The ad said that Gantt, an African-American, had joined a group of investors in purchasing a local television station under a Federal Communications Commission program designed to encourage minority ownership of broadcasting stations. Soon after the purchase, however, Gantt had sold his share of the company. The implication of the ad was that Gantt had unethically taken advantage of an affirmative action program for his own personal profit.

The Gantt campaign's response ad was a purely ad hominem attack; essentially it said that the television station ad was "another Jesse Helms smear campaign." Although that claim may or may not have been true, consider what the

Gantt ad did *not* say. It did not say that Gantt had not helped purchase that station; it did not say that the station had not been purchased through an affirmative action program; it did not say that he had not profited from a quick resale of his share of the station. It gave no *reasons* for viewers to believe that Gantt had acted ethically; it only claimed that Helms had acted unethically.

Politics, of course, makes large use of such mudslinging, ad hominem attacks, but ad hominem appeals are also common in all too many debating situations. First, we know that a person's ethos—that is, the speaker's credibility—can be important in the audience's decision-making process, and so ad hominem attacks are tempting because they are often effective. Second, when we are arguing with someone, there is a tendency to connect our self-esteem with our arguments. Attacks on our arguments become attacks on us personally, and the temptation is to respond with a counterattack on our opponent.

Yet, we cannot dismiss all ad hominem appeals as fallacious reasoning. For example, in Chapter 4 we noted that source is a valid test of evidence. If the source is biased or dishonest, isn't that a valid point to raise against the source's evidence? If the person's character is an integral part of the decision to be made —should this person be ratified to the Supreme Court?—aren't ad hominem attacks valid reasons to consider in our deliberations?

Ad hominem appeals are fallacious when one of two conditions occurs: (1) the ad hominem attack is designed to arouse the audience's emotions against the person so that the audience ignores other parts of the reasoning process; or (2) the quality of the person's character is irrelevant to considerations of the evidence, reasoning, or claim being made. Ad hominem attacks may be justifiable in some cases, but they should be considered carefully before being used; they should not be used inflammatorily; and they should not replace other pertinent parts of the reasoning process.

Indignant Language

Like ad hominem appeals, the **fallacy of indignant language** replaces reasoning with inflamed passions. "I won't dignify that with an answer," or "I am insulted that anyone would suggest such a thing" are two typical uses of indignant language. Like ad hominem appeals, indignant language is a strategy too often resorted to in the heat of a debate. As we take our opponent's attacks personally, it is easy to respond with hurt, pride, and anger. Indignant language does all three well.

Yet, to say there is no place for passion in our reasoning process is unrealistic for we cannot park our feelings at the doorway of discussion. Passion, however, should *grow out of* our reasons instead of *replacing* them. It is important to remember that we can be passionate without raising our voices, or that we can be emotional while still explaining the reasons for our emotions. In argumentation especially, we should take care to explore and examine our opponents' reasons as fully as possible rather than yield to the temptation to dismiss that reasoning with an indignant "How dare they!" It may be psychologically satisfying to resort to an abrupt, passionate condemnation, but it abandons our ethical responsibility to engage in reason-giving discussion.

This is hardly an exhaustive list of all the possible fallacies of reasoning, but it should be helpful to have examined some of the most common ones. Perhaps the most important point of this discussion is that we must be *careful* in our reasoning to consider each situation individually with all its accompanying complexities. Although we can understand the present and guess the future only by what we have "experienced" in the past, we must also be willing to see the peculiarities of each unique situation as we reason our way through it.

Conclusion

In this chapter we have examined two types of reasoning: interpretive and causal. Interpretive reasoning guides us toward understanding what our world is about. There are four methods of interpretive reasoning: induction, deduction, reasoning from sign, and reasoning from analogy. All are common methods of reasoning and are important to understanding how we make inferences. Causal reasoning is used to determine the existence of cause-effect relationships. Two methods are used in causal reasoning: the associational method and the connectional method. The strongest causal arguments are typically those that make use of both methods.

Finally, we examined several common fallacies of reasoning. Such fallacies do not occur because we follow some improper "form" of reasoning but because we use the methods of reasoning simplistically or inappropriately to the particular situation. Reasoning—done well or done poorly—constitutes much of the "stuff" of any argument, and an appreciation of the reasoning process can help us prepare our arguments better and prepare ourselves better to respond to others' mistaken, fallacious, or misguided reasoning.

Notes

1. In Chapter 9, as we discuss the use of criteria, these are called "standards." Standards are observable *signs* that certain qualities (health, safety, adequate preparation) have been obtained.
2. We take these terms from Otis M. Walter and Robert L. Scott, 136–54.

3. If we were creating a complete argument for reducing the presence of handguns, we could also use the associational and connectional methods for arguing that handguns also "cause" more deaths and injuries than alternative, nonfirearm weapons, such as knives, chains, bombs, and so on.

4. Although not always as fully developed in policy debate, standards may still be significant components in such debates and are certainly important parts of everyday policy argumentation.

5. The exception, of course, would be when the proposition is one of fact. See our discussion of propositions in Chapter 6.

Selected Bibliography

Arnold, Carroll. "What's Reasonable?" *Communication Quarterly* 19 (1971): 19–23.

Berube, David. "Hasty Generalization Revisited, Part One: On Being Representative Examples." *CEDA Yearbook* 10 (1989): 43–53.

Fisher, Walter R. "Toward a Logic of Good Reasons." *Quarterly Journal of Speech* 64 (1978): 376–84.

Hample, Dale. "Dual Coding, Reasoning, and Fallacies." *Argumentation and Advocacy* 18 (1982): 59–78.

Newell, Sara E., and Richard D. Rieke. "A Practical Reasoning Approach to Legal Doctrine." *Argumentation and Advocacy* 23 (1986): 212–22.

van Eemeren, Franz H., and Rob Grootendorst. "Unexpressed Premises, Part I." *Argumentation and Advocacy* 19 (1982): 97–106.

———. "Unexpressed Premises, Part II." *Argumentation and Advocacy* 19 (1983): 215–25.

Walter, Otis M., and Robert L. Scott. *Thinking and Speaking.* 2nd ed. New York: Macmillan, 1984.

Discussion Questions

1. Examine some interpretive reasoning you have done. Which method— induction, deduction, sign, or analogy—did you use?

2. Construct a hypothetical cause-effect relationship about the economy. How could you go about defending that relationship associationally? How could you do it connectionally?

3. Pick a fallacy of reasoning and develop two examples. In the first, develop an example of fallacious reasoning. In the second, use the same form of reasoning appropriately.

STRATEGIES OF REFUTATION

*I*n many respects, we have been discussing the tactics of refutation in each of the preceding three chapters. To know how one defends a position is to know how one can attack that position. For example, I can bolster the credibility of my evidence by qualifying the credentials of the source; I can attack the credibility of my opponents' evidence by discrediting the source of their evidence. I construct a logical case by demonstrating the link between my warrant, data, and claim; I can attack the logic of my opponents' case by showing that their warrant, data, and claim are not appropriately linked. These, however, may all be termed *tactics* of refutation; they are specific arguments one may make for refuting an opponent's argument. In this chapter, we discuss the *strategies* of refutation—the general approaches for constructing a refutation and the strengths and weaknesses of those approaches. In our discussion, we look at three aspects of any refutative strategy: its nature, its scope, and its focus.

The Nature of the Refutation

One method for conceptualizing our strategy of refutation is to ask what the nature of the refutation is; that is, in general argumentative terms, what is the audience left with after the refutation is finished? Strategies of *attack* aim to remove or reduce the credibility of our opponents' claims. If our refutation is successful, the audience retracts its belief that our opponents' arguments are true. In contrast, strategies that *advance* a position attempt to construct arguments of our own that contradict or compete with the claims of our opponent.

105

When this strategy of refutation is successful, the audience *replaces* its belief in our opponents' claims with belief in our own position. In this section of the chapter, we examine these two kinds of refutation.

Attacking the Opponent's Arguments

We *attack* our opponents' arguments directly when we claim that their data and/or reasoning give us insufficient grounds for accepting the conclusion that has been drawn. When we question the credibility of our opponents' evidence, argue that they have misinterpreted that data, or contend that their reasoning is fallacious, we are attacking our opponents' argument.

Attacking an argument can be strategic; if our opponents "drop" or do not try to refute an argument or piece of evidence, they have tacitly admitted that the argument or evidence is true. Many judges count a "dropped" argument as having been won—albeit by default—by the team whose argument was dropped.[1] Attacking our opponents' arguments may also be useful in undermining their credibility; the more they seem to have used bad evidence or fallacious arguments, the more the audience may suspect that most of their evidence or arguments are fallacious.

When you are attacking the opponents' argument, three considerations are important to remember. First, you should make sure that you understand their argument or evidence. Although it may seem painfully obvious, it is a lesson too frequently forgotten: we can construct an effective attack only if we understand what we are arguing against. Second, it is important that you communicate clearly *what* you are attacking. The audience must understand which part of your opponents' overall argument you are attacking at any given moment. Finally, it is important to understand how the argument attacked fits into the overall debate. Attacking your opponents' argument is only part of the equation; you must also communicate clearly *how* their loss of this argument affects their overall case.

Advancing Your Own Position

In *advancing* a refutative position of your own, you construct arguments that either *contradict* the opponents' claims or that *compete* with them. A contradictory position *denies* the specific argument made by the opponent. In contrast, a competitive position argues that there are competing truths that *diminish* the overall importance or validity of the opposition's arguments. These two types of positions are not mutually exclusive; I can directly contradict my opponents' position and also construct a competitive position of my own. Let us look at each of these two types of positions.

Advancing a Contradictory Position   A refutative position is contradictory when it denies the opponents' argument. For example, if my opponents claim that unemployment is increasing, I may counter with evidence that indicates unemployment is decreasing. Or, if my opponent argues that privacy is important and should be valued in our society, I may argue that privacy is not important and is of little value to society.

It may be useful here to differentiate clearly between strategies that "attack" and those that advance a contradictory position. When I attack my opponents' position I am simply saying that they have not really proved their point. In attacking, I examine only their arguments and their evidence and argue that one or both are insufficient for proving their claims. When I construct a contradictory position, however, I not only deny that their case has been proved, but I positively advance the position that the opposite of their case is true. For example, when presidential contender Steve Forbes proposed a 17 percent flat income tax, most of his opponents *attacked* the 17 percent figure, arguing that Forbes had no evidence that a 17 percent rate would raise the needed tax revenue. Most of his opponents also *advanced contradictory positions*—that is, they provided their own estimates of how high the rate would have to be set: 22 percent, 23 percent, 27 percent, and so on.

Generally, it is harder to advance a contradictory position than simply to attack the opponents' argument. Almost any argument can be questioned to a greater or lesser degree, attacked for small inconsistencies in the logic or less-than-perfect evidence. Constructing a position of your own that contradicts the opponents' position is a more difficult task. Simply pointing out Forbes's inadequate data is easier than finding a credible study of your own. Not only must the study be found but it must be presented, explained, and possibly, defended against the attacks of others. Constructing a contradictory position of your own is, however, a stronger strategy of refutation.

First, it is more assertive to say "This is wrong" than to ask "Is this wrong?" The latter position contends that your opponents *may* be mistaken; the former says that they *are* mistaken. Second, *questions* about your opponents' argument may be *answered* later by your opponents. Incomplete reasoning can be completed, questionable evidence can be buttressed or replaced. To advance a position of your own forces your opponents to refute *your* argument. It moves at least part of the debate to *your* reasoning and *your* evidence. Finally, many advocates find it easier to advocate rather than simply to question. It is often easier to frame your argument by saying what you believe to be true rather than by restricting your statements to what you refuse to believe. Advancing a position

—whether contradictory or competitive—gives you something to be *for*, not just something to be *against*.

Of course, attacking your opponents' position and advancing a contradictory position are not mutually exclusive strategies. In fact, most successful refutation will incorporate elements of both, because advancing a contradictory position generally requires some attack on the opponents' position. If my opponents say that unemployment is increasing while I say it is decreasing, not only do I need to say what the evidence is for my claim but I should tell the audience why my evidence is more believable than my opponents'. If I argue that privacy is not important and my opponents say it is, I need to advance some reasons for why my arguments are better than theirs.

It is possible to attack your opponents' position without advancing one of your own, and in certain situations it may be appropriate and effective to do so. Rarely, however, will it be effective to advance a contradictory position of your own that does not also attack the weaknesses of your opponents' argument.

Advancing a Competitive Position   A contradictory position denies the truth of my opponents' specific arguments, but a competitive position says that other truths are operating that invalidate my opponents' ultimate claim. Suppose, for example, you were debating the proposition, "Resolved: that increasing the severity of punishment for violent crimes in the United States would be desirable." Your opponents might construct a case around the argument that increased punishment would diminish the incidence of violent crime in America. You could create a competitive position by arguing that increasing the severity of punishment would reinforce the patriarchal worldview of our society. That is, rather than *helping* people to avoid committing violent acts (a matriarchal approach), focusing on revenge (via punishment) and prevention (via the threat of punishment) is an individualistic, punitive approach to communal relations (a patriarchal approach).

Using this argument, you might then develop the dangers of reinforcing this traditional, patriarchal worldview: society is viewed as a loose aggregate of competitors rather than an interrelated community of cooperators; there is an increased or continued reliance on war and violence as the glue that maintains societal relations; and communal values perpetuate society's preference of the traditionally advantaged male over the traditionally disadvantaged female.

Note that during the construction of this argument you have never contradicted your opponents' claim that increasing the severity of punishments for violent crimes would diminish the incidence of such crimes. Indeed, you could even grant that your opponents' claim is true. What you have constructed instead is a competitive position. You have argued that (1) increasing the severity of punishment would reinforce our patriarchal society; (2) such an effect is less desirable than any advantage we might accrue from the reduced incidence of crime; and therefore (3) although your opponents' specific argument is acceptable, it does not justify belief in the proposition. If your competitive position is granted, then increasing the severity of punishment for violent crimes would *not* be desirable.

There are two distinct advantages to utilizing a competitive position. First, it gives a debater a *distinct* position to be *for,* one that is not simply *against* the opponents' position. Psychologically, this puts the debater in a stronger position with the audience. As we suggested earlier regarding counterdata and advancing competitive positions, it is often more impressive to build a position of your own than to concentrate solely on destroying your opponents' position. Many audiences will want you to talk about what you are for rather than only what you are against. For the advocate, too, it is often easier to construct a coherent refutation if there is a positive position around which to build one's arguments.

In the example above, suppose I had extensively questioned my opponents' evidence as a strategy of attack.[2] The questions would be more effective if combined with my competitive position. We are less likely to believe questionable evidence when we know that there will be negative repercussions if the evidence proves false (and sometimes even if the evidence proves true). Thus, instead of simply saying "my opponents' evidence is questionable," I can now argue that "there is much at stake here; if we accept this argument, we will be perpetuating and strengthening a dangerously patriarchal society in exchange for supposed benefits we have no certainty of achieving." Not only is my overall argument now stronger, but the questions I raised about my opponents' evidence takes on greater importance combined with this competitive position of my own.

The second advantage in using a competitive position as opposed to a contradictory position is that it moves even more of the argument from your opponents' ground to yours. The debate over capital punishment is a good example of this advantage. Typically, the initial dispute over capital punishment centers on whether it deters future criminal acts. The evidence on both sides of the debate is questionable, and arguments about capital punishment often devolve into a muddle of evidentiary claims. Many opponents of capital punishment have found it strategic to develop a *competitive* position. Capital punishment is wrong, they argue, because it is the murder of another person. Developing such a position moves the argument from an issue of expediency (does it reduce crime or not?) to an issue of ethics (what is ethical behavior for us?). This position allows opponents of capital punishment to argue the issue from *their* grounds. In almost any kind of argument, most debaters prefer to debate *their* issues rather than their opponents'. They are usually better prepared to discuss those issues and they usually understand those issues better. Conversely, their opponents may be less prepared to discuss these competitive positions and may understand them less thoroughly also.

The advantages to creating a competitive position are usually overwhelming, but there are two potential problem areas that the debater should be especially aware of. First, constructing a competitive position can be time-consuming, requiring considerable attention and discussion by the debater. The patriarchy/matriarchy example above is representative. Consider the effort that must be devoted to define those terms adequately, demonstrate that patriarchy is linked in substantial ways to our system of criminal justice, establish the significance of the resulting harms, and then show that those problems will be reduced or eliminated by changing the system.

In Chapters 11, 12, and 13 we discuss the rather extensive requirements for building an affirmative case. These same requirements must be met when we construct a competitive position. Of course, time devoted to constructing a position of your own is time taken away from directly refuting your opponents' arguments. Moreover, it is all too easy to become so concerned with building your own position that you ignore the position being constructed by your opponents. In some instances, your position may be so strong that what your opponents do with their case is immaterial to the final outcome of the debate. In most situations, however, it is bad strategy and bad debating to be oblivious to the opposing arguments.

A second potential problem with creating a competitive position is that it may not be competitive. It is possible to construct a position that we *believe* indirectly refutes our opponents' case when in fact the arguments presented by the two sides are *not* mutually exclusive. In the example above, suppose our argument centered on rehabilitation rather than on patriarchy and matriarchy. We might construct a position that said rehabilitation, not severity of punishment, is the key to preventing repeat criminal behavior. Drug treatment, education, and socialization programs have all proven effective, we might argue, and improving those efforts will do more to reduce the incidence of violent crime than will increasing the severity of punishments.

Although our argument may be entirely correct, it is not competitive with our opponents' position. That is, as our argument is currently framed, increasing the severity of punishment and improving rehabilitation programs are not mutually exclusive reforms. Society could undertake both reforms simultaneously. Indeed, in their refutation of our argument, our opponents might "turn" our position by arguing that lengthening prisoners' sentences will provide them with more time to be exposed to the various rehabilitation programs. The longer the exposure, our opponents might argue, the greater the chances that the lessons learned will "stick." Because our position is not competitive with our opponents' case, we have not successfully refuted it, even though our specific claims may be true.

Our argument could have been made competitive, though, if we had shown that rehabilitation programs work best when the criminal is imprisoned for a short-to-moderate sentence. Or, we could have argued that (1) there is a finite amount of money that society is willing to pay regarding the criminal justice system; (2) imprisonment is extremely costly; therefore, (3) increasing the severity of punishment will directly limit our ability to offer rehabilitation programs to prisoners. With either argument, we would have constructed a position that *is* competitive with our opponents' case.

We should note here that the construction of noncompetitive positions is a frequent problem. Any time we engage in refutation, there is a danger that we will become so focused on the specific arguments we are making that we lose sight of how those arguments fit—or don't fit—the positions our opposition has been taking. It is important with competitive as well as contradictory refutation that we first make sure we understand our opponents' argument and then that we understand the relationship between their argument and ours. If we do so, we will be able to construct sound arguments that provide us with an appropriate competitive *or* contradictory position to advance.

The Scope of Refutation

In addition to considering the nature of their refutative strategy, arguers must also choose the scope, or the breadth of the response, of their refutation. Some debaters elect to argue every claim made by their opponents. Others are more selective in the rebuttals they advance. Yet a third approach is to advance several arguments in conjunction but with each argument contingent upon the "success" of the last. In this section we examine three different strategies of refutation, each of which embodies a different *scope* of refutation: the shotgun attack, the selective approach, and disjunctive arguments.

The Shotgun Attack

Also called a **spread attack,** the **shotgun** approach contradicts an opponent on every point he or she makes. Many scholars attack this strategy as being intellectually impoverished because it treats all the arguments as if they were of equal strength and importance. Those objecting to the strategy claim that it develops no skills for *evaluating* arguments; they argue that it requires one to have skill only in *generating* arguments, no matter how frivolous the argument may be. The more arguments one can generate, the more successful the shotgun attack usually is. Despite widespread criticism of this approach—criticism with which we agree—this strategy remains popular with many debaters for three reasons.

First, the shotgun approach replicates the "brainstorming" stage of idea development. In brainstorming, one uncritically generates as many ideas as possible. After this creative stage is completed, the ideas generated are evaluated for their validity and worth. Similarly, many debaters use the shotgun approach to see which arguments "stick"—that is, which ones work. In the rebuttal stage, the debaters then become selective, pursuing those arguments that worked best and dropping those that proved invalid or ineffective. If you are uncertain of which arguments are better than others or which ones will "work," the shotgun approach can be very appealing.

Second, the shotgun approach is often used to damage the opponents' credibility. Under the impression that "where there's smoke, there's fire," audiences sometimes equate the quantity of arguments with their quality. The more we force our opponents to defend their arguments, the more the audience might think that they have much *to* defend. Many politicians know from painful experience that the more they defend themselves against mudslinging charges, the more voters think there must be mud there someplace. In academic debate, too, debaters may lose credibility as they scramble to defend themselves from a large quantity of attacks, regardless of the quality of those attacks.

Finally, the shotgun approach is most often used for creating "dropped" arguments. As discussed above, a "dropped" argument is often counted as a "won" argument for the team whose argument was dropped. Using the shotgun approach, I may play the counting game as I compare the number of arguments I win (because they were dropped) versus the number my opponents win. I may also play the "landmine" game, where, in my rebuttal, a dropped argument suddenly becomes the "key" to the entire debate, as I use this "won" argument to counter various parts of my opponents' case.

There may be some intellectual justification for the first use of the shotgun approach as there can be value to "trying out" ideas. There is a great deal of real-world application in regard to the second reason because many arguers, especially in courtroom trials, use the same kind of strategy. Outside the world of academic debate, however, there is little application for the "dropped argument" justification. Few real-world audience members count a dropped argument as an automatic win for the arguer, nor does a debater enhance his or her credibility by sneaking an argument through until the last possible moment in a debate. This justification turns on the rules of the game rather than on the nature of argumentation, and many observers find this artificiality objectionable.

The Selective Refutative Strategy

The opposite of the spread attack is the **selective refutative strategy.** In this strategy, the arguer makes certain select arguments rather than contradicting every item of the opponents' case. When employing the selective refutative strategy, there are three questions to keep in mind.

First, *how do the arguments affect the opponents' case as a whole?* In making selective arguments, it is imperative to keep the "big picture" in view. Suppose my opponents have presented two independent reasons that explain why the resolution is justified. Perhaps they have argued that stricter sentencing is desirable in cases of violent crime because it will reduce the incidence of crime and it will satisfy the community's desire for justice. If I focus my attacks entirely on one of those reasons, I may win that argument but lose the overall debate. Say I argue—convincingly—that stricter sentencing will not reduce the incidence of crime. My opponents' second reason—that it satisfies a community's need for "justice"—may serve independently to sway the audience or justify the adoption of the resolution.

Or suppose I attack my opponents' criterion but fail to replace it with a criterion of my own. My opponents may then supply another criterion that also fits their case. As either example illustrates, I may win the particular argument I elect to attack but lose the overall debate. For this reason, it is critical to keep in view the overall features of the argument, much like the "picture" provided by Toulmin's model. Only then can you be sure that you have attacked your opponents' case well enough to invalidate it.

Second, besides making arguments that will invalidate the case, *are these the strongest arguments available?* Part of the value of a selective refutative attack is that one can and should pick and choose the strongest arguments from those available. Which ones do the best job of damaging the opponents' case? Which ones are the easiest to explain and support? Which ones have the strongest reasoning backing them up? The strongest evidence? Which ones are the easiest to defend? Put simply, you want to select arguments that will inflict the greatest damage in the most efficient manner possible. Not only does that make the best use of your speaking time but by concentrating your refutation on the strongest arguments you have, you invite the debate to take place on *your* ground. You invite your opponents to leave their strong points and focus the discussion on yours instead. That can happen only if you have chosen the strongest arguments and developed them in your refutation.

Finally, in addition to choosing the strongest arguments that effectively invalidate the opponents' case, *are these arguments the most appealing ones for the audience?* It is important to realize that audiences rarely listen to a speaker uncritically. Most of us simultaneously listen and evaluate arguments as we hear them. We may find some parts of a case very believable; other parts we may find less credible. The arguer must realize that the audience is rarely a blank slate; they have often already begun to refute parts of the case themselves. If one's refutation fits their preconceived arguments, it *reinforces* the audience's beliefs and is much stronger psychologically. Conversely, if one's refutation contradicts the audience's preconceptions, greater explanation may be needed as to why this argument is germane and valid.

When performing this kind of audience analysis, the arguer should remember three points. First, *what do you know about this specific audience or judge?* Do you know their preferences for types of arguments, evidence, criteria, or cases? Do you know what their likely response is to parts of the argument? Second, *what do you know about audiences or judges like this generally?* Do you know what these audiences or judges are probably thinking in response to your opponents' case? Third, *should the agreement be made explicitly, or implicitly?* Often, it is better to leave the agreement with the audience implicit while making the differences explicit. If your selective refutation agrees with the audience's likely response, the stronger move is often to let *them* supply the conclusion that says "he or she thinks like I do."

If, however, your selective refutation disagrees with the audience's likely response, the more effective course is usually to note the probable disagreement as a prelude to explaining your perspective on the argument. Making such disagreements explicit allows you to show an appreciation for the opinions of others and allows you to demonstrate selectively why, in this particular case, you disagree with those opinions.[3] When you are making disagreement explicit, it is usually better to avoid *telling* the audience what they're thinking. Saying something like "Now I know you're thinking that . . ." can appear extremely presumptuous. Instead, a more preferable course is to soften your statement by phrasing it more as a suggestion: "Now, you may be thinking that . . . ," or "I wouldn't be surprised if your reaction was to say . . ."[4]

In sum, when making your selections from the available arguments for refutation, choose them with an eye toward (1) your opponents' case as a whole, (2) the strongest of the available arguments, and (3) the audience's preconceptions about your arguments and those of your opponents. You can then make *intelligent* choices for your selective refutative attack.

Disjunctive Arguments

The disjunctive argument form of refutation is less selective than using a selective refutative strategy; in some senses it straddles the line between a selective strategy and a spread attack. In a **disjunctive argument**, essentially two arguments are made in refutation; we can call these the primary and secondary arguments. First, the advocate advances a primary argument. The advocate then makes a secondary argument, which is meant to be considered in the event that the primary argument does not defeat the opponent's original argument. The refutation is thus phrased disjunctively: *if* the primary argument is not effective, *then* the audience should consider the secondary argument.[5]

As an example, suppose my opponent has argued that workfare is preferable to welfare because it does more to develop the recipient's social and personal independence. I might respond with a primary argument contending that developing the recipient's personal characteristics is outside the purpose of any workfare/welfare program and therefore should not enter into our decision making about which type of program is most desirable. I might then make a disjunctive argument: that *even if* the audience decides personal growth is a relevant benefit to consider, there is no credible evidence that workfare does in fact do more to develop such growth.

The advantage of a disjunctive argument, of course, is that it allows you to cover your bases or hedge your bets. Because we can never be certain which arguments an audience will believe, it is often difficult to be narrowly selective in the refutative case we construct. However, there is a twofold danger in using a disjunctive argument. First, in supposing that the primary argument is not true, the advocate psychologically lends support to the conclusion that the primary argument is *not* true. That is, admitting the possibility that your argument is faulty will very often invite the inference that it *is* faulty. Even if you are very clear in delineating the hypothetical nature of the secondary argument, the disjunctive argument has the tendency of weakening the primary argument. Second, in creating a disjunctive argument, it is very easy to construct a contradictory case. Returning to the welfare/workfare example above, suppose that I responded with a primary argument that my opponent had not provided a definition of workfare. Without a definition to distinguish workfare from welfare, I argue, it is impossible to make claims as to which performs better in the area of personal development. I might then make a disjunctive argument: that *even if* my opponent can provide such a definition to distinguish the two, workfare has not been tried on a national scale. Because local systems may be idiosyncratic, I argue, we cannot say definitively and generally which is the preferable system, welfare or workfare.

The contradiction in my disjunctive argument should be clear: if there is no definition to distinguish welfare from workfare, then how do I know that it has not been tried on a national scale? Although this contradiction should be obvious, it is the kind of logical error committed all too often in a disjunctive argument. Consequently, although a disjunctive argument is often an appealing way out of deciding which refutative argument to select, and it can be an effective and appropriate refutation in certain situations, we caution debaters to use it judiciously and carefully as a refutative strategy.

We have looked at the potential scope of refutation by discussing three distinct refutative strategies: the shotgun attack, the selective attack, and the disjunctive argument. We have suggested that the selective approach should predominate because the shotgun approach is less effective and less intellectually rigorous, and the disjunctive argument is preferable only in situations where it is specifically appropriate.

Focus of Refutation

In addition to thinking about refutative strategies in terms their nature (attacking or advancing) and their scope (shotgun, selective, or disjunctive), it is also useful to consider the focus of one's attack. As outlined in the preceding chapters, arguments contain two components: evidence and reasoning; one's refutation may focus on either or both of those components. Refuting evidence raises different concerns from those involved in refuting reasoning, and strategies that address evidentiary issues are constructed differently from those that address questions of reasoning. Although we may blend the two strategies in our overall argument, at any particular time we will be presenting one or the other kind of refutative argument.

Evidentiary Attacks

In this section, we examine three different kinds of evidentiary attacks: the evidence press, counterdata, and the evidence turn.

One kind of evidentiary attack is called the **evidence press,** a strategy by which you simply question the opponents' evidence. When they are employed in questioning the credibility of the evidence, evidence presses use one or more of the tests of evidence discussed in Chapter 4. Is the source reputable or biased? Is the evidence recent enough to be valid for today's situation? What was the context from which the evidence was taken? You may also question the opponents' interpretation of the evidence. In these cases, the press takes some form of a single question: Does the evidence really say what the opponent says it does?

Questioning the evidence is often considered the weakest kind of evidentiary attack because it does not "forward" a position of its own; by nature it only *attacks*. Your opponents can readily counter such presses in two ways: by answering the questions (the evidence is reputable, it is recent enough, it does say what we say it does), or by replacing the questioned evidence with other data.

Evidence presses are most effective when debaters follow several guidelines. (1) *The press is stated as a positive claim.* You are in a stronger position to say the source is disreputable, the evidence isn't recent enough, or the data do *not* say what the opposition claims rather than to be asking whether these claims are true.[6] (2) *The evidence press significantly damages the credibility of the opponent's evidence.* Some evidence presses lessen the credibility only slightly; it is often best to reserve presses for those situations where they can substantially reduce the credibility of the evidence. (3) *The opponents' case routinely misuses and misinterprets evidence.* Evidence presses can be effective when they go beyond showing that a piece or two of evidence lacks credibility and instead indicate a *pattern* of poorly used or badly interpreted evidence. Then the evidence press can call into question the credibility of the opponents' entire case. (4) *The evidence press is combined with contradictory data.* If you are countering your opponents' data with evidence of your own, it may be useful to include an evidence press that lessens the credibility of the opposing data. Again, this is a tactic that should probably be used selectively, when the point is an important one to the overall debate, and when the press can be formulated as a statement rather than as a question. Although it can be time-consuming to construct, a well-developed evidence press can significantly undermine the credibility of your opponents' data and thus ultimately weaken the foundation of their argument.

A second kind of evidentiary attack is to employ **counterdata.** Here you use data of your own either to contradict or subvert the opponents' evidence. Evidence *contradicts* the opponents' evidence when it reaches an opposite conclusion. If your evidence claims that the federal government is fiscally wasteful, mine is contradictory if it states that the federal government is fiscally careful. When using contradictory evidence you must explain why your evidence is better or more credible than your opponents' data. Too often, debaters rely solely on source and timeliness to make such claims, when all six tests of evidence can be used to differentiate your evidence from that of your opponent. As we stressed in Chapter 4, which tests of evidence you should use depends on the particular data you are debating. Avoid using one test of evidence simply because it is the easiest to use or because it is the test of evidence you "always" use.

Evidence *subverts* an opponent's evidence when it admits that the opponent's evidence is accurate but claims that it is incomplete. Given other evidence, this argument says, we see that the evidence is true as far as it goes, but it does not go far enough. For example, my opponent may note that the republics of the former Soviet Union have, in aggregate, ten times as many nuclear missiles as does the United States. From this, my opponent may then claim that increased military spending is desirable because we need to "catch up" with the former Soviet republics. I may respond with data of my own showing that on each nuclear missile, the former Soviets have one to two nuclear warheads, while U.S. missiles carry ten to twelve warheads apiece. There is, I could conclude, no "catching up" to do; we are currently even in the number of nuclear warheads that each side has.

When we admit in our evidentiary attack that the opponents' evidence is true, many of the tests of evidence are not relevant to assessing their evidence. The problem is not that the opponent's evidence is wrong; the problem is that it has been wrongly interpreted because it is incomplete. The result of this error of interpretation is that your opponents' claim is not supported by the data. In this instance, the test of *context* may be a useful one to keep in mind as you explain why *your* evidence is complete while your opponents' is not. The test of *precision* may also be important, as the details *not* provided by your opponents become critical to your subversion of the data.

Unlike the situation with the evidence press, your opponent cannot respond to your attack with more of the same kind of evidence. An effective response to your attack will fall into one of three categories: (1) attack your explanation of why your evidence subverts your opponents'; (2) counter your data with evidence that *contradicts* it; or (3) counter your data with evidence that *subverts* yours. The most common of these responses are the first two; rarely will an opponent respond to your "big picture" argument by admitting that it is true, but then moving on to an even "bigger" picture. It is, however, one possible response.

The third and final kind of evidentiary attack can be called an evidence turn. Whether it involves evidence or reasoning, a **turn** occurs when you admit that a part of your opponent's argument/evidence is true but then use that part to justify a completely opposite conclusion. Say, for example, that you are debating "Resolved: that an increase in U.S. defense spending is desirable" and that most of your opponents' evidence argues that the United States has fallen woefully behind in its military expenditures. We are extremely weak defensively, your opponents argue, and so, they conclude, increased military spending is desirable. A refutation that turned the evidence would be one that admitted that the country is indeed "woefully behind" in its military spending. So behind, the argument would go, that any attempt to "catch up" to our potential enemies would probably trigger a preemptive attack by them before we could complete our buildup. Rather than trigger war by increased military spending, we should *decrease* it (so we become even less threatening) and focus instead on diplomatic missions that increase the likelihood of maintaining the peace.

A similar kind of argument can be found in the debate about gun control. Some observers point to the increase in gun-related robberies, assaults, and homicides and call for tighter gun control and less gun ownership. Others, of course, see the same increase of crime and turn those numbers: the increased crime means that there is a greater need to defend ourselves; guns are an effective means for doing so; therefore, there should be *less* gun control and *greater* gun ownership.

Turning your opponent's evidence can be an effective strategy of refutation because it utilizes your opponents' own data, data that cannot then be abandoned by your opponents without seriously damaging their credibility as advocates. In a sense, it removes the argument from your *opponents'* evidence and moves it to *yours*. Consider the two turns outlined above. In each case they acknowledge the truth of the opponents' data, but they then require some significant evidence of your own: that other countries will become concerned about a U.S. military build-up, that they would strike preemptively, that the results would be disastrous, that diplomacy will work, or, in the second example, that gun ownership protects one from violent crime. Turning the evidence often requires substantial use of evidence on your part. If that evidence is available to you, however, the advantage is that the argument moves to *your* ground and *your* evidence, and away from the evidence of your opponents.

Reasoning Attacks

As with evidentiary attacks, attacks that focus on the opponents' reasoning can be constructed in several ways, each with their own strengths and responsibilities. The first strategy of refutation is to demonstrate that *the opponents' reasoning is incomplete.* In an argument of this type, you contend that one or more key steps is missing in the opponents' logic. Suppose, for example, that your opponent has argued in support of tighter restrictions on handguns in the United States and has done so by constructing this case: (1) government should protect its citizens from violent crime to the greatest extent possible; (2) violent crimes involving handguns have been increasing significantly; and (3) therefore, tighter restrictions on handguns are desirable. At least one refutative argument against this case would be that its reasoning is incomplete. That is, we could grant that claims 1 and 2 are completely correct, but those two claims together do not yield the conclusion (3).

Missing from the reasoning, we could argue, is a claim that says tighter restrictions on handguns will result in decreased violent crime. The adoption of tighter restrictions does not guarantee that government has protected its citizens. It may be that either (1) tighter restrictions have no effect on violent crime, or (2) tighter restrictions *increase* the incidence of violent crime because citizens, obeying the law, are now disarmed but criminals are not. In the first instance, the tighter restrictions have not helped government protect us. In the second instance, the government—through these laws—has actually done the *opposite* of what it is supposed to do.[7]

When you are constructing a refutation contending that the opponent's case is incomplete, it may be useful to recall the discussion of Toulmin's model in Chapter 3. Refutations charging incompleteness need to be constructed with awareness of the various components of the argument. Do the components fit together to yield the conclusion they claim to produce? Are there missing pieces that need to be supplied? Like the evidence press, a weakness of this argument is that your opponent may answer your arguments with the pieces that "fill in" the logic. In academic debate, one may argue that such a response is "too late" and "against the rules," but in real-world argumentation, such a rejoinder won't hold. Even in academic debate, there may be considerable differences of opinion as to what constitutes the "rules" and when it is too late for debaters to amend their original logic.

Still, the refutation that the opponents' argument is logically incomplete is a strong one. It forces the opposition to reconceptualize that argument and to advance and defend new points in order to complete their logic. Although the refutative charge of incompleteness may not determine the final disposition of that argument, it can be termed a necessary starting point. Technically, you could argue that there is little to gain in discussing anything else about an argument if it is logically incomplete. Often, however, debaters will employ a disjunctive argument when using a refutative strategy of logical incompleteness; that is, they will note the lack of completion in the opponent's logic and argue that the conclusion is therefore unsupported. They then argue, however, that *if* the opponent can later complete the logical substructure of the argument, here are the other problems with the conclusion. Again, it is important to avoid contradictions within the disjunctive argument. If the secondary argument cannot be made without admitting that the opponent's argument is true, it may be better to develop only the stronger of the two refutative arguments: either the argument is invalid because the logic is incomplete *or* the logic is valid but there are other significant problems with the argument.

The second refutative strategy is to argue *that the opponent's reasoning is invalid*—that although the opponent's argument is complete, it is still fallacious. Here, the fallacies of reasoning discussed in the previous chapter as well as the Toulmin Model of Argument are appropriate to consider. Does the opponent's argument account for all the complexities of the situation, or is it a fallacy of composition or division? Has the opponent looked at a single example of the resolution in operation and committed a hasty generalization? Has the opponent used faulty standards? Does the argument contain poor causal reasoning? All these are questions that address the validity of the opponent's argument and reasoning.

As we stressed in the previous chapter, the fallacies of reasoning that might apply depend entirely on the specific situation and the particular argument being made. It may be useful, however, to examine one refutative argument that illustrates this strategy: *reductio ad absurdum.*

In this argument, the advocate takes a premise or claim from the opponent's argument and draws a logical conclusion that is "absurd." Suppose, for example, that my opponents support increased restrictions on handguns by noting that handguns are present in many household accidents, arguing therefore that gun owners should be required to attend safety training classes so as to reduce the number of accidents. I might use reductio ad absurdum to illustrate the oversimplification present in their argument. Bathtubs, too, figure prominently in household accidents, I may argue. Should we also require safety training classes before allowing people to purchase a bathtub? Stairways pose a significant household danger: better not let anybody have one who hasn't taken a safety training class.

My opponents would probably respond by adding complexity to their argument, which distinguishes handguns from the "absurd" examples of bathtubs and stairs. First, handgun accidents frequently involve innocent bystanders. Safety training classes are therefore useful from the standpoint of safeguarding the community. Second, handguns are more complex in their construction than are bathtubs and stairs. A better analogy, my opponents might argue, would be elevators. Those *are* licensed and regulated, and owners have to use *licensed* and *trained* technicians to operate them.

It is illustrative of reductio ad absurdum that as my opponents' argument becomes more complex, my counterargument becomes less effective. Reduction ad absurdum is most effective in countering simplistic reasoning. If the reasoning is sophisticated and germane to the situation, reductio ad absurdum will probably not be an effective argument. When appropriate, it can be a devastating strategy, and it illustrates again the importance of engaging in careful, appropriately complex reasoning.

Because of the complexity inherent in the reasoning process, there is no simple way to delineate how one argues that the opponent's reasoning is wrong. However, it is important to note that this refutative strategy is probably the most commonly used. Substantial portions of the remaining chapters are devoted to examining specific arguments and reasoning that are appropriate to academic debate; but here, we simply note that this is an important and significant method of refutation within a strategy of attacking the opponent's reasoning.

Finally, as explained in the section on evidentiary attacks, it is possible to turn an opponent's reasoning, just as one may turn the evidence. When turning an opponent's reasoning, I accept one or more of the premises but then supply new data or reasoning myself that then reaches the opposite conclusion of my opponent. For example, my opponent may argue that the most important need a person has for developing a sense of self is self-control. Without control over ourselves, my opponent argues, we cannot develop fully as human beings. Indeed, without such control, all other qualities of life are diminished because we cannot utilize them to our fullest potential. In regard to drug testing, therefore, my opponent argues that regardless of the economic benefits it may create, the loss of control that accompanies the invasion of personal privacy impairs our ability to enjoy those increased economic benefits. Therefore, drug testing in the workplace is undesirable.

I might turn that argument by agreeing that self-control is indeed fundamental to our development as human beings but noting that drug use and addiction are far greater threats to a sense of self-control than the occasional loss of privacy that accompanies drug testing. To eliminate drug testing, as my opponent desires, would thus *decrease*—not increase—society's sense of self-control generally. Thus, I argue as I turn my opponent's argument, not only is the position that drug testing is undesirable mistaken; precisely the *opposite* is true: because control of self is so important to us all, drug testing is absolutely *desirable*.

In sum, three general approaches are available for refuting an opponent's evidence: (1) the evidence press, (2) counterdata, and (3) turning the evidence so that it supports an opposing claim. There are three parallel approaches for refuting an opponent's reasoning: (1) that the argument is incomplete, (2) that the reasoning is faulty, or (3) by turning the reasoning to prove that the opposite conclusion is true.

Conclusion

In this chapter we have surveyed the nature, scope, and focus of various refutative strategies. The nature of one's refutation may assume one of two major forms: attack the opponents' position or advance a position of one's own which either contradicts or competes with the opponents' position. Within a strategy of attacking or contradicting, the advocate must select the appropriate scope of refutation: the shotgun approach—contradicting the opposition on every point; the selective argument approach—concentrating on those arguments that are most important or strongest for refuting the opponent's case; or the disjunctive argument—advancing a secondary, backup argument contingent on the persuasiveness of a primary argument. Finally, an advocate may choose one of two foci: refuting the opponent's evidence—using evidence presses, counterdata, or turning the evidence; or refuting the opponent's reasoning—arguing that the logic is incomplete, claiming that it uses faulty reasoning, or turning the reasoning. These two foci are not, however, mutually exclusive.

Throughout this chapter we have argued that to construct effective refutations, debaters must understand the arguments they are refuting and the relationship between their arguments and the arguments of their opponents. We have also suggested that refutation is better when it is selective rather than scattered and when it can be built around positive claims rather than simply being "against" the opposition.

Notes

1. This "rule" is based on the burden of rebuttal, a concept we discuss in Chapter 7.
2. We will discuss particular strategy, called an **evidence press**, later in this chapter.
3. As always in the study of communication, there are exceptions. Frederick Douglass, for example, in his famous 1852 Fourth of July address, said that opinions against the abolition of slavery deserved to be met with "bit-

ing ridicule, blasting reproach, withering sarcasm, and stern rebuke"—not with respect. The theme of his address, however, centered on America's (and his audience's) hypocrisy; an "appreciation for the opinions of others" would have been out of place in his address.

4. We will return to this concept in our discussion of psychological presumption in Chapter 7.
5. Sometimes this argument is called a **conditional** or **hypothetical** argument because, for the "sake of argument," the secondary argument "supposes" that the primary argument is not true.
6. It is true that many real-world advocates phrase evidence presses as questions rather than statements, but that often occurs when they know that the evidence is in fact appropriate and valid. Posing evidence presses as questions then implies that the evidence is inaccurate, an implication that may never be cleared up. Senator Joseph McCarthy made extensive use of this tactic.
7. When we contend that our opponents' case overall is incomplete, we are making a **prima facie** argument. We discuss this concept in Chapter 8.

Selected Bibliography

Bridges, Dick A., and John C. Reinard, Jr. "The Effects of Refutational Techniques on Attitude Change." *Journal of the American Forensic Association* 10 (1974): 203–12.

Irvin, Charles E. "An Intelligent Guide to Refutation." *Quarterly Journal of Speech* 25 (1939): 248–53.

Mister, Steven M., and Greg Tolbert. "An Examination of Turnarounds in Competitive Debate." *CEDA Yearbook* 8 (1987): 1–7.

Discussion Questions

1. Why is it usually stronger to advance a positive claim rather than simply to attack your opponents' argument?
2. What are the justifications for using a shotgun approach? What are the criticisms of that approach?
3. In what instances would it be most appropriate to use a disjunctive argument?
4. Contrast the advantages and disadvantages of using an evidence press as compared to counterdata.
5. Construct an example of an evidence or reasoning turn.

DEBATE PROPOSITIONS

*E*very argumentative encounter has a central idea or issue that is being contested. In debate, that idea or issue is called the debate proposition. In this chapter we discuss the functions a debate proposition performs and the characteristics of a properly formulated proposition. We also describe the two primary types of propositions used in debate—policy propositions and nonpolicy propositions—and identify the basic components of each type of proposition. Because nonpolicy propositions can be formulated either as propositions of fact or propositions of value, we further distinguish between these different propositional formulations. Finally, we describe a test that debaters can use to correctly identify propositions of fact and propositions of value.

Functions of the Debate Proposition

In its most basic sense, a debate proposition is a claim. It is an assertion and thus requires evidence and warrants, it is likely to be contested, and it can be modified by qualifiers and rebuttal. At the same time, the debate proposition is not an ordinary claim, it is the *ultimate claim* in any debate—*the* focal point of the debate. Everything the affirmative and negative debaters do in a debate is designed either to prove—for the affirmative—or disprove—for the negative—the debate proposition.

In addition to being the overall focal point, the proposition performs three primary functions in debate. First, it identifies the general and specific subject area for the debate. For example, the debate proposition, "Resolved: that compulsory national service for all qualified United States citizens is desirable," indicates that the debate is to be about issues related to "compulsory national service" generally, and to focus specifically on those issues related to "compulsory national service" for "*all qualified United States citizens.*" Although this function of a proposition may seem obvious, it has significant implications for the debate process. By identifying the general and specific subject areas for the debate, the proposition enables debaters to develop systematic and efficient research plans, thereby enhancing their ability to collect the necessary evidence to support, analyze, and refute claims presented in the debate. In this way, the proposition makes it possible for debate to be reason-giving and reason-testing discourse of the highest order.

Second, the proposition clarifies the debaters' role as advocates. By this, we mean that the proposition denotes the major responsibility of the affirmative and negative advocates. For example, the proposition, "Resolved: that activism in politics by religious groups harms the American political process," designates that the affirmative debaters must advocate that "activism in politics by religious groups *harms* the American political process," whereas the negative debaters must advocate that "activism in politics by religious groups *does not* harm the American political process." Similarly, the proposition, "Resolved: that the United States should reduce substantially its military commitments to NATO member states," defines the affirmative burden to justify a substantial reduction in commitments while it denotes that the negative will argue against that general action. The proposition does not prescribe exactly how the affirmative or negative teams must fulfill their roles, but it does establish the general nature of their roles. By establishing the major advocacy roles, the proposition enhances the prospect that the debate will be a more productive and thorough examination of alternative and conflicting points of view.

Third, the proposition helps clarify the legitimate argumentative boundaries for the debate. The proposition does this by providing a general benchmark the debaters and judge can use to determine whether particular claims should be included in the debate or considered in the decision-making process. Thus, the proposition establishes a general dividing line the debaters or judge can use to exclude or include claims in the debate. For example, the proposition, "Resolved: That United States higher education has sacrificed quality for institutional survival," divides the legitimate argumentative ground for the debate in such a way that claims about "higher education in *France,*" or about "United States *public middle schools*" would not be judged relevant to the debate whereas claims regarding "state universities in the United States" would be judged relevant.[1] By clarifying the legitimate argumentative boundaries, the proposition helps focus the debaters' advocacy and the judges' decision making to ensure that debate can be used to arrive at meaningful and purposeful judgments.

Characteristics of Debate Propositions

The proposition performs vital functions in debate. To do this, it must be carefully crafted. A haphazardly written proposition would likely confuse more than clarify. In this section we discuss three primary stylistic characteristics of debate propositions including the requirements that the proposition be *debatable, written in appropriate form,* and *formulated with appropriate terminology.* Understanding these characteristics can enable you to analyze debate propositions more effectively and to construct more debatable propositions.

First, the proposition must focus on a debatable subject area. Recall that one of the primary functions of a proposition is to identify the general and specific subject area for the debate. To have a meaningful debate, however, the proposition must do more than simply identify the subject area; it must focus the debate on a subject area that is truly debatable. To be debatable, the subject area in the proposition must *reflect a genuine controversy* between alternative points of view. The proposition, "Resolved: that the legal protection of accused persons in the United States unnecessarily hinders law enforcement agencies," reflects a genuine controversy because there are clearly conflicting points of view that responsible advocates might take about that subject. On the other hand, the proposition, "Resolved: that in the 1992 presidential election Ross Perot received the largest number of popular votes of any independent candidate in the history of United States elections," does not reflect a genuine controversy. There are no legitimate conflicting points of view in that subject nor is it necessary to engage in a debate to resolve the issue. The issue can be resolved easily by consulting appropriate reference sources.

To be debatable, there must also be *sufficient evidence available about the subject area* in the proposition. The operative words in that statement are *sufficient* and *available.* Debate, as we have attempted to emphasize, is a reason-giving and reason-testing process. Debaters are required to analyze the proposition and their opponents' position critically, to present clearly articulated positions, and to defend those positions against attack by their opponents. Ultimately, fulfilling these responsibilities requires that debaters gather and utilize sufficient and appropriate supporting material. If the subject area in the proposition is one about which little authoritative information exists or is available to the debaters, the ability of the debaters to engage in productive reason giving or effective reason testing will be seriously undermined. They would have little legitimate basis on which to construct, support, contest, or defend their claims.

The second stylistic characteristic of a well-structured proposition is that it must be written in an appropriate form. Recall that one of the major functions of a proposition is to help clarify the role of the debaters as advocates and that doing so increases the likelihood that debate will be a more productive and thorough examination of alternative and conflicting points of view. To accomplish this, however, the proposition must not only clarify the advocacy roles of the debaters but must also focus those roles as much as possible. Thus, the proposition must be written so that it sets the debaters as opposing advocates about a *single idea*. The proposition, "Resolved: That unauthorized immigration into the United States is detrimental to the United States," makes the affirmative responsible for advocating that "unauthorized immigration into the United States *is* detrimental" while it makes the negative responsible for advocating that "unauthorized immigration into the United States *is* (*not*) detrimental." Thus, the proposition focuses the debater's advocacy responsibilities on a single issue. However, the proposition, "Resolved: That the trend toward increasing foreign investment in the United States is detrimental to this nation, and abortion is morally justified," does something very different; it diversifies the debater's advocacy responsibilities. Inevitably, a proposition formulated in such a way forces the debaters to split their attention and time between two very different issues and makes it difficult for either the affirmative or negative to fulfill their responsibilities as advocates. Moreover, such a proposition would seriously decrease the degree to which either issue—foreign investment or abortion— could be thoroughly examined within a debate.

To be written in the proper form, the proposition must be a *simple declarative statement*. If it is to identify the advocacy roles of the advocates, the proposition must express the opposing sides of the controversy as clearly as possible. It must be straightforward and must give an unambiguous signal to each debater about his or her role as an advocate. The proposition, "Resolved: What has been the effect on higher education of challenges to institutional survival?" is not properly formulated because it does not indicate the specific advocacy responsibility of either the affirmative or the negative. Neither the affirmative team nor the negative team can reasonably infer from the proposition exactly what they are required to defend. However, when that proposition is written as a declarative statement, "Resolved: That United States higher education has sacrificed quality for institutional survival," the advocacy roles of the debaters are clear. The affirmative know they must demonstrate that "United States higher education *has* sacrificed quality for institutional survival," and the negative know they must argue against that position.

The final stylistic characteristic of a proposition is that it must be formulated in appropriate terminology. One recurring theme throughout our discussion of the functions of a proposition is clear: language choices and uses are critical to the way the proposition can and does function in debate. Choosing and using appropriate terminology will enable the proposition to fulfill its critical functions in debate, whereas poor choices and uses will undermine that ability.

To be appropriate, the terminology used to construct a proposition must be *neutral*. Neutral terminology enhances the perception of legitimate controversy and makes the advocacy roles of the debaters more equitable. For example, the proposition, "Resolved: That activism in politics by religious groups harms the American political process," is formulated with generally neutral terminology. As such, the proposition embraces a legitimate controversy—activism is/is not harmful—and it distributes advocacy roles within that controversy in a roughly equitable manner. Thus, the affirmative advocates that activism *is* harmful, the negative advocates that activism *is* (*not*) harmful, and neither the affirmative nor the negative assumes an undue burden as an advocate simply because of the way the proposition is worded. Similarly, the proposition, "Resolved: That the federal government should significantly curtail the powers of labor unions in the United States," is formulated in neutral terminology and clearly demarcates and distributes the debaters' general advocacy roles.

"Loaded" or emotionally charged terminology undermines both those functions. If the proposition were to say, "Resolved: that unjustified activism in politics by fanatic and ill-informed religious groups harms the American political process," the proposition would have a very different effect. There would be no clear perception of legitimate controversy: if the activism is "unjustified," "fanatic," and "ill-informed," would there be serious question about whether it is or is not harmful? Moreover, advocacy roles would be far from equitable. No doubt the affirmative would find it much easier to demonstrate that any activism that is "unjustified," "fanatic," and "ill-informed" is indeed also harmful while the negative would be hard pressed to show that "unjustified," "fanatic," and "ill-informed" activism *is* (*not*) harmful.

Loaded language not only undermines the ability of the proposition to function effectively in debate, but it also diminishes the overall meaningfulness of any decision produced in the debate process. Loaded language presumes prejudgment. Decisions reached, even after lengthy debate, about any concept that is prejudged to be "unjustified," "fanatic," and "ill-informed" are unlikely to reveal any significant insight about the subject.

Finally, loaded terminology undermines the educational value of debate. The entire debate process is designed to ensure that debaters have equal rights and assume equal responsibilities as advocates. However, the language used to construct the proposition can undermine an equitable distribution of rights and responsibilities. If the debate proposition were worded in nonneutral language —"Resolved: that the federal government should significantly curtail the harmful and unnecessary powers of labor unions in the United States"—the responsibilities of the advocates would be drastically skewed. In that situation, the affirmative debaters would have a massive argumentative advantage whereas the negative would shoulder an almost impossible task. When argumentative rights and responsibilities are skewed by the language of the proposition, debaters lose any opportunity to understand more fully what it means to engage in thoughtful, critical assessment of conflicting ideas and the fundamental nature of the process itself is irrevocably altered.

Classifying Debate Propositions

In this section, we describe the primary types of debate propositions—policy propositions and nonpolicy propositions; we identify the components of each type and explain how to distinguish among them. It is important for students of argumentation and debate to be able to classify the debate proposition properly for two major reasons. First, understanding how to classify the type of proposition being debated increases the probability that the debaters will be successful advocates. Because the proposition is the focal point in any debate, the nature of the debate itself is significantly influenced by the type of proposition being debated. In turn, how debaters fulfill their role as advocates is influenced by the type of proposition they are debating. As we explain in Chapter 9, debaters contest different stock issues for different types of propositions, and they are also likely to find different types of supporting material to be appropriate for different types of propositions.

Second, knowing how to classify the type of proposition being debated enhances the student's understanding of the process of debate. By being able to distinguish among the types of propositions, students develop a more complete and accurate understanding of the general nature of argumentation and debate. They are able to distinguish among the different forms of debate and are able to analyze the specific requirements that the type of proposition being debated imposes on any given debate.

Debaters also discover very early in their careers the importance of understanding the basic structure of the proposition itself. Correctly identifying the basic components of the debate proposition is critical to developing definitions, criteria, and plans of action. Moreover, debaters need to have a clear understanding of the relationship between the components of a proposition and the corresponding roles those components play in defining the responsibilities and obligations debaters assume as advocates.

Policy Propositions

Policy propositions are frequently used for academic debate as well as in less formal, everyday argumentative encounters. A policy proposition generally asserts that some type of action—policy—needs to be undertaken. Policy propositions may address virtually any issue and prescribe a wide range of actions, including establishment of new regulations or programs or abolition of existing regulations or programs. In academic debate, policy propositions are generally easy to classify because they typically are constructed with the phrase *should.* The following are examples of policy propositions that have been used in intercollegiate debate.

> *RESOLVED:* that the federal government should significantly strengthen the regulation of mass media communication in the United States.
>
> *RESOLVED:* that the United States should reduce substantially its military commitments to NATO member states.
>
> *RESOLVED:* that the federal government should control the supply and utilization of energy in the United States.
>
> *RESOLVED:* that one or more United States Supreme Court decisions recognizing a federal constitutional right to privacy should be overruled.

Policy propositions generally contain three components: the **agent of action,** the **action qualifier,** and the **policy directive.** The agent of action specifies *who* is responsible for taking action. The designated agent of action might be a specific person (such as the President of the United States), an organization (such as the Consumer Product Safety Commission), or a governmental structure (Congress, or the federal government). In the proposition, "Resolved: that the United States should significantly increase the development of the earth's ocean resources," the agent of action is designated to be "the United States."

In some propositions, the agent of action will be implied rather than designated. In the proposition, "Resolved: that executive control of United States foreign policy should be significantly curtailed," the agent of action is implied to be some structure—presumably either Congress or the Supreme Court—that can exercise direct control over the executive branch. Similarly, in the proposition, "Resolved: that United States law enforcement agencies should be given significantly greater freedom in the investigation and/or prosecution of felony crime," the agent of action is implied to be some structure—presumably Congress, the executive branch, or the Supreme Court—that is capable of taking the specified action. When the agent of action is implied, you can identify the appropriate agent of action by determining who has the legitimate authority and power to take the action specified in the proposition. Similarly, when the agent of action is designated as a broad, multifaceted entity such as "the United States," you can determine who the appropriate specific agent of action is by first determining exactly who within the more broadly conceptualized agent has the specific authority to execute the action in the proposition.

The policy directive is a critical component of all policy debate propositions. The policy directive establishes the general nature of the policy action to be implemented. For example, in the proposition, "Resolved: that the United

States federal government should adopt a policy to substantially decrease consumption of marine resources," the policy directive specifies that some sort of program *should be adopted.* That directive requires a policy or series of action steps to be implemented, and the result of the action taken must be the formal establishment of a policy not in place prior to initiation of the action. Similarly, in the proposition, "Resolved: that the United States should reduce substantially its military commitments to NATO member states," the policy directive requires that the action taken constitute a *reduction* from the present level of commitments. Thus, the result of any action taken must constitute some decrease in the commitments honored by the United States prior to the action. Or, in the proposition, "Resolved: that one or more United States Supreme Court decisions recognizing a federal constitutional right to privacy should be overruled," the term "overruled" is the policy directive because it specifies the action that should be taken.

The final component of a policy proposition is the action qualifier. The action qualifier describes or qualifies the basic nature of the policy directive. One way the action qualifier functions is to qualify the magnitude of the policy directive. For example, in the proposition, "Resolved: that the United States should significantly increase the guarantee of privacy for all citizens," the policy directive is to "increase the guarantee of privacy" beyond existing levels and the action qualifier "significantly" denotes the magnitude of the increase that must occur: the increase must be significant.

The action qualifier can also define the general nature of the policy directive by describing important characteristics of that action. The action qualifier can do this in three ways: by indicating who is to be affected by the policy, where the policy is to be implemented, or how the policy is to be implemented. For example, in the proposition, "Resolved: that the federal government should provide a program of comprehensive medical care for all citizens," the phrase "for all citizens" denotes who should be affected by the policy directive; the policy must affect all citizens.

The action qualifier can also specify where the policy directive is to be implemented. In the proposition, "Resolved: that the federal government should significantly strengthen the regulation of mass media communication in the United States," the phrase "in the United States" describes where that policy directive should take effect. Similarly, in the proposition, "Resolved: that the United States federal government should significantly increase exploration and/or development of space beyond the earth's mesosphere," the phrase "beyond the earth's mesosphere" denotes an important action qualifier—the locale—of the policy directive.

Finally, the policy directive can specify how the policy directive is to be implemented. In the proposition, "Resolved: that the federal government should reduce nonmilitary consumption of fossil fuels in the United States by expanding the use of nuclear power," the phrase "by expanding the use of nuclear power" qualifies the way the policy directive to "reduce nonmilitary consumption of fossil fuels" is to be achieved.

Nonpolicy Propositions

Nonpolicy propositions are also frequently used in academic debate as well as in everyday argumentation. Nonpolicy propositions differ from policy propositions in that they do not assert that a particular action should be taken. Nonpolicy propositions do not define a policy directive and require the advocates to demonstrate that the directive should or should not be implemented. Rather, these propositions are generally concerned with judgments about accuracy or worth. Like policy propositions, nonpolicy propositions can focus on virtually any concept or issue. Following are some examples of nonpolicy propositions that have been used for academic debate.

> *RESOLVED:*   that individual rights of privacy are more important than any other constitutional right.
> *RESOLVED:*   that significant government restrictions on coverage by United States media of terrorist activity are justified.
> *RESOLVED:*   that federal government censorship is justified to defend the national security of the United States.
> *RESOLVED:*   that compulsory national service for all qualified United States citizens is desirable.
> *RESOLVED:*   that advertising degrades the quality of life in the United States.

Every nonpolicy proposition has two major components, an **object of focus** and a **judgmental term.** The object of focus is the entity (person, concept, event) that is being judged or evaluated. In the proposition "Resolved: that violence is a justified response to political oppression," "*violence*" is the object of focus because it is the concept designated in that proposition to be judged. Similarly, in one of our previous examples, the proposition "Resolved: that activism in politics by religious groups harms the American political process," the object of focus is "activism in politics by religious groups" because it is the concept being judged.

Whereas the object of focus identifies the entity to be evaluated or judged, the judgmental (or evaluative) term specifies the judgment or evaluation the advocate is required to make. In the proposition "Resolved: that the American judicial system has overemphasized freedom of the press," the judgmental term is "*overemphasized;*" it is the judgment debaters are required to make. Similarly, in the proposition "Resolved: that violence is a justified response to political oppression," the term "justified response" is the judgmental term because the proposition specifies that it is the judgment that must be made about the object of focus, "*violence.*"

In addition to the object of focus and the judgmental term, a nonpolicy proposition may have two other components: a **situational qualifier** and/or a **judgmental qualifier.** A situational qualifier specifies the situation or context within which the object of focus is to be judged. In the proposition, "Resolved: that significantly stronger third party participation in the United States presidential elections would benefit the political process," the phrase "the political process" is a situational qualifier because it describes the context within which the object of focus is placed. That is, it requires that the object of focus, "significantly stronger third party participation in the United States presidential elections," be judged within the context of its effect on the "the political process."

On the other hand, a judgmental qualifier is a term or phrase that clarifies the nature of the judgment to be made. In the proposition "Resolved: that the United States Supreme Court, on balance, has granted excessive power to law enforcement agencies," the phrase "on-balance" is the judgmental qualifier as it specifies that the judgmental term, "has granted excessive power," must be warranted by the totality of the actions of the United States Supreme Court (object of focus). Thus, the judgmental qualifier requires that debaters contest the overall or "on-balance" effect of Supreme Court decisions rather than any single decision. We discuss each of these components, object of focus, judgmental term, situational qualifier, and judgmental qualifier more fully in Chapter 12 and explain the role each plays in developing criteria for a nonpolicy proposition. Ultimately, to be a successful advocate, every nonpolicy debater should be able to identify the basic components of the nonpolicy debate proposition.

As you can tell from the examples used thus far, nonpolicy propositions may be formulated to reflect very different types of judgments. Some nonpolicy propositions require judgments about the accuracy of a stated observation; others require judgments about the worth or value of some object of focus. Because they can be formulated to require very different types of judgments, nonpolicy propositions can be classified more specifically either as **propositions of fact** or **propositions of value.**

Historically, not all theorists have used the terminology *fact* and *value* to classify nonpolicy propositions; however, most theorists and practitioners now do so.[2] We believe the classifications "proposition of fact" and "proposition of value" are appropriate. These basic classifications are generally discrete and each reflects a significant reason for nonpolicy debate. Furthermore, when considered collectively, the classifications provide a meaningful way to distinguish between policy and nonpolicy advocacy. In the following sections, we describe more fully the nature of these different types of nonpolicy propositions.

Propositions of Fact   A proposition of fact posits what is or is not the case. Most often, propositions of fact attempt to determine whether a prescribed judgment is correct/incorrect, accurate/inaccurate, or true/false. Although virtually all theorists agree that a proposition of fact asks, in one form or another, whether something is or is not so, not all propositions of fact are functionally equivalent. Propositions of fact vary based on the *type of issue* with which they deal and the *temporal context* within which they place the judgment that something is or is not so. As a result, to fully understand the nature of this fundamental type of nonpolicy debate proposition, it is important to develop significant subclassifications of propositions of fact.

We use both these factors—type of issue and temporal context—to develop subclassifications for propositions of fact. Using the type of issue exposes substantive differences between types of propositions of fact. That is, propositions are classified according to the nature of the questions they raise and the nature of the arguments that must be sustained for successful advocacy. Using temporal context to classify propositions does not establish a substantive difference among types of propositions of fact, but it does identify distinctions *within* those substantively defined classifications. Thus, using the temporal context allows a more complete understanding of the total range of types of propositions one may encounter in nonpolicy argumentation and debate.

A proposition of fact may address three primary types of issues. The first and most basic issue a proposition of fact can address is **being.** Propositions that address this issue are typically concerned with whether an object of focus exists or whether an action occurred. The proposition, "Resolved: that the United States has a comprehensive medical care delivery system for the elderly," deals with the question of existence as it asks whether it is or is not the case that a comprehensive medical care delivery system exists in the United States. The proposition, "Resolved: that the United States has neglected the needs of homeless persons in this country," deals with the question of occurrence; it asks whether it is or is not the case that the United States has neglected the needs of homeless persons.

Second, propositions of fact can address issues of **relationship.** These propositions of fact typically deal with cause and effect. The proposition, "Resolved: that third parties increase political activism in the United States," posits a question of cause; it asks whether it is or is not the case that third parties cause an increase in political activism. The proposition, "Resolved: that regulating nuclear research programs in North Korea has significantly diminished the threat of nuclear war," posits a question of effect as it asks whether it is or is not the case that a significantly diminished threat of nuclear war (the effect) has been produced by regulating nuclear research programs in North Korea (the assumed cause). Propositions of relationship differ from propositions of being primarily because propositions of relationship focus on the interaction between the object of focus and a presumed outcome or effect whereas propositions of being simply ask whether the object of focus exists or some specified action occurred.

Third, propositions of fact can address issues of **designation**. These propositions are concerned with naming or classifying an object of focus. For example, the proposition, "Resolved: that the United Nations is an obsolete organization," asks whether it is or is not the case that the United Nations can be classified as an obsolete organization. Unlike propositions of fact that deal with issues of relationship, propositions of fact that deal with issues of designation do not presume an interactive relationship between the object of focus and a particular outcome or effect. Nor do they ask whether the object of focus exists or has performed a specified action as does a proposition of fact that deals with issues of being. This type of proposition of fact simply asks whether it is or is not the case that the object of focus can be described in a particular way.

Each of the types of propositions of fact—being, relationship, and designation—can be framed within past, present, or future temporal contexts. For example, a proposition of fact that addresses the issue of being can posit whether it is or is not the case that the object of focus existed in the past, exists now, or will exist in the future. Similarly, a proposition of fact that addresses the issue of relationship can posit whether it is or is not the case that the object of focus caused a particular effect in the past, is causing a particular effect now, or will cause a particular effect in the future. Finally, a proposition of fact that addresses the issue of designation can posit whether it is or is not the case that the object of focus should have been described in a particular way in the past, should be described in a particular way now, or likely should be described in a particular way in the future. By merging the primary classification—being, relationship, and designation—with the past, present, and future temporal contexts we can identify nine different types of propositions of fact that may arise in nonpolicy argumentation and debate. The types of propositions of fact are illustrated in Table 7.1.

Propositions of Value   A proposition of value generally posits some sort of evaluative judgment about the object of focus. For example, a proposition of value may require debaters to determine whether the object of focus is *good, bad, desirable, undesirable, sound, beneficial, important,* or *unimportant.* In some ways, these terms are misleading because they are not actually values. Rather, they are evaluative terms used to construct what we call a proposition of value.

According to Zarefsky, the evaluative judgment embodied in a proposition of value may take either of two forms. First, the proposition of value may require a **composite evaluation** of the object of focus versus some similar entity with which it directly conflicts. A proposition of value formulated in such a way

TABLE 7.1   Classification of Propositions of Fact

Category	Being	Designation	Relationship
Past	Resolved: that Congress has neglected the needs of homeless persons in the United States.	Resolved: that the Reagan administration's drug control policy was inept.	Resolved: that third parties increased political activism during the 1970s.
Present	Resolved: that the United States has a comprehensive medical care delivery system for the elderly.	Resolved: that the United Nations is an obsolete organization.	Resolved: that covert military operations are harming U.S. diplomacy.
Future	Resolved: that the United States will continue to lead the world in the quality of life enjoyed by citizens.	Resolved: that the two-party political system will become inappropriate in this country.	Resolved: that a strong U.S. military presence in the Middle East will be necessary to ensure peace.

requires that a prescribed evaluative judgment be made by comparing or contrasting the object of focus with that opposing object (entity, goal, value, end state) with which it conflicts. For example, "Resolved: that protection of the national environment is a more important goal than the satisfaction of American energy demands," is a proposition of value that poses a direct conflict between goals. It requires that the evaluative judgment "more important" (judgmental term) be made by comparing or contrasting "protection of the national environment" (object of focus) with "satisfaction of American energy demands" (the goal with which it conflicts). Similarly, the proposition, "Resolved: that improving relations with the Soviet Union is a more important objective for the United States than increased military preparedness," is a proposition of value that embodies a presumed conflict between national objectives—"improving relations with the Soviet Union" (object of focus) versus "increased military preparedness."

Second, the evaluative judgment may embody a **singular evaluation** of the object of focus. A proposition of value formulated in this way requires that a prescribed evaluative judgment be made about the object of focus proper. The object of focus may not have a clearly identified opposite, nor is it necessarily presumed to be in conflict with any opposite object. For example, "Resolved: that John Kennedy was a good president," is a proposition of value that embodies a singular evaluation of the object of focus. In that proposition, nonpolicy advocates are required to make the prescribed judgment ("good") about "John Kennedy" (the object of focus). The proposition does not identify any other object with which "John Kennedy" must be compared; the prescribed evaluation can be made without comparing "John Kennedy" to other presidents. Nor does the proposition presume a conflict between "John Kennedy" and any other object. Similarly, "Resolved: that a United States foreign policy significantly directed toward the furtherance of human rights is desirable" is a proposition of value that embodies a singular evaluation of the object of focus. The proposition directs the advocate to make an evaluative judgment about the object of focus, but it does not require that the object of focus be compared to any other similar object or presume that the object of focus is in conflict with any other similar object.

Although a singular evaluation of the object of focus does not presume any sort of direct comparison, contrast, or conflict, value conflicts will inevitably emerge in debates about such propositions. This is because value conflict is inherent in the selection of standards used to formulate the criterion by which the object of focus is evaluated. Selecting any standard for the criterion used to make an evaluative judgment—"desirable," "beneficial," "important"—implicitly establishes a presumed hierarchy; the standards included within a criterion are presumed to be preferred to their opposites and to any other standards that might reasonably have been included within that criterion. For example, in the proposition, "Resolved: that John Kennedy was a good president," one might formulate the criterion for the qualitative judgment, "good," with two standards: (1) the ability to portray strength in foreign relations (standard), and (2) the ability to portray compassion in domestic issues (standard). Making such a choice presumes that "strength in foreign relations" and "compassion in domestic issues" are preferred—more important in judging the "goodness" of a president—to their opposites, "weakness in foreign relations" and "insensitivity in domestic issues." Thus, value conflict inherently emerges, even when the conflict is not explicitly identified in the proposition of value. Although we discuss standards and criteria in much more detail in Chapter 12, we raise the issue now so that you will clearly understand that there is some type of value conflict embedded within every proposition of value, regardless of the specific form of the proposition.

Distinguishing between Propositions of Fact and Value

Although we hope that you understand the definitional differences between a proposition of fact and a proposition of value, it is not always easy to properly classify actual examples of these types of nonpolicy debate propositions. There are two reasons for this difficulty. First, we have generally presumed that all nonpolicy debate propositions must be phrased as a declarative sentence. Resolving a dispute about a declarative statement means determining whether that statement "is or is not so"—the basic characteristic of a proposition of fact.

Thus, when phrased as a declarative sentence, propositions of value appear to be very much like propositions of fact.

Second, many debate propositions contain judgmental terms that have evaluative connotations but do not necessarily require evaluative judgments. For example, terms such as *overemphasized,* and *obsolete* have evaluative connotations, but they need not require evaluative judgments. Propositions of fact, particularly those that deal with issues of designation, may contain such judgmental terms and actually appear very much like propositions of value. Thus, because propositions of value can appear very similar to propositions of fact and vice versa, it is important that debaters understand how to make accurate distinctions between the primary types of nonpolicy debate propositions.

One way debaters can more accurately classify nonpolicy debate propositions is to apply a **redundancy rule.** To use the redundancy rule, first locate the judgmental term in the proposition and then add the phrase "and that is good" or "and that is bad" to the proposition. If the added phrase is not redundant with the judgmental term, you are likely debating a proposition of fact. However, if either of those phrases is redundant with the judgmental term, you are likely debating a proposition of value. For example, "Resolved: that United States higher education has sacrificed quality for institutional survival," would be a proposition of fact because the phrase "and that is bad" could be added without being redundant with the judgmental term, "has sacrificed." That is to say, adding the phrase "and that is bad" adds a new judgment to the proposition; "Resolved: that United States higher education has sacrificed quality for institutional survival *and that is bad*" requires a substantively different judgment than "Resolved: that United States higher education has sacrificed quality for institutional survival." Similarly, "Resolved: that continued U.S. covert involvement in Central America would be beneficial" would be classified as proposition of value, as the phrase "and that is good" is substantively redundant—does not require a different judgment—with the judgmental term, "beneficial." Depending on the exact wording of the nonpolicy proposition, debaters might also use the redundancy test by adding phrases such as "and that is wrong" or "and that is right" in addition to "and that is good," or "and that is bad."

Many nonpolicy propositions, particularly propositions of fact that focus on issues of relationship (for example, "Resolved: that regulating nuclear research programs in North Korea has significantly diminished the threat of nuclear war") and propositions of value that embody a conflict (for example, "Resolved: that protection of the national environment is a more important goal than the satisfaction of American energy needs") can be readily classified without applying the redundancy test. However, the redundancy test can be useful in coping with the inherent confusion caused by framing all propositions as declarative sentences. It is also particularly useful for separating those propositions that have judgmental terms with evaluative connotations but do not require evaluative judgments from those propositions that have judgmental terms that do require evaluative judgments.

Conclusion

The proposition is the focal point of debate. It identifies the general subject area for the debate, clarifies the role of the debaters as advocates, and helps set the legitimate argumentative boundaries for the debate. Well-written debate propositions share basic structural and stylistic characteristics. There are two major types of debate propositions: policy propositions and nonpolicy propositions. Nonpolicy propositions are further divided into two major categories: propositions of fact and propositions of value. Propositions of fact can be further classified according to the type of issue they address and the temporal context in which they are placed. Propositions of value may require a singular evaluation of the object of focus, or they may require that the object of focus be compared to other similar objects. Debaters can distinguish between propositions of value and propositions of fact by using a redundancy test.

Notes

1. Claims about higher education in France or U.S. middle schools could be judged relevant only if the debater argued that events in those situations were *analogous* to what happened or was happening in U.S. higher education. Even then, the propositional term, "U.S. higher education" defines the legitimate argumentative ground.
2. For example, Terris and Verch and Logue identify questions of fact and value as components of the more general proposition of "judgment." Similarly, Windes and Hastings describe questions of fact and value as dimensions of the more general proposition of "belief."

Selected Bibliography

Bartanen, Michael. "The Role of Values in Policy Controversies. *CEDA Yearbook* 3 (1982): 19–24.

Matlon, Ronald. "Debating Propositions of Value." *Journal of the American Forensic Association* 14 (1978): 194–204.

———. "Debating Propositions of Value: An Idea Revisited." *CEDA Yearbook* 9 (1988): 1–14.

Mills, Glen. *Reason in Controversy.* Boston: Allyn & Bacon, 1964.

Murphy, Thomas. "The Legitimacy of Non-Truth-Based Standards in Competitive Academic Debate." *CEDA Yearbook* 15 (1994): 1–9.

Murphy, Thomas, and Melinda Murphy. "Resolutional Relevance: A Primary Standard for Evaluating Criteria in Non-Policy Debate." *CEDA Yearbook* 11 (1990): 1–8.

Rokeach, Milton. *The Nature of Human Values.* New York: Collier Macmillan, 1973.

Terris, Walter. "The Classification of Argumentative Propositions." *Readings in Argumentation.* Eds. Jerry Anderson and Paul Dovre. Boston: Allyn & Bacon, 1963. 129–38.

Verch, Steven, and Brenda Logue. "Increasing Value Clash: A Propositional and Structural Approach. *CEDA Yearbook* 3 (1982): 25–28.

Windes, Russell, and Arthur Hastings. *Argumentation and Advocacy.* New York: Random House, 1965.

Zarefsky, David. "Criteria for Evaluating Non-Policy Argument." *CEDA Yearbook* 1 (1980): 9–16.

Discussion Questions

1. Why is it important to identify the debate proposition accurately?
2. How do the components of a proposition affect the nature of debate about that proposition?
3. Can the redundancy rule be used to identify propositions inherent in everyday argument? If so, how?

ARGUMENTATIVE CONSTRUCTS

*A*rgumentation occurs in many different types of situations and about many different types of issues. Some argumentation is fairly informal; other argumentation is more formal and rule based. Whether one is engaged in a friendly discussion with a roommate about which of two professional basketball teams is "best," in a spontaneous exchange with a speaker about the "accuracy" of her claims, or in a prepared formal public debate about the "desirability" of affirmative action programs, every episode of argumentation is similar to every other episode in at least one major way: each proceeds on the basis of shared assumptions about the process. We call these assumptions **argumentative constructs.** In this chapter, we discuss the five fundamental argumentative constructs: presumption, the burden of proof, a burden of proof, prima facie, and the burden of rebuttal. Together, these constructs explain the major roles and responsibilities of advocates and help clarify how those roles and responsibilities can be met.

Presumption and the Burden of Proof

Presumption and the burden of proof have long been regarded as fundamental constructs of argumentation and debate. Anglican Archbishop Richard Whately developed the construct of presumption over a sixteen-year period during the nineteenth century as he studied how argumentation was used to attack and defend existing institutions. Drawing both from the legal and public forums, Whately surmised that existing institutions had an argumentative "benefit." He noted that an existing institution was the occupant of argumentative ground and that it would remain on that ground until sufficient reason was established to justify its removal. Because the initiator of the argumentation sought to remove the existing institution from its argumentative ground, Whately further surmised, the initiator assumed a corresponding "argumentative responsibility" to provide reason sufficient to justify removal of the existing institution from its argumentative ground. Whately termed the argumentative "benefit" **presumption** and the argumentative "responsibility" **the burden of proof**.

Presumption lies with an existing institution or belief because human beings will, by nature, continue with the familiar rather than adopt the unfamiliar. Unless we perceive some compelling reason to change, we tend to hold those beliefs and perform those actions that have served us adequately in the past. The old adage "If it ain't broke, don't fix it" summarizes neatly the basic idea of presumption. Generally, we like to have some "good reasons" for abandoning old beliefs and behaviors for new ones.

The burden of proof is the corollary to presumption. Once presumption is located in any argumentative encounter, the burden of proof is automatically affixed to the side opposite presumption. In addition to existing institutions, Whately noted, an argumentative presumption should also be extended to possession of property, the written word, and prevailing opinion. Thus, in an argumentative encounter involving any of those objects garnering presumption, the burden of proof would automatically fall on the opposing side.

Presumption and the burden of proof are important constructs across all types of argumentation. Consider the following very different types of argumentative episodes:

> You and your roommate frequently talk about professional basketball and have generally agreed that the Bulls are the best team. While watching a game on television, however, your roommate says that he has changed his mind and now believes that "the Knicks are the best team in the NBA this year." You challenge your roommate to explain why he believes the Knicks are best.
>
> When listening to a speech, you believe the speaker misinterprets some of the evidence she uses. You interrupt the speaker and state your claim. The speaker challenges you to demonstrate why her interpretation is inaccurate. You present your reasons and the speaker is forced to defend her original interpretation.
>
> You are a student in a political science class and have been assigned to develop an extended argument on why the electoral college should be abolished. Another of your classmates has been assigned to develop an extended argument on why the electoral college should not be abolished. You and your classmate are further required to present your arguments to the class. You are given the opportunity to speak first.

In each episode, the role and responsibilities of the advocates were determined in large part by the presumption and burden of proof constructs. When your roommate asserted that "the Knicks are the best team," he initiated an argumentative encounter by challenging the existing belief that, "the Bulls are the best team." Because it was the existing belief, "the Bulls are the best team" occupied the existing argumentative ground and was granted presumption. As the initiator of the argument, your roommate assumed the burden of proof to demonstrate why the prevailing opinion should be removed from its existing argumentative ground. Because you defended the existing belief, which had presumption, you were able to challenge your roommate to meet the required burden of proof.

Your role in the second episode was much different. When you challenged the way the speaker interpreted her evidence, you initiated the argumentation. You attempted to encroach on her presumptive argumentative ground and in so doing, you assumed the burden of proof. Thus, the speaker was perfectly justified in demanding that you demonstrate why your claim—that she misinterpreted the evidence—was correct *before* she acknowledged that it was incumbent on her to offer a defense of her interpretation. After you provided proof for your claim, the speaker was required to respond to that proof to retain her presumptive argumentative ground.

In the third episode you played a very similar role. You initiated the argumentation by asserting that an existing institution—the electoral college—should be abolished. As an existing institution, the electoral college occupied argumentative ground and a corresponding presumption. Because you were trying to remove the existing institution from its argumentative ground, you assumed the argumentative responsibility of the burden of proof. As the defender of the existing institution, your classmate theoretically had the argumentative advantage of presumption. Thus, you were given the opportunity to speak first so you could fulfill the burden of proof by establishing sufficient reason to justify removal of the existing institution from its argumentative ground, thereby mitigating the argumentative advantage of presumption your classmate held. It would make little sense for your classmate to speak first because until you met the burden of proof, there were no "good reasons" to remove the existing institution from its presumptive argumentative ground.

Presumption and the Burden of Proof in Debate

To this point, we have discussed presumption and the burden of proof in very general terms and attempted to illustrate that these constructs function in virtually all types of argumentative situations. It is equally clear that scholars regard presumption and the burden of proof as critical constructs in the debate process. In this section we further explain how these important constructs are used in formal academic debate.

For many years, scholars have treated presumption as a fixed or *stipulated* convention of the debate process. Presumption is stipulated to a particular entity (belief, action, institution, person, and so on) before the interaction begins, and that entity is assumed to retain its argumentative ground until the burden of proof is fulfilled. Debate scholars have frequently used other models of formal argumentation to determine where to assign or stipulate presumption in a debate. Two such primary models have been used to explain where presumption resides in a debate. First, many debate scholars use the **legislative model** to assign presumption in a debate. The legislative model is drawn literally from the legislative process. It is, thus, a composite of the general procedures and expectations used to structure argumentation and advocacy about public policy. Within that model, much as Whately observed, existing institutions or policies are thought to occupy argumentative ground and thus presumption. For example, in congressional debate, the status quo or the existing policies are presumed to remain in place until some good and sufficient reasons are established to justify change. Thus, defenders of the status quo have the argumentative advantage of presumption and advocates of change have the burden of proof. When the legislative model is used to explain where to stipulate presumption in an academic debate, presumption is invariably assigned to the existing policy or institution and the negative team as defenders of the existing order enjoy that argumentative advantage.

The second model frequently used to explain where to stipulate presumption in a debate is the **legal model.** The legal model is drawn from the established rules and procedures of our judicial system. Within this system, the person accused of a crime is presumed innocent until proven guilty. Thus, the accusers—the prosecution—are required to prove beyond a reasonable doubt that the defendant is guilty. The prosecution has the burden of proof and until that burden of proof is met, the defendant will continue to be presumed innocent. When the legal model is used to stipulate presumption in a debate, the affirmative is generally regarded to be the accuser—the prosecution—and the negative is generally regarded to be the defendant. Thus, the argumentative advantage of presumption is stipulated to the negative and the affirmative assumes the argumentative responsibility of fulfilling the burden of proof.

It is obvious that whether one uses the legislative or the legal model, presumption is generally stipulated to reside with the negative in a debate. However, the reasons for that stipulation are different. With the legislative model, presumption is assigned in this way because of the unpredictability of change. One assumes that it is impossible to predict accurately all the consequences of a change and that to justify the risk of unanticipated deleterious effects, there should be a compelling reason to initiate change. The legislative model carries no assumption that the status quo is good, only that the change might be worse. However, with the legal model, the reason for the stipulation resides in our effort to avoid false conviction. The presumption of innocence is granted to the defendant to avoid the possibility that an innocent person might be falsely convicted of a crime. Thus, in the legal model we acknowledge that it is better to let some guilty persons go free than to falsely convict a single individual.

Using the legislative and legal models to determine how to stipulate presumption in a debate has both strengths and weaknesses. On one hand, using these or any other models provides a consistent and reasoned approach to stipulating presumption. The models prescribe clear and time-tested approaches to argumentation within their respective contexts. It is also the case that in many instances, the type of argumentation occurring in a debate closely parallels that of particular models. On the other hand, neither the legislative nor the legal model duplicates academic debate. For example, although debate about policy propositions bears a strong resemblance to the legislative model, primarily because of the subject matter of the dispute, there is no such resemblance when the debate is about a nonpolicy proposition. Similarly, while the legal model offers some primary guidance for debate about nonpolicy propositions, particularly those that address issues of fact, its application to debates about policy propositions is artificial at best. In addition, both the legislative and legal models are derived from processes that differ significantly from that of academic debate.

Debate scholars have also treated presumption as a *psychological* concept. *Psychological presumption* reflects what a particular person values and what that individual is likely to consider a "good reason" to be. In many ways, psychological presumption accounts for the general unwillingness of humans to change the old ways that we discussed above. Thus, while stipulated presumption is a clearly stated convention of the process, psychological presumption is an inherent predisposition or preference every auditor brings to the argumentative encounter. It is a decision-making "rule," but it is a "rule" that is individually constructed, interpreted, and applied.

The difference between these two views of presumption is illustrated in the following example. The legal presumption that "one is innocent until proven guilty" is a stipulated presumption. Over the centuries, our society has decided that justice is best served by making the state prove claims against the defendant, and we therefore assign a legal presumption of innocence to anyone charged with a crime. Studies about communication in the legal setting, however, indicate that most juries have a psychological presumption that the defendant is guilty. That is, most jurors believe the prosecutor would not have arrested and brought the defendant to trial unless the defendant was guilty. Defense attorneys routinely stress the stipulated presumption of innocence to counteract the psychological presumption of guilt. For a number of years, theo-rists were unable to resolve the dispute between these two very different views of presumption, primarily because they assumed stipulated and psychological pre-sumption to be mutually exclusive "types" of presumption.

Recent scholarship reconciles these different points of view in the Holistic Model of presumption (Hill 1989, 1994). According to the Holistic Model, stipulated and psychological presumption are not mutually exclusive "types" of presumption; they are simply different dimensions of the same major construct. Nor do the dimensions perform the same functions. The **stipulated dimension** is the structural component of argumentation; it provides form and order for the process. The **psychological dimension** is the evaluative component; it explains how judgments are made. Because each performs a different function, both dimensions are included as necessary components of presumption in the Holistic Model. In the following sections, we discuss this model in more detail. First, we explore the stipulated and psychological dimensions more fully and the corollary burden of proof associated with each. Second, we demonstrate how the presumption and the burden of proof constructs function in argumentation and debate.

The Stipulated Dimension

The stipulated dimension is designed to provide form and structure to nonpol-icy argumentation; it is quite similar to Whately's early view of presumption as a guiding principle or construct imposed on argumentative episodes. However, whereas Whately derived the notion of a rule-based presumption largely on assessment of argument in the legal forum, within the Holistic Model, the stip-ulated dimension is derived from our understanding of the basic nature of argu-mentation as a *process*. Argumentation scholar Gary Cronkhite describes what we mean by the stipulated dimension of presumption and its corollary burden of proof in the following way:

> The right to do no more than ask "Why?" is presumption; the obligation to respond is the burden of proof. More formally: (1) Presumption is the right of any opponent of a stated proposition to refrain from argument in the absence of a prima facie case supporting that proposition. (2) The burden of proof is the inher-ent alternative of one who states a proposition (argumentative thesis) either to offer a prima facie case in its support or to see it remain unsupported. (3) The assumption of the burden of proof is thus inherent in the statement of a proposi-tion. (4) The presumption is unavoidably forfeited by one who states a proposi-tion to the occupant of any other position. Therefore the person (or agency) who

initially advances an argumentative point of view automatically takes upon himself the burden of proof. (274)

The stipulated dimension is derived from the fundamental roles of advocates within the process. The advocate who defends the existing institution or belief garners the presumption associated with the preoccupation of argumentative ground, and the advocate who initiates the argumentative episode assumes the burden of proof. The advocate with presumption has no responsibility to justify her or his preoccupation of argumentative ground until the advocate with the burden of proof provides sufficient reason to question that preoccupation. Thus, in our previous examples, you were able to challenge your roommate to prove that "the Knicks are the best team" before you were required to respond, the speaker was able to demand that you prove she "misinterpreted the evidence" before she was required to defend her interpretation, and you were required to speak first in the debate before the negative was required to defend affirmative action.

When applied to the stipulated dimension, three important qualities are associated with the terms *presumption* and *the burden of proof.* First, both are descriptive. In addition to describing the roles of advocates within the process, presumption accorded via the stipulated dimension describes the argumentative relationship between the opposing positions supported by those advocates. The position that is challenged occupies presumptive argumentative ground, and the position of the advocate who initiates the argumentation is the encroacher upon that ground. Second, neither presumption accorded via the stipulated dimension nor its corollary burden of proof is evaluative. To say that the challenged position occupies presumptive argumentative ground does not mean that the position is presumed to be more important, better, or more valid than the encroaching position; nor does saying that the encroaching position has the burden of proof mean that position is assumed to be less probable, inferior, or weaker than the challenged position. Presumption and the burden of proof accorded via the stipulated dimension do not suggest that it is more or less likely that the speaker misinterpreted the evidence; they do not suggest that it is more or less likely that affirmative action promotes deleterious hiring practices. Rather, presumption accorded via the stipulated dimension and its corollary burden of proof simply mean that adequate reasons must be established before the encroaching position will be allowed to remove the existing institution or belief from the presumptive argumentative ground.

Third, both presumption accorded via the stipulated dimension and its corollary burden of proof remain constant across all argumentative episodes. Regardless of the subject matter of the argumentation, the capabilities of the advocates, the formality of the interaction, or the context for the interaction, presumption accorded via the stipulated dimension and its corollary burden of proof are assigned to advocates prior to the interaction and remain affixed throughout it. The advocate who initiates the argumentation always has the burden of proof and the advocate who defends the challenged position always has presumption. In a formal debate, the negative always has presumption assigned via the stipulated dimension and the affirmative always has the corollary burden of proof. Because presumption and the burden of proof accorded via the stipulated dimension are based on the nature of the process of argumentation, are descriptive, are nonevaluative, and remain constant, they are designated in the Holistic Model as **PRESUMPTION** and **THE BURDEN OF PROOF** and are illustrated in Figure 8.1.

The Psychological Dimension

As the stipulated dimension apportions PRESUMPTION and THE BURDEN OF PROOF and provides form and order to the process of argumentation and debate, the psychological dimension apportions presumptions and burdens of proof and reflects the evaluative component of argumentation and debate. Presumption apportioned via the psychological dimension and its corollary burden of proof are neither rule based nor imposed on the process. Rather, they reflect the nature of human decision making by helping to explain how auditors process, interpret, and evaluate the arguments presented by advocates. Within the Holistic Model, they are denoted as **<presumption>** and **<the burden of proof>.**

The psychological dimension is an inevitable and everpresent characteristic of argumentation precisely because all argumentation is ultimately a human communication experience. Meaning in any sort of human communicative activity is partly a product of the perceptions and interpretations of the auditor. How a person processes and understands another's messages is greatly influenced by what he or she "knows," "thinks" to be important, "believes" to be consistent with past experiences, and "assumes" the general purpose of the interaction to be.

In the Holistic Model, <presumption> is accorded via the psychological dimension by the auditors of the argumentative episode. Auditors process argumentative episodes through various perceptual **screens.** A screen reflects a preference, predisposition, understanding, or bias that the auditor has about the subject, the nature of the arguments being presented, or even the process of argumentation itself. Auditors may have any number of screens they use to process an argumentative episode. Each screen identifies a potential psychologi-

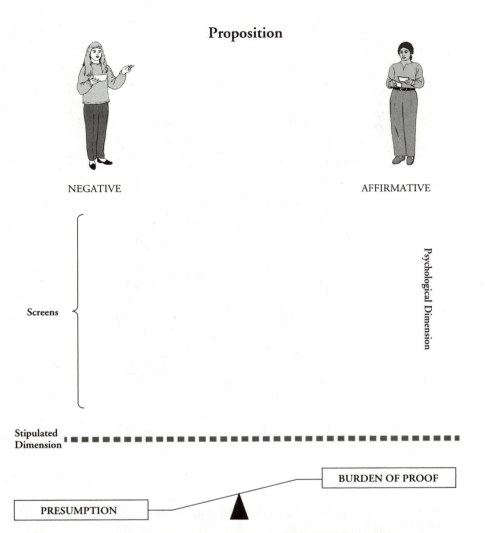

FIGURE 8.1   The Stipulated Dimension of the Holistic Model of Presumption

cal <presumption> that might be accorded by the auditors as they process the argumentation.

A psychological <presumption> is accorded when the auditor processes some portion of the argumentative episode—a claim, evidence, type of reasoning, piece of information, appeal—that embodies the concept represented in a screen. As an example, assume that in a formal debate one of the auditor's screens reflected a preference for evidence based on experimental research. The

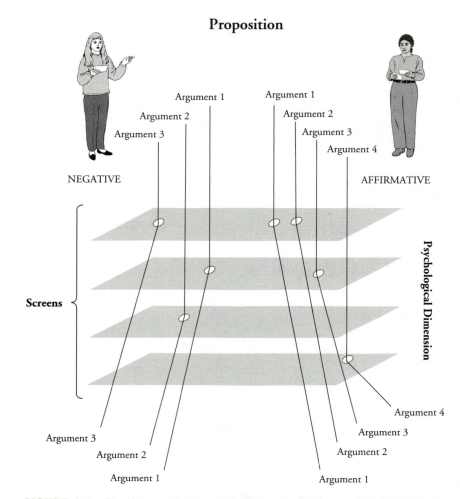

FIGURE 8.2   The Nature of Screens in the Psychological Dimension of the Holistic Model of Presumption

affirmative presents evidence about quotas imposed through affirmative action that is based on the results of experimental research. That evidence is filtered through the screen reflecting a preference for experimental research and is accorded a psychological <presumption> by the judge. The basic way screens function in argumentation and debate is illustrated in Figure 8.2.

Not all psychological <presumptions> exert equal influence on argumentation. Some carry more or less **weight** than others. The weight of any psychological <presumption> is determined by two factors. First, the weight is proportional to the strength of the concept embodied within the screen. In the previous example, if the weight of the preference for experimental research in the screen is 5, theoretically the weight of the argument corresponding to that screen could be up to 5. Second, the weight of the argument is affected by the degree to which the argument directly corresponds to that screen; the more closely the argument replicates the concept embodied in the screen, the more likely it will be to garner the full weight of that psychological <presumption>. If the psychological <presumption> for experimental research has a value of 3 and the judge determines that the argument the negative side presents is based on actual experimental research, it is likely that the negative team's argument will garner a psychological <presumption> of 3.

Consider another example from a less formal argumentative episode. John is your friend and listens to the exchange between you and your roommate. John, the auditor, believes that the most important measure of a basketball team is its ratio of points scored versus points allowed. That belief becomes a screen through which John processes the exchange between you and your roommate. Your roommate presents a number of reasons for his belief that the "Knicks are the best team," including their win-loss percentage, the lifetime record of their coach, their turnover rate, and the like. He does not, however, mention their ratio of points scored versus points allowed. While responding to your room-mate, you not only attack the reasons he presents but you also point out how your favorite team, the Bulls, compares in each of those categories. In addition, you point out that the Bulls have a better ratio of points scored versus points allowed than do the Knicks. When you make that point, your argument is processed through John's screen and is accorded a psychological <presumption>. Because John strongly believes this statistic to be the most important indicator of the caliber of a basketball team, your argument is given a "strong" weight and will likely be the most important factor in John's judgment of who "wins" and who "loses" the exchange. The variable weight of screens used in any argumentative episode is illustrated in Figure 8.3.

The screens through which arguments are filtered can be imposed by the auditor, as in the previous examples, or they can be constructed by the advocate. For instance, in the debate example, the judge might have no preference for information generated through experimental studies, but the negative debater could construct such a screen for the judge to use by demonstrating why experimental research should be considered more valuable than other sorts of evidence. Or, in the exchange between you and your roommate, John might not have a preference for "the ratio of points scored versus points allowed" as the best indicator of caliber, but you could make an argument for why it should be considered so. If John agreed with your argument, a screen would be constructed that would in turn be used to evaluate subsequent arguments you and your roommate presented.

Of course, any argument an advocate makes to construct a screen is filtered through existing screens and may garner psychological <presumptions> or incur

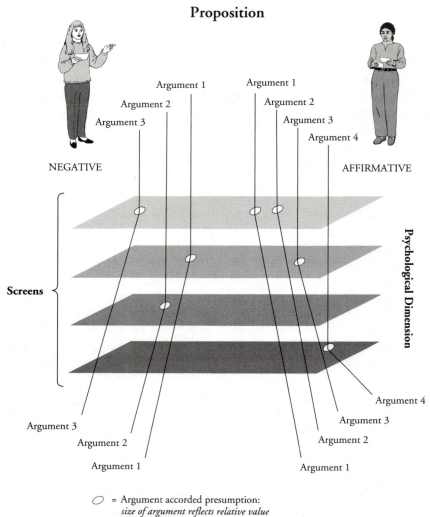

FIGURE 8.3 The Weights and Screens in the Psychological Dimension of the Holistic Model of Presumption

<burdens of proof>. For example, a debater who attempts to construct a screen that preferences experimental research might garner a psychological <presumption> if the argument for constructing such a screen is processed through an existing screen that preferences scholarly research over informal evidence. Conversely, the debater's argument might incur <the burden of proof> if it is filtered

through an existing screen that preferences "common sense" over "ivory tower research."

The <presumptions> derived through the psychological dimension carry with them a corresponding <burden of proof>. If John grants you a psychological <presumption> regarding the ratio of points scored versus points allowed, your roommate is automatically assigned <the burden of proof> to overcome that <presumption>. Similarly, if the affirmative side is accorded a psychological <presumption> regarding the evidence from experimental studies, the negative side has <the burden of proof> to overcome that <presumption>. The affirmative would retain that <presumption> until the negative could fulfill the <burden of proof>.

The <burden of proof> corresponding to a psychological <presumption> is slightly greater than the weight of the psychological <presumption>. For example, if the psychological <presumption> accorded to the negative is 3, <the burden of proof> the affirmative would have to meet would be slightly greater than 3. Theoretically, if the affirmative were not able to fulfill <the burden of proof> to that degree, the negative would retain the psychological <presumption> accorded to its argument. If the psychological <presumption> of your argument is "very great," <the burden of proof> your roommate would have to meet is slightly more than "very great." If your roommate could meet or exceed that <burden of proof>, he would successfully overcome the psychological <presumption> you were accorded.

We associate three primary qualities with <presumption> accorded via the psychological dimension and its corollary <burden of proof>. First, both vary according to the nature of the interaction. Both the psychological dimension of <presumption> and its corollary <burden of proof> are influenced by the subject matter, context, advocates, and auditors of nonpolicy argumentation. For example, had the auditor to the exchange between you and your roommate been someone other than John, this auditor may not have granted any psychological <presumption> to "the ratio of points scored versus points allowed." Second, neither <presumption> accorded via the psychological dimension nor its corollary <burden of proof> is assigned exclusively to any advocate. Any advocate in an argumentative encounter may be accorded a psychological <presumption> or may incur the corollary <burden of proof>. Moreover, an advocate may simultaneously be accorded a psychological <presumption> regarding a particular portion of his case—claim, evidence, reasoning—and incur the corollary <burden of proof> regarding another portion. Third, the amount of <presumptions> and <burdens of proof> in an argumentative episode is variable. Any advocate may be accorded multiple psychological <presumptions> or incur multiple corollary <burdens of proof>, or neither advocate may be accorded a psychological <presumption>.

Combining the Stipulated and Psychological Dimensions

To understand fully the two constructs discussed thus far, it is important to clarify the relationship between PRESUMPTION and <presumption> and THE BURDEN OF PROOF and <the burden of proof>. There are significant differences between PRESUMPTION accorded via the stipulated dimension and <presumption> accorded via the psychological dimension. There can be many <presumptions> accorded via the psychological dimension in any argumentation and such <presumptions> may be accorded to any advocate. However, there can be only one PRESUMPTION and it is always accorded to the advocate defending the challenged position. Thus, in a debate, the negative always has PRESUMPTION, although either the negative or affirmative might be accorded singular or even multiple <presumptions> via the psychological dimension.

PRESUMPTION and <presumption> also influence the outcome of argumentation in different ways. An advocate can retain a <presumption> or even <presumptions> accorded via the psychological dimension and still lose the encounter because it is possible to "win" some arguments in a debate and still "lose" the overall proposition. However, if an advocate retains PRESUMPTION, it means that the advocate who initiated the argumentation did not successfully encroach upon the existing argumentative ground and that the existing argumentative ground remains in place. When the existing argumentative ground is retained, the initiator of the argumentation has lost the encounter. Thus, in a debate, if the negative side retains PRESUMPTION, they should always "win."

Similarly, there are significant differences between <the burden of proof> arising out of the psychological dimension and THE BURDEN OF PROOF arising out of the stipulated dimension. There can be many <burdens of proof> arising out of the psychological dimension and any advocate may incur one or more of such burdens. However, THE BURDEN OF PROOF is always a singular construct and it is always assumed by the initiator of the argumentation. Thus, in a debate the affirmative side always has THE BURDEN OF PROOF, although both the affirmative and negative debaters can incur <the burden of proof> related to specific portions of their or their opponents' case. Moreover, an advocate can fulfill <the burden of proof> or even multiple <burdens of proof> and still "lose" the encounter. However, if the initiator of the argumentation fulfills THE BURDEN OF PROOF, she has successfully encroached on the existing argumentative ground and replaced the position occupying that ground with the position she advanced. Thus, in a debate, either the affirmative or negative side can fulfill <the burden of proof> and still "lose" the debate, but if the affirmative debaters fulfill THE BURDEN OF PROOF, they should be designated the "winner."

By now, you should have a fairly clear understanding of the Holistic Model and how the stipulated and psychological dimensions are combined within that model. The model is illustrated in its entirety in Figure 8.4.

Other Constructs

Although presumption and the burden of proof are clearly significant, they are not the only constructs for argumentation and debate. In this section, we discuss three additional constructs—**prima facie, the burden of rebuttal,** and **a burden of proof**—that further help define the roles of advocates in argumentation and debate. In most instances, it is necessary to explain each of these concepts by describing its relationship to either PRESUMPTION or THE BURDEN OF PROOF. Each of these constructs helps clarify how advocates fulfill their primary roles; thus, each is important to argumentation.

Prima Facie

The term *prima facie* means "on its face," or "on first glance." It is closely related to THE BURDEN OF PROOF because prima facie describes the threshold or basic requirements that an advocate who initiates argumentation must meet to fulfill THE BURDEN OF PROOF initially and force the argumentation to proceed. In a sense, the prima facie requirement is a quality check on the advocate who initiates a dispute because it requires this advocate to present reasons of "sufficient strength" to require his or her opponent to defend the PRESUMPTION of the challenged position. Thus, in our previous examples, your roommate would be required to present a prima facie case to prove that "the Knicks are the best team" if he is to challenge seriously the PRESUMPTION accorded to the existing belief that "the Bulls are the best team." Similarly, you would be required to present a prima facie case to seriously challenge the PRESUMPTION accorded the belief that "the speaker did not misinterpret the evidence." In nonpolicy debate, the affirmative is always required to present a prima facie case in order to challenge the PRESUMPTION accorded to the negative as defenders of the existing order. Ultimately, the advocate who initiates the argumentation can only overcome PRESUMPTION by fulfilling THE BURDEN OF PROOF, and to fulfill that burden, he or she must present a prima facie case.

Determining which advocate must assume the responsibility of presenting a prima facie case is fairly simple. Determining exactly what constitutes a prima facie case is much more complicated. Generally, for reasons to be prima facie, they must possess two characteristics. First, they must be *reasonably complete.*

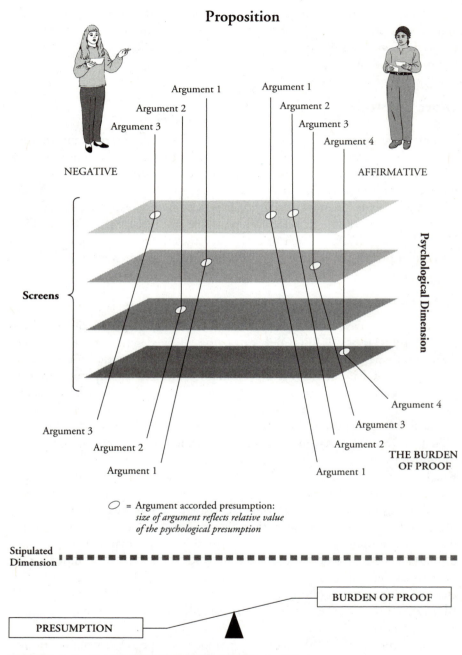

FIGURE 8.4 The Complete Holistic Model of Presumption

That is, the reasons offered by the advocate who initiates the challenge must address the major stock issues of the particular type of proposition being debated. We discuss the concept of stock issues fully in Chapter 9. For now, however, it is useful to think of stock issues simply as requirements an advocate must fulfill when engaging in a specific type of argumentation. For example, when your roommate asserted that "the Knicks are the best team," he implicitly assumed the responsibility to meet two requirements: (1) to explain what "best" means, and (2) to demonstrate that the Knicks can be characterized in that particular way. Similarly, in another example when you asserted that the speaker misinterpreted the evidence she used in her speech, you assumed the task of explaining how to determine when something is "misinterpreted" and then demonstrating that this is what the speaker did. If either you or your roommate did not fulfill the task you assumed, we could say that you did not present a prima facie case because your case is not complete.

Second, what you say must be of *reasonable strength*. By this we simply mean that you must present reasons that are generally consistent with the principles of sound argument construction, use of evidence, and reasoning discussed in Chapters 3, 4, and 5. At the most basic level, your claims must be relevant to the challenge being advanced. You might correctly note that "the speaker relies extensively on emotional appeals" but that observation does not constitute a prima facie reason that she misinterpreted a specific piece of evidence. Your claims also have to be adequately supported. We would not judge your roommate's assertion that "every coach in the league agrees that the Knicks are the best team" as prima facie without some form of evidence to substantiate that assertion. You also need to use sound reasoning. It may very well be correct that the speaker is a "member of the religious right," but using that affiliation to reason that she must have misinterpreted the evidence because "those religious fanatics always bend the truth" would not constitute a prima facie case to support your challenge.

Regardless of the standards someone uses to determine whether a case is a prima facie case, the advocate who initiates the dispute will always be required to present prima facie reasons to fulfill THE BURDEN OF PROOF. Failure to present prima facie reasons invariably will mean that the PRESUMPTION will not be overcome.

The Burden of Rebuttal

Unlike the prima facie requirement, which is a requirement placed on the advocate who initiates the argumentation, the burden of rebuttal is a responsibility placed on each advocate in an argumentative encounter. In its most basic sense, the burden of rebuttal is simply the responsibility to respond to the opposing advocate's case or claims. For example, assume that your roommate presented a claim that "the Knicks have the toughest defense in the league" and he used the results of a recent coaches' poll as evidence to support that claim. When your roommate introduced the claim and evidence, the burden of rebuttal fell to you —you were required to respond to the claim and evidence. Assuming the responsibility imposed by the burden of rebuttal broadens the role of advocates in argumentation by forcing them to do more than simply present their own case or claims; it also requires each advocate to answer the case or claims presented by the opposing advocate. In this way, the burden of rebuttal ensures that one of the primary purposes of the process of argumentation—to examine seriously and test all competing claims—is fulfilled.

In addition to imposing the basic responsibility upon each advocate to respond to her or his opponent's claims, the burden of rebuttal also requires that response be direct and meaningful. To fulfill the burden of rebuttal, a response must warrant reconsideration of the claim it was levied against. Consider the previous example: your roommate presents a claim that "the Knicks have the toughest defense in the league" and he uses the results of a recent coaches' poll as evidence to support that claim. You present a counterclaim stating that "defense is an unimportant indicator of the overall quality of a team" and support that claim with statistical evidence showing that offense has been a more important predictor of the NBA champion over the last ten years than was defense. Your counterclaim forces reconsideration of the claim it was leveled against because accepting the counterclaim precludes acceptance of your roommate's claim. In short, you fulfilled the burden of rebuttal. Of course, because the burden of rebuttal shifts from advocate to advocate, your roommate would have the burden of rebuttal to respond to your counterclaim.

You might also fulfill the burden of rebuttal by launching a substantive attack, such as challenging the way the questions in the coaches' poll were formulated as a way to assault the evidence your roommate used. Although such an attack would not necessarily preclude acceptance of your roommate's claim as the counterclaim would, it would force your roommate either to demonstrate that your challenge is unfounded or to present other satisfactory evidence to support his claim. In either event, your challenge is certainly sufficient to require reconsideration of your roommate's claim; thus, it fulfills the burden of rebuttal. In most instances, an advocate can generate direct and meaningful responses by employing virtually any of the tests of argument construction, evidence, and reasoning explained in Chapters 3, 4, and 5.

To this point, we have illustrated how an advocate might fulfill the burden of rebuttal. It is also important to understand how an advocate might fail to fulfill that burden and what the argumentative consequences of such a failure might be. An advocate might fail to fulfill the burden of rebuttal in either of two ways. First, an advocate can simply *not provide any answer or response* to the opposing advocate's claim. In the previous example, you would fail to meet the burden of rebuttal in the most obvious way if you completely ignored your roommate's claim. Second, an advocate can fail to fulfill the burden of rebuttal by being *nonresponsive*. A nonresponsive answer is actually a nonanswer; it either has no direct bearing on the claim it was directed toward or is so inconsequential that even if correct, it does not force reconsideration of that claim. For example, if you challenged your roommate's claim that "the Knicks have the best defense in the league" by presenting a counterclaim stating that "the Bulls have the lowest number of turnovers," you would be nonresponsive; even if your counterclaim were completely correct, it does not force any sort of reconsideration of the claim it was directed against. Or suppose you challenged the way the coaches' poll questions were constructed and your roommate answered your challenge—fulfilled his burden of rebuttal—by explaining that the poll questions were in the proper form. To answer your roommate and fulfill your new burden of rebuttal, you repeat your original challenge about the form of the poll questions. This answer is nonresponsive because it does not force any reconsideration of your roommate's explanation that the poll questions were in the proper form.

Assume you took a different approach to answering your roommate's original claim that the coaches' poll demonstrates that the Knicks are the best team in the league. This time, you responded to your roommate's claim by asking these questions about the poll: "When was it taken?" "How were the questions formulated?" "Have you been responsive?" Although these questions are related to substantive tests of evidence you might employ, simply asking questions does not force any sort of reconsideration of the claim they are leveled against. You might be able to use the answers to formulate responsive attacks, but the questions themselves are essentially nonresponsive. An advocate cannot fulfill the burden of rebuttal simply by asking a question. Overall, any response that is irrelevant to the claim it is directed against, that is irrelevant given the subsequent explanation of the claim, or that is not formulated as an attack is likely to be nonresponsive and to undermine the ability of an advocate to fulfill the burden of rebuttal.

Certainly it will not often be the case that an advocate fulfills the burden of rebuttal for *every* claim advanced by the opponent. An advocate may focus his or her efforts on some of the opponent's claims and ignore others, be unable to respond to particular claims, or judge particular claims as unworthy of response. Any time an advocate fails to fulfill the burden of rebuttal, however, he concedes that argumentative ground to his opponent. In essence, failing to fulfill the burden of rebuttal results in granting your opponent's claim by default.

The consequences of losing argumentative ground vary from situation to situation and generally depend on both the importance of the claim conceded and the formality of the argumentative context. Obviously, the more important a specific claim is to the overall case being constructed, the greater the argumentative consequences an advocate suffers from failing to fulfill the burden of rebuttal. Generally, the consequences will also probably be greater in formal argumentative contexts than in less formal contexts. In academic debate, for example, judges typically attempt to keep a very complete record of each of the claims advanced by the affirmative and negative sides and each of the answers given to those claims. When either advocate fails to fulfill the burden of rebuttal, the claims for which the burden of rebuttal was not fulfilled are considered irretrievably "lost." Although debate judges certainly weigh the relative importance of the lost claims to the overall case, the precise record keeping they employ calls immediate attention to the affirmative or negative side's failure to fulfill the burden of rebuttal; such lapses can have a significant effect on the decision in the round. In less formal argumentative contexts, such as the exchange between you and your roommate, it is unlikely that there will be a judge keeping such a precise record of the interaction.

A Burden of Proof

The final argumentative construct is a burden of proof. In many ways, this is the simplest of all argumentative constructs. A burden of proof is the responsibility imposed upon any advocate who asserts a claim to provide adequate reasons to support that claim. In the previous examples, your roommate had to provide support for his claim that "the Knicks have the toughest defense in the league," just as you had to provide support for your counterclaim that "defense is an unimportant indicator of the overall quality of a team." In a formal debate, if the negative side argues that "affirmative action programs have not decreased the quality of the faculty in colleges and universities," they would have a responsibility to provide adequate reasons suggesting that to be the case. Overall, a burden of proof is a safety check on the process of argumentation. By requiring every advocate to be able to prove what she or he asserts, a burden of proof ensures, to the greatest degree possible, that argumentation will remain a reason-giving and reason-testing process.

A burden of proof should not be confused with <the burden of proof> and THE BURDEN OF PROOF. Every advocate shoulders a burden of proof to support his or her claims. Only the advocate who initiates the argumentation has THE BURDEN OF PROOF. Further, THE BURDEN OF PROOF applies only to the ultimate claim or proposition being argued (such as "the Knicks are the best team," "the speaker misinterpreted the evidence," or "Resolved: that affirmative action promotes deleterious hiring practices") whereas a burden of proof applies to any claim introduced by any advocate at any time during the argumentation. A burden of proof is also different from

<the burden of proof>. Any advocate can have both a burden of proof and <the burden of proof>, but advocates *assume* a burden of proof for their own claims and *are assigned* <the burden of proof> when their opponents' claims are granted a psychological <presumption>. Thus, an advocate should be prepared to meet a burden of proof for each claim he or she presents, but will be required to meet the burden of proof only for the opponent's claims that garner a psychological presumption.

Conclusion

Argumentative constructs are important in all types of nonpolicy argumentation and debate. They help define the roles of advocates, the requirements advocates must meet, and the ways advocates can attempt to meet those requirements. Understanding PRESUMPTION, THE BURDEN OF PROOF, <presumption>, <the burden of proof>, prima facie cases, the burden of rebuttal, and a burden of proof is critical to understanding what nonpolicy argument is and how it is practiced. Serious students of argumentation and debate will not only thoroughly familiarize themselves with what these constructs mean, but they will also think about how they as advocates might use these constructs in their nonpolicy argumentation and debate.

Selected Bibliography

Balthrop, William V. "The Debate Judge as 'Critic of Argument': Toward a Transcendent Perspective." *Journal of the American Forensic Association* 20 (1983): 1–15.

Bartanen, Michael, and David Frank. "The Issue-Agenda Model." *Advanced Debate: Readings in Theory, Practice and Teaching.* Eds. David A. Thomas and Jack Hart. Lincolnwood, IL: National TextBook, 1989: 408–16.

Brydon, Steven. "Presumption in Non-Policy Debate: In Search of a Paradigm." *Journal of the American Forensic Association* 23 (1986):15–22.

Burleson, Brant R. "On the Analysis and Criticism of Arguments: Some Theoretical and Methodological Considerations." *Journal of the American Forensic Association* 15 (1979): 137–47.

Burnett, Nicholas F. "Archbishop Whately and the Concept of Presumption: Lessons for Non-Policy Debate." *CEDA Yearbook* 13 (1992): 37–43.

Cronkhite, Gary. "The Locus of Presumption." *Central States Speech Journal* 17 (1966): 270–76.

Fisher, Walter. *Human Communication as Narration: Toward a Philosophy of Reason, Value, and Action.* Columbia: U of South Carolina, 1987.

Hill, Bill. "An Evolving Model of Presumption for Non-Policy Debate." *CEDA Yearbook* 15 (1994): 43–64.

———. "Toward a Holistic Model of Presumption for Non-Policy Debate." *CEDA Yearbook* 10 (1989): 22–32.

Rowland, Robert. "The Function of Presumption in Academic Debate." *CEDA Yearbook* 13 (1992): 20–24.

Sproule, J. Michael. "The Psychological Burden of Proof: On the Evolutionary Development of Richard Whately's Theory of Presumption." *Communication Monograph* 43 (1976): 115–29.

Tuman, Joseph S. "Getting to First Base: Prima Facie Arguments for Propositions of Value." *Journal of the American Forensic Association* 24 (1987): 89–94.

Tuman, Joseph S. "Natural Value Hierarchies and Presumption: Merging Stipulated/Artificial Presumption with Natural/Psychological Presumption." *CEDA Yearbook* 13 (1992): 10–19.

Vasilius, Jan. "Presumption, Presumption, Wherefore Art Thou Presumption?" *CEDA Yearbook* 1 (1980): 33–42.

Whedbee, Karen. "Using Presumption as a Decision Rule in Value Debate." *CEDA Yearbook* 13 (1992): 25–36.

Winebrenner, T. C. "Relocating Presumption: Shifting Burdens of Proof in CEDA Debate." *CEDA Yearbook* 13 (1992): 1–9.

Young, Gregory W., and Paul C. Gaske. "On Prima Facie Value Argumentation: The Policy Implications Affirmative." *CEDA Yearbook* 5 1984: 24–30.

Discussion Questions

1. Are the stipulated and psychological dimensions of presumption always of equal importance, or are there situations in which one more directly influences the nature and outcome of a debate than does the other?
2. How might the Holistic Model be applied to everyday argument?
3. Is it important to have clearly defined constructs such as prima facie, burden of proof, and burden of rebuttal, or do such constructs make argumentation and debate more complicated than necessary?

CHAPTER 9

ISSUES AND ANALYTICAL MODELS

*T*o be a successful advocate, debaters must assess the critical questions of the debate proposition systematically and completely. If the debate is to be an exercise in meaningful argumentation and reasoned judgment, judges must incorporate the debaters' advocacy about those critical questions in their decision making. Clearly, the critical questions of the proposition are central to both the role of debaters as advocates and the purposefulness of the process of debate. But what are these "critical questions"?

In this chapter, we discuss the stock issues—the critical questions—of policy and nonpolicy propositions. We begin by discussing the nature of stock issues and the functions they perform in argumentation and debate. Next, we discuss six major analytical models and illustrate the stock issues contained in each. Two of those models, the traditional needs model and the comparative advantage model, are used primarily for policy debate propositions. Two models, the criteria-application and the issue agenda model, were developed primarily for nonpolicy propositions. One model, the classical stasis system, is a general system of analysis for argumentation that can be readily adapted to debate propositions. The final model, the narrative paradigm, is a broadly constructed paradigm for communication that can be adapted for either policy or nonpolicy debate propositions.

Stock Issues

The debate proposition, as we explained in Chapter 7, is the focal point of a debate; it is the ultimate claim that advocates in the debate hope to have accepted. **Stock issues** are the fundamental questions that must be answered if a proposition is to be accepted or rejected. Stock issues are generally presumed to be the set of questions a thinking, reasonable person would ask and would need to have answered to make a reasoned decision about a particular issue.

Stock issues perform three major functions in debate. First, *stock issues help you prepare to debate.* Initially, they provide a broad framework that advocates can use to determine the types of claims to construct for their case. Each stock issue, in turn, identifies a major aspect of the proposition that you must be prepared to debate. For example, assume that you must be prepared to debate—to offer claims about—the method used to determine which of two movies is "best," and which movie's characteristics more closely conform to those identified in the method. The stock issues do not prescribe the specific claims you must present; they do not, for example, specify *what method* you must advocate. However, they do describe the major themes your claims must address and, thus, help you determine the general types of claims you must develop for a debate.

Stock issues can also be used to prepare for a debate by serving as an organizational framework for your case. Although we discuss how to organize a case more fully in Chapters 11, 12, and 13, it is important to understand this very pragmatic function of stock issues. Debaters can use the stock issues of the proposition as the structural divisions of their case. In doing that, they would develop claims for each of the stock issues and then use those issues as the major divisions of their case. Using the stock issues as a framework for the organization helps ensure that your case will be organized in both a purposeful and systematic manner.

Second, *stock issues help clarify what the key logical constructs mean in each debate.* As you recall from Chapter 8, two key logical constructs in debate are THE BURDEN OF PROOF and prima facie case. Stock issues help clarify what both these constructs mean in any given debate. Because the stock issues are the critical questions that must be answered before a proposition can be accepted, they define operationally what the affirmative side has to prove to fulfill THE BURDEN OF PROOF. In turn, by defining the basic components of THE BURDEN OF PROOF, the stock issues define operationally the substantive components of a prima facie case. The affirmative side is required to present a case that, at first glance—that is, on its face—is sufficient to justify acceptance of the proposition. To do that, the affirmative team must address each of the stock issues of the proposition in the case. The case cannot be prima facie without including each stock issue because each must be answered if acceptance of the proposition is to be justified; omitting any stock issues renders the case incomplete and incapable of justifying acceptance of the proposition.

Third, *stock issues provide a framework for advocacy in a debate.* Therefore, they can be used to anticipate the types of claims your opponents might present. The stock issues do not identify the specific claims your opponents will present, but they do provide a framework debaters can use to anticipate the general nature of those claims. Negative debaters, for example, can use stock issues as a general indicator of the types of claims the affirmative will present to fulfill THE BURDEN OF PROOF. Negative debaters know that to justify acceptance of the proposition—fulfill THE BURDEN OF PROOF—the affirmative will have to address each of the stock issues of the proposition, and thus the negative can use the stock issues to anticipate the major issues they will encounter. Similarly, the affirmative team can use the stock issues to predict the sorts of counterclaims the negative could present. In our previous example, the affirmative knows that the negative could present counterclaims about the method or about the specific characteristics of the movie *Clear and Present Danger*. Using that framework, the affirmative might anticipate that the negative could present such specific counterclaims as "there is no objective method," "any method should consider total revenue earned," "*Clear and Present Danger* has superior acting," or "*Clear and Present Danger* has a more interesting plot." Once you know the stock issues, you can brainstorm about those general issues to predict the types of claims your opponent might present.

Analytical Models:
Foundations in the Stasis System

Before embarking on a discussion of the various analytical models used in academic debate, we should first examine the idea of **stasis**. The concept of stasis, we will see, is one of the fundamental underlying principles for all analytical models of debate.

The term *stasis* originally comes from Greek, meaning "standing" or "standstill." Today in English, the word means "a state of balance or motionlessness." In argumentation theory, stasis (or a state of balance) is achieved when two advocates are arguing the same "kind" of argument. To ensure that stasis is achieved, the disputant must (1) systematically search the available arguments to discover the **topoi** (lines of argument) and then (2) select those topoi that argue at the same level as the opponents' argument. Thus, any system based on stasis theory has two important principles: (1) there is a finite set of topoi that, broadly, can be identified independent of the particular situation; and (2) these topoi occupy different "levels." We discussed the notion of "levels" in more formal terms in Chapter 6. As you recall from that chapter, advocates must present arguments on the same level as their opponent in order to fulfill the burden of rebuttal.

An illustration may clarify the essentials of stasis theory. According to stasis theory, when advocates are arguing different kinds of arguments, on different levels or planes, their arguments pass each other like two ships in the night, and stasis is not achieved. Suppose I argue that our city should finance a new reservoir because it will enhance economic development. Another citizen, however, says that, legally, the city is barred by state law from building reservoirs. Stasis theory points out that we cannot resolve our differences until we "meet" or "**clash**" with each other's arguments. Further, stasis theory would point out that, logically, my opponent's argument must be resolved first before we could proceed to my argument. That is, if the city is indeed legally barred from building a reservoir, any benefits that might result from building the reservoir are irrelevant to the argument at hand: "the city should build a reservoir." We must first determine the legality of the proposal, and only then can we discuss the merits.

Stock Issues of the Model

While Hermagoras (late second century B.C.E.) is credited with first formulating stasis theory, it is Cicero, in his book *De Inventione* (c. 86 B.C.E.), who articulated the theory so impressively that he influenced scholars for centuries.[1] Although each writer formulated the theory a bit differently, basically the classical system of stasis held that there were four types of arguments: conjectural (fact), definition, quality, and jurisdiction. These four types of questions make up the stock issues of the model.

Conjectural issues concern the facts of the matter. For example, has person Y been killed and do the available data demonstrate that person X likely killed person Y? **Definitional issues** would speak to the relevant definitions of the issue. What, for example, are the technical differences between first degree and second degree murder, voluntary and involuntary manslaughter, not guilty by reason of insanity, and self-defense? We may agree that X killed Y, but which crime X might be charged with will depend in part on how we define those six terms. The charges (and later the verdict) against X will also be dependent on the **qualitative issues.** These are the events in the situation that might influence our interpretation of the act. In addition to influencing the charges and verdict, the quality of the act may influence the particular sentence X receives. For example, we may agree that X killed Y but conclude that X did so because Y threatened X with a gun. The threat, then, is an integral part of the total context of the action; it is a qualitative issue that bears upon any judgment we may reach about X. Finally, **jurisdictional issues** address the question of "who decides"? Too much pretrial publicity may dictate that the trial's venue be changed from one county to another. If X killed Y as a part of an organized conspiracy, charges may be brought in federal court rather than at the state level.

A simple, everyday example may illustrate not only the four types of issues but also the extent to which we intuitively use stasis theory in common argumentation. Several children are playing backyard baseball one summer day. The batter hits a ball into the outfield and tries to stretch it into a double. The ball is thrown to the second baseman, who tags the runner at about the same time the batter reaches base. An argument ensues as to whether the batter is safe or out.

At first, the two players involved argue about whether the fielder tagged the runner before the runner reached the base (question of fact). They reach a point at which they agree that it was a very close play, and a third player points out that "ties go to the runner"—a point of definition. After a discussion that convinces the other players that this is indeed the rule, the second baseman argues more vociferously that the batter was tagged before reaching second base (back to a question of fact). A bystander suggests that the batter was tagged before reaching second. The issue of fact now seemingly resolved, the batter points out that second base had been kicked out of place in the play preceding the disputed one. Second base "wasn't where it was supposed to be." The resulting delay was what caused the batter to reach second after the tag. The issue is now one of quality—was the batter safe *in the spirit* of what it means to be "safe"? The players on both sides now agree that second base had been moved into a position that gave an advantage to the fielder and a disadvantage to the batter, and so they declare her "safe." The issue of quality resolved, the fielder now points out that the bat and the ball are his, and that *he* says the batter was out. The fielder has attempted to make the issue one of jurisdiction: group consensus should not decide safes and outs; ownership of the equipment should. As he stalks off the field, the batter declares that Mom gave the bat and ball to *both* of them, and she heads home to let their parent decide the argument. She has matched his jurisdiction argument with two of her own: "I own it, too, and we'll let Mom decide."

Using the Model

The classical stasis system is most readily adaptable to forensic, or judicial, issues: What is the law (definitional)? What are the facts of the case (conjectural)? How do the facts meet the definition of or the spirit of the law (qualitative)? Who adjudicates the case (jurisdiction)? It can, however, be used to identify the relevant issues for the kinds of sociopolitical arguments typical of nonpolicy debate.

Consider, for example, the proposition, "Resolved: that U.S. membership in the United Nations is beneficial." Some issues are definitional: What constitutes "membership in the United Nations"? Some issues are factual: What does the United Nations do? What successes has it had? What failures? Some issues are qualitative: Have the successes been beneficial for the United States? Are all failures necessarily detrimental to the United States? Have U.N. policies overall benefited the United States? Are there conditions under which we should consider "indirect" rather than "direct" benefits? Although many other issues could be identified, they can all fit within one of the broad categories of conjecture, definition, and quality. For academic debate, of course, the issue of jurisdiction is irrelevant. The judge in the round has been stipulated as the adjudicator, so appeals to other jurisdictions are not usually germane. In other deliberative settings, the question of "who decides" is extremely relevant.

Several theorists have argued that the classical stasis system is an appropriate method for analyzing nonpolicy questions. Raymond Nadeau, for example, has argued that Hermogenes, a second-century Greek scholar, articulated six "issues" on which deliberative speakers can focus their arguments for or against change: the *lawful* (Is it legal?), the *just* (Does it promote justice?), the *expedient* (Is it cost beneficial?), the *possible* (Can it be done?), the *honorable* (Is it moral and ethical?), and the *anticipated effect* (What will be the likely result of the change?).

However, while Hermogenes's list of issues has been termed a "stasis system," it is instructive to note the difference between this system and the more traditional system of Hermagoras and Cicero. Whereas Hermogenes provides a systematic list of issues by which to discover the relevant topoi, the issues do not all work at different levels. Some of the issues are located on different planes; for example, we must resolve "possibility" before discussing "anticipated effect." "Legality," like jurisdiction, may take precedence because it says whether we are allowed to decide the debate. Other issues, however, do not seem incompatible. You might argue that a certain change is honorable while I argue that it is not expedient. Both issues address our evaluation of the act—and it is now up to us to decide which of the two qualities is more important to us. Should we be honorable or should we be practical?

Like Hermogenes's list of issues, any stock issues approach occupies theoretical ground similar to that of stasis theory. Cole (1987) argues that stasis theory and recently proposed analytical models, such as the criteria-application model, typically have two elements in common. First, both the classical and contemporary systems provide multilevel modality of analysis and synthesis; that is, both systems begin with universal categories that discover the relevant areas of clash and then move to a second level that defines the specific issues. Second, Cole argues that both types of systems propose sequential steps of analysis: conjecture, definition, and quality. Advocates first discover that a phenomenon occurs, then they define that phenomenon, and finally they evaluate the qualities of the phenomenon. Cole's analysis of the stasis system is significant in that it illustrates the close bond between stasis theory and contemporary analytical models of debate.

Although some scholars find such lists of possible issues useful, others argue against employing them. Robert P. Newman, for example, is particularly adamant in insisting that the advocate should search for relevant issues within the particular argument situation. The stock issues doctrine, he claims, is "a mechanical model for analysis" (171). Such mechanical models may be useful for directing scientific inquiry (hypothesis—experiment—theory), but deliberative (policy and nonpolicy) argument is too complex for these models. Because each investigation will be unique to the topic or the proposition. Newman argues, no formal, mechanical model "can encompass the organic growth of an argument" (180).

Of course, Newman's attack is primarily on the modern practice of using "stock issues." He does not, for example, address the utility of conceptualizing arguments as occurring on planes or levels, or of identifying the stock issues that operate within a specific analytical model. His criticism is really about how we discover the relevant issues, and most scholars would agree with Newman that our method of discovery should not be too rigidly defined. However, it is still useful to understand the principle of stasis: that there are different kinds of arguments available to us as advocates, and that the kinds of arguments we select may indeed pass our opponents' arguments like "ships in the night." One way to ensure that we utilize these principles in our debating is to understand the different analytical models that are commonly used and to learn the stock issues contained within each model.

Analytical Models for Academic Debate: An Overview

The term **analytical model** denotes an organized way or procedure for analyzing, reasoning, and debating about debate propositions. Analytical models prescribe the critical questions—stock issues—of the proposition. Developing clear analytical models is important to both the theory and practice of debate. Analytical models help define the nature of debate by prescribing the critical issues that must be addressed in the debate. Furthermore, by identifying those critical issues, analytical models provide a framework debaters can use to guide their research, develop claims, prepare refutation, and organize their cases. Analytical models also provide a foundation for the development of theories about debate as they clarify the relationship between and among the critical constructs of the process.

As important as they are to virtually every aspect of the debate process, analytical models must be used carefully. Models have an alluring appeal because they offer seemingly clear-cut methods for analyzing a debate proposition; they should not, however, be treated as a prescriptive formula. Successful advocacy is born out of an understanding of the complexities of the substantive dimensions of a controversy as much as it is out of an understanding of the formal requirements of the process in which that advocacy occurs. Models help clarify the latter, but they cannot be used as a substitute for the intensive research and critical thought necessary to develop the former. Also, no model is capable of providing a completely thorough and accurate representation of the process in every conceivable situation. Debate is a highly interactive and dynamic process; by their very nature, models and paradigms are static and incapable of capturing all the subtle nuances of an intense interaction between skillful advocates. Models and paradigms do help us understand how the debate process might be viewed, but they cannot completely and accurately characterize how that process evolves in every debate. Moreover, models and paradigms cannot predict exactly how individuals will process, interpret, and respond to the highly subjective data used to resolve disputes about complex and controversial issues.

Debaters should also understand that not all models and paradigms are equally comprehensive. Because policy propositions have been used so extensively in academic debate, the analytical models used for that type of proposition are well developed. Conversely, nonpolicy propositions have achieved widespread use much more recently, and the analytical models used for that type of proposition are less well developed and understood. It is clear, however, that argumentation and debate theorists are focusing extensive effort on developing analytical models for nonpolicy debate.[2] Moreover, some paradigms such as the narrative paradigm have only recently begun to be applied to either type of proposition.

In the remainder of this chapter, we discuss five analytical models for debate. Each of these approaches is designed to illuminate the stock issues that must be sustained for successful advocacy. The first two models, the **traditional needs model** and **the comparative advantage model,** are most applicable to policy propositions. They have been widely used in academic debate and theorists have fully developed the tenets of each. The next two models, the **criteria-application model** and the **issue agenda model,** were specifically developed for nonpolicy propositions. They offer coherent ways to understand nonpolicy propositions but have not been as fully developed as their policy counterparts. The final model we discuss, the **narrative paradigm,** was developed as a contemporary paradigm for human communication rather than for academic debate specifically. Debate theorists, however, have begun to use the narrative paradigm as the exemplar metaphor for academic debate. The narrative paradigm can be used for either policy or nonpolicy propositions and, we believe, offers a globalized way of understanding argumentation and debate.

Analytical Models for Policy Propositions: The Traditional Needs Model

Among all analytical models for debate, the traditional needs model has been used most extensively. This model is composed of a series of questions presumed to be universally applicable to policy considerations. The model prescribes four such questions and, thus, identifies four stock issues of a policy proposition. The first two stock issues in the model deal with an assessment of the problem; the last two issues deal with an assessment of the proposed action. According to the logic of the model, one must first assess the problem to determine whether taking *any* action is justified and, assuming that the problem is such that some action appears to be warranted, one would then determine the suitability of the specific action being proposed.

The Stock Issue of Ill

The first stock issue, or critical question, in the traditional needs model is the question of **ill**. This stock issue focuses on assessment of the seriousness of the problem to determine whether it is serious enough to justify action. According to the logic of the model, there is little reason or need to consider taking any action unless you can demonstrate that a problem of sufficient seriousness exists. A reasonable decision maker, the model assumes, would probably not consider banning unions in this country unless the advocate of that action could demonstrate some compelling need to do so. Nor would one likely consider prohibiting trade between the United States and a foreign country unless there was some critical reason for the ban. In contemplating any policy action, the problem is presumed to be a motivator and must be of sufficient magnitude to provide the impetus necessary for the action to be taken.

In academic debate, the ill issue is usually termed **significance**. Debaters can establish significance in three ways. First, they can address the *quantitative dimension* of the problem. The quantitative dimension usually refers to the scope of the problem, such as the number of people affected, or the frequency with which the problem occurs. You might argue that air pollution is a significant problem because millions of people are exposed to air-borne pollutants or that air pollution is a serious problem because 65 percent of emissions are potentially toxic to humans.

Second, debaters can address the *qualitative dimension* of a problem to establish significance. The qualitative dimension typically focuses on the consequences of the problem. One way to assess consequences is to demonstrate the level of harm produced by the problem. For example, you could argue that erosion of freedom of expression is a significant problem because that right is a critical principle in our society. In so doing, you focus the assessment of significance on the intrinsic value of the principle rather than on the number of instances in which some erosion of the principle occurs. Presumably, the argument goes, *any* erosion of the principle constitutes a significant problem because that principle is a key component of our vision of a free and democratic society. Or, returning to the previous example about air pollution, you might argue that air pollution is a serious problem because it ultimately deteriorates the quality of life.

The third way to establish significance is to use a *combination approach.* In using this approach, debaters focus on both the quantitative and qualitative dimensions of a problem. They attempt to demonstrate that the problem is serious in both scope and level of harm. For example, you might argue that voter apathy is a significant problem because the number of people who give up the right to vote is widespread (quantitative) and because the right to vote is the cornerstone of the democratic process (qualitative). Or you might argue that discrimination based on gender is a serious problem in the workplace because a substantial number of people are affected (quantitative) and because discrimination devalues our basic conception of equality (qualitative).

In most debates, debaters will not be able to establish significance simply by addressing the qualitative or the quantitative dimension. Skillful opponents are likely to demand that you demonstrate *both* aspects of the harm. Because the combination approach is the most complete method of establishing the significance of a problem, debaters who use this approach will usually be able to create the most compelling need for taking action.

The Stock Issue of Blame

The second stock issue or critical question in the model is the question of **blame.** This issue focuses on assessment of the relationship between the problem and the *status quo*. The term *status quo* is important in debate and every debater should understand what it means. The status quo is the existing system —the policies, laws, priorities, regulations, and decision makers who are in place.

In assessing the issue of blame, debaters attempt to determine the degree to which the problem *inheres*—is caused by or exacerbated by—the status quo. In addition, debaters will seek to determine whether mechanisms within the status quo can correct the problem or reduce its significance to a tolerable level. In assessing this relationship, debaters will determine whether the problem is *self-correcting* or *self-perpetuating*. A self-correcting problem is one that is likely to be remedied with no change in existing policies whereas a self-perpetuating problem is one that is caused or exacerbated by existing policies and, therefore, is likely to continue as long as the status quo remains unchanged.

According to the logic of the model, the justification for taking corrective action is less compelling for self-correcting problems than it is for self-perpetuating ones. For example, there would be little reason to implement a program of compulsory wage, price, and interest rate controls to correct seasonal fluctuations in inflation because those fluctuations are presumably self-correcting; predictable changes in consumer purchasing will probably correct the problem. However, there may be sufficient justification to undertake military action to alleviate global terrorism (the problem) if a foreign country such as Iraq can be shown to be consciously instigating terrorism as part of its foreign policy. Presumably, because Iraq's motivation to promote terrorism will be ongoing, there is a need to alter the status quo. The issue of blame, then, when combined with the issue of ill, completes assessment of the problem: those two issues require that the problem be shown to be serious and likely to continue if no action is taken.

In academic debate, the issue of blame is typically referred to as **inherency**. To demonstrate inherency, debaters must be able to identify the causes of the problem; they must have a clear understanding of the causes of a problem to be able to assess whether the problem is self-correcting or self-perpetuating. Ultimately, debaters must be able to demonstrate that as long as the status quo remains unchanged, the problem will continue to exist (the problem is self-perpetuating).

Debaters can use three approaches to demonstrate that the problem is inherent. First, they can establish *structural inherency*. Structural inherency focuses on the operating structures (laws, procedures, policies, and so on) of the status quo as the causes of the problem. You can presume when arguing structural inherency that one or more of the operating mechanisms of the status quo either causes the problem to exist in the first place or makes fixing the problem impossible without a change in the status quo. For example, you could argue that because unions operate on the basis of a seniority system, workers at the bottom of the seniority ladder who also celebrate their Sabbath day on Saturday will always be forced to choose between expressing their religious beliefs and keeping their jobs. The problem—compromising freedom of religion—is structurally inherent because it results from (is caused by) a fixed component of union operating procedure (the seniority system). Similarly, you could argue that the ineffectiveness of the current welfare system (the problem) is structurally inherent because those who receive assistance are not required to enroll in any sort of work-training program to ensure that they become self-supporting. In this case, the problem is structurally inherent because it results from the incompleteness of the status quo; the body of existing mechanisms provides no remedy for the problem.

Second, debaters can establish *attitudinal inherency*. Whereas structural inherency derives from the policies, procedures, and regulations of the status quo, attitudinal inherency is found in the attitudes and predispositions of the decision makers who operate the status quo. Attitudinal inherency exists when those who have power in the status quo, either through their motives or their incompetence, cause the problem to exist or prevent the problem from being remedied. For example, you could argue that the problem of discrimination on the basis of race or sex is attitudinally inherent by demonstrating that corporate executives consciously attempt to maintain a "good old white boy network" among their top management. Similarly, you might argue that fraud in the Medicare system is attitudinally inherent by demonstrating that doctors prescribe unnecessary tests and submit duplicative bills because they believe they will not be caught.

In many cases, establishing attitudinal inherency is much more difficult than establishing structural inherency. Establishing attitudinal inherency presupposes that you have properly identified the attitudes and predispositions of decision makers. Accurately assessing what others think and believe, however, is always a problematic endeavor. Establishing structural inherency is certainly not a completely objective task; it is easier to demonstrate the causal force of those things we can objectively observe—policies, regulations, stated procedures—than those things we must subjectively infer—the beliefs, attitudes, and motives of others.

Third, debaters can establish inherency through a *combination approach*. When using this approach, debaters attribute the causes of the problem both to the mechanisms within the existing system and the predispositions of the decision makers to perpetuate or fail to remedy the problem. Such an approach is a realistic way to assess inherency because it acknowledges that the structures of the existing system are interpreted, applied, and enforced by the decision makers.

In our previous example, we identified the predispositions of the corporate decision makers as the attitudinal cause of the problem of gender and racial discrimination. It would probably be more accurate to say, however, that those deleterious attitudes are able to cause discriminatory practices because the existing system does not have adequate safeguards to ensure that workers are treated equally. Thus, the attitudes give rise to the problem, but the inadequate structures allow the problem to exist and flourish. As is the case with using the combination approach to establish the significance of the problem, using the combination approach to establish inherency typically offers the most complete assessment of the causal factors associated with the problem and creates the most compelling need for change.

The Stock Issue of Cure

The third stock issue, the **cure** issue, begins assessment of the specific change being proposed. This issue focuses on the ability of the proposed plan to remedy the problem. According to the logic of the model, it makes little sense to take an action—no matter how serious the problem—unless that action can be shown to remedy the problem. For example, voter apathy may be a serious problem, but implementing a proposal to increase the number of televised debates among presidential candidates (solution) would make sense only if doing so would increase interest among voters and, in turn, increase the number of people who vote. Similarly, if we could demonstrate that outbreaks of a particular childhood disease had reached serious levels, mandating vaccinations against that disease as a prerequisite for attendance in public and private schools would make sense because that action is presumably a direct remedy for the problem.

In academic debate, this issue is usually referred to as **solvency**. After a compelling need to change the status quo has been established, it is reasonable to expect the proponent of change to be able to demonstrate that the proposed change will remedy the problem. To demonstrate solvency, debaters should be able to show that the proposed change meaningfully alters the causes of the problem. Debaters can approach that task in two ways.

First, they can demonstrate that the proposed change is *countercausal*. A countercausal change is one that directly eliminates the causes of the problem. If an advocate showed convincingly that ineffectiveness is structurally inherent in the current welfare system because that system does not provide recipients with long-term job training, a plan mandating such training would be countercausal as it directly corrects the presumed cause of the problem. Or we could propose a countercausal change by mandating that unions be precluded from using the seniority system (presumed cause of the problem) to determine who will work on weekends and holidays.

Second, debaters can demonstrate that the proposed change is *causal circumventing*. A causal-circumventing change is one that does not eliminate the cause of the problem from the status quo, but it does diminish the capability of that factor to continue to function as a cause of the problem. Recall the example of the problem of discrimination in the work place. The cause of that problem is the predisposition of corporate decision makers to give preference systematically to white over nonwhite and male over female workers. It would be difficult to impose a countercausal measure that would affect that problem because we cannot readily mandate a change in decision makers' cognitive and affective predispositions. However, it would be possible to implement a causal-circumventing measure that diminished the capability of corporate decision makers to further engage in actions based on those predispositions. For example, we could mandate that nonwhites and females be proportionately represented at management levels. Imposing such a change does not directly eliminate the presumed cause of the problem as it does not directly change the predisposition; it does, however, limit the degree to which that presumed cause can result in further acts of discrimination.

The Stock Issue of Cost

The fourth stock issue, the **cost** issue, completes the assessment of the proposed action. This issue focuses on the costs and outcomes of taking the recommended action. According to the logic of the model, we must determine the costs of a proposed action before deciding whether to take that action. The greater the costs associated with implementing a proposed change, the less likely the change is to be implemented. For example, although lack of adequate health care is generally acknowledged to be a serious problem in this country, and providing government-subsidized care for all citizens would be a direct remedy to that problem, debate about implementing such a plan invariably focuses on the financial costs of the plan. Similarly, when deciding whether to undertake a massive unilateral military response in Bosnia, our military and political leaders would consider the costs associated with such an action as an integral part of the decision-making equation.

In academic debate, this issue is usually referred to as **disadvantages.** Disadvantages, or costs, can be derived from two primary types of measures. First, disadvantages can be derived from *material costs* associated with implementing the action. Material costs typically include such items as the money, personnel, and time required to put the proposed change in place. For example, if an advocate proposed to implement a federally subsidized medical care system to provide comprehensive care to all citizens, the material costs necessary to take that action would constitute a disadvantage: the enormous amount of funding required to provide fully subsidized care to all citizens, the argument would go, would create a financial nightmare for the country.

Disadvantages can also be derived from the *effects* produced by making the change. Effects describe the outcomes that result from implementing the proposed action. Many types of effects can result from taking an action (such as undermining basic rights; or placing individuals, groups, or nations in immediate harm), but most can be categorized either as *direct* or *indirect* effects of implementing the plan. Direct effects are outcomes that flow directly from implementing the plan—the proposed action is the sole or major causal factor. You might argue that implementing a rating system on music might have the direct effect of—it might directly cause—erosion of basic First Amendment rights of free expression. You also might argue that undertaking an immediate, unilateral invasion in the Bosnia crisis would intensify—directly cause—human rights atrocities.

Effects can also be indirect. Indirect effects are outcomes that do not result directly from implementing the proposed change but from a sequence of events triggered by the change. You could argue that banning the use of seniority systems by unions would start a series of events that would lead unions to lose their fundamental power, which would ultimately jeopardize the ability of the unions to ensure safe conditions for workers.

In the traditional needs model, solvency and disadvantages work in tandem to complete assessment of the proposed change. Both of these issues are critical to debates about policy propositions and, consequently, occupy much of the time and effort expended by debaters. In Chapter 14, we address these issues in more detail and elaborate fully on how debaters construct arguments about them.

The traditional needs model provides a reasonably clear and straightforward approach for determining the stock issues of a policy proposition. However, not all theorists agree that the model is the only way to assess the stock issues of policy propositions. In the next section, we discuss a popular alternative to the traditional needs model: the comparative advantage model.

Analytical Models for Policy Propositions: The Comparative Advantage Model

The comparative advantage model was developed largely in response to perceived limitations in the traditional needs model. In one such limitation, although the stock issues that must be addressed in a policy proposition are specified in the traditional needs model, a literal interpretation of those issues may not accurately reflect how decisions about policy issues are or should be made. For example, one perplexing question debaters confront when addressing solvency or the cure issue is determining how much of the problem the proposed change must remedy. A literal interpretation of the cure issue in the traditional needs model implies that if the proposed change does not solve the problem—*all* the problem—it should not be implemented. However, because policy debate propositions deal with complex sociopolitical issues, it may be unreasonable to expect that any proposed change could meet such a rigorous standard. Real-world decision makers do not reject proposals simply because they are not perfect, and there appears to be little justification to do so in debate about policy propositions. To align academic debate more closely with real-world decision making, theorists developed the comparative advantage model.

The comparative advantage model typically uses the goals and objectives of the status quo and argues that implementing the proposed change will provide some advantage related to attainment of those goals and objectives. For example, if you could demonstrate that banning cameras in the courtroom would enhance the judicial process in some measurable way, that *comparative advantage* could theoretically be used to justify changing the status quo. The justification for change in the traditional needs model resides in the eradication of some problem whereas the justification for change in the comparative advantage model is based on some resulting comparative advantage.

A Significant Advantage: The Ill Issue Revisited

The comparative advantage model addresses the same basic stock issues addressed by the traditional needs model. The primary difference between the comparative advantage model and the traditional needs model is in the way those stock issues are applied. The ill issue is essential to the comparative advantage model; however, the focus of the issue is on the significance of the *advantage* rather than the significance of the *problem*. Thus, rather than demonstrating that a significant problem exists so as to justify implementing a change, as is the case in the traditional needs model, debaters in the comparative advantage model are required to demonstrate that the advantage derived from making a change is significant. In the traditional needs model, a debater who sought to justify banning cameras in the courtroom (proposed action) would first demonstrate that the defendant's right to a fair trial is threatened in the status quo (problem); in the comparative advantage model, a debater would justify banning cameras in the courtroom (proposed action) by demonstrating that a significant beneficial effect, such as enhancing protection of the defendant's right to a fair trial (advantage), would result from taking that action.

A Unique Advantage: The Issue of Blame Revisited

The issue of blame is incorporated in the comparative advantage model in a different form from that in the traditional needs model. In the traditional needs model, debaters must demonstrate that the problem is inherent in order to justify implementing some corrective action. Thus, debaters must demonstrate that the problem will continue to exist if no action is taken. In the comparative advantage model, debaters are not required to demonstrate that the problem is inherent; rather, they are required to demonstrate that the advantage is *unique* —that the advantage can be produced only by implementing the plan.

In the traditional needs model, if the problem could be solved without changing the status quo, that problem would not be inherent; in the comparative advantage model, if the advantage could be achieved through some mechanism other than the proposed action, the advantage would not be unique. To demonstrate inherency in the traditional needs model, a debater would be required to demonstrate that voter apathy (problem) is caused by skepticism in the two-party system and that skepticism will continue to exist as long as the status quo (two-party system) remains intact. In the comparative advantage model, a debater would demonstrate uniqueness by proving that voter apathy (advantage) can be decreased only by institutionalizing third parties (proposed action). In either case—demonstrating inherency or uniqueness—debaters must still assess the cause-effect relationships within the topic area of the policy proposition.

An Achieved Advantage: The Cure Issue Revisited

The issue of cure is also used in the comparative advantage model in a different form from that of the traditional needs model. To demonstrate solvency in the traditional needs model, a debater must be able to prove that implementing the proposed action would eradicate the problem. In the comparative advantage model, a debater must demonstrate that the advantage is achieved when the proposed action is taken. For example, in the traditional needs model, a debater would be required to demonstrate that mandating auto manufacturers to install alcohol-interlock systems on all new cars (proposed action) would in fact *eliminate* deaths and accidents caused by driving and drinking (problem); in the comparative advantage model, a debater would be required to demonstrate that the number of persons injured or killed in wrecks caused by drivers drinking would be *reduced* (advantage) if auto manufacturers were mandated to install alcohol-interlock systems on all new cars (proposed action). In either case— demonstrating solvency for the problem or solvency for the advantage—a debater must be able to prove that taking the proposed action satisfies the condition (problem or advantage) used to justify that action.

Disadvantages Resulting from Change: The Cost Issue Revisited

The cost issue of the traditional needs model is also integral to the comparative advantage model. In the comparative advantage model, disadvantages are assessed in virtually the same way they are in the traditional needs model: they are determined by assessing the material costs and the direct and indirect effects associated with implementing the proposed change. Once those costs or disadvantages are determined, they are compared with or weighed against the advantages achieved by implementing the proposed action. To justify implementing the proposed action, the advantages achieved must be greater than the disadvantages incurred. A debater might claim that by prohibiting U.S. unilateral military intervention in foreign countries (proposed action), fewer U.S. military personnel would be killed (advantage). At the same time, the opposing advocate might suggest that by taking that action the United States will lose the ability to protect its strategic interests around the world and that such a loss will be deleterious to our national interest—a *disadvantage*. In such a situation, to show that there is a *comparative advantage* attained by implementing the proposed action, the advocate of change would be obligated to demonstrate that the good resulting from decreasing the loss of life of U.S. military personnel would be greater than the harm that would result from loss of the ability to protect strategic U.S. interests around the world.

Assessing and Comparing Advantages and Disadvantages

Comparison is clearly a critical element of the comparative advantage model. According to the analytical framework of the model, advocates are required to enumerate the advantages and disadvantages and then to compare them to each other to demonstrate which—the advantages or the disadvantages—offers the most compelling justification for the respective positions they are used to support. Debaters cannot simply list the respective advantages and disadvantages of implementing the proposed plan of action; they have to show that the advantages are more compelling than the disadvantages, or vice versa, to sustain their argument.

Advantages and disadvantages are outcomes derived from implementing or not implementing a proposed plan of action. Comparing the outcomes is a two-stage process. First, debaters must establish a value assessment for each outcome. To do this, they must demonstrate the *probability* that the outcome will materialize and the *magnitude* of the outcome once it does materialize. Debaters assess probability by explaining the likelihood that the stated outcome (advantage or disadvantage) will happen. For example, if they claim that establishing mandatory minimum sentences for specific crimes would result in a deterrent effect for those crimes, they must establish the likelihood or degree of certainty that the deterrent effect would result.

Debaters assess magnitude by explaining the significance of the outcome if it does materialize. To demonstrate magnitude in the previous example, a debater would establish the significance of the deterrent effect—how much crime will be reduced—if the deterrent effect actually materializes. Thus, the magnitude of an outcome hinges on this fundamental question: Assuming the outcome happens, what is it worth? Debaters would demonstrate the probability and magnitude for disadvantages in exactly the same way.

Second, debaters would compare the value assessments of the outcomes. They would compare the assessments (probability plus magnitude) for the advantages and the disadvantages to determine which—the advantage or the disadvantage—offers the most compelling justification. Assume the following situation: debater A claims that as a result of implementing her plan, drug-related street crime will decrease (advantage); her opponent argues that if the plan were implemented, the right of citizens to be protected against unwarranted searches and seizures would be compromised (disadvantage). In such a situation, both debaters would have to establish the value assessment of their outcome: they would establish the probability and magnitude of the outcome. Once the value assessment of each outcome is established, those indexes can be compared to determine whether the value of the advantage (probability plus magnitude) is greater than, equal to, or less than the value of the disadvantage (probability plus magnitude). Theoretically, if the value of the advantages is greater than the value of the disadvantages, the plan should be implemented. However, if the value of the advantages is less than the value of the disadvantages, the plan should not be implemented. These decision rules are illustrated in the following equations, in which V = value assessment (probability and magnitude), a = advantages, and d = disadvantages.

If Va is > Vd, proposal should be implemented

If Va is < Vd, proposal should not be implemented

Although these equations appear to offer clear decision rules for deciding the comparative advantages of a proposal, determining probability and magnitude are subjective assessments. Each measure of the value assessment in its own right is likely to be a highly complex and debatable issue. Establishing the probability of an outcome, for example, requires an analysis of causal relationships that may be multifaceted, complex, or even undetectable. Similarly, establishing the magnitude of an outcome is often speculative and dependent on highly debatable assumptions and standards.

It is no easier to compare outcomes once value assessments based on probability and magnitude have been calculated. In fact, such comparisons can prove to be quite interesting. Some outcomes might have extremely high magnitude dimensions (such as nuclear war) but relatively low probabilities; others have much less severe magnitude dimensions (such as endangering the spotted owl) but relatively high probability dimensions. How does one compare outcomes of one sort to outcomes of the other sort? Does an outcome with high probability and lower magnitude outweigh an outcome with lower probability but higher magnitude? We raise these questions to illustrate a point we made at the beginning of this chapter. Analytical models provide a *framework* debaters can use to determine what the issues of the proposition are and how they should formulate their positions. Analytical models do not provide a *formula* for resolving the complex controversies about which we debate, nor are they a substitute for responsible judgment and skillful advocacy. Regardless of the degree to which any analytical model is developed, debaters must interpret and *debate* about the substantive issues within the proposition.

The comparative advantage model was clearly an innovation in debate. However, not all theorists and practitioners regarded the model as legitimate when it was first introduced. Some critics argued that it actually diminished the responsibility and burdens of the advocates of change, that it was easier for debaters to demonstrate that some comparative advantage would be derived from a change than it was to fulfill the requirements associated with the stock issues of the traditional needs model. These concerns have proven unwarranted largely because the stock issues of the comparative advantage model and the traditional needs model are so similar. Over the past twenty years, the comparative advantage model has become widely used and accepted as a legitimate analytical model for policy propositions.

Analytical Models for Nonpolicy Propositions: The Criteria-Application Model

The first analytical model developed specifically for nonpolicy debate was the criteria-application model. As early as the 1960s, theorists (Mills; Windes and Hastings) established the basic analytical framework of the model, and prominent contemporary theorists (Matlon; Zarefsky) have refined the model and demonstrated its applicability for nonpolicy debate. Much of the theory that has been developed for nonpolicy debate thus far has either assumed or explicitly advocated use of the criteria-application model.

Stock Issues of the Model

This analytical model focuses on two critical questions advocates must answer to make appropriate nonpolicy judgments: (1) How does one make the type of judgment prescribed in the particular case? (2) Using that method, do the available data demonstrate that such a judgment about the object of focus is warranted? Consider that you are about to engage a friend in an informal debate about the comparative merits of two movies. You believe that *Forrest Gump* is the best movie released in 1994, but your friend believes that *Clear and Present Danger,* which was also released in 1994, may be the best movie ever. Obviously, you and your friend hold incompatible positions—*Forrest Gump* cannot be the best movie released in 1994 if *Clear and Present Danger* is the best movie ever, and debate would be an appropriate method to resolve the controversy.

The informal proposition you and your friend are contesting might be stated as follows: "Resolved: that *Forrest Gump* is the best movie released during 1994." Before you begin the debate, you attempt to identify the critical questions that must be answered for that proposition to be accepted or rejected, and you conclude that there are two such questions in the proposition: (1) How (by what method) does one determine which of two movies is "best?" (2) Does *Forrest Gump* have more of the qualities prescribed in that method than does *Clear and Present Danger?* By identifying those critical questions, you have determined the "stock issues" of the proposition you are about to debate and have established the questions you must answer to prevail in the debate. Formally stated nonpolicy debate propositions also have such critical questions or stock issues, and those issues have come to be termed the **definitive** and **designative** stock issues of nonpolicy debate (Matlon). Theorists generally regard the definitive and designative issues to be applicable to each of the types of nonpolicy propositions we discussed in Chapter 7 (Zarefsky).

The criteria-application model is an analytical model in the most basic sense: it prescribes the stock issues for nonpolicy propositions but does not specify what assumptions should be made about nonpolicy debate or nonpolicy judgment. For example, it does not prescribe how advocates should determine an appropriate method for making nonpolicy judgments; it only defines the general importance of constructing *some* method. Also, the criteria-application model does not attempt to describe the process of nonpolicy debate metaphorically as would a paradigm.

The criteria-application model is a relatively straightforward analytical model. The stock issues of the model are easy to understand and relatively easy to apply. Moreover, the stock issues have an intuitive appeal because they appear to be reasonable and obvious questions advocates would be expected to address in virtually any nonpolicy debate situation. As a result, the criteria-application model has become the most prevalent analytical model used by practitioners in nonpolicy debates.[3]

Using the Model

The definitive issue focuses on the criteria for the nonpolicy judgment. As you recall from Chapter 7, every nonpolicy proposition has a judgmental term: *desirable, beneficial, obsolete, overemphasized,* or something similar. The definitive issue requires the advocates to specify *how* they intend to make that judgment. For example, in the proposition, "Resolved: that throughout the United States, more severe punishment for individuals convicted of violent crime would be desirable," the definitive issue focuses on how one determines what is or is not *desirable* (judgmental term) in a particular case. We illustrated the definitive issue in less formal argument in our example at the beginning of this section. In the debate about *Forrest Gump* versus *Clear and Present Danger*, the definitive issue focused on how, or by what method, one determines a particular movie to be "better" than another movie. We discuss this stock issue more extensively in Chapters 12 and 14.

The designative issue always emerges after the definitive issue. In the designative issue, the advocate is required to demonstrate how the criteria established in the definitive issue are satisfied with respect to the particular object of focus. Assume that in the proposition, "Resolved: that membership in the United Nations is no longer beneficial for the United States," the affirmative team satisfies the definitive issue by prescribing two conditions that must be met to demonstrate something is no longer *beneficial* (judgmental term): (1) membership does not enhance the economic power of a country, and (2) membership does not enhance national security. The affirmative side would then be required to fulfill the designative issue by demonstrating that both those conditions exist with respect to the United States' membership in the United Nations: they must show that membership in the United Nations does not enhance the economic power or the national security of the United States. As you can infer from this example, the definitive issue conceptually defines the designative issue because it identifies what an advocate must demonstrate in the designative issue.

Analytical Models for Nonpolicy Propositions: The Issue Agenda Model

The issue agenda model, like the criteria-application model, was also developed specifically for nonpolicy debate. It was originally conceived by Michael Bartanen and later refined by Bartanen and his colleague David Frank. Bartanen and Frank base the issue agenda model on the concept of agenda building used in political science and public deliberations. They argue that issues emerge on public agendas when those who set the agenda determine that the issue is sufficiently important to warrant consideration, deliberation, and action. Issues that are not judged sufficiently important—have no clear and compelling exigence —have more difficulty gaining agenda status and thus are less likely to be seriously considered, debated, and acted on.

Stock Issues of the Model

Bartanen and Frank use the concept of agenda setting to formulate the key stock issue of their model: determination of the significance of the exigence. This stock issue requires that debaters determine *why* it is important to discuss the issue embodied in the nonpolicy proposition and that they be prepared to explain and justify the significance of the issue. For example, in the proposition, "Resolved: that imposing more severe penalties on persons convicted of violent crimes throughout the United States would be desirable," debaters might choose to focus their case on a particular type of violent crime such as rape, assault of police officers, or crimes committed with handguns. According to the issue agenda model, the debater would be required to demonstrate the importance of discussing any of those particular foci by demonstrating the significance of the problem—the significance of rape, the significance of assaults on police officers, or the significance of crimes committed with handguns. The model does not prescribe *how* the debater should demonstrate significance of the issue, but it does require some justification of its general importance before the issue—rape, assaults on police officers, crimes committed with handguns— is granted agenda status and discussed in the debate.

This stock issue is virtually identical to the ill issue in the traditional needs model for policy debate, discussed earlier in this chapter. You will probably find it useful to review the discussion in that section of the three ways a debater can establish the significance of a problem.

Although the concept of agenda setting is clearly the heart of the issue agenda model, determining the significance of the exigence is not the only stock issue the model prescribes. Bartanen and Frank complete their model with three additional stock issues: (1) **definition of key terms**, (2) **identification of audience-centered criteria**, and (3) **comparison of germane values with potential countervalues**. Definition of key terms has always been assumed to have primary importance in argumentation and debate. If debate is to be a truly meaningful exercise in reason giving and reason testing, there must be a shared understanding of the meaning of the terms being discussed. Debaters, as advocates, must assume the responsibility for creating that shared meaning by defining their terms precisely and reasonably. The issue agenda model does not prescribe guidelines for defining key terms, but it clearly institutionalizes the importance of that task by including it as a stock issue of nonpolicy debate.

The next stock issue, identification of audience-centered criteria, is derived from the criteria-application model. Bartanen and Frank recognize the central role criteria play in nonpolicy judgment, and they formalize the demand for criteria as a requirement of nonpolicy debate. At the same time they borrow this stock issue from the criteria-application model, Bartanen and Frank also refine it. They note that unlike those in the criteria-application model, the criteria in the issue agenda model must be *audience centered,* or formulated in ways the audience can both understand and accept. Thus, while the criteria-application model requires debaters to formulate *some* criteria, Bartanen and Frank suggest that debaters should formulate those criteria their audience would likely agree to be most suitable.

The final stock issue, comparison of germane values with potential countervalues, adds a dimension to nonpolicy judgment not incorporated in the criteria-application model. Nonpolicy debaters have routinely used strategies based on value comparison to both construct and refute cases. One popular approach for negative debaters has been to present "value objections," or countervalues to the affirmative. In the issue agenda model, however, the notion of value comparison takes on a broader meaning. Debaters are expected not only to identify the values to which they subscribe, but they are ultimately required to prioritize their values relative to any other values their opponents advocate. In our previous example, the affirmative side might choose to defend capital punishment as a desirable punishment for those convicted of rape. The debaters could base their case on the core value of individual privacy by arguing that rape is a violation of individual privacy and that the threat of capital punishment would deter potential rapists, thereby helping to protect the right to privacy. In such a situation, the affirmative team would be required to prioritize their core value, individual privacy, relative to any other value the negative could demonstrate as potentially being abridged by imposing capital punishment on those convicted of rape.

Value Hierarchies and Nonpolicy Judgments

At this point, it is important to discuss the major theoretical and practical implications of using value hierarchies to make nonpolicy judgments. When we compare values with potential countervalues, we have established a **value hierarchy**. Joseph Tuman ("Getting to First Base,"; "Natural Value Hierarchies") has argued that value hierarchies are central to any debate about a proposition of value. In fact, Tuman classifies the establishment of a value hierarchy as a prima facie requirement for nonpolicy debate. Tuman's position assumes that making the judgment prescribed in a proposition of value always involves consideration of value hierarchies. That assumption is consistent with our view of the nature of propositions of value. In Chapter 7, we argued that value conflict is embedded within each proposition of value, whether the proposition requires value assignation to the object of focus ("Resolved: that John Kennedy was a good president") or explicitly notes a value comparison the advocate must make ("Resolved: that privacy is more important than national security"). Thus, every proposition of value either implicitly or explicitly requires some consideration of a value hierarchy.

Although value hierarchies do seem to play a pivotal role in debates about propositions of value, they must be used appropriately if used to render meaningful nonpolicy judgments. To be used appropriately, a value hierarchy must be properly conceptualized for the specific decision-making situation in which it is prescribed. The basic notion of a value hierarchy assumes that the core field-invariant values can be isolated. These are values that have the same general degree of importance across all contexts and situations of human interaction and decision making. Although many theorists, philosophers, and ethicists have developed general value hierarchies, no *general* value hierarchy necessarily prescribes the *particular* value hierarchy decision makers will use to make a specific nonpolicy judgment.

Any generalized value hierarchy is subject to reordering, depending on the nature of the situation in which it is being used.[4] Rhetorical scholar Walter Fisher, who developed the narrative paradigm we discuss in the final section of this chapter, concludes that even the most generalized value hierarchy is subject to reordering when it is applied to a specific decision-making situation. As Fisher notes, "how a value operates depends on time, place, topic, and culture" (*Human Communication* 114). This is not to say that value hierarchies cannot be used to make nonpolicy judgments in specific situations, but it does suggest that generalized value hierarchies cannot be *imposed* on the decision-making process. Any prescribed value hierarchy must account for the unique characteristics of the situation in which the nonpolicy judgment is being made. Certainly, this notion is consistent with Bartanen and Frank's concept of audience-centered criteria.

Some debaters use value hierarchies to construct criteria in nonpolicy debate. Such a globalized construction proceeds by identification of some generalized value—such as "life," "rights," the "quality of life"—and assertion that the team demonstrating the greatest degree of attainment of that value "wins" the debate. A generalized value such as "life" might be used to construct a criterion such as "to promote the preservation of life" and a standard such as "that which saves the most lives." By this criterion and standard, the team that "saves the most lives" is declared the winner because they attain the highest degree of the generalized value, "life."

Although using a generalized value is a simple and direct way to construct standards for criteria in nonpolicy debate, it is problematic. To say that "life is the highest value" presumes that the worth of that value transcends contexts; debaters assume that the value they claim to be the "highest" would be judged as such regardless of the nature of the proposition (the object of focus, the judgmental term, and any situational or judgmental qualifiers) being debated. However, as we explain in Chapter 12, Toulmin indicates that we should not presume a generalized value such as "life" to be the highest value in every situation. Most people would agree that there are sacrifices of life that are justified, even when such sacrifices result in the net loss of life. As one instance, many observers would argue that the American Revolution was a justified war. The British Empire did not threaten colonialists' lives, so we must conclude that the war was not fought to save lives. The war was fought, many would argue, to preserve liberty and freedom and was therefore justified.[5] For these decision makers, "life" *in this situation* was not of greater value than liberty and freedom; it did not occupy a higher priority in the value hierarchy, and the standards derived from it did not render the most meaningful field-dependent judgment. However, *in other situations* these same decision makers would undoubtedly be willing to sacrifice some freedom and liberty to preserve life.

Value hierarchies should not be assumed *carte blanche* to be sources of standards for criteria in nonpolicy debate; appropriately conceptualized value hierarchies—hierarchies that are shown to be relevant to the particular decision-making situation—can be profitably used. For example, if "privacy" is shown to be the preferred value and the purpose of the object of focus can be shown to be "promoting privacy," field-dependent standards (such as "the ability to protect individual privacy") might be derived from the value. Here, one might use a general value to formulate standards for criteria but only after demonstrating that a legitimate purpose of the object of focus is to achieve that value. The issue agenda model does not prescribe how to construct a value hierarchy or how to resolve disputes about conflicting hierarchical arrangements. It does, however, clearly make value hierarchies a central component of nonpolicy debate about propositions of value.

By focusing formal consideration on value hierarchies, the issue agenda model loses some of its utility as a complete analytical model for nonpolicy debate. Unlike the stasis system and criteria-application model, which have been shown to be appropriate analytical models for both propositions of value and propositions of fact, the issue agenda model seems most appropriate for propositions of value. Propositions of fact, as explained in Chapter 7, do not directly invoke consideration of value hierarchies. Propositions of fact may *precede* value assignation or value comparison, but they turn on the accuracy of descriptions of being, relationship, or designation. Debaters need not establish value hierarchies to make the judgments prescribed in propositions of fact, nor is the hierarchical placement of any value or values necessarily critical to the resolution of any particular stock issue implicit within a proposition of fact.

This does not mean that we judge the issue agenda model to be inferior to either the stasis system or the criteria-application model. To the contrary, the issue agenda model is an important and timely analytical model for nonpolicy debate. However, no analytical model should be used outside the parameters for which it was intended. Debaters can profitably use the model when debating propositions of value, but forcing the model on debates about propositions of fact would be problematic.

A Paradigm for Policy and Nonpolicy Propositions: The Narrative Paradigm

When analytical models do more than identify critical questions—when they prescribe a method of decision making for debate—they are classified as **paradigms.** Paradigms not only prescribe the stock issues and decision-making assumptions but they also usually describe debate metaphorically.

The narrative paradigm was proposed by Walter Fisher as an "alternative paradigm for human communication" ("Narration as Human Communication" 1). The foundation of the narrative paradigm is Fisher's belief that "man is in his actions and practices, as well as in his fictions, essentially a story-telling animal" (qtd. from MacIntyre 201). That is, humans communicate and reason through narratives, or stories. Fisher identifies five presuppositions of the narrative paradigm:

> (1) humans are essentially storytellers; (2) the paradigmatic mode of human decision-making and communication is "good reasons" which vary in form among communication situations, genres, and media; (3) the production and practice of good reasons is ruled by matters of history, biography, culture, and character . . . ; (4) rationality is determined by the nature of persons as narrative beings—their inherent awareness of narrative probability, what constitutes a coherent story, and their constant habit testing narrative fidelity, whether the stories they experience ring true with the stories they know to be true in their lives; (5) the world is a set of stories which must be chosen among to live the good life in a process of continual recreation. (Fisher, "Narration as Human Communication")

Fisher characterizes the narrative paradigm as a paradigm because it offers a globalized way of understanding how humans communicate across contexts, situations, and purposes. He argues that the narrative paradigm incorporates within itself other existing paradigms for human communication, rhetorical criticism, and argumentative analysis ("Narration as Human Communication" 3).

The key distinguishing feature between the narrative paradigm and more traditional analytical models—needs, comparative advantage, stasis system, criteria-application, and issue agenda models—is its assumption about the nature of "rationality" or what constitutes sound and reasonable argument. The narrative paradigm challenges the assumptions that reasoned discourse must be expressed in traditional argumentative form and that the soundness of arguments must be determined by traditional standards of either formal or informal logic.

Fisher argues against traditional models on two levels. First, he criticizes them as formulas that prescribe ways to construct "sound" arguments, suggesting instead that we need a broad perspective to understand how humans reason and determine the "soundness" of argumentative discourse. Second, Fisher argues that the "logic of reason" (such as traditional tests of reasoning or evidence) does not provide a complete method to assess argument. To Fisher, most of our communication is "value laden;" we explicitly and implicitly advocate value preferences, assume value preferences in our arguments, and attempt to move others to accept what we say by aligning our positions with accepted values. We might use the "logic of reason" to assess some aspects of argument—tests of verifiability, precision, context; when used in isolation, however, the "logic of reason" does not provide a complete method for assessing argument because it does not explain how values and value preferences influence judgments about the "soundness" of argument.[6] Thus, Fisher rejects both the "traditional reality" and its reliance on the "logic of reason," replacing them with **"narrative rationality"** and the **"logic of good reason,"** which form the critical core of the narrative paradigm.

Stock Issues of the Paradigm

Fisher argues that narrative rationality is a natural part of human experience; it evolves naturally out of the experiences every person has. As a result, narrative rationality is a *public-based* rationality because all persons regardless of their status, position, or power can use it to assess their own stories and the stories others construct for them. In short, the rules of the game inhere within each individual, and all individuals can participate in the game as equal players. [7]

Narrative rationality is composed of two major elements: **narrative probability** and **narrative fidelity;** these become the stock issues of the paradigm. According to Fisher, narrative probability refers to judgments about the structure of a story—whether the story considered as a story is coherent and free of internal contradiction. Fisher identifies three dimensions of coherence that can be used to assess narrative probability. First, you can assess the *argumentative or structural coherence* by examining the elements of the story to determine whether they are internally consistent within themselves and with each other. This dimension is very similar to the general test we explained in Chapter 4 of internal consistency that can be used to evaluate the credibility of evidence.

The second dimension is *material coherence.* To assess this dimension, Fisher says to compare the story to other similar stories to determine its relative completeness; that is, whether "important facts may be omitted, counterarguments ignored, and relevant issues overlooked" (*Human Communication* 47). This dimension is similar to the tests of precision and external consistency explained in Chapter 4.

The third dimension is *characterological coherence.* Fisher argues that characterological coherence "is one of the key differences between the concept of narrative rationality and traditional logics" (*Human Communication* 47). To determine characterological coherence, assess the motives and actions of the characters in the story to determine whether these are consistent with the characters' previous motives and actions. Characterological coherence ultimately determines the believability of a story and is thus critical to the narrative paradigm.[8] Thus, a story is said to have narrative probability if it recounts events in a consistent manner, provides sufficient detail in explaining the events, and attributes to the central characters in the story actions and motives consistent with the known actions and motives of those same characters.

Whereas narrative probability is concerned with the coherence of a story, the second stock issue—narrative fidelity—is concerned with the plausibility of a story, or how likely the various elements of the story are to be true. A story with narrative fidelity is said to "ring true" ("Narration as Human Communication" 8) to those who assess it. To assess narrative fidelity, look at the story microscopically to determine whether the individual components of the story are "accurate assertions about social reality" (*Human Communication* 105) and use the logic of good reason to make such assessments.

Fisher identifies five criteria in the logic of good reason that could be used to assess narrative fidelity. First, identify the implicit and explicit values in the argument. Fisher calls this the **question of fact** and it is similar to the question of fact in the stasis system. Second, determine how relevant those identified values actually are to the argument and the ultimate decision likely to result from the argument. In short, you must determine whether the identified value is the actual value assumed in the argument or if some other value is more relevant to the argument. Fisher calls this the **question of relevance.** Third, determine what effect adhering to the identified value would have. You would determine what outcome is likely to be produced by subscribing to the value. Fisher calls this the **question of consequence.** Fourth, determine what outcome has actually been produced by subscribing to the value in the past. To do this, you would compare the predicted consequences of adhering to the value with the actual consequences observed in situations where you, respected others, groups, or society have previously adhered to the value. Fisher calls this the **question of consistency.** Fifth, determine whether the values advocated are the most suitable values. Assuming that the predicted consequences are validated by previous experience, you must determine whether those consequences enhance the individual, group, or society to the fullest degree possible. To do so, you would determine whether subscribing to another value would produce more desired consequences. Fisher calls this the **question of transcendence.**

Fisher does not deny that one may select "bad stories," even when judging those stories by the standards of narrative rationality—narrative probability and narrative fidelity. He does claim, however, that assessing the narrative probability and narrative fidelity of a story minimizes the chance that a bad story will be selected because using these standards "engenders critical self-awareness and conscious choice" ("The Narrative Paradigm" 349).

Applying the Paradigm to Debate Propositions

Hollihan, Baaske, and Riley first applied Fisher's narrative paradigm to debate, arguing that it is an "exemplar model" for academic debate. These authors argue that using the narrative paradigm as an exemplar model would help correct a wide range of shortcomings they perceive to exist in debate. Ultimately, they suggest that academic debate would become a more valuable educational experience if advocates formulated, analyzed, and defended their arguments within the parameters of the narrative paradigm.

Kristine Bartanen, applying the paradigm specifically to nonpolicy debate, views the narrative paradigm as a "new metaphor" for nonpolicy debate. She argues that the narrative paradigm provides debaters with a more effective and useful way of resolving value disputes than do currently available analytical models and that adopting the narrative paradigm as the "new metaphor" would promote more humane and ethical practices among nonpolicy debaters.

Building on the work of Hollihan, Baaske, and Riley, we can illustrate how debaters might use the narrative paradigm, specifically narrative probability and narrative fidelity, in debate. In the remainder of this section, we explain in some detail how debaters might use the stock issues of the paradigm—narrative probability and narrative fidelity—in debate about both policy and nonpolicy propositions.

Using Narrative Probability

Narrative probability concerns the coherence of the story and is assessed on three dimensions. First, debaters would demonstrate the *argumentative or structural coherence* of the story (their case). To achieve narrative probability, the components of the case—claims, assumptions, evidence, reasoning—would need to be internally consistent. Argumentative or structural coherence would be compromised if contradictory elements (such as values, assumptions) are used to construct a story, or if elements (such as assumptions, values) used to defend a story contradict those originally used to construct the story. For example, if a story suggested simultaneously that covert operations are harmful to the United States and that openness in government is desirable, that story would be structurally coherent because the assumption of the former dimension—covert operations are harmful—is consistent with the value implied in the second dimension—openness in government is desirable. However, if a story suggested simultaneously that mandatory drug testing in the workplace is desirable and that we must protect citizens from any and all invasions of privacy, it would not be structurally coherent because the assumption of the former dimension is inconsistent with the value subscribed to in the latter dimension.

The second dimension is *material coherence*. Hollihan, Baaske, and Riley argue that debaters need to include all "pertinent" information—information about the historical, cultural, or biographical context within which the story should be interpreted—to demonstrate the material coherence of their stories. For example, debaters who construct a story that says the presence of third parties in presidential elections increases public involvement in the political process would need to include in their construction some account of the contextual factors such as the role of problems and issues (historical context), trends toward activism and involvement (cultural context), and the charismatic appeal of third party spokespersons (biographical context) to interpret the story accurately. Similarly, they might use those contextual factors as the bases to explain why their story offers the most complete and coherent account about the effects of third parties in presidential elections. Establishing the material coherence is important so that both their judge and the opposing advocates will be able to assess accurately and completely the individual arguments and the cumulative effect of all of the arguments used to construct the story.

The third dimension is *characterological coherence*. Debaters are expected to portray primary and secondary actors in their story in ways consistent with how those actors have behaved in the past, or how they would most likely be predicted to act in the future. Hollihan, Baaske, and Riley provide an excellent example of how this dimension might be used in debate. They write:

> [A] negative who argues that the American military establishment would willingly surrender to the Soviet Union if ordered to do so by their Commander in Chief, is arguing a position which might seem inconsistent with the character impressions that many of us have of our military. A rival story which suggested instead that those military leaders would lead a coup d'etat might seem more likely. Similarly, advocates who contended that the opening of a single adult bookstore in New York could create enough furor to distract the national media from the Reagan administration's Iranscam nightmare, are probably not presenting a portrayal of media representatives which would be consistent with most people's perceptions. (188)

A debater might consider three particular aspects of characterological coherence: (1) the known actions of the actors, (2) the presumed and stated motives of the actors, and (3) the capabilities of the actors. Without action, there would be no story. To develop a coherent story, a debater would need to be able to identify accurately the significant and relevant actions and accurately attribute those actions to the primary actors. In addition, debaters should be able to offer a plausible explanation of the actor's motives. Although assessing motives is always problematic, debaters would attempt to develop as complete an understanding as possible about why the primary actors act as they do. The more completely debaters can account for the motives of primary actors, the more thoroughly they will understand the episodes that give rise to the story, and the more effectively they will be able to construct the story for the critic. Finally, debaters would need to account for the capabilities of the actors. Although motive is the impetus for action, capability is the vehicle. To develop a coherent story, debaters must go beyond their assessment of the motives of the actors and be able to demonstrate that the motivated actors in fact had the capability to perform the primary actions in the story. Along with motive, capability becomes the primary basis debaters can use to project the likelihood that their story will continue into the future.

Using Narrative Fidelity

Narrative fidelity is tested both by the traditional "logic of reasons" and Fisher's logic of good reasons. The "logic of reasons" is used no differently in the narrative paradigm from the way it is in any analytical model for academic debate; tests of claims, evidence, and reasoning are applied to the specific arguments debaters present in their story. The five questions of the *logic of good reasons*— fact, relevance, consequence, consistency, and transcendent issue—can be utilized in the following ways.

First, debaters would be required to address the issue of fact by clearly and completely identifying the values pertinent to their story. As the proponents of a story, debaters would have to identify the implicit values on which their story is built as well as the end values to which their story suggests they aspire. The values should be identified at the outset of the story and expressed in clear and readily understandable terms. For example, in the proposition, "Resolved: that imposing more severe penalties on persons convicted of violent crimes throughout the United States would be desirable," a debater might construct a story arguing that people who commit violent crimes inflict significant psychological and material harm on society, and they, in turn, should suffer significant consequences for their actions. In such an argument, one of the assumed values is retribution—people should be punished in kind for their crimes. The debaters would need to identify that value and clearly explain what "retribution" means.

Debaters would have a similar responsibility in debating a proposition of policy. In debating the proposition "Resolved: that the U.S. federal government should significantly reform ocean shipping policy," debaters might construct a story arguing that current policies allow practices that threaten ocean life. Such a story would likely be based on an environmental value, such as preserving environmental systems. In constructing this story, debaters would need to define the nature of that value clearly so that both the opponents and the judge would understand what the value means and how it functions as the foundation of the story.

Second, debaters would be required to address the question of relevance by demonstrating that (1) the value identified is the value assumed in the argument, and that (2) the identified value is relevant to the judgment about the object of focus. If "retribution" were the only value identified in the previous argument, the debaters would have to explain why that is the sole value assumed in the argument. If their opponents could demonstrate how another value is assumed in the argument, the opponents would cast doubt on whether the story constitutes a "good reason" to judge the object of focus—"imposing more severe penalties"—to be desirable. Similarly, if debaters could demonstrate that some value other than environmental protection is assumed in the proposition, they would cast doubt on whether that story constitutes a "good reason" to implement the policy stated in the proposition.

In addition, debaters would need to demonstrate that the identified value is indeed relevant to the judgment being made about the object of focus of the proposition. The primary way to demonstrate this aspect of relevance is to use the concept of field-dependence discussed in Chapter 12. Proponents of a story need to demonstrate that the identified value is relevant to the judgment being made about the object of focus within the field in which the object of focus is placed. In the previous example, the debaters might use a purpose-based construction and place the object of focus, "imposing more severe penalties," in the argument field of "vehicles designed to punish." That being the case, proponents of the story would then be required to demonstrate that the value, "retribution," is relevant to judgments made about "imposing more severe penalties" when that object of focus is viewed as a "vehicle designed to punish."

Third, debaters would address the question of consequence by identifying the predicted effect of adhering to the pertinent value. As proponents of a story, debaters would be required to demonstrate how the value used in the story affects or is likely to affect the way a persons thinks, feels, and acts. In the previous example, proponents of the story would need to identify what effects subscribing to "retribution" might produce in individuals, groups, or society at large. They might argue that by subscribing to the value of retribution, society would send a strong message to people who commit violent crimes and that the result of this message would be to reduce the incidence of violent crime throughout the United States.

Determining consequences that stem from adherence to the foundational value of a story is also important in debating policy propositions. For example, debaters might argue that adhering to the value of preserving environmental systems is potentially detrimental because doing so would be excessively costly. Demonstrating the degree of such costs places a particularly heavy burden on the advocates of the story to justify the story's foundational value. In addition, demonstrating that adverse consequences will indeed arise from adherence to the foundational value of the story creates a powerful basis to question whether the story is acceptable.

Fourth, to address the question of consistency, debaters would compare the predicted consequences with actual consequences observed in previous situations. They would compare the actual outcomes of previous instances in which persons subscribed to the value with the outcomes predicted in the story. The substantive difference between the test of consistency and consequence, therefore, is that the test of consistency requires the proponents of the story to demonstrate that the predicted consequences are in fact the *probable* consequences, whereas the opponents of the story attempt to demonstrate that the predicted consequences will likely not materialize. In the previous example of the nonpolicy proposition, the proponents of the story would be required to demonstrate that the incidence of violent crime throughout the United States would likely decrease if the value, "retribution," was subscribed to and implemented by the imposition of more severe penalties. On the other hand, the opponents of the story might argue that subscribing to the value of retribution, perhaps through the imposition of capital punishment, has not historically resulted in a decrease in the incidence of violent crime throughout the United States. By taking this approach, the opponents in essence create an alternative story arguing that the predicted effects did not materialize when the advocated value was in fact embraced.

Similarly, in debating the policy proposition, the proponents of the story would be required to demonstrate the degree to which adhering to the value of preserving the environmental system would result in the predicted positive consequences. In doing that, the proponents would likely draw from examples of other situations when the positive consequences did materialize; they would use those occurrences from past stories to demonstrate the probability that similar consequences would emerge in the present story. Of course, in using such evidence, the proponents would need to be able to show similarity between the conditions in the past story and those described in the present story. The opponents of the story would obviously attempt to deny that the predicted positive consequences would result, and they would attempt to demonstrate that predicted negative consequences would more likely result. The opponents would also draw evidence from past examples to establish the probability that their predicted outcomes would emerge.

Fifth, debaters would address the question of transcendent issue by demonstrating the comparative importance of the value used in their story with other possible values. As proponents of a story, debaters would be required to demonstrate that, assuming the predicted outcomes do occur, the value they advocate is the best possible value for individuals, groups, and society. Ultimately, debaters would be required to demonstrate that their value outcomes are superior to other possible value outcomes. Proponents of the story could not be expected to introduce every conceivable comparison when they initially construct their story; however, they must be prepared to defend the value used in their story against any reasonable comparison opponents might suggest. For example, the opponents in the previous situation might argue that "justice" is a better value than "retribution." To do so, they might demonstrate that the outcome produced by subscribing to "justice" is "equal treatment under the law for all persons" and that ensuring equality under the law is more important to our nation than reducing the incidence of violent crime throughout the United States. Should the opponents of the story make such an argument, the proponents would be forced to demonstrate that reducing the incidence of violent crime throughout the United States is more important to the nation than ensuring that all persons are treated equally under the law.

In the policy proposition example, the opponents might suggest that strengthening economic systems is a more important foundational value for a story than is preserving environmental systems. In creating such an argument, the debaters would compare the consequences likely to be derived from adhering to the economic value with those attained by adhering to the environmental value. In making such a comparison, the debaters would invariably discuss issues of probability and magnitude similar to those described in the discussion of the comparative advantage model earlier in this chapter. Ultimately, the opponents' task would be to demonstrate that more is attained from adhering to the economic value whereas the proponents' task would be to demonstrate that adhering to the foundational value of preserving environmental systems is more desirable.

Overall, debaters can use the dimensions of narrative probability and the criteria for *narrative fidelity* in several ways. First, the dimensions of narrative probability provide a guide debaters can use to construct the stories they will present. For example, debaters should employ the general dimensions of narrative probability as the necessary structural elements of their story. In addition, the specific bases of material coherence—historical context, cultural context, and biographical context—and characterological coherence—the known actions of the actors, the presumed and stated motives of the actors, and the capabilities of the actors—can indicate to debaters the types of information they might need to include when constructing the story.

Second, debaters can use the questions of the *logic of good reason* as a guide to explain basic burdens they must meet when constructing and defending a story. For example, the questions of fact, relevance, and consequence are basic responsibilities debaters must fulfill when initially constructing a story; the questions of consistency and transcendent issue identify types of elaboration that might be required to defend a story after it has been constructed.

Third, the dimensions provide the basis on which debaters can construct arguments to challenge a story. Used in this way, the dimensions become tests; debaters use the tests to assess the story and as a basis to advance claims to demonstrate why the story is unsatisfactory. For example, debaters might assess a story that says members of the Nuclear Regulatory Commission suppress data about unsafe nuclear power plants on the basis of *characterological coherence* by arguing that there is no apparent motive for such action.

Fourth, debaters can use the dimensions of *narrative probability* and the questions of *narrative fidelity* as the decision-making criteria to resolve the debate. A team might argue that they should "win" the debate because their story—as measured by the dimensions of argumentative, material, and characterological coherence—has more narrative probability than the story constructed by their opponents. Or debaters might argue that they should win the debate because their opponents' story lacks narrative fidelity. The narrative fidelity of the opponents' story could be challenged by demonstrating that the value used in the story is unclear (question of fact) or is of questionable relevance or consequence.

Not all theoreticians judge the narrative paradigm to be suitable for argumentation and debate. Rowland ("Narrative Mode") argues that narrative rationality is not adequate to test reasoning. He argues that stories can be coherent and plausible but also false (for example, Hitler's mobilization of Nazi Germany), and stories can be incoherent and implausible, but still be true (for example, electing a peanut farmer, Jimmy Carter, to the presidency of the United States and then electing a former actor, Ronald Reagan, to that office). Warnick advances a slightly different criticism when she argues that narrative rationality cannot be used to help us decide between stories that are equally probable-plausible. Rowland also argues that we cannot test probability and fidelity without resorting to traditional tests of evidence and reasoning. Both Rowland ("On Limiting") and Warnick criticize the presumed subjectivity of narrative probability and narrative fidelity. Rowland writes:

> The key critical terms of the paradigm, the tests of narrative probability and fidelity, are difficult to apply and quickly reduce themselves to an idiosyncratic evaluation of the credibility or coherence of a work for a particular audience and a test of informal logic. This is not to say that these tools are useless in all situations. When a work either explicitly tells a story or draws upon a story, narrative probability and fidelity are useful standards, not so much for testing the argument in the work as for testing its potential credibility for a particular audience. However, at least as these critical terms have been developed so far, they lack generalizability. (52)

Proponents argue that using the narrative paradigm in debate will produce a number of important advantages. In general, proponents argue that the narrative paradigm can enhance the educational value of debate by doing the following: (1) making academic debate a more public and less elitist activity; (2) redefining the role of the judge from dispassionate arbiter to concerned educator; (3) encouraging the debaters to develop and refine speaking styles more appropriate to real-world advocacy situation; (4) forcing debaters to present more realistic arguments. In addition, proponents argue that the quality of argumentation would be enhanced because judges would become more active in decision making and there would be more emphasis on argument consistency if the narrative paradigm were used. Ultimately, proponents suggest, the value of debate as a laboratory for teaching argumentation would be better appreciated if the narrative paradigm were used.

Conclusion

To be successful advocates, debaters need to have a thorough understanding of the concepts of stasis and stock issues. In addition, debaters need to be familiar with the analytical models for policy and nonpolicy propositions. Whereas the traditional needs model and comparative advantage model can be readily used for policy propositions, debaters might use either the criteria-application model or issue agenda model for nonpolicy propositions. Among these models, each prescribes a different set of stock issues for debate propositions. The traditional needs model incorporates four stock issues: ill, blame, cure, and cost. The comparative advantage model uses these same basic issues but applies them in slightly different ways. The criteria-application model was specifically developed for nonpolicy debate and incorporates two primary stock issues: the definitive and the designative. The issue agenda model, also developed specifically for nonpolicy debate, incorporates four stock issues: definition of key terms, establishing the exigence, identification of audience-centered criteria, and comparison of germane values with potential countervalues. The issue agenda model builds on the criteria-application model by clearly making value hierarchies a focal point of nonpolicy debate. Finally, the narrative paradigm is a broad paradigm for human communication that can be readily adapted to either policy or nonpolicy propositions. It is a dramatic departure from the other analytical models because it redefines the nature of rationality. In the narrative paradigm, debate becomes a clash between competing stories. The stories are judged on the basis of two broad stock issues—narrative probability and narrative fidelity —and each of these issues, in turn, has specifically defined dimensions and criteria.

Notes

1. The *Rhetorica ad Herrenium* (c. 90 B.C.E.), long mistakenly attributed to Cicero, was also important in articulating and sustaining stasis theory.
2. Some theorists and practitioners claim that as a field, the nonpolicy community has failed to generate appropriate theory and analytical models

rapidly enough (see, for example, Thomas L. Murphy and Melinda L. Murphy).

3. The common practice in nonpolicy debate has been to use the framework of the definitive and designative issue to guide case construction and determine requirements for a prima facie case. For a general indication of the acceptance of this approach, see Tim Dixon and Chris Leslie.

4. The exception to our rule here would be the case of a religious or ethical absolutist—someone who consistently holds to a single, rigid ethical standard regardless of the situation. Most people, however, recognize the role that situation plays in any ethical decision. For example, for most Christians and Jews, the Mosaic commandment "Thou shalt not kill" does not mean "thou shalt not kill in any situation." Usually, even the most orthodox believer would see self-defense or the protection of innocent lives as justification for killing another person. However, this is not to say that most people are ethical relativists. For most, the *process* can remain consistent even if there is no one overriding *rule* that transcends and governs all situations.

5. A similar argument could be constructed for Northern involvement in the Civil War.

6. Some argue that the relationship Fisher proposes between the "logic of reason" and his "logic of good reason" is equivocal. Warnick, for example, traces the development of the relationship and concludes that "Fisher ["Toward a Logic of Good Reasons"] seemed to feel that the logic of reasons and the logic of good reasons could exist alongside each other, that neither one was to be preferred. More recently, in 1984, Fisher's attitude toward rationality has become decidedly less friendly and more ambivalent. He has argued that rational standards for examining texts have limited usefulness when compared with the standards of narrative rationality, and he has concluded that one is justified in asking whether narrative rationality is 'a more beneficial way to conceive and to articulate the structures of everyday argument'" (174).

7. Fisher contrasts the narrative paradigm with what he calls the "rational world paradigm." According to Fisher, the rational world paradigm is inherently laden with hierarchies which preference elitist decision making at the expense of widespread public involvement. Thus, its "rationality" is *power based;* it must be learned and can only be learned when those in power agree to divulge the rules of the game. The elites maintain their dominance simply by refusing to release the rules of their "rationality" (Fisher, "Narration as Human Communication").

8. As Fisher explains, "Central to all stories is character. Whether a story is believable depends on the reliability of characters, both as narrators and as actors. Determination of one's character is made by interpretations of the person's decisions and actions that reflect values. In other words, character

may be considered an organized set of actional tendencies. If these tendencies contradict one another, change significantly, or alter in 'strange' ways, the result is a questioning of character. Coherence in life and in literature requires that characters behave characteristically. Without this kind of predictability, there is no trust, no community, no rational human order. Applying this consideration of coherence is an inquiry into motivation. Its importance in deciding whether to accept a message cannot be overestimated. Determining a character's motives is prerequisite to trust, and trust is the foundation of belief" (*Human Communication* 47).

Selected Bibliography

Bartanen, Michael. "The Role of Values in Policy Controversies." *CEDA Yearbook* 3 (1982): 19–24.

Bartanen, Michael, and David Frank. "The Issue-Agenda Model." *Advanced Debate: Readings in Theory, Practice, and Teaching.* Eds. David Thomas and Jack Hart. Skokie, IL: National Textbook, 1987: 408–16.

Bartanen, Kristine. "Application of the Narrative Paradigm in CEDA Debate." *Advanced Debate: Readings in Theory, Practice, and Teaching.* Eds. David Thomas and Jack Hart. Skokie, IL: National Textbook, 1987: 417–28.

Cole, Terry W. "The Role of Stasis in Non-Policy Analysis." *The Forensic of Pi Kappa Delta* 72 (1987): 57–64.

Dieter, Otto. "Stasis." *Speech Monographs* 42 (1950): 345–69.

Dixon, Tim, and Chris Leslie. "Propositional Analysis: A Need for Focus in CEDA Debate." *CEDA Yearbook* 5 (1984): 16–23.

Fisher, Walter. "Clarifying the Narrative Paradigm." *Communication Monographs* 56 (1989): 55–58.

———. *Human Communication as Narration.* Columbia: U of South Carolina, 1987.

———. "Narration as Human Communication: The Case of Public Moral Argument." *Communication Monographs* 51 (1984): 1–22.

———. "The Narrative Paradigm: An Elaboration." *Communication Monographs* 52 (1985): 347–67.

———. "Toward a Logic of Good Reasons." *Quarterly Journal of Speech* 64 (1978): 376–84.

Hollihan, Thomas, Kevin Baaske, and Patricia Riley. "Debaters as Storytellers: The Narrative Perspective in Academic Debate." *Journal of the American Forensic Association* 23 (Spring 1987): 184–93.

Hultzen, Lee. "Stasis in Deliberative Analysis." *The Rhetorical Idiom.* Ed. Donald C. Bryant. Ithaca, NY: Cornell UP, 1958: 97–123.

MacIntyre, Alasdair. *After Virtue: A Study in Moral Theory.* Notre Dame, IN: U of Notre Dame P, 1981.

Matlon, Ronald. "Debating Propositions of Value." *Journal of the American Forensic Association* 14 (1978): 194–204.

Matlon, Ronald. "Debating Propositions of Value: An Idea Revisited." *CEDA Yearbook* 9 (1988): 1–14.

Mills, Glen. *Reason in Controversy: An Introduction to General Argumentation.* Boston: Allyn & Bacon, 1964: 53–74.

Murphy, Thomas L., and Melinda L. Murphy. "Resolutional Relevance: A Primary Standard for Evaluating Criteria in Nonpolicy Debate." *CEDA Yearbook* (ed. Walter Ulrich) 11 (1990): 1–8.

Nadeau, Ray. "Hermogenes on 'Stock Issues' in Deliberative Speaking." *Speech Monographs* 25 (1958): 59–66.

Newman, Robert P. "Analysis and Issues—A Study of Doctrine." *Readings in Argumentation.* Eds. Jerry M. Anderson and Paul J. Dovre. Boston: Allyn & Bacon, 1968. 166–80.

Pierce, Donald C. "The History of the Concept of Stasis." *The Forensic of Pi Kappa Delta* 72 (1987): 75–81.

Rowland, Robert. "Narrative: Mode of Discourse or Paradigm?" *Communication Monographs* 54 (1987): 264–75.

Rowland, Robert. "On Limiting the Narrative Paradigm: Three Case Studies." *Communication Monographs* 56 (1989): 39–54.

Tuman, Joseph. "Getting to First Base: Prima Facie Arguments for Propositions of Value." *Journal of the American Forensic Association* 24 (Fall 1987): 84–94.

———. "Natural Value Hierarchies and Presumption: Merging Stipulated/Artificial Presumption with Natural/Psychological Presumption." *CEDA Yearbook* 13 (1992): 10–19.

Warnick, Barbara. "Arguing Value Propositions." *Journal of the American Forensic Association* 18 (Fall 1981): 109–19.

Windes, Russel, and Arthur Hastings. *Argumentation and Advocacy.* New York: Random House, 1965: 162–68 and 218–33.

Zarefsky, David. "Criteria for Evaluating Non-Policy Argument." *CEDA Yearbook* 1 (1980): 9–16.

Discussion Questions

1. In what ways do analytical models increase the reliability of argumentation and debate as decision-making tools?

2. What are the most significant ways in which the comparative advantage and issue agenda models differ from the traditional needs approach?
3. Based on your experiences, is the narrative paradigm a practical way to assess everyday argument? Why, or why not?
4. What are the major strengths and weaknesses of each of the models and paradigms presented in this chapter?

PREPARING TO DEBATE:
Format, Responsibilities, and Process

*D*ebating involves a number of different skills and abilities; debaters must be able to do many things and do them well. In this chapter, we discuss a number of tasks debaters must accomplish and how they can do them. We begin by describing the debate format and discussing the general responsibilities associated with each speaking position in a debate. Next, we address two critical tasks debaters must accomplish—selecting and using evidence and presenting refutation—and explain how debaters might accomplish those tasks more effectively. Finally, we discuss the process of note-taking and explain how debaters might work to improve their note-taking skills.

Format and Responsibilities

Because academic debate is argumentation in a formal setting, there are rules and norms that govern how the argumentation will be conducted. Some of these rules concern the format of the debate and within this format are rules and norms that establish the responsibilities for each speaker. The affirmative and negative cases are surely the substance of any debate. In this section, we discuss the debate format and the major responsibilities associated with each speaker. Debaters must understand both the format and their individual responsibilities in order to be effective advocates.

The Debate Format

One idea we have stressed throughout this book is that debate occurs within a clearly structured format. The debate format specifies the number of speeches that will be given, the order in which the speeches are given, and the maximum amount of time allocated to each speech. Having a clearly structured format helps ensure fairness by giving all participants prior notice about their roles and responsibilities; it also helps balance the argumentative advantages and responsibilities any debater incurs. In this chapter, we focus on the most traditional type of debating involving four persons—two affirmative speakers and two negative speakers.

Every debate has four distinct phases, the **constructive** phase, the **cross-examination** phase, the **rebuttal** phase, and the **preparation** phase. In the constructive phase, the debaters advance and develop their cases, or "construct" their arguments—the reason this phase is so named. The constructive phase includes the first four speeches in the debate, and each debater presents one of those speeches. The person who presents the first speech for the affirmative side is designated the first affirmative; the person who presents the first speech for the negative side is designated the first negative. The other debaters are designated second affirmative and second negative, respectively.

In the cross-examination phase the debaters are engaged in a question-answer interaction. This phase of the debate is interspersed with the constructive phase; at the conclusion of each of the constructive speeches, the debater who gave the constructive speech is asked questions by one member of the opposing team. For strategic reasons explained later in this chapter, questions are usually asked by the member of the team who is *not* preparing to present the next constructive speech. For example, the first affirmative speaker is usually cross-examined by the second negative speaker because the second negative speaker does not follow the first affirmative in the designated speaking order.

In the rebuttal phase, the debaters present their final responses to the arguments advanced in the constructive phase as well as the final summary of their respective cases. Like the constructive phase, the rebuttal phase includes four speeches and each debater presents one of them. The rebuttal phase begins following completion of the cross-examination of the second negative speaker. Thus, the first negative rebuttal speech marks the beginning of this phase of the debate. Although not as long as the constructive phase, the rebuttal phase is usually critical to the outcome of the debate. Ultimately, debaters will need to develop superior skills of refutation and summarization to excel in their rebuttal speeches.

The preparation phase of the debate is the only part in which the debaters are not speaking to or directly interacting with their opponents. During this phase, a debater may use time to prepare before presenting the next speech. Each team is allocated an equal amount of total preparation time the team may use. Either member of the team may use preparation time and may use as much of the team's total time as he or she chooses. However, any time used by one debater is subtracted from the team's total remaining time. Thus, time allocated

TABLE 10.1   Speaking Order and Time Allocations for Debate

Speech	Cross Examination Debate Association	National Debate Tournament
First Affirmative Constructive	8	9
Cross-examination by Second Negative	3	3
First Negative Constructive	8	9
Cross-examination by First Affirmative	3	3
Second Affirmative Constructive	8	9
Cross-examination by First Negative	3	3
Second Negative Constructive	8	9
Cross-examination by Second Affirmative	3	3
First Negative Rebuttal	5	6
First Affirmative Rebuttal	5	6
Second Negative Rebuttal	5	6
Second Affirmative Rebuttal	5	6
Total Preparation Time	10	10

for preparation should always be considered as part of the cumulative time allocated to the team.

The preparation phase is invoked during the debate at the debater's request. For example, if the second affirmative speaker needs time to prepare before presenting his or her constructive speech, that debater would simply request the time and use it as necessary. Although there are no "rules" that govern how debaters use the preparation time they are allocated, generally the affirmative debaters use the bulk of their preparation time before the second affirmative constructive speech and the first affirmative rebuttal; the negative debaters use the bulk of their time before the first negative constructive speech and the second negative rebuttal. The affirmative would never use preparation time before the first affirmative constructive speech, nor should the negative side need preparation time before the first negative rebuttal speech.

Whether debating a policy or a nonpolicy proposition, the format for your debate will likely include each of the four phases just discussed. There may be some differences in total time allocated to each phase. Depending on the time constraints of the class, your instructor may need to allocate less time to each phase than would be the case in a formal tournament setting. Even in a formal setting, the tournament director may choose to use time allocations suited to the particular needs of the tournament. Time allocations may also differ depending on which national organization has sponsored the tournament. Debates sanctioned through the Cross Examination Debate Association (CEDA) typically have shorter time allocations for both constructive and rebuttal phases than do debates sanctioned through the National Debate Tournament (NDT). In Table 10.1, we have specified the format for a formal debate by listing each speech of the debate in order. For the purpose of comparison, we have also given the time allocations subscribed to by the Cross Examination Debate Association (CEDA) and the National Debate Tournament (NDT).

Basic Speaker Responsibilities

Every debate is in many ways a unique communicative experience, but basic speaker responsibilities for debaters are generally constant from one debate to the next. By basic speaker responsibilities, we mean those general tasks associated with the respective speaking positions in a debate. Recall that there are four speaking positions in a debate—first affirmative, first negative, second affirmative, and second negative—and the debater in each of those positions presents two speeches in the debate—a constructive and a rebuttal. In this section, we discuss the basic responsibilities associated with each position for both constructive and rebuttal speeches. We explore the responsibilities associated with each position in the order in which speeches would be given in a debate.

The initial speech in a debate is the first affirmative constructive speech. Its primary function is to present the affirmative case. As we explain in Chapter 11, the affirmative case should contain an introduction, definitions, criteria (for a nonpolicy resolution), and the rationale. The case might also contain preliminary and summary components such as an overview or underview. In two important ways, the first affirmative constructive speech is a unique speech in a debate: it is usually the only speech that can and should be completely prepared ahead of time and presented from a manuscript, and it is the only speech in the debate that focuses almost exclusively on constructing rather than constructing *and* refuting arguments. We say almost exclusively because this affirmative speech may contain introductory or summary components designed to preempt negative arguments.

The first affirmative constructive speech is followed by the first negative constructive speech. The primary purposes of this speech are to establish the foundation for the negative position and to refute the affirmative case presented in the first affirmative constructive speech. The first negative speaker can respond to the affirmative case in many different ways and should choose those approaches that create the strongest and most convincing negative case. In most cases, the first negative speaker will introduce the basic negative position or philosophy statement for the debate, launch the major attacks on the definitions and criteria, and make critical responses to the major claims in the affirmative case. In some debates, the first negative might also present disadvantages (policy resolution), value objections (nonpolicy resolution), or a counterplan. We discuss each of these options in detail in Chapter 14.

The next speech in the debate is the second affirmative constructive. The debater in this position needs to fulfill two distinct responsibilities. First, the second affirmative speaker needs to rebuild the affirmative case that was presented in the first affirmative constructive speech. The second affirmative speaker should proceed from the beginning of the affirmative case to the conclusion and respond to the arguments presented in the first negative constructive speech. The second affirmative should, if at all possible, refute any attack made against the major components of the case, including the definitions, criteria, or rationale, as well as repair any challenge made against the preview or underview if either of those components were included in the case. The second affirmative speaker also has the responsibility to respond to any additional arguments—negative philosophy, disadvantages, value objections, or counterplan—that were presented in the first negative constructive speech. If time allows, the debater in this position should also further develop the affirmative case. The second affirmative can do this by presenting new evidence to support the claims contained in the case and by supplying additional explanation of the case. The amount of time the second affirmative debater will be able to devote to this task will, of course, vary from debate to debate depending upon how much time must be spent rebuilding the basic affirmative case. Generally, when the second affirmative attempts to further develop a component of the case, he or she should do so immediately after rebuilding that same portion of the case rather than rebuilding the entire case and then backtracking to further develop selected components.

The final speech of the constructive phase of the debate, immediately following the second affirmative constructive, is the second negative constructive. The speaker in this position should fulfill two general responsibilities. First, the second negative debater should complete development of the negative case. The basic foundation of the case is established in the first negative constructive. In the second negative constructive, any additional arguments to be levied against the affirmative case must be presented. The second negative speaker can focus his or her efforts on any portion of the affirmative case and advance those arguments most appropriate to the specific component being attacked (such as advancing solvency arguments or disadvantages to attack the plan in a case developed for a policy resolution). The second responsibility associated with this position is to rebuild selected portions of the arguments launched in the first negative constructive speech. We say *selected* portions because the second negative speaker should not attempt to rebuild every argument the first negative speaker launched: doing so will surely undermine both the ability of the second negative to fulfill his or her major responsibility—completing development of the negative case—and the importance of the first negative rebuttal speech. In many debates, however, the second negative debater may need to rebuild some arguments presented in the first negative constructive to complete the development of the negative case. For example, if the second negative debater wanted to further develop a disadvantage presented in the first negative constructive speech, it would be necessary to rebuild the disadvantage—to answer any attacks on the disadvantage made in the second affirmative constructive speech —before the disadvantage could be more completely developed.

The next speech in the debate, the first negative rebuttal, marks the beginning of the rebuttal phase of the debate. The singular responsibility associated with this speech is to rebuild the key portions of the negative case launched in the first negative constructive speech. We say *key* portions because the first negative speaker may choose not to attempt to rebuild every argument presented his constructive speech. As a general rule, the first negative speaker should attempt to rebuild as many of the arguments presented in his or her constructive speech as possible but is not obligated to rebuild every one. The first negative debater should focus on those arguments that are most critical to the negative case and most "winnable." In rebuilding arguments, the first negative debater would refute those attacks launched in the second affirmative constructive speech.

The next speech in the debate is the first affirmative rebuttal. In many ways, this is the most demanding speech in the debate. This speech is the only one that follows two consecutive opposition speeches—the second negative constructive and the first negative rebuttal. Thus, the first affirmative speaker faces the difficult task of refuting the major arguments from this combined negative "block." Although the particular circumstances of the debate may dictate otherwise, the first affirmative debater will usually first attempt to refute the major arguments developed in the second negative constructive speech and then refute those arguments emphasized in the first negative rebuttal. In the case of new arguments developed in the second negative constructive speech, the first affirmative debater will actually establish the affirmative's response; in the case of arguments emphasized in the first negative rebuttal speech, the first affirmative will likely extend responses originally presented in the second affirmative constructive. The first affirmative debater will not be able to attack every minute detail of the entire block of negative arguments. Thus, it is critical for the first affirmative debater to focus on the most crucial aspects of the negative arguments and to present the most concise and efficient responses to them.

The first affirmative rebuttal speech is followed by the second negative rebuttal. This speech is the final speech for the negative team, and the second negative debater has the significant responsibility of summarizing the negative team's case clearly. The second negative debater needs to present the final negative position about the critical issues in the debate. To do that, the second negative debater would refute the responses made in the first affirmative rebuttal to the critical negative arguments. The second negative debater may address whatever arguments he or she judges to be most important and may allocate as much or as little of the speech time as desired to those arguments. In addition to addressing the critical issues in the debate, the second negative debater must explain to the judge why the negative team should be accorded a victory in the debate. To do that, the second negative debater needs to prioritize the critical issues in the debate and explain why the negative positions on those issues are singularly or collectively sufficient to refute the affirmative position. The second negative debater needs to be clear and convincing in summarizing the negative team's position.

The final speech in the debate is the second affirmative rebuttal. The second affirmative debater needs to summarize the entire debate from the standpoint of the affirmative team. It is critical that the second affirmative debater address each of the issues emphasized in the second negative rebuttal. In addition, the second affirmative debater will likely focus on other arguments advanced in the first affirmative rebuttal and the second affirmative constructive. The negative debaters have the latitude to be selective in terms of the arguments they address —they need not "win" every argument; the affirmative, however, must be much more comprehensive. The second affirmative debater needs to convince the judge that the affirmative team has provided sufficient justification to "win" each of the major issues in the debate. The second affirmative debater must be clear, concise, and convincing. The responsibilities for each speaker are summarized in the following general outline.

Outline of Basic Speaker Responsibilities

1st Affirmative Constructive (1AC)
1. Present the introduction
2. State the proposition
3. Define the key terms in the proposition
4. Establish reason for change
5. Present the affirmative plan
6. Demonstrate solvency

1st Negative Constructive (1NC)
1. Introduce the basic negative philosophy or position
2. Challenge definitions (optional)
3. Challenge affirmative case claims
4. Introduce other negative response strategies (optional)

2nd Affirmative Constructive (2AC)
1. Respond to negative philosophy/position
2. Respond to definition challenges
3. Rebuild affirmative case
    A. Identify claims/evidence that was not attacked
    B. Answer challenges to claims/evidence
4. Extend case as feasible
5. Respond to alternative negative response strategies

2nd Negative Constructive (2NC)
1. Assess affirmative plan (policy proposition)
    A. Present solvency arguments
    B. Develop disadvantages
2. Develop negative position (nonpolicy proposition)
    A. Develop value objection
    B. Present Counterexamples
3. Respond to critical issues introduced by 1NC
4. Respond to 2AC challenges to alternative strategies

1st Negative Rebuttal (1NR)
1. Respond to 2AC answers to key 1NC arguments
    A. Identify key challenges that were dropped
    B. Answer responses to other arguments
2. Summarize the key issues from the negative perspective

1st Affirmative Rebuttal (1AR)
1. Respond to all arguments presented in 2NC
2. Respond to major arguments presented in 1NR
    A. Emphasize dropped case arguments
    B. Answer responses by 1NR
3. Briefly summarize debate from affirmative perspective

2nd Negative Rebuttal (2NR)
1. Rebuild most critical arguments from 1NR and 2NC
    A. Identify dropped arguments
    B. Answer 1AR responses
2. Explain why negative team should win the debate

2nd Affirmative Rebuttal (2AR)
1. Answer critical arguments from 2NR
2. Rebuild critical aspects of affirmative case
    A. Emphasize what has been dropped
    B. Respond to 1NR and 2NR
3. Explain why affirmative team should win the debate

The Process of Selecting and Using Evidence

As shown in Chapters 3 and 4, evidence is a critical component of any argument because it provides the foundation from which an advocate can advance and gain acceptance of claims. Debaters should use the criteria explained in Chapter 4 to assess the strengths, credibility, and potential weaknesses of all evidence they collect, but it is vitally important that debaters carefully select and use their evidence. In this section, we discuss those two key aspects of evidence with which affirmative and negative debaters alike must grapple. In addition, we explain the basic process debaters should follow in advancing refutation in a debate.

Selecting Evidence

In a sense, the issue of selecting evidence is really a composite of the other issues: how to find the available evidence and how to select from it the evidence that best supports the various claims to be presented. In Chapter 4, we provided a detailed discussion of the former issue when we described the research process, pointing out examples of general and specific reference materials you can use to locate evidence. In this section, we focus on the latter issue: once you have collected your evidence, how you decide what to use in a debate. To make that determination, debaters should follow five principles.

First, debaters should incorporate at least one piece of evidence for each claim they advance. As you recall from Chapter 8, all debaters have a burden of proof; they must provide support for their claims. Although this principle should be self-evident, we include it to remind debaters that unless they provide a foundation of evidence, there will be no basis on which they can successfully advocate acceptance of their claims.

Second, debaters should use evidence from a variety of sources. Particularly when researching very specialized aspects of a proposition, debaters will frequently locate one or two sources from which they draw a number of pieces of evidence. Although evidence should not be rejected because it comes from a source from which other evidence has been drawn, debaters should always attempt to include as many different sources of evidence as possible. We do not advocate that debaters sacrifice quality of evidence for variety in sources; they should always use the best evidence available. However, we do subscribe to the notion that the overall credibility of evidence is enhanced when the same conclusions, information, or predications are made by different sources of information. In short, utilizing evidence from a variety of sources adds an element of internal corroboration and thus enhances the overall credibility of your position.

Third, debaters should use a variety of types of evidence. If there is one tendency debaters have regarding the use of evidence, it is that they rely very heavily—at times almost exclusively—on expert testimony. Expert testimony is an important type of evidence, but it is by no means the only type debaters can use. Debaters can and should use statistics, examples, and other types of evidence in conjunction with expert testimony. Although they should apply this principle across their entire case, using a variety of types of evidence to support individual claims is critical. Having a variety provides different and interrelated levels of support for the claim. For instance, supporting a claim with an example gives a specific occasion in which the claim was validated. Combining statistics with that example extends the degree of support from a specific instance to a number of instances or to a general population. Incorporating expert testimony can establish the proper context in which to interpret the example and statistics and can help establish the general degree of confidence a listener should have in the claim. Thus, the more variety debaters use for types of evidence, the stronger their claims are likely to be.

In addition, using a variety of types of evidence to support a claim helps give debaters a strategic advantage because it forces their opponents to adopt multiple response strategies. If the affirmative team supports a claim with just one type of evidence (expert testimony), the negative might well use a single response strategy to attack that evidence (challenge expertise of the source). However, if the affirmative uses multiple types of evidence to support a claim, they force the negative to respond to different levels of support, thus making the negative's burden of rebuttal more difficult. Obviously, the same principle holds for evidence used by the negative and the corresponding burden of rebuttal for the affirmative.

Fourth, debaters should only use evidence they are capable of defending. Debaters find out very early in their careers that there is no such thing as the perfect piece of evidence. All evidence has some potential weakness or is used in a way that makes it vulnerable in some respect. Debaters should carefully assess the potential weaknesses in their evidence and how that evidence might be attacked. They should then determine whether they can successfully defend the evidence if their opponent launches a serious attack against it. Debaters should not include in their speech a piece of evidence they cannot defend against substantive attacks. Moreover, they should not be so naive as to assume that their opponents will not detect the weakness in the evidence. Rather, debaters should assume that their opponents will be no less diligent and capable in assessing the evidence than they themselves are. Debaters should not advance claims for which they have insufficient evidence.

Finally, debaters should use evidence that is as complete as possible. They often feel an irresistible urge to use evidence in its most condensed and succinct form. To a large extent, the concern with brevity, like every other part of a case, is legitimate as debaters must work within very limited time constraints. However, they must balance the need for efficiency with the overall credibility and forcefulness of their evidence. In many instances, the credibility of a piece of evidence is ultimately reducible to the core assumptions and explanations that provide a foundation for the evidence. For example, a piece of expert testimony that states "The United States has a significant need to develop the full potential of ocean thermal power" may initially sound impressive, but ultimately its credibility will be determined by the *reasons* the expert had for drawing the conclusion that is quoted as evidence. To maximize the effect of the evidence in generating acceptance of a claim, the debaters should also quote—in so far as possible—a statement of the reasons that led to the conclusion. When it is not feasible to quote these reasons directly within a reasonable amount of time, debaters should be prepared to provide a brief summary of the reasons in conjunction with presentation of the evidence. When it is not possible to provide a statement of the reasons because they are not directly given in the document from which the conclusion is taken, debaters should carefully assess the advisability of introducing the conclusion as "evidence."

Using Evidence

Not only should debaters carefully select evidence for a debate, but they should also use their evidence in the most effective manner possible. Because debate is an oral communication activity, *how* a debater actually presents evidence greatly affects how well the evidence is understood, how credible the evidence appears, and how auditors will use the evidence in the decision-making process of the debate. Using evidence effectively in a debate involves much more than simply reading it. Debaters should present their evidence in ways that help establish both its credibility and the context in which it should be interpreted. Debaters should consider the following basic principles to enhance the effectiveness with which they use evidence.

First, they must clearly state their claim in conjunction with presentation of evidence. Evidence does not in and of itself constitute an argument, nor does it constitute a "claim." Rather, evidence is one component of an argument and it functions as a foundation from which debaters may gain acceptance of a claim. As a result, debaters should not attempt to use their evidence as a complete argument; they should not assume that presenting evidence is tantamount to constructing claims or that their claims can easily be inferred from their evidence. Without a clearly identified claim, presenting evidence in a debate serves no purpose as there is nothing for the evidence to support. To use their evidence effectively, debaters must first identify the claim the evidence is intended to support.

Second, debaters must establish the initial credibility of their evidence. How well any piece of evidence functions as support for a claim is primarily dependent on the credibility that the auditors—or judges—attach to it. Although major questions about the credibility of evidence will likely emerge in a debate through your opponents' response to your evidence, you should attempt to establish with the judge a positive initial evaluation of its credibility. By presenting strong, believable evidence, you can often preempt potential objections or questions your opponents might raise about it. Apart from the "strategic" advantage achieved by doing this, establishing the qualifications of sources of evidence is a fundamental requirement of sound argumentation and responsible advocacy.

Third, debaters should clarify the relationship between their evidence and the claim that the evidence is intended to support. Every piece of evidence introduced into a debate has the same primary purpose: to provide sufficient support for a claim. For the evidence to function as adequate support for a claim, there must be a direct and clearly understood relationship between it and the claim. To establish a relationship between evidence and a claim, two primary questions must be answered: (1) Is the evidence relevant to the claim? (2) How does the evidence demonstrate the likely accuracy of the claim?

To demonstrate the relevance of evidence to a claim, a debater must be able to show that the operative concept in the evidence is equivalent to the operative concept in the claim. Suppose the claim says, "The number of incidents of human rights violations has increased dramatically," and the supporting evidence reports that "between 1991 and 1995 there was a 32 percent increase in the number of reported incidents of serious physical or mental injury inflicted by state-sponsored agents on presumably innocent civilians worldwide." To demonstrate the relevance of the evidence to the claim, the debater would need to demonstrate the similarity between the operative concept of the claim, "incidents of human rights violations," and the operative concept in the evidence "incidents of serious physical or mental injury." That evidence can function as adequate support for that claim only to the degree that the operative concepts are indeed similar. If the judge does not understand the similarity between the operative concepts, the evidence will have little utility in supporting the claim. Debaters should not assume that others will automatically judge the particular operative concepts in their claim and evidence to be similar. Thus, when presenting evidence, debaters should be prepared to provide a brief statement that clearly establishes the similarity for their auditors.

Debaters should also be prepared to address the second question: How does the evidence demonstrate the likely accuracy of the claim? In many ways, this question requires a more generalized judgment than the first; it focuses on the overall relationship between the information contained in the evidence and how that information demonstrates that the conclusion advanced in the claim is true. In the previous example, this question would focus on the ability of the information contained in the evidence—"a 32 percent increase worldwide"—to demonstrate adequately the likelihood of the conclusion advanced in the claim: "incidents of human rights violations have increased dramatically." In some cases, as here, this aspect of the relationship between the claim and the evidence will be fairly obvious; in others, it will be less so. As a general rule, debaters should remember that any time they do not explain how their evidence demonstrates the likely accuracy of their claims, they are assuming that others will automatically interpret and apply that evidence in a manner similar to the way they linked the evidence and claims. Interpretation—even within the context of an academic debate round—is a highly subjective process (see Chapter 8), and debaters should avail themselves of every opportunity to minimize differences in interpretation. Briefly explaining how the evidence supports particular claims is one way to do that.

The Process of Refutation

Throughout our description of the general responsibilities associated with each speech in the debate, we consistently emphasized the importance of "refuting" arguments presented by the opposing team. We discussed the concept of refutation in some detail in Chapter 6 and identified a number of strategies of refutation that can be used by debaters regardless of the position they are debating. At this point, we would like to clarify the *process*, or steps, debaters should follow when refuting arguments.

First, be sure to *identify what you are refuting*. State the specific component of your opponents' speech that you intend to refute. For example, you might say, "We want to challenge the piece of evidence from Professor Small that the negative team reads to support their claim that televised commercials do not affect antisocial behaviors of teenagers." For your refutation to be effective, both your opponents and the judge must clearly understand exactly what you are contesting. Provide any signposts your opponents used to demarcate the argument you are about to refute.

Second, *state the specific basis for the refutation*. You need to identify the grounds you will offer to challenge your opponents' arguments. Remember, your challenge is essentially a claim, and like any claim, it must be clear. You might say, "We will challenge the credibility of the evidence from Professor Small on the grounds that he is not an expert in the field the evidence encompasses." Explaining the basis of the refutation adds precision and context to your challenge; it makes your refutation clearer and better enables you to defend your position. It is also sound argumentation because the basis of your refutation is actually the claim you are advancing.

Third, *prove the challenge*. To be meaningful, you must be able to prove the basis of the challenge. The challenge is your claim, and you have a responsibility to demonstrate why it should be accepted. You might say, "Professor Small is an expert in the field of economics, but training in economics is not sufficient to establish expertise in psychology, the field of my opponents' claim." Debaters have the same responsibility to offer evidence to prove their claims of refutation as they do to prove the claims they are using to construct or defend their case.

Fourth, *explain the effect of the refutation*. To maximize the impact of your refutation, you need to explain how your challenge—assuming it is demonstrated—undermines your opponents' argument. You might say, "Without having established the expertise of Professor Small, the negative has no reasonable basis to believe that his conclusion is warranted. As the evidence from Professor Small is all that the negative offers to support their claim, that claim is unsubstantiated." It is important that debaters attach some degree of importance to their refutation; they need to explain what ultimate effect the refutation will have on their opponents' case if the refutation is accepted.

Following these steps in the process will not automatically ensure that every bit of refutation you offer will be successful. Certainly, the substance of your refutation will affect that outcome dramatically. However, understanding and following this basic process will help ensure that you get the most effect out of the refutation you have.

The Process of Note-Taking

Being an effective note-taker is important in most academic and professional settings. In debate, the notes a debater takes are critical to advocacy. Debaters' notes constitute their only written record of the debate; the notes record the arguments and evidence presented in the debate. In addition, they provide a record of the refutation presented during the debate and a visual account of how specific claims and advocacy of those claims have evolved during the debate. It is easy to understand the dramatic effect notes can have during a debate by simply visualizing a debater standing to present his speech, referring to his notes to state the opponent's argument that he is about to refute, and not being able to determine from his notes what the argument is. If the debater cannot recount the argument he is about to refute and do so accurately, the effect of any refutation he provides will be needlessly undermined. The only thing that might be worse for the debater would be for his listening skills to be so poor that he did not even realize his opponent had presented an argument!

Nature of Notes in a Debate

Although taking notes during a debate is a very important part of the debater's responsibilities as an advocate, it may be one of the most difficult skills for a beginning debater to master. The debate process is a very specialized communicative interaction, and that specialization affects the way debaters take notes. One effect specialization has on taking notes is with the name of the notes. In debate, notes are typically called a **flow** and the process of taking notes is called **flowing**. This is not an arbitrary name as the primary purpose of a debater's notes is to indicate how the arguments in the debate evolved or progressed—

hence "flowed"—across the various speeches in the debate. Another effect specialization has on note-taking relates to the rate at which debaters have to take notes. In many debates, debaters present numerous claims and evidence during the time allotted for their speeches. Although debaters should always make every effort to present their case in a clear and understandable manner, some speak at a faster than normal rate. Thus, for the debater attempting to flow an opponents' case, note-taking will probably occur at a faster rate than in a lecture in an average college class. A final effect specialization has on the note-taking process is with the terminology itself. Debaters will use terms during a debate that they probably are not accustomed to using on a regular basis in everyday conversation—terms such as *contention, presumption, cost-benefit analysis, paradigm, stock issues* as well as the countless technical and specialized terms inherent in the issue they are debating. Thus, debaters will have to develop their familiarity with the terminology and be able to incorporate that terminology within the notes they take.

Taking notes during a debate, or the process of flowing, is a very individualized skill. There are some general practices most debaters follow when flowing a debate, yet virtually every debater's flow has some sort of idiosyncratic notations, shortcuts, or style. We illustrate the most commonly used approaches to flowing but fully assume that as you become more experienced you will develop your own flowing techniques. One general approach to flowing is to create separate flows for the major types of arguments in the debate. Thus, debaters separate the arguments about the affirmative contentions from the arguments about the affirmative plan as well as from the implications of the value assumptions implicit in the affirmative or the negative contentions. Most debaters refer to this division or separation as **case** (affirmative contentions) and **off-case** (arguments about the plan, value assumptions implicit within the affirmative contentions, or negative contentions).

The case and off-case flows are then further divided among the various speeches that occur during the debate. Each division in the case and off-case flows creates a space where arguments presented by a debater can be recorded. As you recall from our discussion of speaker responsibilities earlier in this chapter, the case arguments in a debate will typically be addressed in seven speeches: the first affirmative constructive, the first negative constructive, the second affirmative constructive, the first negative rebuttal, the first affirmative rebuttal, the second negative rebuttal, and the second affirmative rebuttal. Most debaters use 8½" by 14" legal-size paper for their flows and set up the case flow horizontally on that paper. Thus, the case flow for a debate would generally be set up as shown in Figure 10.1.

The off-case flow looks different from the case flow, but it is set up in precisely the same manner. As you recall, most debates have four speeches that deal directly with off-case arguments: the second negative constructive, the first affir-

Sample Case Flow

1st Affirmative	1st Negative	2nd Affirmative	1st Negative Rebuttal	1st Affirmative	2nd Negative	2nd Affirmative

FIGURE 10.1 Sample Case Flow Layout

Off-case Flow

2nd Negative	1st Affirmative Rebuttal	2nd Negative	2nd Affirmative

FIGURE 10.2 **Sample Off-Case Flow Layout**

mative rebuttal, the second negative rebuttal, and the second affirmative rebuttal. Because there are only four speeches—thus divisions—required on the off-case flow, most debaters set that flow up vertically, again using 8½" by 14" legal-size paper. The off-case flow would be set up as shown in Figure 10.2.

There are also some general conventions debaters follow in recording arguments on their case and off-case flows. Most debaters attempt to record both the major and supporting claims their opponents present. Although it may not be possible or feasible to record those claims word for word, it is important to have an accurate representation of what they are. To satisfy this demand, you will need to develop some shorthand for recording the wording of the claims, and you will need to demarcate accurately and separate the major claims from the supporting claims. Most debaters also attempt to record the evidence presented to support the claims. At a minimum, debaters attempt to record the source of the evidence, the date of the evidence, and a brief paraphrase of the critical portions of the evidence. Most also attempt to record the evolution of arguments about major and supporting claims and evidence as precisely as possible. To do this, they typically record arguments about a claim directly beside that claim and further establish the reference point for the argument by using an arrow to link each argument to the claim or evidence the argument addresses.

To understand how arguments in a debate might be recorded, assume that the first affirmative speaker presents a major claim that says, "Labor-related violence is a significant problem in society." To support that claim, the first affirmative speaker presents a supporting claim that "statistically, the problem is significant." The first negative speaker makes two arguments about that supporting claim: (1) that statistics of incidence of violence are misleading and (2) that there is no consistent definition of what is counted as an act of violence. The second affirmative speaker responds to those two arguments by asserting that precise numerical estimates are irrelevant—any degree of violence is unacceptable; also, there is no need to provide precise definitions of the characteristics of acts of violence to be able to understand generally that there is a problem. Such an exchange might be recorded on a flow as illustrated in Figure 10.3.

Note in the illustration how shorthand is used to record the claims and evidence. Note further how the source of the evidence, *US News and World Report*, is indicated in parentheses simply as (USNWR) and the date of the issue is noted. You can also see how the note-taker demarcates the arguments by underlining the major claim and noting the supporting claim as "A." Similarly, the two arguments given by the first negative speaker are separated—"1 and 2"—as are the two arguments presented by the second affirmative speaker. Finally, notice how the arrows begin at the argument being refuted—the reference point—and proceed to the refutation or argument being presented in response to that reference point.

You would use the same sort of process for the off-case flow. Consider, for example, that the second negative speaker presents a value objection, arguing that "Liberty is the most important value." To support that major claim, the second negative speaker presents three supporting claims: (1) the affirmative intends to restrict freedom of choice, (2) people at large value freedom of choice more than other freedoms, and (3) trade-offs that restrict freedom of choice are unacceptable to the general public. The second and third supporting claims are bolstered with evidence. In response to that value objection, the first affirmative rebuttal speaker makes four arguments: (1) overall, liberty is not a major concern for most people; (2) the evidence presented to support the importance people attach to freedom of choice is outdated and no longer accurate; (3) the public has always accepted the need for trade-offs regarding rights; and (4) increasing national security, which the affirmative proposes to do, is more

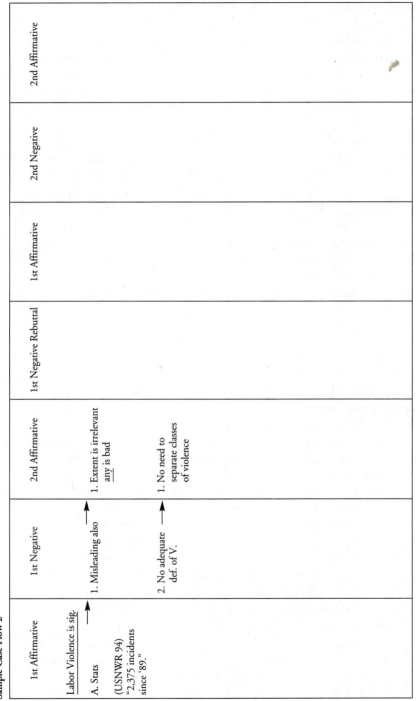

FIGURE 10.3 Sample Flow of Case Arguments and Responses

Off-case Flow 2

2nd Negative	1st Affirmative Rebuttal	2nd Negative	2nd Affirmative
Liberty is paramount A. Affirmative ⟶ restricts free choice B. People value free ⟶ choice (Cohen 84) "people judge it to be most important" C. Trade-offs are ⟶ unacceptable (Yellig 95) "will pay a heavy price in freedom trade-offs"	1. Overall not a major concern 1. Source is outdated 1. Public accepts trade-offs 2. National security more important		

FIGURE 10.4   Sample Flow of Off-Case Arguments and Responses

important to the public than personal liberty and freedom of choice. That exchange might be recorded as illustrated in Figure 10.4.

The process used to record arguments would proceed through each of the speeches in the same manner we have illustrated thus far. For example, the arguments in our two examples might evolve as shown in Figures 10.5 and 10.6.

Note in each example that we have illustrated how the arguments about only one major claim or value objection might be recorded on the flow. You would follow the same process for each component of the affirmative case— definitions, criteria, major claims, and argument, value objections, or disadvantage presented by the negative.

Sample Case Flow 3

1st Affirmative	1st Negative	2nd Affirmative	1st Negative Rebuttal	1st Affirmative	2nd Negative	2nd Affirmative
Labor Violence is sig.						
A. Stats	1. Misleading also	1. Extent is irrelevant <u>any</u> is bad	1. Minor V. is insig. ≠ change	Any violence justifies change	Problem must be compelling	Current level is sig to justify change
(USNWR 94) "2,375 incidents since '89."	2. No adequate def. of V.	1. No need to separate classes of violence				
	3. What was M. of USNWR study? (Thompson 91) "violence method is questionable"		1. The methodology was dropped.			
			2. There is no reason to vote AFF.			

FIGURE 10.5 Sample Progression of Case Arguments during a Debate

Off-case Flow 3

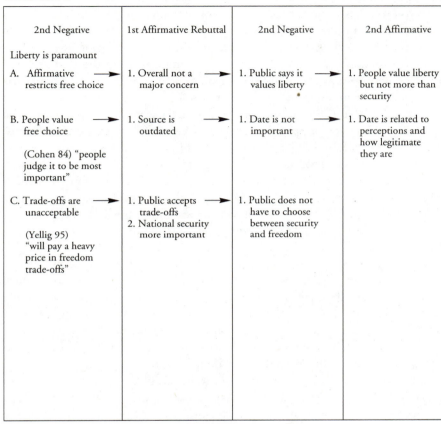

2nd Negative	1st Affirmative Rebuttal	2nd Negative	2nd Affirmative
Liberty is paramount			
A. Affirmative restricts free choice	1. Overall not a major concern	1. Public says it values liberty	1. People value liberty but not more than security
B. People value free choice (Cohen 84) "people judge it to be most important"	1. Source is outdated	1. Date is not important	1. Date is related to perceptions and how legitimate they are
C. Trade-offs are unacceptable (Yellig 95) "will pay a heavy price in freedom trade-offs"	1. Public accepts trade-offs 2. National security more important	1. Public does not have to choose between security and freedom	

FIGURE 10.6   Sample Progression of Off-Case Arguments during a Debate

Principles of Flowing

Every debater will develop his or her own preferred techniques for flowing a debate, there is not one "right" or "best" way to flow. Develop the techniques with which you feel most comfortable and capable. As you experiment, how-ever, be certain to keep in mind three major principles of note-taking during a debate: *accuracy, completeness,* and *usability.*

Regardless of your method, you must be able to take notes accurately. Remem-ber that your notes are a record of what has occurred in the debate and that record provides the context from which you develop and present arguments. If you are not able to record accurately what your opponents say, it will be difficult if not impos-sible to recall precisely what their case is, which of your arguments have been responded to and which have been ignored, or precisely how to develop the arguments you will present during the debate. Any inaccuracy in your notes can have a multiplier effect during the debate, skewing both the relevance and cogency of your responses and ultimately undermining the effectiveness of your advocacy.

Part of making certain your notes are accurate is to ensure that they are complete. Because arguments in a debate are presented orally, it will be impossible for you to record every utterance your opponents make. You will have to be selective in what you record, but you need to make certain that you record the vital information your opponents present. Major claims, supporting claims, sources of evidence, and at least a paraphrase of key pieces of evidence need to be recorded in most debates. Direct responses to claims, key ideas emphasized by the opponents, and key components of your case that your opponents have ignored also need to be systematically noted. The more information you have available on your flow, the better will be your account of the debate and the better prepared you will be to restate, interpret, and respond to your opponents' case and defend your own.

Finally, you need to ensure that your notes are usable. Your note-taking system is *your* system, but you must make certain that it enables you to produce notes you can use effectively and efficiently during the debate. In addition, there are many instances during a debate when your partner will need to use your flow to get an argument, make a response, or understand a portion of your opponents' case. Thus, your note-taking system must also be accessible to your partner. Most debaters speak from their flow; the flow functions much as an outline does for a public speaker. For it to be useful as an outline, it must be legible, indicate adequately the major divisions of argument (major claims, supporting claims, evidence), and provide a clear visual map of the debate. Time spent trying to decipher the flow is valuable time wasted.

As you become more experienced in debate, your note-taking skills will improve and they will work hand in hand with improvement in your listening skills. You will, however, need to *work* on improving your note-taking skills. Do not take note-taking for granted. It is important, and all debaters should consciously continue to improve their note-taking abilities. As you work to develop and refine these skills, you may find it useful to incorporate the following guidelines for effective note-taking.

Guidelines for Effective Note-Taking

1. *Use plenty of paper.* Don't attempt to crowd your notes on a single page or two. Dedicate a separate piece of paper for each major component of your opponents' case. Remember that you can never fully anticipate how many argu-

ments will be presented about a particular portion of a case and you need to allow plenty of space to account for uncertainty.

2. *Separate affirmative and negative arguments visually.* One of the most fundamental requirements of a flow is to record so that you can easily distinguish your arguments from those of your opponents. Most debaters use different colored pens to record arguments—one color for their arguments and the other for their opponents' arguments.

3. *Do as much pre-flowing as possible.* By pre-flowing we mean recording specific arguments or blocks of arguments including both claims and evidence before the debate takes place. Certainly you cannot pre-flow the entire encounter, but you can do portions of every debate. For example, affirmative debaters should have their entire case flowed before the debate begins. Flowing the affirmative case on a slip of paper attached to the flow with paper clips can save much time and ensure more accuracy and completeness. Similarly, negative debaters can develop such clip-ons for major off-case arguments they anticipate using.

4. *Develop a shorthand system and use that system consistently.* Debaters should develop a system of shorthand for their flowing. You will need a way to distinguish major from supporting claims, claims from evidence, and sources of evidence from the evidence proper. You should also have a shorthand system for key recurring terms in debate such as *significance, inherency, criteria, disadvantage, presumption,* and *paradigm.* You should also become familiar with the key recurring terms in the subject matter of the proposition and develop shorthand for those terms. Once you develop a shorthand system, use it consistently; don't reinvent your system every time you debate.

5. *Develop a system of referent markers for your flow.* You will need to be able to indicate basic points of reference on your flow. For example, you will need to be able to link your opponents' arguments and your responses to those arguments. Many debaters use arrows as we did in our illustrations to establish this reference point. You could use lines or enclose the arguments in a block. Similarly, you should be able to indicate when the chain of advocacy about a particular argument has been broken—when one of the debaters has failed to respond to or "dropped" an argument that had thus far been carried through the debate. Many debaters simply draw a circle or a box and place an "X" through it to indicate that the evolution of the argument has stopped.

6. *Practice note-taking every chance you get.* Note-taking is a skill that develops with time and practice. Always be serious about your note-taking and use every possible opportunity including scrimmage debates to practice.

7. *Check the accuracy of your notes during the debate.* Clarify your notes during the debate itself. You might need to check the accuracy or completeness of your notes by asking your opponent questions during cross-examination, or you might need to confer with your partner during preparation time.

Conclusion

Debate is a multifaceted activity. Debaters need to develop a broad understanding of both the process and the complementary skills they will use as participants in the process. Debates occur within a prescribed format and each debater is expected to fulfill basic responsibilities associated with her or his designated position. Not only must debaters have a good understanding of the basic principles of evidence and refutation that are used in everyday argumentation but they must also know how to effectively select and use evidence for a debate and how to properly introduce refutation. Finally, debaters must understand the importance of effective note-taking and must make a concerted effort to enhance their skill as note-takers to enhance their success as advocates.

Selected Bibliography

Trapp, Robert. "The Need for an Argumentative Perspective for Academic Debate." *CEDA Yearbook* 14 (1993): 23–33.

Winebrenner, T. C. "Authority as Argument in Academic Debate." *Contemporary Argumentation and Debate* 16 (1995): 14–29.

Discussion Questions

1. How might the format used in a debate affect the advocacy strategies that debaters use?
2. Do the responsibilities described for each debater suggest a strategic advantage or disadvantage for any speaker?
3. How might the way evidence is used in a debate affect the weight that evidence is given in the judge's decision-making process?
4. How might a debater improve her or his refutation skills?

CHAPTER 11

DEVELOPING AN AFFIRMATIVE CASE:
The Basics

*T*he case is both the formal statement of the affirmative side's arguments about the proposition and the foundation from which the argumentation in the debate will proceed. Affirmative debaters cannot hope to be successful advocates unless they are able to develop an adequate case, and to do that they must fully understand the various components used to construct a case. In this chapter, we discuss three general components included in affirmative cases for both policy and nonpolicy propositions: the preliminary and summary component, the definition component, and the rationale component. We explain how to construct each component and suggest general principles the affirmative side should follow when developing these components for their case.

The Preliminary and Summary Component

Whether the debate involves a policy or a nonpolicy proposition, all affirmative cases have similar preliminary and summary components. Two types of preliminary components—the introduction and preview—and one type of summary component—the underview—might be included in an affirmative case. In this section, we describe the basic functions of each component and illustrate how they can be constructed. We also suggest basic principles debaters should use when constructing these components for their affirmative case.

The Introduction

Every affirmative case, regardless of the type of proposition being debated, should include a well-developed introduction. The introduction includes two basic elements: (1) a description that establishes a rhetorical context for advocacy of the proposition, and (2) an exact statement of the proposition being debated. The following is a well-constructed introduction that includes both these elements.

> (*Rhetorical context*) The Second Amendment of the United States Constitution lies at the heart of any debate on the validity of gun control. In light of this controversy's importance, and because we believe that the proper interpretation of the Second Amendment would allow increased restrictions, Dave and I stand (*formal proposition*) Resolved: that increased restrictions on the civilian possession of handguns in the United States would be justified.[1]

Establishing the rhetorical context for advocacy of the proposition is important to the affirmative team. Debate is ultimately an oral communication activity. Therefore, establishing a rhetorical context for the advocacy of the proposition helps identify the thematic core of the affirmative's case and helps the judge better understand the broad perspective the affirmative will use in their advocacy of the proposition. In short, the rhetorical context helps the debaters communicate more effectively with their audience.

Debaters might use many types of description to establish a rhetorical context for advocacy of the proposition. For example, they might incorporate statistics that give a general sense of the urgency of the issue, an actual example of some aspect of the issue on which the case will focus, a statement of testimony about some critical aspect of the issue, or an original summary of the key aspects of the issue.

Debaters should also include in the introduction of the affirmative case an exact statement of the proposition being debated. Although both the judge and opponents should be fully aware of the proposition before the debate begins, the statement of the proposition in the introduction makes a formal record of the proposition for that debate and provides a formal beginning for the advocacy of that proposition by the affirmative.

Debaters should consider three major principles when constructing the introduction for their affirmative case. First, *the introduction should capture the attention of the judge.* The affirmative should select a method for establishing the rhetorical context that pronounces a clear theme for their case and that critically and emotionally motivates the judge to listen intently to their arguments. The introduction should be compelling and convincing. Moreover, the introduction should be constructed in a manner consistent with both the content and purposes of the specific affirmative case and the affirmative's unique debate style.

Second, *the introduction should be concise.* Although the introduction needs to be rhetorically powerful, it should also be as brief as possible. Long quotations, overly detailed and complex examples, tedious statistics, or extended original overviews can confuse rather than clarify and minimize rather than enhance attention. The affirmative should not spend undue time on the introduction at the expense of developing the other major components of their case.

Third, *the proposition should be stated accurately.* Debaters are expected to debate the proposition as it has been officially worded; they do not have the option of reformulating that proposition within the context of their introduction. The proposition should be stated in the introduction exactly as it has been written. Do not paraphrase, or add or delete words from the proposition.

The Preview/Underview

Previews and underviews perform essentially the same function in an affirmative case, so we discuss them simultaneously here. Previews/underviews are usually designed to fulfill either of two purposes. First, they may be used to clarify how the judge should interpret the affirmative case. When debating a nonpolicy proposition, for example, the affirmative might construct a preview that explains the way a particular value should be interpreted, establishes a priority order for the competing values that will be discussed in the debate, or establishes the legal parameters within which the examples used in the case should be judged. Because a preview is usually presented immediately after the introduction, it should be used to establish an appropriate context for interpretation. The following is an example of a preview that establishes a priority order for a central value the affirmative will defend in its case.

> We will defend the basic position in today's debate that life is the most important value that can be considered. Life is more important than all other values; no other value has meaning for an individual who has lost life. For example, preserving freedom, privacy, or equality is of little consequence to a person who has lost life. Those values are important as long as one has life, but they have little or no meaning once life has been taken away.

Second, a preview or underview can be used to delineate parameters regarding either standard procedural issues or specific substantive issues in the debate. When debating a policy proposition, for example, the affirmative might establish specific tests that evidence should meet to be considered legitimate for the debate, or the preview/underview could identify conditions or obligations that the negative counterplan must meet to be considered competitive. Previews/ underviews used to fulfill this function are generally intended to establish obligations that the negative should meet when refuting the affirmative case. The following is an example of an underview the affirmative might use to establish standards for evaluating arguments the negative is likely to present.

SAMPLE UNDERVIEW

In this debate we have established the psychological and behavioral effects produced by watching televised violence. We have done that by citing and clearly explaining the methodology of a number of carefully controlled scientific studies. If the negative cites counterstudies about these effects, they should be held in their defense of the studies to the same standards we have imposed upon ourselves. They should

1. explain the operational definition of televised violence used in the study
2. identify the specific population studied
3. identify significant limitations described in the study

Without meeting these requirements, the negative team will have no legitimate basis to claim either that their studies are relevant to this issue or that they are substantively superior to ours.

Although previews/underviews are optional components of an affirmative case, they must be properly constructed when they are used. There are three major guidelines debaters should follow when constructing a preview or an underview. First, *previews and underviews must be complete.* Regardless of the purpose the preview/underview is intended to fulfill, it is composed of a series of claims. The preview or underview is, for all practical purposes, a claim the debaters are using to enhance their advocacy of the proposition. For example, if they construct a preview that offers a priority ordering of the competing values that might emerge in the debate, as our example did, they are actually advancing a claim or a series of claims intended to demonstrate that a particular value is "more important" than some other values.

As they do for any other claim in a debate, the affirmative team must provide support for the claims in their previews and underviews. In every case, the debater assumes full responsibility to provide adequate support (evidence) for the claim embodied in the preview or underview and further assumes the responsibility for defending that claim against any attacks the opponents may launch. Simply because a claim is advanced within the confines of a preview or underview does not give that claim any presumptive truth or immunity from scrutiny by any other debater.

Second, *previews and underviews should be reasonable.* Affirmative debaters have a right to include a preview or underview in their case; however, they do not have any legitimate authority to use either a preview or underview to place the negative in an untenable position. In our example of an underview, we established three criteria the negative side should meet when presenting counterstudies about the effects of watching televised violence. We argued that our criteria were reasonable because we had imposed the same standards on ourselves and because they were central to determining the relevance and quality of the studies.

It would be difficult to defend the underview we used in our example as reasonable if it specified standards we could not meet for our own studies, or if it established such restrictive standards as to make using *any* counterstudy virtually impossible for the negative team. If we claimed in our underview that "every study must be longitudinal," that "only studies with a population of those least susceptible to violent behaviors could be used," and finally that "no study that had any significant limitation could be used," the negative debaters could rightly argue that our standards are so restrictive it would be impossible for them to cite any study that is not limited by one or more of those conditions. Such restrictive standards, they could rightly argue, are unreasonable. Affirmative debaters should always remember that credibility can contribute immensely to the success any advocate enjoys, and one sure way to damage credibility is to include in an affirmative case a preview or underview designed to make a debate essentially a nondebate.

Third, *previews and underviews must be meaningful.* Previews and underviews can serve a legitimate purpose when they clarify the way arguments in a debate should be interpreted or outline how particular types of arguments should be constructed. However, simply having a preview or underview component in an affirmative case does not necessarily enhance the quality of that case. Including that component in an affirmative case takes away time that might be better spent developing other critical parts of the case, such as the definitions or rationale. Debaters should always make a careful and thoughtful judgment about the overall purpose served by a preview or underview before deciding on its inclusion in their affirmative case. Use a preview or an underview if it is likely to make you a more successful advocate; refrain from using either if the likely benefits are minimal.

Definitions

Whether debating a policy or a nonpolicy proposition, affirmative debaters must include a definitions component in their case. In this section, we first discuss the major functions definitions perform in the affirmative case and in the debate. Next, we discuss four different methods debaters can use to construct viable definitions for either policy or nonpolicy propositions. Finally, we suggest major principles debaters should follow when developing their definitions.

Functions of Definitions

It is important for you to understand the major functions definitions perform in your affirmative case and ultimately in the debate. We emphasize three primary functions. First, *definitions enhance successful advocacy.* Debaters are advocates who attempt to convince others to accept a particular point of view about the proposition being debated. To be successful advocates, debaters must present a clear message that depicts the point of view they are advocating. Definitions are a primary tool debaters use to clarify their message and thus increase their effectiveness as advocates. For example, it would be very difficult for a debater to successfully advocate the adoption of "stricter gun control laws" without specifying exactly the meaning of "stricter gun control laws."

Not only should debaters attempt to be effective advocates but they also have a special responsibility to be ethical advocates. As we explained in Chapter 2, an ethically responsible advocate demonstrates respect for the individual by attempting to clarify rather than confuse the intended meaning. While our language is not so precise that any advocate will ever be able to exactly replicate the intended meaning of a message, definitions can enhance the degree to which your opponents and the judge share a common and accurate understanding of the message. For example, while there may be many connotations associated with the term *crime of passion,* providing a simple denotative definition such as "a crime likely to be committed spontaneously and precipitated by an intense emotional reaction to another person or situation" does increase the possibility that all will have a similar understanding of how that term is being used. Ultimately, ethically responsible advocates use definitions to enhance shared meaning and they resist success bred out of vagueness or intentional misleading.

Second, *definitions enhance critical inquiry.* Debate is inherently an exercise in critical inquiry because it is primarily a reason-testing activity. Every advocate is given the responsibility to support—to provide reasons that justify—the claims they present. Once a claim and corresponding support have been introduced into the interaction, they are subjected to critical inquiry. For critical inquiry to be meaningful, the claim and support being assessed must be clear. Thus, the terminology used in the claim and the support needs to be defined. For example, it would be impossible for anyone to assess accurately a claim such as "Discovery of covert military operations undermines United States diplomacy" without knowing what is meant by the term *covert military operation.* The greater the uncertainty about the definition of that term, the less precise and relevant the critical assessment of the claim would be. Without a clear definition, the advocates would not know what their inquiry was to be about. For this reason, debaters have a fundamental responsibility to define clearly the major concepts they discuss to enable their opponents to assess critically the arguments they advance.

Third, *definitions enhance decision making.* In every debate, the judge must render a decision that declares one team the "winner" of the debate. To arrive at the most reasonable and reasoned decision possible, the judge must have a clear understanding of the intended meaning of the terms in the proposition, the terminology used to construct the claims, and the terminology contained in the data. Definitions are used to establish the intended meaning of terms and create for the judge an accurate understanding of the point of view being advocated. In turn, the intended meaning established through definitions explains *how* the debater wants the judge to understand arguments and helps shape the decision-making process the judge will use.

Of course, understanding the role that definitions play in debate is only the first step in developing an affirmative case. Ultimately, to actually construct your case, you must be able to use an appropriate method to define terms and be able to assess the quality of your definitions. We address the first of those concerns in the next section.

Methods of Definition

The key terms in a debate may be defined in a variety of ways. In this section, we explain four primary methods debaters frequently use to define key terms: *standardized reference, contextual usage, example,* and *negation.* Each of these methods can be productively used to define the terms for an affirmative case for either a policy or nonpolicy proposition. Each method of definition has its own strengths and weaknesses. We encourage debaters to select the method that is most appropriate for the nature of the terms they are defining and which they feel most capable of defending. We also encourage debaters, when possible, to use a variety of methods to define the key terms.

Using a standardized reference to define a term is a common practice in both everyday argument and formal debate. The first way most people learn to define terms is by consulting a standardized reference such as a dictionary or encyclopedia. Definitions contained in standardized references are widely regarded as authoritative because they are developed by people considered to be experts on the common usage of terms. As a result, we have become accustomed to give deference to standardized references to resolve disputes about definitions.

Debaters may draw definitions from two sorts of standardized references. Standardized reference works such as the *New American Webster Dictionary* and the *Random House Dictionary* provide the accepted **common usage** of a term because they denote how that term can be used generally or how the term is likely to be used across a variety of contexts. For example, when debating the proposition, "Resolved: that the United States should significantly increase development of the earth's ocean resources," many debaters defined the term *increase* to mean to "make greater; extend in bulk, size, number, degree, and so on." That definition is the common usage of the term as prescribed in the *New American Webster Dictionary.*

On the other hand, standardized reference works such as *Black's Law Dictionary, Words and Phrases, Corpus Juris Secundum, Ballantines Law Dictionary,* and the *Encyclopedia of Philosophy* denote the **specialized meaning** of a term within the particular field for which the standardized reference work was developed—such as law, medicine, science, or philosophy. Definitions contained in standardized reference works such as these may be more precise and technical than the definitions found in standardized reference works that denote common usage. For example, *Webster's Third New International Dictionary* defines the term *nation* as "a community of people composed of one or more nationalities and possessing a more or less defined territory and government" (1505), while *Ballantines Law Dictionary* defines the same term as "A body politic or society of mankind united together for the purpose of promoting their mutual safety and advantage by their combined strength, occupying a definite territory and politically organized under one government" (830). As you can see, *Ballantines Law Dictionary* identifies specific purposes of a nation as a defining characteristic, whereas *Webster's Third New International Dictionary* does not.

The second common method for defining terms in debate is through contextual usage. Definitions derived from contextual usage denote how a term is actually used by experts within a particular field. Contextual usage is likely to coincide with definitions from specialized reference sources, but it may not precisely replicate the definition. Because we assume that experts within the field have the most complete and current understanding of a term, contextual usage is widely regarded in debate to be a sound method of definition. Noted economist Milton Friedman provided a contextual definition of the term *free enterprise* in his address entitled "The Future of Capitalism."

> In talking about freedom it is important at the outset to distinguish two different meanings on the economic level, of the concept of free enterprise, for there is no term which is more misused or misunderstood. The one meaning that is often attached to free enterprise is the meaning that enterprises shall be free to do what they want. This is not the meaning that has historically been attached to free enterprise. What we really mean by free enterprise is the freedom of individuals to set up enterprises. It is the freedom of an individual to engage in an activity so long as he uses only voluntary methods of getting others to cooperate with him. (245)

Contextual definitions might also be stipulated by experts and included in formal documents such as reports, policies, hearings, or scientific studies. In such cases, the experts who compose the definition attempt to codify exactly what they presume a term to mean and exactly how that term is used within the context of the document in which it is reported. One famous example of a stipulated contextual definition is the definition of "obscenity" provided by the Supreme Court of the United States in the landmark *Miller v. California* decision in 1973.

"Obscene" means that to the average person, applying contemporary standards, the predominant appeal of the matter, taken as a whole, is to prurient interests, i.e., a shameful or morbid interest in nudity, sex, or excretion, which goes substantially beyond customary limits of candor in description or representation of such matters and is matter which is utterly without redeeming social importance. (17)

Contextual definitions stipulated in documents generally provide a precise and binding definition of the term within the parameters of the document. Such definitions are presumed to be the only definition recognized within the boundaries of the document to be legitimate. Whether such definitions are applicable in other contexts, of course, depends on the similarity between the circumstances prescribed in the document and those outside the document to which the definition is being applied.

The third method a debater might use to define terms is through example. When using example to define a term, debaters will provide an actual instance of the term as a way of clarifying what they intend for that term to mean. In debating the nonpolicy proposition, "Resolved: that continued United States covert involvement in Central America would be undesirable," the affirmative might define the term *covert involvement* by example:

By covert involvement, we mean the type of activity such as occurred with the Sandinista freedom fighters in which our government provided military support on an ongoing basis to an indigenous, nongovernment-sponsored group.

A definition by example establishes a general similarity between the characteristics and conditions of the given example and the intended usage of the term. It does, however, presume that the major characteristics and conditions of the given example accurately describe those in the term being defined.

Using an example can add concreteness to a definition since it identifies an actual occurrence of the term being defined. However, the effectiveness of this method of definition is ultimately related to others' familiarity with the given example. If the judge or opponents are unfamiliar with the example being used, it is unlikely that they will be able to extract a clear understanding of the term being defined. Thus, debaters should be prepared to delineate the specific primary characteristics and conditions of the given example, and further, they should be prepared to defend those characteristics as reasonable descriptors of the term being defined.

The final primary method debaters use to define terms is negation. When using negation, a debater explains what a term does *not* mean. For example, when debating the proposition, "Resolved: that advertising degrades the quality of life in the United States," the affirmative might use negation to explain that they do not intend for the term *quality of life* to mean the "basic standard of living commonly measured in increases and decreases of disposable income." From this example, it is apparent that using the method of negation does not enable a debater to establish the definition of a term directly; a debater cannot precisely establish what a term does mean by saying what it does not mean. Explaining what a term does not mean, however, can reduce potential ambiguity about the intended meaning of the term. Thus, when the method of negation is used in conjunction with another method, it can be an effective tool to clarify the intended meaning of a term.

In one of our previous illustrations, the debaters used the method of example to define the term *covert involvement.* Their intended meaning of the term could have been further clarified had they combined the definition by example with the method of negation. Such a construction could have been presented as follows.

> By covert involvement, we mean the type of activity such as occurred with the Sandinista freedom fighters in which our government provided military support on an ongoing basis to an indigenous, nongovernment-sponsored group (method of example). We do not mean activities sponsored solely for the purpose of gathering information vital to our national security (method of negation).

Combining the method of negation with the method of example provides a much clearer sense of the intended meaning of the term because it eliminates one possible misinterpretation: that the term *covert involvement* refers to vital intelligence gathering activities as well as paramilitary operations.

Principles for Defining Terms

In developing the definition component of their case, debaters should consider six major principles, discussed here. First, *the affirmative must assume their responsibility to define the key terms.* As the initiator of the dispute and the initial source in the communicative interaction, the affirmative side has the responsibility of defining the crucial terms in the debate. Remember, defining terms is a basic requirement that every affirmative team must meet.

Second, *the affirmative should define all key terms.* To make the debate as meaningful as possible, the affirmative team should define every term critical to its advocacy of the proposition. That responsibility extends to both the key terms in the proposition and the key recurring terms the affirmative uses in their advocacy of that proposition.

Third, *the affirmative should not over-define terms*. Definitions are critical to the debate; however, the best definition is not always the most complex one. Definitions should be complete and thorough, but the affirmative team should not unnecessarily complicate definitions either by defining unimportant terms or by presenting overly complex and tedious definitions.

Fourth, *the affirmative should present clear definitions*. Definitions are valuable only if they help clarify meaning. To do that, definitions must be understandable, less abstract than the term they are defining, and clearly stated. Definitions that are ambiguous, poorly presented and explained, or obtuse can undermine the communicative interaction, the advocacy, and critical inquiry of the debate process.

Fifth, *the affirmative should present reasonable definitions*. Definitions are designed to provide a mutually understandable basis for advocating a point of view about the debate proposition. While the affirmative team wants to ensure that the definitions they provide are consistent with and complementary to the advocacy approaches they use, definitions should not be used primarily to gain strategic advantage. Definitions that are too narrow and unduly restrict negative ground can damage the credibility of the advocates, undermine critical inquiry about the proposition, and subvert the educational value of the debate process.

Finally, *definitions must have some basis of support*. When the affirmative side presents a definition, they are in essence presenting a claim about the meaning of a term. As with all claims presented in a debate, the advocate of the claim must be able to provide an adequate basis of support for the claim. Thus, although the affirmative members might "believe" or "think" that a particular definition is appropriate, they must ultimately be able to provide sufficient support to demonstrate that to be the case.

The Rationale

The rationale is the largest component of the affirmative case. It includes those claims and evidence that the affirmative team advances to develop their point of view about the proposition. In this respect, therefore, the rationale components of an affirmative case for either a nonpolicy or a policy proposition are fundamentally similar. In this section, we discuss the general task of developing claims that every affirmative debater—regardless of the proposition type being debated—must address.

At the same time, however, the claims contained in the rationale must address the stock issues of the particular proposition type being debated; thus, the nature of the claims included in the rationale are somewhat different for cases designed for a nonpolicy proposition and those developed for a policy proposition. In addition, the rationales for nonpolicy and policy propositions will differ in other significant ways: the rationale of an affirmative case for a nonpolicy proposition will include a criteria component; the rationale for a policy proposition will include a specific plan of action. In Chapters 12 and 13 we elaborate on those unique aspects of the rationale components for nonpolicy and policy propositions, respectively.

Developing Claims for the Rationale

Whether a team is debating a policy or a nonpolicy proposition, a most basic task is to develop the claims that will be included in the affirmative case. As you recall from Chapter 3, a claim is the specific idea for which one side is trying to gain acceptance in the debate. Virtually every affirmative case is constructed with three specific types of claims: the **ultimate claim**, **major claims**, and **supporting claims.** The ultimate claim is the overall idea argued by the affirmative side as the idea that should be accepted. In every affirmative case, that overall idea is expressed in the formal debate proposition. Thus, in a debate of the policy proposition, "Resolved: that the United States should significantly increase the development of the earth's ocean resources," the ultimate claim for the affirmative case would be "the United States should significantly increase the development of the earth's ocean resources." Similarly, in debating the nonpolicy proposition, "Resolved: that significant reform of U.S. ocean shipping policy would be desirable," the ultimate claim would be that *significant reform of U.S. ocean shipping policy would be desirable.*

Major claims are those broad ideas the affirmative team attempts to demonstrate to justify acceptance of the ultimate claim. For example, in debating the proposition, "Resolved: that continued United States covert involvement in Central America would be undesirable," the affirmative might construct such major claims as "covert involvement undermines diplomatic relations" and "covert involvement precipitates direct military intervention" to support its advocacy of the ultimate claim—"continued United States covert involvement in Central America would be undesirable." The major claims are generally referred to as "contentions" and are demarcated as distinct divisions of the affirmative case. For example, the two previous major claims would be structured in the affirmative case in the following way.

> **CONTENTION 1:**   Covert involvement undermines diplomatic relations.
> **CONTENTION 2:**   Covert involvement precipitates direct military intervention.

Supporting claims are the ideas the debater advocates to support the major claims. In debating the proposition, "Resolved: that significantly stronger third party participation in the United States presidential elections would benefit the political process," the affirmative might construct a major claim such as "third party participation would increase voter turnout." To support that major claim, the affirmative might construct supporting claims such as "third party participation rekindles interest among voters who feel disenfranchised," and "third party participation motivates issue-specific voters." As you can see, the supporting claims—assuming the affirmative is able to offer adequate data to support them and is further able to defend the data and claims from attacks offered by the negative—actually function within the affirmative case as support for the major claims.

Just as the major claims are demarcated as distinct divisions within the affirmative case, so too are the supporting claims separated within the structure of the major claim. In the previous example, the major claim and supporting claims might be structured in the affirmative case in the following way.

CONTENTION 1:   Third party participation would increase voter turnout. Supporting Claim A: Third party participation rekindles interest among voters who feel disenfranchised. Supporting Claim B: Third party participation motivates issue-specific voters.

Major and supporting claims can be designed to function as either *independent* or *dependent justification*. A claim offers independent justification for a superseding claim (for example, major claim for the ultimate claim and supporting claim for the major claim) when, assuming it is proven, that claim can stand alone as justification for the superseding claim. In the previous example, we offered two supporting claims for the major claim, "Third party participation would increase voter turnout." Both of those supporting claims provide independent justification for the major claim because they focus on distinctly different cause-effect relationships of the issue—disenfranchised voters and single-issue voters.

Claims that must function in conjunction with other claims provide dependent justification. In our first example in this section, we used the following major claim: "Covert involvement precipitates direct military intervention." To develop that claim we could offer the following supporting claims: (1) the number of covert involvements is increasing; (2) the greater the number of involvements, the greater is the likelihood of discovery; and (3) discovery increases the likelihood of direct military intervention. These supporting claims function in conjunction with each other as support for the major claim because neither can stand alone as adequate support for the major claim.

There are strengths and weaknesses inherent in using claims that function either independently or dependently as justification for a superseding claim.

Claims that function as independent justification provide more flexibility for the affirmative side. Because the affirmative need to win only a single independent claim to support the superseding claim, they gain more latitude in deciding how to focus their advocacy; they can choose to emphasize one independent claim almost to the exclusion of another. Conversely, when the claims are dependent, the affirmative team has less latitude because they must win all the dependent claims. However, dependent claims generally offer a more complete basis of support for the superseding claim. Dependent claims explore multiple dimensions and provide greater detail about a single aspect of the issue. They more thoroughly explain the basis of support for the superseding claim. Conversely, independent claims will be more general.

Principles for Constructing Claims

Constructing major and supporting claims is an exceedingly important part of developing an affirmative case. Claims should be carefully constructed and properly formulated. Affirmative debaters should incorporate the following four principles when constructing the major and supporting claims for their affirmative case.

First, *construct a reasonable number of major claims.* Remember that every major claim must be accompanied by sufficient supporting material and explanation to be accepted. The more major claims the affirmative team include in their case, the less completely developed each claim is likely to be. Although affirmative debaters may believe that some strategic advantage is to be gained by presenting numerous major claims in their rationale, they are likely to discover that the negative side benefits from having claims to refute that are less developed.

Second, *make certain all claims are clearly worded.* Every claim should be stated as specifically and succinctly as possible. Claims should encompass a single major theme and should be phrased in the simplest possible terms. As far as possible, claims should be phrased as a declarative statement and be void of potentially confusing technical terminology.

Third, *claims should be carefully selected.* The affirmative debaters should carefully consider what claims to include in the case. Only those they can support and defend should be presented. Claims should be included if they correlate with the stock issues of the particular type of proposition being debated and if they further add to or explicate the affirmative team's point of view about that proposition. All major claims must be clearly relevant to the ultimate claim just as the supporting claims must be relevant to the major claim.

Fourth, *the body of claims must be as thorough as possible.* Because of time constraints in a formal debate, it will not be possible to include every conceivable major and supporting claim in your case. It is necessary, however, for the body of claims you do present to constitute a solid foundation of support—a prima facie case—for the ultimate claim—the formal proposition. To ensure that and thereby fulfill THE BURDEN OF PROOF, your major claims must address the requisite stock issues inherent in the type of proposition you are debating.

Conclusion

How well the affirmative debaters develop their case will be critical to their success. The affirmative case must be developed carefully and completely. Decisions about what to include in the case should be based on informed choice rather than haphazard guesswork. Whether the debate concerns a policy or a nonpolicy proposition, every affirmative case will contain preliminary and summary components, definitions, and a rationale. The preliminary and summary components as well as the definitions will usually be constructed in similar ways, whether the case is developed for a policy or a nonpolicy proposition. The rationale component will also be similar to the extent that it will consist of a series of major and supporting claims.

In a case for a nonpolicy proposition, the rationale will consist of criteria; in a policy case, it will consist of a plan and a justification of the plan. In the following chapters we elaborate more fully on the differences between affirmative cases for nonpolicy and policy propositions.

Note

1. *1989 National CEDA Tournament Final Round,* transcripts edited by James Brey. The affirmative case was presented by William DeForest and Dave Hansen of Gonzaga University.

Selected Bibliography

Ballantines Law Dictionary. 1969 ed.

Cantrill, James G. "Definitional Issues in the Pursuit of Argumentative Understandings." *CEDA Yearbook* 9 (1988): 45–53.

Friedman, Milton. "The Future of Capitalism." *Contemporary American Speeches.* Eds. Wil Linkugel, R. R. Allen, and Richard Johannsen. Dubuque, IA: Kendall-Hunt, 1978.

Jensen, Scott, and E. Sam Cox. "An Alternative Method for Approaching Non-Policy Propositions." *The Forensic of Pi Kappa Delta* 77 (Spring 1992): 1–14.

Micken, Kathleen F., and Patrick H. Micken. "Debating Values: An Idea Revisited." *CEDA Yearbook* 14 (1993): 54–71.

Murphy, Thomas L., and Melinda Murphy. "Resolutional Relevance: A Primary Standard for Evaluating Criteria in Non-Policy Debate." *CEDA Yearbook* 11 (1990): 1–8.

413 U.S. Supreme Court. Miller v. California. 1973.

Webster's Third New International Dictionary. 1965 ed.

Discussion Questions

1. Is any method a debater might use to define terms likely to be more effective than another? Why?
2. What potential pitfalls should a debater avoid when constructing the preliminary and summary components for an affirmative case?
3. After constructing some sample claims for the rationale for your case, evaluate those claims according to the principles discussed in the chapter. How might your claims be improved?

CHAPTER 2

DEVELOPING AN AFFIRMATIVE CASE FOR A NONPOLICY PROPOSITION

*E*very affirmative case includes a preliminary and summary component, a definition component, and a rationale. There is little difference in the preliminary and summary components for affirmative cases for policy or nonpolicy propositions. There are differences, however, in the definition and rationale components, depending on the type of proposition being debated. In this chapter, we discuss the unique aspects of constructing the definition and rationale components for affirmative cases for nonpolicy propositions. First, we identify the key terms of a nonpolicy proposition that need to be defined. Second, we discuss fully how to construct criteria for the rationale component of an affirmative case for a nonpolicy proposition. Finally, we will explain how to complete the rationale component by constructing claims related to the criteria.

As you read this chapter, keep in mind that it is a continuation of Chapter 11. To understand how to develop an affirmative case for a nonpolicy proposition, you must be familiar with the principles contained in both chapters.

Defining Terms for a Nonpolicy Case

Before writing a successful definition component, debaters must first identify the terms that need to be defined. Two major types of terms need definition in any affirmative case: *key terms of the proposition* and *key recurring terms of their advocacy*. In this section, we discuss how to locate each of these types of terms in a nonpolicy proposition and explain why each must be adequately defined.

As you recall from Chapter 7, nonpolicy propositions can contain four types of terms: the *object of focus,* the *situational qualifier,* the *judgmental qualifier,* and the *judgmental term.* Each of those terms would need to be defined if a listener were to understand clearly the affirmative debaters' interpretation and advocacy of the proposition. The object of focus, the situational qualifier, and the judgmental qualifier are usually defined in the definitions component of the affirmative case. The judgmental term, however, is typically defined within the rationale of the case, and specifically within the criteria component of the affirmative case. We discuss development of criteria for the rationale of the case more fully in the next section of the chapter.

Because the object of focus in a nonpolicy proposition is the concept being evaluated, it must be clearly and precisely defined. The affirmative must state exactly what they intend for that term to mean. We have, to this point, given numerous examples of objects of focus in nonpolicy debate propositions (such as "covert military operations," "imposition of more severe penalties," "mandatory drug tests," and "the right to privacy"). As you can tell from those examples, the object of focus in a nonpolicy debate proposition is likely to be a broad concept that might be defined in more than one way. For example, "covert military operations" may entail many different sorts of involvement—providing high-level advisers, infiltrating enemy decision making, providing weapons or supplies, and so on. Similarly, there are a number of ways to "impose more severe penalties"—mandatory minimum sentences, structured sentencing, "three strikes and you're out" sentencing, or even capital punishment for persons convicted of felony crimes. The affirmative will need to provide clear definitions so that others will understand the specific meaning intended for the term.

It is also important to define the situational qualifier in a nonpolicy proposition because it specifies the context within which the object of focus must be judged. In the proposition, "Resolved: that membership in the United Nations is no longer beneficial to the United States, "*to the United States*" is a situational qualifier because it specifies the context in which the object of focus is to be judged. That is to say, "*membership in the United Nations*" (object of focus) must be shown to be no longer beneficial (judgmental term) "to the United States" (situational qualifier). It would be impossible to assess accurately the relevance of specific claims and support, or the overall probable truth of the proposition without knowing exactly what "to the United States" means.

It is necessary to define the judgmental qualifier because it clarifies the nature—usually how encompassing—the judgment must be. For example, in the proposition, "Resolved: that the United States Supreme Court, on balance, has granted excessive power to law enforcement agencies," the phrase "on-balance" is the judgmental qualifier because it specifies how encompassing that judgment (excessive) must be. Thus, to determine whether an advocate's case demonstrates the probable truth of that proposition, it would be absolutely essential to know exactly what "on-balance" means in order to determine how encompassing the claims and support presented must be.

After identifying the key terms used to construct the debate proposition, debaters should next define any key recurring terms that emerge in their advocacy of the proposition. We say key recurring terms "emerge" to indicate that they usually follow from the particular advocacy of the proposition. Key recurring terms appear in claims or evidence presented in a debate and have a direct bearing on how those claims or evidence are understood and interpreted. For example, in the nonpolicy proposition, "Resolved: that covert military operations undermine the national security interest of the United States," one key recurring term likely to emerge in the debate is *"plausible deniability."* Both affirmative and negative debaters will probably advance claims that focus on the consequences occurring when covert military operations are discovered. The ability or inability to "plausibly deny" a covert operation can have a significant impact on post-discovery effects. Obviously, it would be impossible to assess critically the claims either side makes without clearly understanding what constitutes "plausible deniability."

Criteria: An Overview

Criteria, as we illustrate throughout this chapter, are critical to nonpolicy debate. In this section, we explain the role of criteria in nonpolicy debate and how debaters can develop criteria. To accomplish those purposes, we discuss the key functions of criteria in nonpolicy judgment, explain the process debaters should use to develop criteria, and compare the two primary methods debaters can use to construct criteria. To ensure that you understand thoroughly what a criterion is and why the use of criteria is integrally related to reasoned decision making, we begin our discussion by illustrating the role of criteria in everyday argument and public advocacy.

Criteria in Decision Making

Criteria give us the yardstick by which we determine what judgments should be made and how they should be made. For instance, you may decide to buy a particular car for any number of "reasons"—it costs very little to operate, it promises to last a long time with low maintenance expenses, it will have excellent resale value, or it has the color and styling you desire. Whatever reasons you have for purchasing a specific car, those reasons make up the yardstick you used to determine how to make the judgment. The criterion is a value statement; it declares what is important to you in this particular situation. By using a criterion, you can sort through various competing reasons and select only those that will best help you to meet your goal, or criterion. If you cannot decide between a cost-efficient car and a sporty, great-looking model, your indecision probably stems from either (1) unclear criteria about what you are looking for in an automobile or (2) indecision about which of the two criteria should take precedence.[1] Together with deciding on common definitions, establishing clear criteria—the goals we wish to meet—is a first step in any rational, effective decision-making process.

In public advocacy, we use criteria in the same way—as the yardstick by which we determine which claims are important. Criteria identify the general values or goals an advocate maintains that (1) we aspire to and (2) are relevant to the issues at hand. Further, we use criteria to decide whether a behavior or belief is warranted and to decide which among several competing, warranted beliefs is the most compelling.

In any public advocacy, at least one set of criteria must be present. Sometimes these criteria are implicit, in which case the advocate has assumed that the audience agrees with the implied goals. In his Atlanta Exposition Address of 1895, Booker T. Washington presumed that his audience was interested in material gain. He assumed that his listeners would accept that criterion and judge it to be important. Given the setting—an exposition celebrating the commercial progress of the post–Civil War South—Washington's assumption was probably warranted. Throughout the speech, Washington used an "economic prosperity" criterion to justify his recommendations to African-Americans and to white Southerners. Implicitly, Washington felt that African-Americans *needed* to learn to dignify and glorify common labor because *prosperity*—exemplified through the criterion of material gain—was the audience's goal. Similarly, he argued that Southern whites should help African-Americans achieve economic prosperity because the economic well-being of both groups was inextricably tied together. Prosperity was desired and it should be pursued, his argument went, and so whatever helped meet that goal—helped them prosper—was good.

Where Booker T. Washington implicitly incorporated his criterion into his speech, other persuaders will explicitly state and defend their criteria. W. E. B. Du Bois's speech on disfranchisement, delivered to the National American Woman Suffrage Association in 1912, provides an illustrative case (230–38). In this speech, Du Bois argued on behalf of voting rights for African-Americans. In doing so, he chose to rebut five oppositional arguments: that African-Americans (1) were too ignorant to vote intelligently, (2) were too inexperienced to be trusted to vote responsibly, (3) would misuse the privilege, (4) did not need the right to vote, and (5) did not want the right to vote. Du Bois grounded his rebuttal in a simple criterion: any law that affects the governance of a nation should be measured against how well or how poorly it sustains and improves democracy. Within that criterion he embedded a particular standard of democracy: democracy functions best when every citizen's voice is heard through the ballot. He justifies the criterion and standard through reasoning by identifying the characteristics that differentiate democracy from other forms of government, and through history by tracing the evolution from monarchy to democracy.

Having firmly established his criterion, Du Bois is then able to use that criterion to develop rebuttals to each of the opposition's arguments. African-Americans are too ignorant? It is the responsibility of a democratic government to educate them, so that all might bring their knowledge to the further benefit of democratic government. Further, no matter how "ignorant" one is according to an educated person's standards, each person—educated or not—knows the world from his or her own unique perspective. Indeed, it is this "unique perspective" that democratic government is designed to recognize and use; therefore, each person must be allowed to vote if democratic government is to work fully.

African-Americans are too inexperienced to be trusted to vote? Every individual and every class of individuals was inexperienced in voting at one time. They were given the vote because, again, no one could vote in a way that represented another's unique perspective and knowledge. African-Americans would misuse the privilege? Perhaps it is only by allowing them to misuse it that they will learn how to use it correctly, a use that is important if democracy is to achieve its full potential.

African-Americans do not need the ballot? Du Bois's theory of democracy argued that it is not so much the voter who needs the ballot but the government that needs the voter's participation. If the body politic is to gain from African-Americans' knowledge, then society must insist on extending the right to vote to all excluded groups.

African-Americans do not want the right to vote? Du Bois disputes that on factual grounds, but his theory of democracy also means that voting is not a right—it is a responsibility. It is only through the involvement of all its citizens that a democracy attains its fullest measure of strength and justice.

Du Bois's speech is a representative example of an advocate's use of criteria. Moreover, his criteria closely resemble "argument fields," discussed later. He does not say that the promotion of democracy is the ultimate goal in every situation. His criterion—the promotion of democracy—applies only to decisions about "how to govern." For those decisions, his criterion is relevant; or, put another way, his criterion is drawn from the argument field of "government and governance."

Our purpose in discussing these speeches is not to suggest that criteria used in everyday argument and public advocacy are developed in precisely the same way as criteria used in nonpolicy debate. In some cases there will be similarities; at other times the methods of developing and using criteria will differ greatly. For example, a debater should not use implied criteria as Washington did, nor will a debater have the time to justify "the promotion of democracy" through a grand, sweeping history of the evolution of government as did Du Bois. Regardless of these differences, however, criteria are important components of everyday argument and public advocacy. Criteria are no less important in formal debate. In the next section we discuss their importance more fully.

Functions of Criteria

Criteria are widely recognized to be an indispensable component of nonpolicy debate. Specifically, criteria perform three functions in nonpolicy debate: (1) they clarify the decision-making process that will be followed, (2) they help identify the important issues in the debate, and (3) they help instruct the development of claims for a case. Because of their integral role in nonpolicy judgment, criteria represent a stock issue of nonpolicy debate.

The first function of criteria in nonpolicy debate is to *clarify the decision-making process to be used.* Criteria do this by specifying the standards that will be used to make the judgment. For example, in the proposition, "Resolved: that the United States is justified in providing military support to nondemocratic governments," we might include in the criterion for "justified" the standard "that which promotes peace and stability is preferable." The next general step of the decision-making process is now clear: the affirmative needs to demonstrate that providing military support to nondemocratic governments promotes peace and stability. If the negative accepts the affirmative's criterion, then their argumentative path is also clear: to show that providing military support to nondemocratic governments does not promote, or perhaps even deters, the achievement of peace and stability. In this way, criteria can be said to clarify the decision-making process that debaters will follow.

The second function of criteria is to help *identify the potential issues of the debate.* Each standard included in the criterion becomes a potential issue that will likely be disputed in the debate. In the example given above, the issues will be "peace" and "stability." Which actions promote peace? Which ones yield stability? Which alternatives might better produce one or both of those? On the other hand, if the affirmative's criterion was "that which improves economic relations between the United States and nondemocratic countries is desirable," then the issues debated will be different ones. Now the discussion is focused on market forces, international economics, and government-subsidized trading. Thus, criteria help define the range of potential issues that might be considered in a nonpolicy debate.

The third function of criteria is *to guide the development of a complete and coherent case.* Considering the criterion "that which promotes peace and stability is preferable," the affirmative would be required to develop claims to demonstrate how each standard—peace and stability—is satisfied. For example, they could claim that military support creates the incentive for better diplomatic relations, which in turn yields the improved likelihood of peace and stability. Or the affirmative could argue that, empirically, such military support has been necessary in the past for ensuring domestic and international tranquility. Because the world has not changed, the argument would go, such military support will clearly be justifiable for the foreseeable future as well. Although many different cases could be developed using the same criterion, in each case the criterion would provide the particular decision-making goals toward which the case works. By providing the specific "destination," it creates a structure for the "journey." In that sense, criteria will always help guide case development in nonpolicy debate.

Because criteria are such an integral component of nonpolicy judgment, they function as a stock issue in any nonpolicy debate. In many debates, the criterion even becomes the primary "voting issue." When both sides have proposed different criteria, and each side has demonstrated that their own case meets their criterion while the other side's does not, then the advocate who "wins" the argument about the criterion "wins" the debate. Even in a debate where the criterion per se is not the primary "voting issue," it will influence how the other substantive voting issues will be resolved.[2] Criteria are thus a valuable, and unavoidable, component of nonpolicy debate.

In discussing the role of criteria in nonpolicy debate, we have emphasized the part they play in the affirmative's case and argument. Note, however, that the negative team may *reject* the affirmative's criteria and, indeed, propose **countercriteria** of their own. In that instance, the countercriterion performs the same three functions for the negative team's case and argument. Or, if the negative side *accepts* the affirmative team's proposed criteria, then the *affirmative* criteria perform the same three functions for the negative as well as the affirmative team. Because they operate as such an integral part of the decision-making process, criteria need to be constructed clearly, carefully, and cogently. Accordingly, we turn now to the process of developing criteria.

Developing Criteria: The Process

The criterion statement in a debate may be either simple or complex, but constructing the appropriate criteria is never a simple matter. Debaters need to keep in mind both the role of criteria in nonpolicy debate and the theoretical underpinnings of criteria in nonpolicy judgment. In this section, we suggest a three-step process that unites theory with practice. The stages of the process are (1) identifying the components of the resolution, (2) constructing the argument field, and (3) developing field-dependent standards. As we discuss stages two

and three, we integrate two theoretical constructs of criteria in nonpolicy judgment that provide the grounding for the process: **argument fields** and **field-
dependence.** The central objective in stage three is to develop standards that are
field-dependent, that is, are drawn from the appropriate argument field. As we
discuss stage three, our goal is to explain how that can be done.

Identifying the Components of the Proposition

Stage one of the process always consists of identifying the primary components
of the debate proposition. This stage is not complicated but it is essential. If the
components of the proposition are not properly identified, constructing the criteria rationally is impossible.

As we explained earlier in this chapter, every nonpolicy proposition has two
major components: an object of focus and a judgmental term. The object of
focus is the entity (person, concept, event) that is being judged or evaluated,
and the judgmental (or evaluative) term specifies the judgment or evaluation
the advocate is required to make about that object of focus. You also know that
two other components may be included in nonpolicy propositions: a situational
qualifier and/or a judgmental qualifier. A situational qualifier specifies the situation within which we are to judge the object of focus; the judgmental qualifier
clarifies the nature of the judgment to be made.

Although identifying the components of the proposition is not particularly
difficult, it is nonetheless critical to the process of developing the criterion.
Identifying the object of focus is important because it is the component of the
proposition for which an argument field must be constructed. Identifying the
judgmental term is important because it specifies the judgment for which
the field-dependent criterion must be formulated. Identifying the situational
qualifier is important because it clarifies the specific situation in which the judgment is to be made and affects how a field-dependent criterion will be formulated. The judgmental qualifier is important because it specifies the force of the
judgment to be made. Put simply, it is impossible to develop an appropriate criterion without first determining what is being judged, what judgment must be
made, the situation in which it must be made, and the nature of that judgment.

Constructing the Argument Field

Stage two in developing the criteria is to construct the **argument field.** Stephen
Toulmin introduced the concept of argument field as a way of better understanding both the "form and merits" of argument (15). In a general sense, the
field is the perspective from which the object of focus is being judged. Thus,
Toulmin holds that we will judge a legal argument using standards appropriate
to the "field" of law, medical arguments using standards appropriate to the

"field" of medicine, diplomatic arguments using the standards appropriate to the "field" of diplomacy, and so on. Many argumentation theorists have studied the concept of argument fields, and there is general agreement that arguments are judged according to the standards of the field of inquiry in which they are made. As argumentation scholar Robert Rowland writes, it "seems obvious that arguments vary by field" (228).

The principle of argument fields is particularly important in understanding and developing criteria in nonpolicy debate. Every nonpolicy judgment consists of two components: the *force of the judgment* and the *criterion used to make the judgment*. According to Toulmin, the force of a judgment—its connotative and denotative meaning coupled with the response it elicits from auditors—is generally similar across fields. Thus, the force of a judgment can be said to be **field-invariant;** that is, it does not change when the argument field changes. Consider, for example, that four people make the following judgments:

- Person 1: "That is a great car."
  Person 2: "That is a great university."
  Person 3: "That is a great book."
  Person 4: "He was a great president."

In each case the judgment is the same—the object of focus is judged to be "great." Across these cases, the "force" of that judgment is, broadly, similar. Whether it be applied to cars, universities, books, or presidents, "great" connotes and denotes a judgment of excellence. In nonpolicy debate, the judgmental term—for example, *would benefit, is desirable, is adequate*—is field-invariant. Regardless of the particular resolution, our connotative and denotative meaning of a judgmental term remains similar across situations.

However, the criteria used to make nonpolicy judgments are field-dependent. Toulmin draws a crucial distinction between the field-invariance of the force of a judgment and the field-dependence of the criteria used to make that judgment:

> It has to be recognized that the *force* of commending something as "good" or commending it as "bad" remains the same, whatever sort of thing it may be, even though the criteria for judging or assessing the merits of different kinds are very variable. (33)

Toulmin's point is aptly illustrated in our previous examples. You would use different standards to judge the "greatness" of a car from those you would use to judge the "greatness" of a university, of a book, of a teacher, and so on. Cars, universities, books, and teachers can all be judged to be "great," but their "greatness" is likely to be a product of vastly different considerations or criteria.

Criteria for nonpolicy judgments also vary according to the field in which they are made. You may judge a covert operation to be beneficial as an intelligence gathering tool but detrimental as a political assassination tool, or you may judge a president to be good with foreign policy but bad with domestic policy. Just as nonpolicy judgments vary according to the field in which they are made, so too must the criteria used to make those judgments.

When a criterion does *not* illuminate those properties relevant to the particular field, no reasonable judgment about the object can be made. For example, you could no more say that an intelligence gathering tool is beneficial because of its ability to eliminate hostile leaders than you could judge an international political assassination squad beneficial because it produces accurate information. Similarly, you would not situate "compulsory national service for all qualified United States citizens" (object of focus) within the field of public policy and use the same criteria to judge that object of focus as you would use to judge that object of focus if it were situated in the field of education. Hence, criteria are used to render field-dependent judgments about the object of focus, and to do that they must themselves be composed of standards that are field-dependent. We discuss criteria and standards more specifically in the third step of the process.

Two distinct methods of defining the argument field have been suggested for nonpolicy debate: **discipline-based construction** and **purpose-based construction.** Regarding discipline-based construction, debate scholar Don Brownlee has identified two meanings of *discipline* that can be used to locate the argument field of the object of focus: (1) the discipline of the preponderance of "experts" who deal with the object of focus, or (2) the discipline in which the object of focus is most regularly studied. For example, in the proposition, "Resolved: that compulsory national service for all qualified United States citizens is desirable," "compulsory national service for all qualified citizens" (the object of focus) might be judged within the field of public policy if the preponderance of expert sources who discuss compulsory national service are policy analysts or if proposals for compulsory national service are most frequently studied within the discipline of policy analysis. However, if most of the evidence about compulsory national service came from politicians, or if it was most frequently studied in the discipline of political science, then the object of focus might be said to reside in the field of political science. Similarly, in the proposition, "Resolved: that United States higher education has sacrificed quality for institutional survival," "United States higher education" (the object of focus) might be considered to be within the field of education if the preponderance of sources of evidence about that object of focus are "education experts" or if the discipline of education is where it is most frequently studied. Typically in non-policy debate, discipline-based constructions would give us argument fields such as public policy, law, economics, criminal justice, political science, ethics, or government. Such argument fields would tend to mirror the disciplines that have been created at colleges and universities.

We do not intend to ignore the obvious overlap between disciplines and the fact that many objects of focus, particularly those contained in nonpolicy debate resolutions, are studied in multiple disciplines. However, even when the same object of focus is studied across disciplines, it is likely to prioritize those various fields (primary fields, supporting fields, tangential fields) and select as the argument field the one in which the object of focus is given *primary* emphasis. For example, "compulsory wage and price controls" (object of focus) might be studied in the fields of political science, economics, and law, but you might reasonably argue that economics is the primary field.

An alternative to the discipline-based construction is the purpose-based construction. To use the purpose-based construction, you need to determine what specific purpose or function the object of focus performs. We conceive of the object of focus as a *vehicle* for achieving a particular outcome, and that purpose or function then defines the argument field of the object of focus. For example, in one recent nonpolicy debate proposition, "Resolved: that membership in the United Nations is no longer beneficial to the United States," "membership in the United Nations" (the object of focus) might have been placed within the argument field of "a vehicle for preserving world peace" as preserving world peace was presumed to be one of the primary purposes of the organization. In another proposition, "Resolved: that increased restrictions on civilian possession of handguns in the United States would be justified," "increased restrictions on civilian possession of handguns" (the object of focus) might have been placed in the argument field of "a vehicle to decrease crime" as that outcome appears to be the primary purpose of the possible restriction. Similarly, "compulsory national service" might be placed in the argument field of "a citizen employment training program" if that is determined to be its function or purpose.

If the proposition contains a situational qualifier, that qualifier will be useful in constructing the argument field, particularly if the debater chooses to utilize a discipline-based construction. For example, in the proposition, "Resolved: that significantly stronger third party participation in the United States presidential elections would benefit the political process," the situational qualifier "political process" indicates that the object of focus would probably be placed in the "political" discipline, as that discipline most directly studies the political process.

Situational qualifiers do not similarly specify the argument field if a purpose-based construction is used. Here, the purpose of the object of focus is still

the element that defines the argument field. However, because situational qualifiers define the nature of the situation in which the judgment is to be made,
they will usually construct boundaries within which the object of focus's purpose must operate. In the previous example, you might employ a purpose-based
construction by arguing that "significantly stronger third party participation in
the United States presidential elections" (object of focus) should be viewed as a
vehicle to ensure that voters make informed decisions in elections. Such a construction is at least minimally acceptable because "ensuring that voters make
informed decisions in elections" clearly falls within what we would call "the
political process." To define "third party participation" as a vehicle for improving the economy (via the advertising revenues spent) would just as clearly fall
outside the boundaries of "the political process." In that sense, the situational
qualifier may restrict the potential functions or purposes from which the
debater may choose.

Regardless of which approach we take, the argument field of the object of
focus explains the context in which we are judging the object of focus.[3] In the
discipline-based construction, the object of focus is being judged *as a member of
a particular discipline;* in the purpose-based construction the object of focus is
being judged *as a vehicle for achieving a particular outcome.* For example, covert
operations (object of focus) might be evaluated as "foreign policy" (argument
field, discipline-based construction) or as "a vehicle for displacing government
leaders" (argument field, purpose-based construction).

Either method for determining the argument field ultimately clarifies the
interpretation of the nonpolicy debate proposition. For example, the proposition, "Resolved: that continued U.S. covert involvement in Central America
would be undesirable," can be stated as either (1) Resolved: that continued U.S
covert involvement in Central America (when viewed as foreign policy) would
be undesirable; or (2) Resolved: that continued U.S. covert involvement in
Central America (when viewed as a mechanism for displacing government leaders) would be undesirable. By determining the argument field, either construction helps clarify our interpretation of the proposition and moves us further
toward developing a cogent and appropriate criterion. In the third stage of the
process, field-dependent standards are drawn from the argument field identified
in stage two.

Developing Field-Dependent Standards

The third stage in the process of developing criteria is to identify field-
dependent **standards**. A *standard* is different from a *criterion*. A standard identifies the *specific* basis to be used in making a judgment. As we use the term, it is
roughly analogous to a *test* to be applied to the object of focus, or a *condition* the
object of focus must be shown to meet the criterion. When the object of focus

meets the standard set forth, the criterion has been satisfied and the judgment called for by the judgmental term of the resolution can be deemed "warranted." When the object of focus does not meet the standard, the criterion has not been satisfied and the judgment is not warranted. For example, if the criterion for "covert operation" is that it should "be a good intelligence gathering mechanism," you might identify two standards for measuring whether a covert operation has met that criterion: the operation must (1) "provide accurate information," and (2) "provide timely information." If the operation significantly meets these two standards, it—the object of focus—can be said to have met the criteria—that it is a "good intelligence gathering mechanism."

A criterion, then, is a composite of, or generalized statement about, all the standards used to judge the object of focus. If we stopped with the criterion itself, such as "it should promote democracy," we are left with a goal that may be desirable but is too vaguely worded for the kind of reasoned discussion called for in nonpolicy debate. By using standards to operationalize what we mean by "promoting democracy" or "good gathering of intelligence information," we answer the question, "How do we know when the goal (or criterion) has been met?"

To better understand the concept of field-dependent standards, consider formulating them like this:

$$X = \text{Object of Focus}$$
$$A, B, C, \text{ and so on} = \text{range of possible argument fields}$$
$$A^1, A^2, B^1, B^2, C^1, C^2, \text{ and so on} = \text{field-dependent standards}$$
$$Z = \text{judgment about the object of focus}$$

If the object of focus X is considered within argument field A, it would be necessary to meet standard A^1 (or A^2, A^3), to render judgment Z about that object of focus. If, however, X is considered within argument field B, then X must meet standard B^1 to warrant judgment Z.

The "covert operations" example could be formulated this way: If *covert operations* (X) are considered an *intelligence gathering mechanism* (A), it would be necessary to demonstrate that covert operations produce *accurate* (A^1) and *timely* (A^2) information to show that covert operations are *desirable* (Z). If, however, *covert operations* (X) are considered a *political assassination tool* (B), then the standards might be that covert operations should be successful in *removing unwanted political leaders* (B^1) and should be *plausibly deniable* (B^2).

There needs to be agreement between the argument field (A, B, or C) of the object of focus and the standards used to judge the object of focus. If X is considered *as A*, then standards B^1 or B^2 are irrelevant and inappropriate to the discussion. They become relevant and appropriate only when we view X *not as A,* but *as B*.

When the discipline-based construction is used, field-dependent standards can be derived from at least three different sources. First, a standard might be derived from the *theoretical assumptions of the discipline*. Theoretical assumptions reflect how the discipline understands those phenomena it studies. For example, we might use the assumption from the discipline of education that "learning occurs experientially" to formulate a standard for evaluating "U.S. higher education." Such a standard might be this: "U.S. higher education" (object of focus) is beneficial (judgmental term) if it can be shown to "make full use of experiential learning techniques" (standard).

Second, a standard might be derived from *norms within the discipline*. Norms reflect expectations about actions or behaviors. We might use the expectation that "publicly funded programs should utilize financial resources prudently" to evaluate "greater restrictions on welfare programs." The following standard might result: "greater restrictions on welfare programs" (object of focus) would be justified (judgmental term) if welfare programs were shown not to "utilize financial resources prudently" (standard).

Third, a standard might be derived from fundamental *philosophical principles of the discipline*. Philosophical principles reflect values to which the discipline subscribes or aspires. We might use the principle from criminal justice that "it is better to let the guilty go free than it is to incarcerate the innocent" to develop the standard to evaluate "cameras in the courtroom." Such a standard could be constructed like this: "cameras in the courtroom" (object of focus) are undesirable (judgmental term) if they can be shown to "jeopardize the rights of the innocent" (standard). The following is an example of criteria with a discipline-based construction.

Discipline-based construction
1. Mandatory drug testing should be viewed within the field of law (argument field).
2. Within the field of law, mandatory drug testing should be assessed according to the following standards (field-based standards):
   A. Legal precedent for such tests
   B. Degree to which tests violate rights

Standards for a purpose-based criterion are developed differently. Throughout this chapter we have provided several examples of such standards; for example, "accuracy" and "timeliness" as standards for an intelligence gathering mechanism; and "promoting diplomatic resolution of conflict" as a standard for a mechanism designed to promote international stability. In each instance, the field-dependent standards were derived from their primary connection to the object of focus when viewed as a particular *vehicle*.

Specifically, when a purpose-based construction is used, field-dependent standards can be drawn from two types of "connections." First, field-dependent standards might be derived from the *primary characteristics* that the particular type of vehicle would be expected to exhibit. The example of "covert operations" illustrates how field-dependent standards might be developed when primary characteristics are used. In that example, we used two characteristics—"accuracy" and "timeliness"—that such a vehicle (an intelligence gathering mechanism) would be expected to exhibit. In this method, we are constructing a *qualitative* judgment; that is, we want the vehicle to achieve a certain quality of product. It is not enough that the covert operation "gather intelligence"; the information must be of a certain quality—*accurate* and *timely*—for the vehicle that gathered the intelligence to be considered desirable.

Second, field-dependent standards might be drawn from *primary tasks* the vehicle is expected to accomplish to fulfill its primary purpose. If the United Nations (object of focus) is viewed as a vehicle to promote international stability, we might delineate three tasks that then become our standards: "achieving diplomatic resolution of conflict," "uniting diverse factions of the international community," and "providing a forum for developing international consensus." In this method, the judgment can be termed *factual* rather than qualitative. The object of focus is a success simply if it accomplishes the primary task. It does not matter what quality of diplomatic resolution the vehicle achieves; what matters is whether such a resolution is accomplished. Similarly, the quality of the forum for developing international consensus is irrelevant. The standard only asks that a forum be provided.

Neither method of deriving field-dependent standards—through primary characteristics or through primary tasks—is superior to the other. In some situations, vehicles will be asked to perform at certain levels of quality. In other situations, they will be successful simply if they accomplish the task. Which method is appropriate depends on the purpose the object of focus is being asked to perform. The following is an example of criteria developed with a purpose-based construction.

Purpose-based construction
1. Mandatory drug testing should be viewed as a mechanism designed to increase workplace safety (argument field).
2. The following standards should be used to assess mandatory drug testing (field-based standards):
A. Ability to detect drug use
B. Ability to deter drug use by employees
C. Reduction in number of workplace accidents

Comparing Discipline- and Purpose-Based Standards

Both discipline-based standards and purpose-based standards offer the debater advantages and disadvantages. There are two important advantages that discipline-based construction offers. First, discipline-based argument fields are often *readily identifiable*. In many cases, the general area of study within which the object of focus typically falls will be obvious. In every case, a discipline of the experts who study the object of focus can be easily ascertained. Second, using the discipline-based construction allows the debater *more flexibility in case development*. Because discipline-based construction creates a broad argument field, debaters who use this method will have considerable latitude in determining particular foci for emphasis within the field and equal latitude in selecting the types of supporting claims they will present in their case. To say, for example, that covert operations is in the argument field of foreign policy provides a broad field within which the debater may choose standards and claims.

Using purpose-based construction may be more difficult. Identifying the primary function or purpose of a complex sociopolitical object of focus often requires a more detailed analysis than simply identifying the broad area of study within which that object of focus falls. Indeed, because purpose-based construction requires that the object of focus be more narrowly conceived, it creates a more specific and constricted argument field for the debater and limits the choices that can be made regarding emphasis and claims. Debaters using a purpose-based construction have fewer options regarding the claims and emphases they are able to make.

Although it may be easier to use a discipline-based construction, this construction has one major disadvantage: *the relationship between the object of focus and appropriate field-dependent standards may be unclear*. Broadly constructed argument fields, such as those produced with the discipline-based construction, promote a rough classification but do not account for potentially subtle differences that may exist among objects grouped within the same classification. Indeed, a broad construction presumes that *any* standard derived from a field should be appropriate to judge *any* object situated within that field. For example, any object located within the field of politics could be judged by any standard deemed "political" as the standards within the "political" field are presumed to link the objects within that field because of their shared "politicalness." As a result, the presumed relationship between the standards and the object of focus is derived from a coincidental classification (both the standards and the object of focus are termed *political*) rather than from the direct relevance of the standards to the object of focus because of its *specific* nature.

However, considering the specific nature of the object of focus may be necessary for determining the appropriate field-dependent standards. For example, although there are numerous "legal" standards—such as the compelling state interest/least restrictive alternative test, the rule of reason test, and the rule of proximate cause—we cannot presume that all "legal" standards are equally well suited to judge any object of focus that happens to fall within the "legal" argument field. Rather, an evaluator needs more information about the specific nature of the object of focus to determine which legal standard would be most appropriate.

In contrast, a major advantage of the purpose-based construction is that it *better clarifies the nature of the object of focus.* Identifying the most appropriate field-dependent standards provides for a more meaningful method of decision making. Creating an argument field based on the purpose of the object of focus segregates the relevant characteristics of the object of focus from the irrelevant ones. This, in turn, illuminates the field-dependent standards on which a judgment should be made. Baier provides an excellent example of this integral relationship:

> In order to know what is the criterion of "running a better mile" . . . [one must] know the purpose of the race. If we know that races are competitions in which people are trying to run as fast as they can in order to win, we know what the purpose of races is. It is then also obvious that we must evaluate miles on the basis of speed. (62)

To extend the reasoning in Baier's example, we could presume that if the purpose of a particular race was determined to be something other than "running a better mile"—such as "promoting friendships"—the race would be located within a different argument field. Evaluating the race on the basis of speed would then make little sense, regardless of how the "preponderance of experts" *typically* evaluates a race. In this case, it is more sensible (and meaningful) to develop a field-dependent standard such as "the degree of interaction promoted among participants" to determine the actual worth of the race.

Other examples further illustrate how our view of the function or purpose of the object of focus influences the selection of appropriate standards. For example, judging whether a particular set of democratic elections is "good" (desirable, beneficial) depends on whether we view the function of the elections as fostering democracy or as electing a suitable candidate. A democratic election could be judged either by adherence to the process or by its product. Depending on the purpose, the 1972 presidential election might be judged "bad" because Richard Nixon was reelected (bad product) or because the Nixon campaign used extensive dirty tricks (bad process). Although the end judgments may be similar, the standards and the decision-making processes used in each instance would, obviously, be quite different. In either case, however, the purpose-based construction of argument field more clearly illuminates the field-dependent standards on which the object of focus could be properly judged.

A second significant advantage of the purpose-based construction is that a debater using it *will typically be able to identify the appropriate field-dependent standards* easily. An argument field constructed according to purpose will usually be narrower than a discipline-based construction because it establishes a more specific and limited focus on the object being judged. For example, placing compulsory national service within the argument field of "a citizen employment training program" (purpose) is a much more specific way of viewing that object of focus than placing it in a discipline-based field such as public policy or domestic programs. Within the more narrowly defined argument field, there will usually be fewer standards available from which to choose. For example, there would be fewer field-dependent standards for employment training programs than there would be for public policy or domestic programs.

Overall, although either the discipline-based or purpose-based construction may be used, we believe it advisable for nonpolicy debaters to select the latter option whenever possible. Apart from advantages of expediency, flexibility, or ease, the most important consideration in constructing an argument field is whether meaningful field-dependent standards can be drawn from that field. On the basis of that consideration, the purpose-based construction is typically the better method for developing field-dependent standards, primarily because it encourages more meaningful discussion and debate.

Incorporating Criteria into the Rationale

The criterion is a necessary component of every affirmative case dealing with a nonpolicy proposition. To have a well-developed case, however, criteria must be carefully integrated with the major claims of the rationale. In addition, they must be carefully crafted and conform to general principles of appropriateness. We discuss both of those issues in this final section of the chapter.

Integrating Criteria and Major Claims

When constructing the major claims for the rationale component of their case, affirmative debaters should carefully correlate their major claims with the criteria. The major claims are a demonstration of the conditions or tests specified in the criteria. Thus, these claims must relate those conditions or tests to the object of focus and must do so in a complete manner: every condition or test specified in the criteria must be accompanied by a major claim. An example may clarify this point. Suppose that for the proposition, "Resolved: that membership in the United Nations is detrimental to the self-interest of the United States," the affirmative side develops discipline-based criteria (field of foreign policy) for determining "detrimental," and those criteria specify two standards. Membership in international organizations may be deemed "detrimental" if (1) it decreases autonomy in decision making, and (2) it reduces response flexibility in crisis situations. The affirmative debaters would then need to include, in the rationale component of their case, major claims that individually or collectively demonstrate how both those standards are met. Most likely, the affirmative would formulate major claims similar to the following.

CONTENTION 1:   U.N. Membership decreases U.S. decision-making autonomy.

CONTENTION 2:   U.N. Membership reduces U.S. response flexibility in crisis situations.

Similarly, if the affirmative team used a purpose-based construction to develop three standards to assess mandatory drug testing—(1) ability to detect drug use, (2) ability to deter drug use by employees, and (3) reduction in number of workplace accidents—they would be required to include at least three major claims in the rationale of the case. Those claims would roughly parallel the following:

CONTENTION 1:   Mandatory drug testing is effective in detecting drug use by employees.

CONTENTION 2:   Use of mandatory drug testing in the workplace deters drug use by employees.

CONTENTION 3:   Use of mandatory drug testing in the workplace results in decreased incidents of drug-related accidents.

General Principles for Constructing Criteria

At this point, we want to explain six important considerations you should keep in mind when developing this critical part of the rationale for an affirmative case. First, *criteria should be developed as a distinct and separate component of your affirmative case.* Criteria should be set apart from the other major components of your case so that you will be able to explain and others will be able to understand and analyze exactly how you intend to make the judgment required in the proposition. Criteria are so critical to nonpolicy judgment that successful advocacy and meaningful critical inquiry about that advocacy demand that criteria be clearly set apart from the rest of the rationale. Usually, the criterion component of an affirmative case will immediately follow presentation of the definitions. Because criteria establish the context for understanding the major claims, they should always be the first element of the rationale in the affirmative case. Both the negative debaters and the judge will be better able to understand the claims and how they should be interpreted if they first understand the criteria to which those claims are correlated.

Second, *your criteria must be clear*. Because criteria form the basis for reasoned decision making in nonpolicy debate, all parties in the debate must be able to understand them. Criteria should not be "discovered" or "evolve" during the debate. They should be definitively stated at the outset of the debate as the basis on which the nonpolicy judgment will be made. To be a successful advocate and to ensure that the most meaningful critical inquiry possible occurs during your debates, you must do everything possible to make your criteria precise, direct, and coherent. Vague or ambiguous criteria cloud reasoned decision making, detract from the credibility of the affirmative debaters, and potentially create significant opportunities for the negative debaters to refute the affirmative rationale.

Third, your *criteria must be complete*. The criteria explain *how* the judgmental term will be operationalized or *how* the judgment will be made. As a result, your criteria must identify the *field* in which you have placed the object of focus and the specific *standards* you will use to make the required judgment about the object of focus as it is considered within that field. We identified both these components in our previous examples. You will not need an elaborate explanation, but it will be important to identify the field clearly, regardless of whether you use a discipline-based or purpose-based construction. Similarly, you must provide a clear statement and any necessary explanation of *each* field-dependent standard you will use to demonstrate the required judgment. Remember, if the object of focus is not placed in an argument field, you cannot develop field-dependent standards; without field-dependent standards, you cannot make any meaningful nonpolicy judgment. Every criterion must contain both components.

Fourth, your *criteria should be as concise as possible*. Criteria inform reasoned decision making, but overly elaborate criteria may complicate the assessment of the argument field, obscure the degree to which standards are field-dependent, and detract from the debaters' ability to apply the criteria clearly to the decision-making process. Complex, overly developed criteria are difficult and time-consuming to explain and tedious for others to process and evaluate. Keep in mind the time constraints in which your entire affirmative case must be presented and make the criteria component as direct and to the point as possible without sacrificing completeness.

Fifth, your *criteria should be integrally related to your case*. Although criteria should be developed as a distinct component, your criteria are not a conceptually independent part of your affirmative case. Criteria are not an "add-on" component of the case that you construct after you have decided which claims you will present in the case. Rather, you must develop your criteria in tandem with development of the claims to ensure that the field and standards within the criteria are relevant to the claims and that the claims actually demonstrate the conditions or circumstances established in the field and standards. Your criteria and claims must be a matched set in order to fulfill THE BURDEN OF PROOF and present a compelling reason to have others accept your advocacy.

Finally, *you must be able to justify your criteria.* The affirmative is given great latitude in selecting the argument field for the object of focus and, ultimately, the field-dependent standards that will be used to make the judgment specified in the nonpolicy proposition. With that latitude, however, the affirmative team also assumes the responsibility for selecting reasonable criteria and being able to justify them. The affirmative side must treat the criteria component for what it is—a series of claims regarding the argument field and a series of claims regarding standards appropriate to that field. Ultimately, as with any claim, the affirmative team assumes a burden of proof to justify their choice of an argument field and further justify the appropriateness of the standards they claim to be field-dependent. In our previous example, we would need to be able to justify both selection of law as the argument field for mandatory drug testing and the standards we used as measures within that field. The task of justifying field and standards is infinitely easier to manage if the affirmative has made reasonable choices. Affirmative debaters will soon learn that any presumed strategic advantage gained by constructing overly restrictive or obscure criteria is more than offset by the increased difficulty they face in justifying such choices.

Conclusion

The affirmative case for a nonpolicy proposition has two unique characteristics. First, the definition component of the case will include definitions of types of terms that are different from those in the definition component of a policy proposition. Second, the rationale component will include criteria. Establishing criteria is always an important first step in any rational decision-making process because criteria provide the mechanism by which nonpolicy judgments are made. The criterion serves to delineate the decision-making process, identify potential issues, and guide case development; because of its central role in decision making, it a stock issue in nonpolicy debate. To establish appropriate criteria, the debater should follow a three-step process: identify the components of the proposition, determine the argument field of the object of focus, and develop field-dependent standards. Debaters need to understand the difference between criterion and standard, and between field-invariant and field-dependent standards. Moreover, they should understand the comparative advantages and disadvantages of the discipline-based and purpose-based constructions for an argument field. Regardless of which approach a debater uses to construct criteria, the criteria must be carefully integrated with the major claims of the rationale and constructed according to basic principles of appropriateness.

Notes

1. One other possible reason for your uncertainty is that you doubt the validity of the data; that is, you are not sure the car is as cost efficient as claimed or that it looks as great as you think it looks.
2. We distinguish "substantive" from "nonsubstantive" voting issues. Substantive voting issues are those issues directly related to the judgment being made (such as stock issues, issues called forth by the criterion). Nonsubstantive voting issues are those relating to the procedural aspects of the debate (such as topicality, justification issues in one of its many forms, and so on).
3. Both methods can be used to identify the "nature of the problem," a "nature" meaning that arguments can be said to occupy the same argument field because they employ data and conclusions "of the same logical type" (Toulmin 13, 14). The discipline-based construction and the purpose-based construction are simply two alternative avenues to discovering the argument field.

Selected Bibliography

Baier, Kurt. *The Moral Point of View*. Ithaca, NY: Cornell UP, 1958.

Brownlee, Don. "Approaches to Support and Refutation of Criteria." *CEDA Yearbook* 8 (1987): 59–63.

Cantrill, James G. "Definitional Issues in the Pursuit of Argumentative Understanding: A Critique of Contemporary Practice." *CEDA Yearbook* 9 (1988): 45–53.

Du Bois, W. E. B. "Disenfranchisement." *W. E. B. Du Bois Speaks*. Ed. Philip Foner. New York: Pathfinder, 1970.

Gill, Ann M. "Catastrophe and Criterion: A Case for Justification." *CEDA Yearbook* 9 (1988): 38–44.

Rescher, Nicholas. *Introduction to Value Theory*. New York: UP of America, 1982.

Rowland, Robert C. "The Influence of Purpose on Fields of Argument." *Journal of the American Forensic Association* 28 (1982): 228–45.

Toulmin, Steven. *The Uses of Argument.* London: Cambridge UP, 1958.

Warnick, Barbara. "Arguing Value Propositions." *Journal of the American Forensic Association* 18 (1981): 109–19.

Washington, Booker T. "An Address Delivered at the Opening of the Cotton States' Exposition in Atlanta" (Sept. 1895). *American Public Addresses 1740–1952.* Ed. A. Craig Baird. New York: McGraw-Hill, 1956.

Zarefsky, David. "Persistent Questions in the Theory of Argument Fields." *Journal of the American Forensic Association* 18 (1982): 191–203.

Discussion Questions

1. Is it important to make field-dependent judgments in everyday argument? Why or why not?
2. In your judgment, what are the most significant advantages associated with the discipline-based argument field construction? The most significant limitations?
3. Is either method of argument field construction more appropriate for every day argument?
4. In what ways might a debater develop improperly constructed criteria?

DEVELOPING AN AFFIRMATIVE CASE FOR A POLICY PROPOSITION

*A*ffirmative cases for a policy proposition differ in two important ways from cases for a nonpolicy proposition. First, because policy propositions are constructed differently from nonpolicy propositions, debaters will need to define different types of terms in the definitions component of the case. In addition, because of the nature of the terms contained in a policy proposition, the affirmative team will be able to incorporate at least one method of definition not generally applicable to nonpolicy propositions. Second, the rationale component of the affirmative case will include a plan; there is no such requirement for affirmative cases dealing with nonpolicy propositions. We discuss both these differences in this chapter. As with Chapter 12, debaters should consider this chapter an extension of Chapter 11: it is important to understand the concepts contained in both chapters to develop a suitable affirmative case for a policy proposition.

Defining Terms for a Policy Case

Policy propositions and nonpolicy propositions are constructed somewhat differently. As a result, debaters will develop a different type of definition component for affirmative cases for policy propositions. In this section, we describe the terms in a policy proposition that must be defined and identify one method of definition uniquely suited to defining the terms in a policy proposition.

Identifying the Terms That Need to Be Defined

Defining the terms contained in a policy proposition is important. As you recall from Chapter 7, policy propositions generally contain three components: *the agent of action, the action qualifier,* and *the policy directive.* The agent of action is the group, entity, organization, or persons charged with undertaking the action specified in a policy proposition. In the proposition, "Resolved: that the United States should significantly increase the development of the earth's ocean resources," the agent of action is "the United States." When the agent of action is a broad, multifaceted entity such as "the United States," specifying exactly to whom ultimate authority and responsibility for the action will be given is important. For example, to say that "the United States" is the combination of the three branches of government—the legislative, executive, and judicial— vests authority for action in a very different agent than if "the United States" were defined as the "combined actions of the fifty separate states." In short, to understand the proposition, we must know precisely who the agent of action is intended to be.

Also critical is for the action qualifier to be clearly defined. As you recall from Chapter 7, the action qualifier denotes the general direction of change specified in the policy proposition and the magnitude of that change. In the proposition, "Resolved: that the United States should significantly increase the guarantee of privacy for all citizens," the words "significantly increase" form the action directive; they specify that the change should be an increase (as opposed to a decrease) in the guarantee of privacy for all citizens, and further indicate that such an increase must be "significant." It would be virtually impossible to assess advocacy in a debate critically or to determine whether the prescribed policy should be implemented without knowing exactly what the action qualifier means. We must know what a "significant increase" is to determine whether such an action has been developed or whether such an action is warranted.

The policy directive is the final component of a policy proposition to be defined. This directive establishes the general nature of the policy action to be implemented. In the proposition, "Resolved: that the United States federal government should adopt a policy to substantially decrease consumption of marine resources," the policy directive focuses on "consumption of marine resources." That directive requires a policy or series of action steps to be formulated specifically regarding the "consumption of marine resources."

Using Operational Definitions in the Affirmative Case

The policy directive, like the judgmental term in nonpolicy propositions, is usually defined separately from the other key terms in the proposition. Typically, the policy directive will be *operationally defined* within the context of the specific provisions of the affirmative plan. In an operational definition, a term is defined by exactly how it is intended to operate. For example, in debating the proposition, "Resolved: that the federal government should establish a comprehensive medical care program for all United States citizens," the affirmative team might define the policy directive—"a comprehensive medical care program for all United States citizens"—by identifying the specific steps of action they will take to implement that directive. In such a situation, the affirmative side might define the term operationally to mean this:

1. All United States citizens will be eligible for comprehensive medical care subsidized by the federal government.

2. All care shall include preventive, diagnostic, and treatment procedures for conditions or infirmities resulting from accident, injury, or illness.

3. All care shall include services rendered by a duly licensed dentist, general practitioner, specialist, or hospital.

4. All care shall include necessary prescription drugs, testing, surgical procedures, and psychiatric counseling.

Operational definitions are commonly used when policy propositions are debated because these definitions provide a clear and direct way for the affirmative team to define the policy directive of the proposition. These definitions may also be used, however, to define other components of policy or nonpolicy propositions. For example, in her address, "The Struggle for Human Rights," Eleanor Roosevelt provided an operational definition for the term *basic human rights* by explaining what that term includes.

> Basic human rights are simple and easily understood: freedom of speech and a press; freedom of religion and worship; freedom of assembly and the right to petition; the right of men to be secure in their homes and free from unreasonable search and seizure and from arbitrary arrest and punishment. (79)

Unlike standardized reference or contextual usage that provides definitions from an authoritative basis (such as the reference work or the expert), operational definitions have no presumptive authority as their foundation. The primary assumption of all operational definitions is that the specified indicators (such as the steps of action in an affirmative plan, the delineation of specific rights included in "basic human rights") are the necessary and sufficient components of the term. Ultimately, the advocate who uses an operational definition must be able to defend individually and in combination the components of the definition.

Defining Key Recurring Terms in Policy Advocacy

In addition to the key terms of the proposition, key recurring terms may emerge in advocacy about policy propositions, particularly in claims and evidence that debaters use to construct and defend their case. For example, in the policy proposition, "Resolved: that the federal government should provide comprehensive medical care for all United States citizens," one term that will almost invariably arise is "universal coverage." That term may be defined in different ways. Some define "universal coverage" quantitatively by designating the total percentage of all citizens covered; in quantitative terms, universal coverage might mean that 97 percent of all citizens would be given coverage, or it might mean that 95 percent of all citizens would be covered. Others, however, might define the same term qualitatively by denoting the types of coverage that would be extended. Some advocates of universal coverage would support plans that provide preventive care and dental care whereas other proponents of universal coverage exclude those very same items. At first glance, it may appear that the differences between 97 percent and 95 percent, preventive care and no preventive care are small. However, when translated into policy implications, even such seemingly small differences can have profound consequences. Within the context of an academic debate, it is impossible to adequately understand and critically assess the claims and evidence that debaters present without clearly understanding precisely what all the key recurring terms mean.

Constructing the Rationale: The Plan

Just as criteria are a distinguishing component of an affirmative case for a non-policy proposition, a plan of action is a distinguishing component of an affirmative case for a policy proposition. In this section, we explain the major components of a plan and some important considerations for developing one for your affirmative case.

Components of a Plan

When debating a proposition of policy, the affirmative team must demonstrate that the change prescribed in the proposition is warranted. To do that, they must explain exactly what specific changes they propose to implement and demonstrate a compelling justification for implementing that proposal. Thus, the rationale component of the affirmative case for a proposition of policy consists of the specific plan of action and some combination of major claims that provide sufficient justification for implementing the plan.

An affirmative plan should include five major components. First, the plan must identify the specific **agent of action.** Your plan is a statement of action and some agent must be responsible for initiating and overseeing that action. The policy proposition will identify an overall agent of action, but most such agents are specified in very general terms (such as the United States, the U.S. federal government). Plans of action are not actually initiated by such general agents but by specific agents. You might specify that your plan will be implemented through the Environmental Protection Agency, the Nuclear Regulatory Commission, the Department of Education, or some other specific organ of the general agent of action identified in the proposition. In some instances, you may choose to create a new organization such as "a special ten-person committee of the top national experts on the effects of media," or "a special commission composed of the top five ranking majority and top five ranking minority members of the House of Representatives and the Senate."

Whomever you designate as the specific agent of action, that agent must meet two tests. First, the agent must be representative of the general agent of action specified in the proposition. If the proposition called for action by the United States, you could not designate the Governor of Arkansas to be the specific agent of action. Actions undertaken by the Governor of Arkansas do not constitute actions by the United States. Second, the agent of action must be capable of performing the action specified in the plan. The agent of action you specify should have some legitimate base of power within the general area of action prescribed in the proposition. If your plan implements a new series of economic stimulus measures, it would be reasonable to consider placing responsibility for that action in the Federal Reserve as that group has a legitimate base of power from which to deal with national economic issues and policies. However, to designate the Federal Reserve as the specific agent of action to implement a new series of air and water pollution controls would make little sense, as that group has no direct and legitimate power in the area of environmental oversight. Although you could theoretically create a new base of power for the agent you specify (you could mandate that the Federal Reserve will now oversee U.S. environmental policy), doing so would unnecessarily complicate your plan and likely make it susceptible to serious substantive attack.

Second, your plan must include a statement of the specific **steps of action** you propose. This component of the plan, commonly called the "mandates," identifies exactly what action will be taken under the plan. In debating the proposition "Resolved: that the federal government should significantly strengthen the regulation of mass media communication in the United States," affirmative teams could develop plans designed to regulate the content of television programs. The specific steps of action, or mandates, included in such plans might be developed as follows:

1. The Federal Communications Commission (FCC) will develop standards to prevent graphic depictions of violent or sexual images on television programs available during prime time to either cable or network viewers in the United States.

2. All current programming will be reviewed by the FCC and subject to the standards it establishes. Broadcasters of current programming that does not

meet the newly promulgated FCC standards will be apprised of the specific nature of the violations and will be allowed twelve months to correct them. Failure to correct the problems within the twelve-month period will result in loss of broadcast rights for the program.

3. New programming will be submitted to the FCC and must receive clearance before it can be broadcast.

The steps of action included in the plan should meet two tests. First, they must be as specific as possible. As the affirmative, you have an obligation to explain in terms that are as clear, specific, and direct as possible exactly what you propose to be implemented. Being vague or ambiguous in the steps of action not only can undermine your credibility as an advocate but can allow your opponents increased flexibility in developing attacks on that action. Second, the steps of action should be as comprehensive as possible. You need to state every action you intend to implement within the plan. As the affirmative side, you have the right to choose the specific ways you will implement the action mandate stated in the proposition, but that right does not extend throughout the debate. Action steps should not evolve as the debate progresses. Rather, the affirmative team must present a thorough statement of the actions they propose at the outset and be prepared to defend those choices throughout the debate.

The third major component of the plan is the statement of **resource provisions**. This component of the plan provides for the basic inputs or resources necessary to carry out the specific steps of action you have established. Plans can require a wide range of resources including personnel to oversee implementation and discharge of the steps of action, funding to enable the steps of action to be performed, and information dissemination mechanisms to serve as a conduit between the administrative structure of the plan and the various publics with which it interacts. This component of the plan might be constructed as follows.

All necessary staffing for the plan will be appropriated through normal personnel acquisition channels. The agency will be guaranteed all support personnel, administrative support, and supplies necessary to carry out the mandates of the plan effectively. The administrative staff will have complete access to all pertinent information collected by other government agencies related to the mandates of the plan. All necessary funding for the plan will be provided through general revenue allocations and will be generated by a combination of cuts in duplicative federal agriculture subsidies and an increase of 1 percent in federal income tax rates.

The specific resource requirements for your plan will be determined by the nature of the steps of action you develop and the administrative structure you establish. The more complex and costly the steps of action you propose, the more important this component of the plan will be. For example, an affirmative plan mandating that all medical care would be provided without cost for all citizens would have to give serious consideration to funding provisions and would have to be prepared to demonstrate the country's capability for funding such an immense action. Similarly, an affirmative plan establishing a national education program to increase public awareness of the dangers of additives in processed foods would have to provide for specific information dissemination channels to be used in conducting such a massive educational campaign.

The affirmative team has the responsibility to develop a plan that is feasible. Remember, there is literally "no free lunch." The affirmative debaters, as the proponents of change, have the responsibility to provide for the resources necessary to implement their proposal, and their resource component must be sufficient to ensure that the plan can operate efficiently and effectively.

The fourth component of an affirmative plan is the **enforcement provision.** The purpose of this component is to provide a reasonable assurance that the specific steps of action will be carried out as provided for in the plan. The enforcement provision should specify what consequences will be imposed on any agent who attempts to disregard or undermine the steps of action. Consequences may include a wide range of penalties such as monetary fines, community-based public work, loss of privileges or position, or even criminal sentences. This component of the plan might be constructed as follows.

> Violations of this plan will constitute a misdemeanor and will be punishable by appropriate fines and imposition of community-based work requirements. Any administrative officer who violates the mandates of this plan shall be removed from office and subject to appropriate criminal penalties including a prison term.

To determine how severe the enforcement provisions of the plan should be, you should assess the probability of possible violations. If there is a strong incentive for people to disregard the steps of action, it will be necessary to construct an enforcement provision sufficient to neutralize that incentive. The Internal Revenue Service code is an excellent example of the need for clearly specified stringent penalties; most people would prefer not to pay taxes, but they do so in part to avoid the penalties established for tax evasion. In this case, the penalties are developed to act as a deterrent to potential violators.

The affirmative team may develop any sort of enforcement provisions they deem appropriate. Enforcement provisions should specify the groups or persons who will be subject to the provisions established, the actions that will constitute a violation of the provisions of the plan, and the consequences that will be imposed on those individuals if they violate the provisions of the plan. The affirmative should always be prepared to defend their enforcement provisions as a socially, pragmatically, and philosophically reasonable response to violation of the plan mandates.

The final component of an affirmative plan is the **clarification plank.** The purpose of this component is to clarify any potentially confusing or vague information about how the plan will be put into place or how it will function. The affirmative team can also establish in this component a procedure to ensure that the plan operates within the parameters of their intent. They might also use the clarification plank to *preempt* possible objections the negative team might raise against the plan. For example, the proposition for debate might be "Resolved: that the federal government should establish a comprehensive medical care program for all United States citizens"; the affirmative team could anticipate an argument by the negative side that the plan is disadvantageous because it restricts the right of citizens to choose their own physician. If the affirmative plan is not intended to restrict physician choice, the affirmative debaters might try to preempt such an attack from their opponents by specifically stating their intention in the clarification plank. In such a situation, the clarification plank might be constructed as follows.

> Affirmative speeches shall be used to clarify intent regarding implementation and operation of this plan. In no case should the mandates of this plan be construed to preclude the right of any individual to obtain adequate preventive medical care from the physician of her or his choice (preempt). Should this plan or any of its mandates be in conflict with any existing federal legislation, the provisions of this plan shall prevail.

The affirmative debaters obviously have great latitude in developing the clarification plank of their plan. They should include in the plank any qualifiers that may prevent possible misinterpretation of their intentions and may help to explain how the plan is meant to function.

Although the affirmative team has broad latitude in interpreting how their plan will function, they should always be reasonable in constructing the clarification plank. They cannot preempt every conceivable negative objection, nor should they try to do so. Overly zealous affirmative debaters can seriously damage their credibility by constructing clarification planks so broad and encompassing that they appear to eliminate reasonable objections the negative team might raise. In the following outline, we illustrate how the major components of an affirmative plan might be structured.

Sample Structure of an Affirmative Plan
1. Agent of Action
2. Action Steps
  A. Step One . . .
  B. Step Two . . .
  C. Step Three . . .

3. Resource Requirements
 A. Personnel . . .
 B. Information . . .
 C. Funding
4. Enforcement
 A. Enforcement Agent
 B. Consequences
5. Clarification Plank
 A. Statement of Intent
 B. Preempt

General Principles for Developing Plans

Obviously, the plan is a critical part of the rationale for any affirmative case for a policy proposition. In fact, in many debates, the plan will become the focal point for much of the critical argumentation about the proposition. We suggest that affirmative debaters pay particular attention to the construction of the plan, and we offer five major principles to guide its development.

First, *the plan should provide sufficient explanatory detail.* Although an affirmative plan is not a formal piece of legislation, it should be treated like a well-developed solution to an identified problem. The affirmative team should provide a complete and meaningful explanation of how they will solve a problem and give sufficient information so that the negative debaters and the judge can understand their approach.

Second, *the plan should not be overly complex.* Although the affirmative team should include all necessary explanatory information in their plan, they should resist the temptation to make the plan too complex. They need not include every minute detail about the operation of the plan, even though they should be prepared to explain those details if asked. The more complex the mandates and provisions of the plan, the greater the likelihood that these may be misunderstood or even purposefully misinterpreted.

Third, *the plan should target the causes of the problem.* The provisions of the plan should formulate as direct an approach as possible to remedying the causes of the problem. In some situations, the nature of the problem will be such that the affirmative team can develop **countercausal** measures, or steps of action that directly eliminate the problem's causes. If the problem is caused by absence of a directive to take an action, the affirmative side could mandate taking that action. If the problem is caused by conflicting statutory requirements, they could eliminate the policy conflicts. If the problem is caused by inadequate or weak regulatory provisions, the debaters could construct a plan that strengthens those provisions.

In other situations, particularly if the problem is caused by attitudinal barriers, the affirmative team may not be able to eliminate those causes directly, but they must develop **causal-circumventing** measures—steps of action that minimize the effects produced by the causes of the problem. If, for example, the problem is caused by lack of acceptance of current policy, prejudice or bias, or some deleterious personal motive, the affirmative side would probably be required to formulate a plan that used causal-circumventing measures. In these instances, they would formulate mandates forcing individuals to comply with current policy, even if those persons disagreed with it, or establish provisions that prevented individuals from acting out of prejudice, bias, or personal motive without necessarily attempting to change those prejudices, biases, or motives. When using either the countercausal or causal-circumventing approach, the affirmative should avoid formulating circuitous, obtuse steps of action, and they should use the most appropriate approach for addressing the causes of the problem they have identified.

Fourth, *the plan should be reasonable.* The affirmative should not include steps of action that are impossible to accomplish. For example, it would not be reasonable for the affirmative team to assume that they could abolish all wars, racial prejudice, or disease. Also, the affirmative plan should not include highly impractical provisions. For example, in their plan to guarantee medical care for all United States citizens, the affirmative team would not want to require that three program physicians certify the need for specific treatments before any care is provided. Such a mandate could be easily argued as wasteful of resources and potentially counterproductive to the health of individuals.

Fifth, *the plan should be defendable.* The affirmative debaters should carefully assess their ability to defend every component before including it in the plan. Ultimately, the affirmative team are responsible for every effect produced by their plan whether the effect is intended or not. Thus, the affirmative should determine beforehand what consequences the negative team might propose as probably arising from operation of the plan and determine how to respond to those objections.

Completing the Rationale: Justifying the Plan

In the rationale of an affirmative case for a policy proposition, the second element is a set of major claims that provides a justification for implementing the proposal. To demonstrate that the proposed change is warranted, the affirmative must prove that there is a significant problem, that the problem inheres within the present system, that the proposed change will alleviate the problem, and that the proposed change does not produce more undesirable than desirable effects. These stock issues are commonly referred to as significance, inherency, solvency, and disadvantage. In this section, we describe two primary approaches debaters can use to justify adoption of their plan: the traditional needs approach and the comparative advantage approach.

The Traditional Needs Approach

As for a nonpolicy proposition, the nature of the major claims that debaters use in this portion of the case is determined primarily by the stock issues of a policy proposition.

The affirmative team might formulate claims to address these stock issues in either of two forms. First, they might use a traditional **needs approach.** This is the most straightforward form for constructing major claims for the rationale component of the affirmative case. When using this approach, the affirmative team constructs major claims that address the significance, inherency, and solvency issues. As with the rationale component for a nonpolicy proposition, these claims are usually called contentions. Examples of contentions addressing each of those stock issues is presented below.

CONTENTION 1:   Environmental degradation is increasing. (Significance)
Supporting Claim A: Air pollution is increasing.
Supporting Claim B: Water pollution is increasing.

CONTENTION 2:   Environmental degradation is harmful. (Significance)
Supporting Claim A: The quality of life is eroded.
Supporting Claim B: Individual health is threatened.

CONTENTION 3:   Environmental degradation will continue. (Inherency)
Supporting Claim A: Current regulations are inadequate.
Supporting Claim B: Financial motives ensure pollution.

CONTENTION 4:   The affirmative plan solves the problem. (Solvency)
Supporting Claim A: Establishing more stringent levels will cut pollution in half.
Supporting Claim B: The plan changes the financial incentive to pollute into a substantial financial disincentive.

Affirmative debaters should consider two important principles when using the needs approach to formulate their rationale. First, the plan may be presented at different points during the rationale. In the original order of the needs approach, the plan was presented following the major claims about significance and inherency and immediately before the major claims about solvency. There is a certain logical appeal to that order: there is a significant problem (major claim), the problem will continue unless action is taken (major claim), here is the action we propose (plan), here is why that action solves the problem (major claim). More recently, and largely because it has become a convention, affirmative debaters present their plan during the first part of the rationale for their case and present the major claims following the plan.

Second, in the needs approach, the affirmative typically does not advance a claim regarding the fourth issue, disadvantage. Rather, they address that issue by responding to the disadvantage arguments launched by the negative side. That does not mean the disadvantage issue is less important than the others. It simply means that in most debates the negative will assume the lead role in advancing specific disadvantages. Once a compelling disadvantage is introduced, the affirmative debaters must refute that disadvantage to fulfill THE BURDEN OF PROOF. However, the affirmative does have the option, if convinced that the negative will launch a particular disadvantage, to include a preemption for the disadvantage in an underview, which would be presented following the major claims of the rationale.

The Comparative Advantage Approach

The second form that might be used to construct the major claims for the rationale component of an affirmative case is the **comparative advantage approach.** This was developed partly as a case form for situations in which the affirmative could suggest improving the current system without necessarily eliminating all or even the majority of a particular problem within that system. In the comparative advantage approach, the affirmative establishes a justification for implementing the action proposed in the proposition by demonstrating that doing so would be advantageous. Rather than showing how their plan of action solves some significant and inherent problem, as would be the case in the needs approach, the affirmative demonstrates that the advantages produced by implementing their plan are sufficient to justify taking that prescribed action.

Although at first glance it appears to be quite different, the comparative advantage approach is actually a modified form of the traditional needs approach. The affirmative side is still obligated to demonstrate the worth of the advantages (significance), to show that the advantages flow uniquely from their plan (inherency), to demonstrate a sufficient probability that the advantages will actually materialize (solvency), and to show that the advantages are superior to any disadvantages that will result from the plan (disadvantage), according to the negative side. Thus, affirmative debaters who use the comparative advantage approach assume essentially the same obligations in fulfilling THE BURDEN OF PROOF as do affirmative debaters who use the needs approach, although there will be some differences in the way the major claims are formulated.

Using the comparative advantage approach does not significantly alter the substance of the major claims of the rationale, but it does affect the form in which those claims are presented. The major claims of the rationale are typically called advantages rather than contentions. Following is an example of how the major claims might be formulated in the comparative advantage approach.

> **ADVANTAGE 1:** Reducing air pollution is advantageous.
> *Supporting Claim A:* Air pollution is increasing. (Significance)
> *Supporting Claim B:* Air pollution is harmful. (Significance)
> *Supporting Claim C:* Without the plan, air pollution will continue. (Inherency)
> *Supporting Claim D:* The affirmative plan decreases air pollution by 50 percent. (Solvency)
>
> **ADVANTAGE 2:** Reducing water pollution is advantageous.
> *Supporting Claim A:* Water pollution is increasing. (Significance)
> *Supporting Claim B:* Water pollution is harmful. (Significance)
> *Supporting Claim C:* Without the plan water pollution will continue. (Inherency)
> *Supporting Claim D:* The affirmative plan decreases water pollution by eliminating the financial incentive to pollute. (Solvency)

When using the comparative advantage approach, the affirmative team will almost always present their plan in the first part of the rationale component of the case. Following presentation of the plan, they will then advance the major claims that accrue from that plan. As with the needs approach, the affirmative will not usually include a major claim regarding disadvantages but will probably deal with that issue by responding to the disadvantages the negative side introduces. As with the needs approach, however, the affirmative debaters might include a preemption for the disadvantage in an underview, which they would present after the major claims of the rationale.

Conclusion

An affirmative case for a policy proposition is different from a case for a non-policy proposition in two major respects: different types of terms must be defined and the rationale component will contain a specific plan of action. Plans are critical to the affirmative case for a policy proposition and must be carefully developed. Plans must contain specific components, and each component should be carefully constructed according to fundamental guidelines. The claims in the rationale component of the case must be correlated to the stock issues of the policy proposition. Either the traditional needs approach or the comparative advantage approach can be used to formulate the claims for the rationale of an affirmative case for a policy proposition.

Selected Bibliography

Flaningam, Carl. "Inherency and Incremental Change: A Response to Morello." *Journal of the American Forensic Association* 20 (Spring 1984): 231–35.

Herbeck, Dale A., and John Katsulas. "In Response to Rowland on 'Realism and Debateability in Policy Advocacy.'" *Journal of the American Forensic Association* 23 (Fall 1986): 102–07.

Reynolds, William. "Harms and Benefits: A Reappraisal." *Journal of the American Forensic Association* 22 (Winter 1986): 152–57.

Roosevelt, Eleanor. "The Struggle for Human Rights." *American Rhetoric from Roosevelt to Reagan.* Ed. Halford Ross Ryan. Prospect Heights, IL: Waveland, 1987.

Discussion Questions

1. Are operational definitions better for policy propositions than the general methods of definition discussed in Chapter 11? Why or why not?
2. How might a debater know when the mandates for his or her plan are sufficiently specific?
3. In what ways might a student apply the basic principles of the comparative advantage approach to decision making outside the debate setting?
4. How might the clarification plank of an affirmative plan be used to give the affirmative debaters too much flexibility in interpreting their intent?

DEBATING THE NEGATIVE

*A*s you prepare to debate the negative side, you will find that many of the principles discussed in the previous three chapters are still relevant. As noted in Chapter 6, effective refutation rarely consists solely of questioning the other side's argument, probing for and exposing its weaknesses. Whether engaged in direct refutation (also called the **on-case** argument) or in indirect refutation (also called the **off-case** argument), the negative team will inevitably find themselves advancing arguments of their own. In doing so, this team will assume the burden of proof for those arguments, and that burden of proof will carry with it many of the same demands placed on the affirmative as they develop arguments for their case.

Despite the many similarities between the two positions, the negative still has characteristics. First, it must be *responsive.* By the conventions of debate, the affirmative is allowed to speak first and thus gives the debate its initial direction. The negative, carrying the burden of rebuttal, must respond to the case the affirmative has outlined. The negative can, of course, introduce any issue or argument that is relevant to the resolution; but it cannot *solely* raise such arguments. Even if the affirmative case is not prima facie or perhaps not topical, the negative *has the burden of pointing that out in response.* Unlike the affirmative, the negative cannot come into a debate, simply advance its own position, and still win the round.[1] It must respond to the affirmative case.

Second, the negative can be *selective* in its rejection of the resolution. Whereas the affirmative must provide a case that justifies the adoption of the complete resolution, the negative does not have to reject every component of the resolution. For example, in the case of the proposition "Resolved: that the United States should substantially reduce its military commitments to NATO member states," the negative might agree that the United States should reduce its overall military commitments but not to NATO member states. Or they might agree that we should reduce our overall commitments to NATO member states, but not our military ones. Or they could agree that we should reduce our military commitments to NATO member states but disagree with reducing them substantially. In all three of those positions, although agreeing with *part* of the proposition, the negative team would reject the proposition because they did not agree with the *entire* resolution. The negative can, of course, advance an off-case position that directly contradicts the proposition—such as arguing that we should substantially *increase* our military commitments.[2] It is always an option for the negative to be selective in its refutation—agreeing with part of the proposition but disagreeing with another part.

This characteristic of selectivity extends to their treatment of the affirmative case. As with the resolution itself, the negative can agree with one or more components of the affirmative argument yet still refute some key parts of it. If this refutation is effective, it can negate the affirmative case. The affirmative side must win all the stock issues to maintain its prima facie case, but the negative side need win only one stock issue to defeat that case.

It is useful to remember these two characteristics of the negative—the obligation to be responsive, but with the option of being selectively responsive—as we discuss the principles for developing a negative position. In this chapter we first discuss the form of negative argument and then examine the construction of on-case and off-case arguments.

The Negative Form of Argument

Because the negative team is responding to the affirmative case, it is important that every negative argument carry with it three components: the link, the rationale, and the impact. Occasionally, it will be useful to include a fourth component as well: a preemptive argument. These components should always be arranged the same way—link, rationale, impact, preemptive argument (if included)—and we discuss them in that order.

Because the negative side carries the burden of being *responsive,* it must make clear at the beginning of each refutation which affirmative argument it is refuting. This part of the negative team's argument is known as the **link,** because it "links" the negative's refutation to the affirmative case. The nature of the link may vary, from a simple transition sentence to an in-depth description of the affirmative argument, but if the negative wants the responsive nature of its argument to be clear, the link, too, must be clear.

The **rationale** consists of the negative side's refutative argument. The link points out which part of the affirmative argument the negative is responding to; the rationale *is* the response. Like the link, the rationale may be short or long. It could be a simple question about the affirmative team's data or an entire off-case position. The rationale may be constructed from questions, reasoning, data, or any combination of those. The rationale is important because it is the heart of the refutation. This is the component of the argument that says "this is our thinking on the issue—thinking that differs from that of the affirmative."

The **impact** statement explains the importance of the refutative argument to the debate as a whole. Recalling our discussion of selectivity above, the impact statement tells the opponent and the judge how this particular negative argument affects the affirmative case and/or the decision to adopt or reject the resolution. The refutation may weaken the affirmative case, call it into question, or contradict it fully. It may attack a single affirmative advantage or the entire affirmative rationale. It may create an entirely different criterion for judging the arguments or it may provide some disadvantages that lessen the attractiveness of the affirmative side's plan. Refutative arguments can vary widely and so have widely differing impacts on the affirmative case; it is the negative side's responsibility to point out clearly what those impacts are.

Link-Rationale-Impact-(Preemptive Argument) Model

(**Link**): Now the Affirmative states that their case is based on the Florida model, and the only data they have suggesting that crime will decrease are the Florida statistics. (**Rationale**): There are two problems here. First, Florida is a single example and, potentially, a unique case. It has a large immigrant population combined with a large retirement community. Can the Affirmative accurately generalize from this one example to the United States as a whole? But there's a second problem: the data the Affirmative give us for this single example are suspect. Dr. Leonard Skinnard, in *Criminal Justice Quarterly,* August 1995, writes that "the statistics gathered for Florida have indicated only the barest of correlations between the adoption of the law and the decrease of crime. Additionally, many variables—some of critical importance—have not been controlled for in any of the statistical studies of the data." (**Impact**): So we can have no confidence that the only example the Affirmative gives us does in fact prove that crime will decrease, and even if it does we have no reason to assume that the data are generalizable to the United States. But, if the Affirmative can't prove that crime will decrease, it removes the only advantage they've claimed that their plan would provide. (**Preemptive Argument**): *(hypothetical argument):* Now the

Affirmative may say that it is important for the government to do something, anything, to demonstrate that it is fighting crime. The perception of crime fighting, they'll tell us, is as advantageous as an actual reduction in crime. *(Preemptive response):* But perceptions eventually catch up with reality, and when they do, citizens will backlash. The resulting loss of confidence in the government will be worse than if the government had done nothing at all. At least when the government does nothing, it can't be caught trying to deceive the public, trying to convince us that an ineffective policy is actually working.

Finally, the negative may choose to include a preemptive argument (often shortened to "preempt") to forestall affirmative responses; that is, a preemptive argument *preempts* disagreement. Essentially, the preemptive argument extends the rationale. It says, "Well, the affirmative is likely to say this about our rationale, but if they do, you need to consider the following arguments."

The form of a preemptive argument is similar to the link-rationale connection. The "link" for a preempt is the *hypothetical argument* the negative proposes, outlining an argument the affirmative may raise. In preemptive arguments, the hypothetical argument is often the most critical part. The negative must be clear in describing this hypothetical link to a future affirmative argument.

If the affirmative team *does* raise that argument later, then the rationale part of the preempt comes into play. The *preemptive response* consists of the same kinds of materials—questions, reasons, evidence—found in any rationale. The preemptive response *is* a rationale—a refutation—to an imagined, hypothetical argument that the opponent *might* bring up in the future.

The "impact" component of a preemptive argument is usually implicit, although it can be explicitly stated as well. If the affirmative team raises the hypothetical argument, the preemptive response is applied to that argument; if it is persuasive, the affirmative argument is invalidated. If an impact component is required, this usually comes in later speeches, after the affirmative has in fact raised the hypothetical argument.

Preemptive arguments are useful in that they develop arguments more fully in the constructive speech, thus saving precious rebuttal time, and because they may discourage the affirmative side from even bringing up the preempted argument. Preemptive arguments also have a cost, however; the negative team may be devoting valuable time to an argument the affirmative side had no intention of raising. For that reason, it is usually best to use preemptive arguments conservatively.

A well-constructed negative argument, then, whether on-case or off-case, will follow the L-R-I-(P) form or model. This model is illustrated on page 284. The argument will be *linked* to the affirmative case, the negative side's *rationale* will be developed, and the *impact* of the argument on the debate as a whole will be explained. Where appropriate, the negative team may choose to include a *preemptive* argument—a refutative argument that anticipates and rebuts an affirmative response. Having discussed the form of the negative side's argument, we turn to the two areas of negative concern: on-case and off-case argumentation.

On-Case Argumentation

Because the negative side's on-case argumentation is a direct response to the affirmative case, the negative team's duties and responsibilities closely mirror those of the affirmative. Generally, the first negative constructive will follow the affirmative case structure most closely, using the same three components: the preliminary or summary component, the definition component, and the rationale. The second negative constructive will almost always extend the preliminary or summary component, will definitely extend any definitional argument, and will sometimes develop additional on-case rationale arguments.[3]

Preliminary and Summary Components

Like the affirmative, either or both negative speakers may choose to begin with an *introduction* that establishes the rhetorical context for viewing the debate or provides an exact statement of the proposition. The latter is rarely seen in debating, as most affirmatives can competently repeat the proposition verbatim. If the affirmative has failed to supply the proposition or has indeed misstated it, this may be usefully included in the negative's introduction. Establishing the rhetorical context is a trickier matter. Many negative teams choose to save time and start right in with a preview or overview; indeed, many affirmative introductions are forgotten and unused after the first affirmative constructive. Establishing a rhetorical context, however, can be meaningful in a debate, particularly if the negative side will be taking an unusual position in its on-case or off-case arguments. The rhetorical context may help the judge and the opponents understand and interpret what the negative team's arguments are and may ultimately help persuade the judge to the negative side's point of view.

The overview and/or underview are more common and usually more critical elements of the negative side's preliminary/summary component. As noted in Chapter 11, the overview/underview can be used to (1) clarify the interpretation of the proposition, (2) delineate the relevant procedural issues, and/or (3) delineate the relevant substantive issues. In all three cases, whether the affirmative places these as overviews or underviews, they are of *vital importance to the overall debate*. For example, if the affirmative interprets the proposition as referring strictly to federal policy, then all the negative team's evidence about state and local policy becomes inapplicable to the debate. Or if the affirmative argues that the presumption, typically assigned to the negative, is assigned by this proposition to the affirmative, then the negative must now assume THE BURDEN OF PROOF for the assertion that the proposition is wrong. Or if the affirmative argues that in deciding the proposition the defense issues are of primary importance, then negative arguments about the civilian sector will be given lesser weight in the round.

Obviously, each of these affirmative arguments would have important implications for what the negative could and could not argue. Although the negative team should not automatically contradict an affirmative overview or underview—after all, the affirmative's parameters might not affect or could even benefit the negative side's argument—it is critically important that the negative take a good look at the affirmative's overview/underview before agreeing to it.

Because this component of the debate can potentially affect every argument made during the debate, most negatives respond to affirmative overviews and underviews as part of their own overview. That is, even if the affirmative chooses to place procedural limits on the negative in an underview, it may be best for the negative to move that argument to the beginning of its constructive.[4] This way, as the negative speaker moves through the rationale part of the on-case argument, she can refer back to these general interpretive/procedural arguments where necessary or appropriate.

In addition to responding to the affirmative's over- and underviews, the negative speaker may establish over- or underviews of her own. These can accomplish the same three functions performed by the affirmative's overview or underview: clarify the interpretation of the proposition, delineate the parameters on procedural issues, and/or delineate the parameters on substantive issues. The second function—establishing procedural parameters—is often an important issue for the negative. This is where the negative side will raise any questions about whether the affirmative case has abided by the "rules of the game." It is here that the negative team should raise prima facie issues—that is, negative arguments making the claim that, at its most basic or "*on its face,*" the affirmative case has substantially failed to meet its BURDEN OF PROOF. Two types of arguments question whether the affirmative case is prima facie: **topicality** and **justification.**

The negative side can argue that an affirmative team has not met its prima facie burdens by saying that the case is *not topical.* By that, the negative is arguing that the affirmative has not stayed within the bounds (or parameters) of the resolution. Suppose the proposition is "Resolved: that the federal government should adopt an energy policy that substantially reduces the nonmilitary consumption of fossil fuels in the United States." If the affirmative has put forward a plan that reduces the use of nuclear power, the negative could argue that the affirmative is not topical because the proposition calls for the reduction of fossil fuel use and nuclear power does not run on fossil fuels. Or suppose the proposition is "Resolved: that violence is a justified response to political oppression." If the affirmative rationale discusses the justification for violence as a response to the increase of crime, the negative might argue that increased crime is not political oppression, so regardless of how justifiable such a response is, the affirmative case has failed to provide a rationale that supports the resolution.

In essence, a topicality argument says the affirmative case has failed to "play by the rules." The rule is that the affirmative will support the agreed-on resolution as worded. The wording of the resolution limits what the affirmative can and cannot argue in the case, and a topicality argument says "the affirmative has violated those limits." The agreement was to debate violence as a justifiable response to political oppression, but the affirmative chose to debate it as a response to the fear of crime. The affirmative has "violated" the agreement by not sticking to the topic—by being "nontopical."

The negative may argue that the entire affirmative case or a segment of it is not topical. Each of the examples above is an example of the former: the affirmative has constructed a case that in its entirety is not topical. In such cases, the negative is telling the judge that, because the affirmative's arguments are "off limits" or "out of bounds," the affirmative's case should be ignored and the judge's decision should be awarded to the negative. It is possible for the negative to argue that only a portion of the affirmative case is not topical and that only that portion should be "thrown out" of the debate. Suppose the affirmative, debating the proposition, "Resolved: that violence is a justified response to political oppression," advanced three situations that justified violent responses: to a dictatorship, to police brutality, and to increased crime. The negative could argue that the third situation—increased crime—is not topical and should not be considered a relevant argument in the debate. The negative might agree that the first two situations—the dictatorship and police brutality—are topical, and in so doing would wait to dispute those two arguments in the rationale portion of its constructive.[5]

In Chapter 8, a prima facie affirmative case was explained as one that is reasonably complete and of reasonable strength. When either of these conditions has not been met, the negative may argue that the affirmative case *has not justified* the resolution—that is, the case either lacks key elements of the argument or does not have sufficient importance to warrant the adoption of the resolution.

Returning to the resolution on justifiable violence, an affirmative case would not justify the resolution if its key elements were that (1) political oppression is significantly evil, and (2) anything that helps decrease or remove a significant evil is justified. The negative team might argue that the affirmative has failed to provide a prima facie case that justifies the resolution because the case is incomplete. The affirmative team has not demonstrated *solvency;* they have not shown that violence helps decrease or remove political oppression.

The negative side may also argue that the affirmative case fails to justify the resolution when it lacks reasonable strength. Consider the affirmative case that argued (1) excessive ticketing for driving offenses is a form of political oppression, and (2) violent reactions to excessive ticketing would effectively curb the practice. Even if the first negative speaker accepted these two affirmative contentions, he might argue that the affirmative case has failed to justify the resolution because (1) it does not show that excessive ticketing by police is a widespread problem—that is, that the problem is *significant;* and (2) it does not demonstrate that the case of excessive ticketing is *representative* of political oppression generally. The negative side could argue, on either count, that the affirmative case does not justify the resolution because it does not have reasonable strength. That is, the affirmative case can be accepted on its face, but it does not justify adoption of the proposition.

A variation of this argument, specific to nonpolicy debate, is the **whole resolution** argument. According to the theory of whole resolution, in nonpolicy debate, the affirmative must justify the adoption of resolution *as a general principle* and not simply a single instance of it. For example, for the proposition, "Resolved: that violence is a justified response to political oppression," a whole resolution standard would hold that the affirmative must construct a case that justifies adopting the resolution as a generalized value. An affirmative case arguing simply that violence was justified in the case of the civil rights movement of the 1950s and 1960s, for example, could be charged with not supporting the whole resolution. The affirmative case should have provided a rationale for generalizing from the case of civil rights to most instances of political oppression.

Whole resolution is not typically argued as a standard for policy debate. In policy debate, the resolution calls for *a* change, and the plan included in the affirmative case is the specific change the affirmative is proposing and willing to defend. A resolution calling for a national land use policy does not, for example, require an affirmative to defend every land use policy ever proposed. Indeed, to defend every plan that would be topical under a policy resolution would often require the affirmative to defend mutually exclusive plans. In contrast, a value proposition asks the affirmative to defend a *value,* a generalized belief about how an individual or society *ought* to act. In a value proposition, whole resolution is a valid prima facie issue.

More problematic is the case of what is sometimes called a "quasi-policy" resolution in nonpolicy debate. Quasi-policy propositions are those resolutions that invite the affirmative to offer a "plan" but that occur in a debate setting that discourages the use of policy debate (in a nonpolicy debate setting). For example, the CEDA topic of 1989, "Resolved: that increased restrictions on handguns are warranted," almost forced affirmatives to propose and defend certain specified restrictions. There were various reasons for this. First, some restrictions (such as banning gun ownership) required the affirmative to attack long-held constitutional rights whereas others (such as waiting periods and gun registration) did not. Would adopting the "value" implied in the resolution conflict with other values (such as the constitutionally guaranteed freedoms)? It depended on which restrictions the affirmative advocated. Second, it is very hard to justify (or warrant) support for the adoption of laws (restrictions) unless there is evidence that the restrictions will *work*. This burden, of course, introduces the issue of solvency, an issue that is difficult to debate unless you are specific about the actions you are proposing. It is far easier to demonstrate that restrictions solve the problem if you are specific about the restrictions. Returning to the whole resolution standard, does it make sense to say that the affirmative team defending the proposition about increased restrictions must justify the adoption of this proposition as *a general rule*—should argue that *most* restrictions on handguns should be supported? Although it is conceivable that an affirmative side could construct a case supporting handgun restrictions that satisfied the whole resolution standard, few affirmative teams did so that year, and few judges or debate theorists are willing to impose that standard on a quasi-policy resolution.

In addition to overviews at the beginning of a constructive speech (and extended through rebuttals), the negative speaker may also choose to include underviews at the end of her speech. Negative underviews perform the same function as affirmative underviews: they may provide additional interpretation that should guide the decision making in the round or attempt to place parameters (restrictions) on what subsequent affirmative arguments should not or cannot be. As with parameters advocated by the affirmative, a negative side's argument for parameters should be complete, reasonable, and meaningful.

The preliminary/summary component is important. Through prima facie arguments, the placing or dismissing of argumentative burdens or the construction of rhetorical lenses through which to view the overall argument, the introductions, overviews, or underviews may provide the deciding element of an entire debate.

Definitions

How the terms of the resolution are defined is as important for the negative as it is for the affirmative—and for the same reasons. Definitions perform the same argumentative functions for either team—enhancing successful advocacy, critical inquiry, and reasoned decision making. The negative does, however, have a greater option about whether to incorporate definitions into the first constructive speech. If the affirmative's definitions are acceptable to the negative, the first negative constructive speaker can indicate that they are and then move on to other case arguments.

If one or more of the affirmative's definitions are *not* acceptable to the negative, those definitions need to be contested in the first negative constructive speech. After all, the reason we define terms is to make certain that all participants to the argument begin on "common ground," with a common understanding of *what* is being debated. A question arises, then, of whether the issue of defining terms should come before any overview the negative might provide or immediately after.

Our answer is that it depends on the overview and the definitions being debated. In some instances, the order will be obvious. An introduction that provides a rhetorical context would almost always precede any definitional argument—and may even be important for providing the context within which the negative is disputing the definition. If the overview disputes the affirmative's topicality and does so based on how a disputed term is defined, the definition would certainly precede the overview.

In other cases, the decision of how to arrange the first negative constructive will be less clear. Some debaters favor starting with the overview—especially if it disputes the affirmative's topicality or justification. Such placement highlights the significance of the argument for the debate. Others prefer beginning with definitional arguments because *technically* it is "impossible" to begin arguing a proposition without a common understanding of the proposition's meaning.

Regardless of the arrangement you prefer, it is important for the first negative constructive speaker that some consideration be given to the order of these arguments. It is also important for the negative side to realize that regardless of the arrangement of any overviews or definitional arguments, they must raise *all* definitional arguments *before* proceeding to the rationale arguments. Finally, the negative team should remember that, by tradition, any affirmative definitions that are not disputed in the first constructive speech will be considered acceptable to the negative. *Very* few judges will allow negative teams to raise definitional issues in later speeches.

Negative definitions should be supported in the same manner as definitions for the affirmative (see Chapter 11). Any of the five primary methods of defining—standardized reference, contextual usage, operation, example, and negation—may be employed by the negative. As with the affirmative, the negative team should choose the most appropriate method for the nature of the term they are defining. Two components of the negative side's argument, however, will not be found in the affirmative's initial definitions.

First, the negative team needs to include a rationale for why its definition is *better* (or more appropriate) than that of the affirmative. This rationale may include an argument regarding the deficiencies of the affirmative's definition, the superior understanding provided by the negative's definition, or a combination of both those arguments. For either argument—about deficiencies or superiority—the negative will probably need to focus on the nature of the term being defined. Rarely do affirmatives make definitional errors of fact—applying the "wrong" definition to a word; almost every definitional controversy arises over which of two viable definitions is best for understanding the term as it is being used/debated in this proposition. It is useful here to remember our discussion of field-dependent and field-independent. The superior definition will usually be field-dependent—that is, the best definition for understanding the word *as it is being used in this particular context.* The discarded definition may also be field-dependent, but rarely will a field-independent definition win over one that has been drawn from the field or context constructed by the proposition.

Second, as with all its arguments, the negative's definitional arguments need an impact component. What is the effect on the debate of whether we accept the affirmative's or negative's definition? Too many definitional arguments in a debate have no impact argued. The negative needs to show the judge where in the debate the contested definition makes a difference in the judgment rendered. Does the negative team's definition make one or more of the affirmative team's advantages nontopical? Does the negative's definition render some of the affirmative's case contentions irrelevant to the proposition? Does the negative's definition broaden the affirmative's definition in ways that allow the negative to introduce important considerations in its off-case arguments?

Because definitional arguments tell us what is appropriate to argue *throughout* a debate, the negative may not be able to develop its impact statement fully until its on-case rationale arguments or its off-case arguments are presented. It is important, however, that the negative clearly link those later impact statements to its earlier definitional argument. By the end of the two negative constructive speeches, the impact of the negative's definitional challenge needs to be clear. As an aid to clarity, it may also be useful to preview the later impact statements; for example, "The importance of using a broader definition of 'beneficial' will be clear when we present our off-case disadvantage arguments."

Finally, note that on occasion, the negative side's definition will supplement rather than contradict the definition of the affirmative side. In those instances, the negative will argue that the affirmative's definition is incomplete, not incorrect. As with definitions that contradict, it will be important for the negative to show why the additional meaning is superior to the affirmative's original, more limited definition, and what impact the supplemented definition has for the debate at hand.

On-Case Rationale Arguments

Because the rationale is the heart and soul of the affirmative case, it is typically the "heart and soul" of the negative's attacks and the debate as a whole. This is certainly true when an affirmative team has presented a topical, prima facie case; for if it has, the affirmative has met its BURDEN OF PROOF. Regardless of any auxiliary arguments the negative might make, the affirmative will win the debate unless the validity of its case is either called into question or thoroughly refuted.

The *substance* of what the negative can argue in its refutation of the affirmative's rationale has already been discussed. The negative may, for example, draw on the material discussed in Chapter 4 and take issue with the affirmative's evidence, perhaps by attacking the credibility of that evidence or by providing contradictory evidence. Or the negative may dispute the affirmative's interpretation of its evidence. Or the negative may choose to draw on the material discussed in Chapters 3 and 5, taking issue with elements of the affirmative's reasoning. It may accuse the affirmative of indulging in fallacious reasoning or of failing to qualify its claims properly. In a nonpolicy debate, the negative may draw on the material discussed in Chapter 12 and challenge the affirmative's criteria. In policy or nonpolicy debates, the negative may draw on material from Chapter 9 to challenge the affirmative's paradigm, or from Chapter 8 to challenge the inherency or the significance of the affirmative's rationale. Whatever the substance of the negative's attacks, however, there are certain points this team should keep in mind when constructing its on-case rationale arguments.

First, the clearest arrangement for these arguments is to follow the order of the affirmative's case. The negative should begin with the affirmative's first contention and follow that arrangement through the second, third, and so on. It is usually confusing, especially for beginning debaters, to jump back and forth between the contentions. Within contentions, too, the negative should follow the affirmative's arrangement, beginning with the A point, then the B point, the C point, and so on.

Remember, though, that it is permissible to skip arguments you accept; the negative does not have to disagree with or refute every single point and subpoint of the affirmative's case. Therefore, the negative could use this kind of transition statement: "Taking a look at the affirmative's second contention, which tries to prove inherency, the A and B points are valid. The affirmative is mistaken, however, in the conclusion they draw in their C point." With these two transition sentences, the negative has not only signaled that she is addressing contention 2, point C, but she has acknowledged the presence and acceptability of points A and B. Rather than leaving those two points unaddressed, she has focused the debate on the argument at issue. She has also foreshadowed the refutation she will use (mistaken reasoning) and the impact of her refutation (inherency).

Second, the negative should remember to use the L-R-I-(P) format as a pattern for arranging each of its individual arguments. How does each refutation relate to the affirmative case? What is the rationale for rejecting the affirmative argument? What is the impact of doing so for the debate? There may be times, of course, when a single link argument lays the groundwork for several refutation arguments. There may also be times when several refutations, taken together, have a unique and important impact on the debate. Thus, there will be instances when the L-R-I-(P) format may be used more loosely than normal. In general, however, it should provide the arrangement for each individual argument made by the negative, and always, all three of the mandatory components —the link, the refutation, and the impact—need to be present at some point in the negative speech.

Third, as discussed in Chapter 6, direct refutation may either question or contradict, or both. Generally, it is clearest if the negative begins with arguments that question the validity or credibility of the affirmative's arguments and then provide reasoning or evidence that directly refutes the affirmative. Suppose the affirmative offered evidence to indicate that drug tests are accurate. In its refutation, the negative might first point out the methodological flaws in the affirmative's evidence, and then provide methodologically superior evidence to support the claim that drug tests are inaccurate. This arrangement would be clearer than first presenting the methodologically superior evidence and *then* discussing the methodological problems with the affirmative's evidence. For the listeners, hearing first a discussion of the affirmative's methodology problems would help make immediately evident the superior nature of the negative's evidence.

The same principle is true in refuting the affirmative's reasoning. Suppose the affirmative had constructed its case inductively, arguing that the United States is justified in providing military support to nondemocratic countries because of the evidence supplied by three examples. The negative could respond by first indicting the affirmative's reasoning, arguing that inductive reasoning is a dubious intellectual method for constructing value judgments and that the affirmative's three choices are limited, narrow, and too similar to allow broad conclusions about values to be drawn. In its on-case arguments, the negative could then present examples that directly contradict those of the affirmative. Later, in off-case argument, the negative might construct a deductively reasoned argument that refutes the resolution. Again, the clearest presentation usually begins with a discussion of the weaknesses or limitations of the affirmative, and uses that discussion as the context for the negative side's on-case (and off-case) arguments. Exceptions will occur, especially if there are pressures of time; it might be strategic to begin with your own refutative arguments if they are stronger and if limitations of time restrict your ability to discuss both kinds of refutations.

Fourth, it is important for the negative side to recognize and understand the basic affirmative case structure. We discuss some of these issues of structure in ensuing sections. For example, do the affirmative's contentions match the standards created by their criteria? Does the plan solve the problems presented in the contentions? Does the significance of the problem/need/advantages presented in the contentions justify the various costs (funding, disadvantages, and so on) of the plan? One simple but important element of the case structure the negative needs to recognize is whether (or which of) the affirmative's contentions or supporting claims are **dependent** or **independent.** A contention or supporting claim is *independent* when, in and of itself, it proves the resolution or larger claim. A contention or supporting claim is *dependent* when it must rely on one or more other contentions or supporting claims to prove that the resolution or claim is true.

Consider the environmental degradation policy example from the preceding chapter.

CONTENTION 1: Environmental degradation is increasing. (Significance)
Supporting Claim A: Air pollution is increasing.
Supporting Claim B: Water pollution is increasing.

CONTENTION 2: Environmental degradation is harmful. (Significance)
Supporting Claim A: The quality of life is being eroded.
Supporting Claim B: Individual health is threatened.

CONTENTION 3: Environmental degradation will continue. (Inherency)
Supporting Claim A: Current regulations are inadequate.
Supporting Claim B: Financial motives ensure pollution.

CONTENTION 4: The affirmative plan solves the problem. (Solvency)
Supporting Claim A: Establishing more stringent levels will cut pollution in half.
Supporting Claim B: The plan changes the financial incentive to pollute into a substantial financial disincentive.

The overall case structure is *dependent.* To justify the adoption of the resolution, the affirmative needs to win all four of the contentions. For example, showing that the condition is significant and growing (contention 1) is not enough to justify adopting the plan; the affirmative also needs to show that the condition is detrimental, inherent, and will be solved by the plan. Proving that the condition is detrimental (contention 2) is not enough to justify adoption of the plan; the affirmative also needs to show that the condition is significantly present, inherent, and will be solved by the plan. If the affirmative proves that the problem is inherent (contention 3), that is not enough, by itself, to justify adoption of the plan; the problem must also be proven significant and the plan valid for solving that problem. Proving the affirmative plan will solve the problem (contention 4) is not enough, by itself, to justify adopting the plan; the problem must also be proven to be significant and inherent. Because the contentions of the affirmative side are dependent, if the negative team effectively refutes *any* of them, it will have won the overall argument.

Note, however, that many of the supporting claims in this example are *independent.* In contention 1, for example, the affirmative need not prove that air pollution (claim A) *and* water pollution (claim B) are both occurring to justify the contention. To defeat the contention, the negative needs to effectively refute *both* those contentions. Similarly, in contention 2, the affirmative has provided two *independent* reasons for believing that environmental degradation is harmful: it erodes the quality of life and threatens individual health. Again, the affirmative need not win both these arguments to win the contention; winning a single subpoint would be sufficient. Either supporting claim—decreased quality of life or threatened health—could be argued as providing sufficient justification for accepting the claim that "environmental degradation is harmful," and the negative would have to refute *both* supporting claims to win the point.

The negative must understand independent and dependent claims to determine which arguments must be contested to refute a claim. Identifying claims as dependent or independent can be tricky, however. Consider, for example, the mandatory drug testing example from Chapter 12.

> **CONTENTION 1:** Mandatory drug testing is effective in detecting drug use by employees.
>
> **CONTENTION 2:** Use of mandatory drug testing in the workplace deters drug use by employees.
>
> **CONTENTION 3:** Use of mandatory drug testing in the workplace results in decreased incidents of drug-related accidents.

In wording and form, the case appears to consist of three dependent contentions: because drug testing detects, it deters; and because it deters, accidents decrease. However, these three contentions could be argued quite independently of one another. This is particularly true if the affirmative has any advantages—increased productivity, increased quality of work, improved quality of life for the employee—that supplement the "decreased accidents" advantage.

A negative debater might be lulled into thinking that the contentions are dependent, and if he proves that drug tests are inaccurate and therefore do *not* detect drug use, he has knocked out the deterrence and accident contentions as well. This is not the case, however. The affirmative debater could argue that the use of drug tests deters drug use because employees *perceive* them to be accurate, *regardless* of whether they are or not. The tests may deter drug use not because they detect it but because employees *fear* detection. In that case, the affirmative's second and third contentions could be true even if contention 1 is false.

Suppose the negative side wins contention 2, proving that drug tests do not deter employee drug use. The affirmative could still argue that (1) drug tests do detect drug use, so (2) drug users, especially in positions susceptible to accident, can be removed from the company or from those positions, and therefore, (3) accidents do decrease with the use of drug tests. Again, the contentions are far less dependent than a cursory examination might reveal.

Even if the negative side effectively refutes the affirmative's third contention, the first two contentions could carry the round—depending on the criteria established in the affirmative plan. Suppose the affirmative defined standards of "beneficial" as (1) decreased risk of accidents, injury, and loss of life on the job and (2) decreased use of hallucinogenic or mind-altering drugs. Losing contention 3 means they have not met standard 1, but winning contention 2 *is* enough to show that they have met the second of the two criteria.

As we noted in Chapter 10, however, the foundation for all affirmative claims *must* be laid in the first affirmative constructive. Few judges will allow affirmative teams to introduce new criteria or new advantages in later constructive or rebuttal speeches. If the affirmative side lost contention 3, it could not argue new criteria (such as criteria 2 above) or new contentions (deterring employee drug use increases productivity) that would make contention 2 sufficient to win the round. Contentions and supporting claims should remain consistently independent or consistently dependent from the first affirmative constructive on; it is up to the first negative speaker, however, to make sure that he or she correctly understands what the affirmative position is.

Finally, it is important for the negative side to consider the **voting issues** in the debate. The term *voting issues* refers to those arguments in the debate that are critical to deciding whether the judge will vote affirmative or negative on the debate. At first glance, you might think that *every* argument in the debate is a "voting issue"; after all, the entire debate round is *about* the proposition and which way the judge should vote on the proposition. In practice, however, each debate has certain arguments that become more important than others, arguments that in fact decide the debate. The preceding discussion of dependent and independent contentions illustrates that point. Suppose in a debate about environmental degradation that the negative did not attack contentions 1 and 2 (significance of the problem) but instead focused their refutation on contentions 3 and 4 (inherency and solvency). Those two contentions would be called "voting issues" because how the judge decided those two arguments would determine—in conjunction with any other voting issues in the round—whether the judge voted affirmative or negative on the proposition.

Voting issues are usually divided into two types: procedural and substantive. Procedural issues are arguments that concern the general conduct (or procedure) of the debate. Topicality, for example, is a procedural issue. An argument about what the affirmative's or negative's responsibilities are in a debate would also be a procedural issue. For example, for a particular proposition, affirmatives will sometimes argue that the PRESUMPTION for the debate actually lies with them and that the BURDEN OF PROOF lies with the negative. This is a switch of responsibilities that few negatives will accept and the point is usually argued vigorously in each constructive and rebuttal speech. This would become a procedural voting issue: who had which responsibilities in today's debate?

That decision would then be used to decide which team had met their responsibilities and which had not.

Debate about the nature of the proposition—whether it is a value, non-policy, or policy resolution—is another common example of a procedural argument that is typically a voting issue. As with a presumption-switch, determination of a proposition's type will indicate what responsibilities are placed on the affirmative and negative. Many debaters and judges treated the proposition, "Resolved: that restrictions on the ownership of handguns in the United States are warranted," as a policy or "quasi-policy" topic.[6] When the resolution is interpreted that way, it places different burdens on the affirmative than when it is interpreted as a value resolution. The argument over which way to interpret the resolution was, in those debates, a procedural voting issue.

Substantive voting issues would be those addressing whether the affirmative or negative team has better met its burdens. The issues discussed in Chapter 13 —such as significance, solvency, and inherency—and those examined in Chapter 12 regarding criteria are examples of substantive issues. Has the affirmative proven a significant problem in the status quo? Is that problem inherent in the status quo? Is the resolution the right answer to that problem? Substantive voting issues are the arguments the affirmative needs to win to prove the resolution true, or needs to lose for the negative to prove the resolution false.

Debaters should keep the voting issues of a round in mind as they prepare and deliver any speech in a debate, but doing so is particularly important in the rebuttals. The first negative rebuttal needs to address the second affirmative constructive's arguments, but she also needs to discuss, even if briefly, where the affirmative's arguments have failed to win the voting issues necessary for winning the debate. The second negative rebuttal speaker needs to review the overall debate, pointing out along the way which voting issues the affirmative has lost and why, thus leading to the conclusion of the speech: that a vote for the negative is warranted.[7] Rebuttals, then, are especially critical speeches for the negative in regard to recognizing, examining, and debating the voting issues of the round.

In this section, we have looked at five general principles for arguing the negative side of the rationale: (1) The clearest overall arrangement is usually to follow the order of the affirmative's case. (2) The L-R-I-(P) format should be used as the pattern for arranging each individual argument. (3) For each affirmative argument the negative is refuting, the most effective procedure is usually to begin with those arguments that call the affirmative's argument into question and then provide the reasoning or evidence that directly counters the affirmative's argument. (4) At the beginning of the debate (first constructive speech) it is important for the negative team to recognize and understand the basic affirmative case structure. (5) By the end of the debate (rebuttals), it is critically important for the negative side to recognize and discuss the voting issues in the round.

Differences between Policy and Nonpolicy On-Case Arguments

The general approaches for negative on-case rationale arguments are very similar in nonpolicy and policy debates. However, a couple of unique considerations and differences should be mentioned.

First, although criteria arguments can be used in policy debate, in nonpolicy debate they usually occupy a central place in the argument. Not only are they important voting issues for determining the debate, but, as we discussed in Chapter 12, they can often consume considerable time in the debate if done well.

They are sometimes labeled off-case arguments (and sometimes termed *overviews* or *countercriteria*), but because they stand in opposition to the affirmative side's criteria, they are best considered on-case arguments. Like definitions, criteria arguments *must* be raised in the first negative constructive speech. Whereas the "link" component of a criterion argument is usually clear—the negative criterion stands in opposition to the affirmative's criterion—arguing the rationale and impact components well is especially important. Again, as with definitional arguments, two key questions should be answered by the negative side's criterion argument: the *rationale* question, "Why is the negative criterion better than the affirmative criterion?" and the *impact* question, "What difference does changing the criterion make in how we judge the arguments in the debate (and, ultimately, the debate itself)?" Debaters arguing the negative side of a nonpolicy proposition should make sure they are well versed in the concepts discussed in Chapter 12.

Second, although the negative teams in both policy and nonpolicy debates will probably raise arguments of solvency, the placement of those arguments is usually different depending on the type of proposition. In policy argumentation, plan attacks are usually argued as off-case arguments. Plan attacks include solvency arguments (Will the plan really solve the problem?) and disadvantages (Do the disadvantages of the plan outweigh the advantages?). We look at solvency and disadvantage arguments in greater detail in the next section, but here we note that solvency arguments are also important components of nonpolicy debate. Because there is no specific plan in nonpolicy debate, however, solvency arguments are typically placed in the first negative constructive's on-case argumentation.

Solvency arguments, in policy or nonpolicy debate, simply ask if the adoption of the proposition will in fact *cause* the results (effects) the affirmative case claims it will cause.[8] As such, our discussion of cause-effect reasoning in Chapter 5 is particularly relevant to solvency argumentation. Negatives should be especially wary of an affirmative's reliance on evidence from authority—quotations that simply assert that the "cause" will result in the "effect," with no discussion of the *reasoning* behind that claim. Has the affirmative provided adequate associational data to demonstrate that the cause has created the effect? Has it provided adequate connectional data? Will adoption of the resolution in fact *cause* the benefits the affirmative claims? These are solvency questions, and solvency is often an important voting issue in the debate.

Nonpolicy Off-Case Arguments

Unlike the negative on-case arguments, where policy and nonpolicy debate have many similarities, the negative off-case arguments look very different for policy debate and for nonpolicy debate. Off-case arguments in policy debate focus solely on plan attacks. In contrast, off-case arguments in nonpolicy debate raise arguments against the proposition that do not apply directly to the case the affirmative has made for it.

Nonpolicy off-case arguments are made up chiefly of value objections, countercontentions, and counterexamples.[9] Value objections and countercontentions, in some senses very similar and often confused in nonpolicy debate, do in fact represent two different approaches to refuting the proposition. Counterexamples, often called counterwarrants, provide a third approach to developing a nonpolicy off-case position. We look at each of these three types of off-case nonpolicy argument below.

Value Objections

Value objections are very similar to disadvantage arguments in policy debate. Essentially, value objections state that if the value contained within the resolution is adopted, certain disadvantages (or *objectionable* effects) will occur. Depending on the criteria adopted in the round, value objections may state that adopting the resolution will create economic, environmental, psychological, educational, physical, or moral harms.

Suppose the affirmative was supporting the proposition, "Resolved: that individual rights of privacy are more important than any other constitutional right." The affirmative could construct a case using three contentions: (1) Governments are formed for the purpose of protecting its individual citizens and should do all they can to accomplish that purpose (criteria). (2) Privacy is a fundamental need for maintaining individuality. (3) Individuality is critical for making the protection of individual citizens meaningful. Therefore, privacy rights are the most important protection a government can provide for its citizens. A negative side could construct an off-case value objection arguing that emphasizing privacy rights leads to an increase of crime. Preferencing privacy rights over other rights, the negative might argue, (1) allows criminals to conduct their business freely through various electronic media such as telephone, e-mail, and fax lines; (2) often results in evidence that cannot be used in court because it is discovered in a search that violates an individual's privacy; and (3) allows for the freer distribution of illegal substances by various modes of transportation.

The negative's value objection, that increased emphasis on privacy increases the incidence of crime, presents a disadvantage or harm that occurs when the value contained in the resolution is adopted. Value objections such as this one need to be combined with on-case attacks that minimize the advantages that accrue if we adopt the resolution's value. Taken together, these arguments can justify rejection of the resolution.

Negative debaters using value objections should remember that at their core, value objections lie within a comparative advantages paradigm (see Chapter 9). That is, the affirmative case has probably enumerated some advantages or benefits that come from adopting the resolution;[10] the negative's value objections are the disadvantages or harms that come from adopting the value contained within the resolution. In this kind of a debate, the first negative speaker attempts to minimize or eliminate the affirmative's claimed benefits while the second negative speaker attempts to maximize the claimed harms. It is a pragmatic/cost-benefit approach to debating values, and although it is a popular paradigm, remember that it is not the only one available.

In a debate of value objections, the negative must remember that comparison of the affirmative side's advantages with the negative side's disadvantages is a crucial voting issue. Although any off-case position the negative advances will be considered in comparison with the affirmative side's case, that comparison will be a particularly close one with value objections. This is because the weight a judge will assign to any particular value objection can be determined only by its relationship to the affirmative case. As decision makers, we are all willing to endure some disadvantages if the advantages outweigh them, or if there is a principle (value) involved that we feel strongly about.

In debating value objections, the debaters should keep in mind the entire negative position. When debaters are developing value objections in the middle of a debate, they can be tempted to favor quantity over quality, figuring that the larger the number of harms caused by the value, the greater will be the overall disadvantage of adopting it. There is a danger in relying on quantity, however;

debaters can easily present conflicting value objections or introduce a value objection that contradicts one of their own on-case arguments. The negative should therefore choose and construct value objections carefully and completely.

Countercontentions

Countercontentions, like contentions in the affirmative case, are major claims that, taken together, create a prima facie argument for rejecting the proposition. As with the affirmative position, the negative side constructing an off case through countercontentions must satisfy certain stock issue requirements: criteria, significance, inherency, and harm. Of these four issues, the one concerning criteria is unique in two ways. First, the negative could choose to adopt the affirmative's criteria. Although it is rare that a negative can construct a competing prima facie off-case using the same criteria as the affirmative, it is certainly possible. Second, the criteria component of the negative's off-case must be developed in the first negative constructive speech. Like definitions, criteria must be challenged at the first opportunity for doing so. The other three components—inherency, significance, and harm—could be developed in the second negative constructive.[11]

If we return to the example of individual rights of privacy, a negative team could construct an off-case countercontention arguing that (1) governments are formed for the purpose of developing and preserving community and should do all they can to accomplish that purpose (criteria); (2) giving primacy to individual rights of privacy places undue emphasis on those rights; (3) undue emphasis on privacy creates antisocial citizens; therefore, (4) individual rights of privacy should not be valued more than other, more socially constructive rights (such as First Amendment freedoms of expression). Except for the first contention, which develops the criteria, the negative side's countercontentions do not *directly* clash with the affirmative's contentions. They do, however, present an alternative perspective—a competing rationale—that justifies rejecting the resolution.

Whereas a negative team arguing value objections compares the advantages to the disadvantages, a team constructing an off-case position through countercontentions is comparing competing interpretations of the resolution. Which team has chosen the best criteria? Which has identified the greatest significance or harm? Which offers the more compelling interpretation of the resolution and the values and effects contained in the adoption of that resolution?[12]

Countercontentions are the riskiest and most difficult of the three off-case approaches to use and to use well. When it is properly developed, however, a negative off-case built on countercontentions has the advantage of presenting a consistent and coherent negative case. Such unity of vision can make arguing the negative position much easier. Also, rather than relying solely on presumption—"the affirmative has not given us sufficient grounds for adopting the resolution"—a countercontention off-case provides the negative side with a positive platform from which to reject the resolution. This, too, can provide a psychological boost to arguing the negative.

Finally, as with the affirmative case, a negative off-case built on countercontentions can be prepared well in advance of the debate. Regardless of the affirmative team's specific approach to constructing its case, the resolution remains constant. A negative off-case position that is directly linked to the resolution (rather than specifically to the affirmative case) can be used in any debate and against any affirmative case. The negative will, however, need to uphold a whole resolution standard, because a common affirmative response will be that they do not have to argue against off-case positions that have not been directly linked to the affirmative case. The negative must be ready to argue that the affirmative is responsible for *all* possible ramifications of adopting the resolution.

Counterexamples

Counterexamples, often called counterwarrants, are arguments describing examples that "negate" the resolution. These are examples demonstrating that in the past, when the resolution has been adopted, problems have resulted. Counterexamples could be used as evidence for value objections or countercontentions, but they are called counterexamples when each example is developed separately as an "instance" in which the resolution failed. In direct contrast to countercontentions, which create a deductively structured off-case based on reasoning and interpretation, counterexamples construct an inductive off-case based on examples.

For the individual privacy resolution, a counterexample might be that freedom of the press is more important than any individual right of privacy. The negative might cite an important court case as evidence, or discuss a specific, actual example in which freedom of the press was more important than a right of privacy. The public's "right to know," the negative might argue, is more important than a public figure's right to privacy. The freedom of the press to intrude on one's privacy is, therefore, greater than any individual right to privacy.

Just as an affirmative case constructed inductively from a series of examples is the weakest kind of case to build, counterexamples are, generally speaking, the weakest of the three approaches to developing a nonpolicy off-case. First, in and of themselves, the counterexamples do not prove that the affirmative's examples are untrue. Indeed, the negative will often accept the affirmative's examples but then argue that there are "other" examples. The crux of the debate becomes a determination of whose examples are most representative or most significant. Although representativeness and significance can certainly be argued, the result can be rather ambiguous and messy arguments. Representativeness especially is a claim that is readily arguable.

Second, counterexamples are also weak because they can be countered by the affirmative with more examples. The debate then becomes "who has the most examples," which is simply another form of the representativeness argument. For example, the affirmative could provide instances when individual rights of privacy have been preferenced over freedom of the press to report whatever it wants. The debate then becomes a game of counting up court cases in which the right to privacy was or was not preferenced over freedom of the press.

Third, deductive arguments by nature are broader in scope than are inductive arguments. Deductive off-cases entail a greater degree of logic and reasoning, and they thus provide a more conclusive reason for rejecting the resolution. Both the examples above of countercontentions and of value objections create more compelling cases than does the counterexample. Counterexamples are limited in their explanatory power, simply listing instances in which the value contained in the resolution proved faulty.

Counterexamples should usually be used as an argument of the last resort, and they are most effective when the affirmative has also structured its case inductively. When the affirmative case is deductively structured, counterexamples may be best used as evidence in the negative's on-case argumentation—as evidence that the affirmative's contentions are false. When used in off-case argumentation, counterexamples are usually best used as evidence for value objections or countercontentions.

These, then, are three approaches to developing an off-case in nonpolicy debate. Value objections, a form of disadvantage, is easily the most commonly employed approach. Countercontentions provide the most thorough arguments for rejecting the resolution but are also the most difficult to construct. Counterexamples, because they inductively attack the proposition, are the weakest of the three approaches and are often most productively used in the other approaches as evidence rather than standing alone as major claims.

Policy Off-Case Arguments

The nonpolicy off-case attempts to construct a negative position that will compete with that of the affirmative whereas the policy off-case is usually devoted to plan attacks. In the second negative constructive speech, the speaker typically makes two basic arguments: the plan won't "work" (solvency); and the plan, if implemented, will create significant disadvantages. Both arguments are common in policy off-case argument. More rare is a third argument: a counterplan. A negative counterplan is a plan proposed by the negative that would solve the problem outlined in the affirmative but does not fit or fulfill the resolution. Each of these is explored in the next sections.

Solvency

Sometimes called plan meets needs (PMN) or plan meets advantages (PMA) arguments, a solvency argument simply contends that the affirmative plan "won't work" the way the affirmative claims it will. Remember that affirmative teams always justify the adoption of their plan on the grounds that it will eliminate or lessen the significant harm outlined in the contentions. The negative side may argue that the plan will *not* solve that problem at all, or it may argue that the plan will solve it *to a lesser extent* than claimed by the affirmative. To demonstrate the validity of its solvency claims, the negative can employ any or all of the arguments that are available to affirmatives for *proving* that the plan *will* work as advertised: logical claims, previous examples, and authoritative testimony.

The negative team may argue that the plan lacks solvency because, *logically*, it will not work. Suppose the affirmative proposed a plan mandating drug tests for job applicants for the purpose of reducing work-related injuries. The negative might argue that unless the plan also mandated follow-up testing, job applicants could refrain from taking drugs long enough to pass the application test but then resume their use of controlled substances. Similarly, the negative team might argue, the lack of follow-up means that an employee may have had no experience with drugs until the time of employment but may begin drug use once on the job. Without follow-up testing, the negative would argue, the deterrence is weak and the affirmative's solvency is minimal.

The negative may also argue that the plan lacks solvency because, in previous instances, plans that were similar or identical have not worked. In the previous example, the negative could use statistics of drug-related accidents that occur in companies that already test employees for drugs. Or the negative might use examples of drug-related accidents that have occurred with railroad engineers, school bus drivers, and other employees who were, at some point previously, tested for drugs. Even ongoing drug tests can be circumvented, the negative might argue. Drug tests used only in the application stage are certain to solve little, if any, of the problem.

Finally, the negative can also use authoritative evidence to support its claims that the plan will not solve the problem. Experts often consider whether hypothetical actions will solve a problem, and such expert speculation may be crucial for the negative if the plan has not been previously attempted. In our discussion of testimony as a type of evidence (Chapter 4), we showed authoritative testimony to be most useful when the expert spells out the *reasons* behind his or her conclusions. That is, authoritative testimony is weakest when it stands alone, asking listeners to believe the claim solely on the basis of the credibility of the source. Authoritative evidence is most effective when it either reiterates the negative's logical claims regarding the plan's solvency or when it points to previous examples as its support for its claims.

When constructing solvency arguments, the negative would do well to recall the discussion about cause and effect reasoning in Chapter 5. The issue of solvency rests entirely on the question of causality: Will the plan *cause* the effects to occur that the affirmative claims it will? The side that can best argue the plan's causality—or lack of causality—will win the solvency issue. Solvency is invariably an important voting issue in a debate. The negative can argue absolute nonsolvency—that the plan will have *none* of the effects claimed by the affirmative—in which case solvency is an "absolute" voting issue; if the negative wins the argument, the resolution has been disproved.

The negative can, however, elect to argue *reduced* solvency instead—that the plan will have fewer beneficial effects than the affirmative claims. Reduced solvency arguments are often combined with disadvantages arguments when attacking a comparative advantages case. Reduced solvency claims that the advantages gained by the affirmative plan are minimal whereas the disadvantages argument claims that the disadvantages caused by the affirmative plan are maximal. These arguments complement each other well when the cost-benefit paradigm is used by the affirmative or the negative.

Disadvantages

Solvency arguments state that the affirmative plan will not do what the affirmative says it will, whereas plan disadvantage arguments say, "But here's the harm the plan *will* cause." The disadvantage argument establishes that some undesirable consequence will either absolutely or likely result from the implementation of the affirmative plan.

These undesirable consequences can take a variety of forms. They might be effects produced by the resource requirements of the plan (fewer resources for the production of consumer goods), effects of the plan on basic human rights (loss of privacy), societal effects produced by the plan (increase in crime), changes in human behavior produced by the plan (less concern about safety when driving), organizational/relational effects produced by the plan (increased tension between the United States and China), or disastrous scenarios precipitated by the plan (increased risk of nuclear proliferation, increased risk of global starvation, increased risk of an ecological calamity).

Regardless of the type of consequence outlined in the plan, the disadvantage must be shown to be *unique*. That is, the effects cited in the disadvantage must be shown to be a direct result of the implementation of the plan. If the disadvantage would have occurred anyway or is currently occurring in similar proportions, then the disadvantage is not unique to the affirmative plan and does not constitute a reason to reject the plan. Uniqueness will probably be established in the link or the rationale section of the argument, but it is *critically* important for the negative to establish uniqueness in order to prove the *impact* of the disadvantage. A disadvantage that would have occurred anyway has no impact; we can adopt the affirmative plan and incur no additional costs because the disadvantage will occur regardless of whether we adopt the plan or not.

The negative can demonstrate the uniqueness of the disadvantage by arguing that we are either "on the brink" or that we are engaged in a "linear progression" toward incurring the disadvantage. In the **on the brink approach,** the negative demonstrates that the status quo is "on the brink" of experiencing the disadvantage and that implementing the affirmative plan will provide the final impetus for the disadvantage to occur. For example, the negative could argue that we are on the brink of a new round of international nuclear proliferation and that adopting the affirmative plan would be the final catalyst needed for that proliferation to occur. In the **linear progression approach,** the negative argues that the disadvantage occurs in a linear fashion: the harmful consequences already exist, but implementing the affirmative plan will exacerbate or magnify the severity of the problem. For example, the negative might argue that crime exists now, but that adopting the affirmative plan will make a particular aspect of the crime problem worse.

In addition to proving uniqueness, the negative team presenting a disadvantage argument must also demonstrate that the disadvantage presents a **compelling reason** to reject the affirmative plan. Like uniqueness, the compelling nature of the disadvantage is critically important for the impact component of the argument. If the disadvantage is not compelling, it will carry little impact on the larger argument of whether to adopt the proposition.

The basis for determining whether a disadvantage is compelling resides largely within two issues: the *probability* that the harmful effect will occur if the plan is implemented, and the *magnitude* or degree of harm created by the effect if it occurs. The most compelling disadvantage argument, of course, is one that has a high degree of probability and a large magnitude of harm. A plan that released unreformed rapists from prison would be a compelling disadvantage. Criminals typically have a high degree of recidivism—many crimes are committed by repeat offenders—and they usually commit the same kinds of crimes.

There is a high probability, then, that such felons would commit additional rapes. The magnitude of the disadvantage—sexual violence committed on the victims, fear of crime experienced even by those not themselves victimized— would be similarly high.

Negative teams do not, however, need to argue that both the probability and the magnitude of the problem are high for the disadvantage to be compelling. If the probability is high but the magnitude is low, the disadvantage may be compelling because of the almost *certainty* that the disadvantage will occur. The magnitude of the disadvantage may be enough, when combined with solvency attacks or low magnitude of affirmative plan advantages, for the cost of the plan to outweigh the benefits of adopting it. Similarly, if the magnitude is high but the probability is low, the disadvantage may be compelling because, the negative argues, "no potential benefits are worth risking the occurrence of this harm."

Indeed, this is exactly the reasoning that makes "disaster scenarios" such popular off-case arguments. It is easy to document the magnitude of nuclear war, global environmental disaster, and other similar events. Negatives count on that magnitude to lessen the degree of probability they need to demonstrate and still have the argument considered compelling. At times, the probability component seems almost to be completely ignored. In general, however, we suggest that the negative presenting a disadvantage argue the highest degree of probability and greatest degree of magnitude possible. Together, they create the most compelling kind of disadvantage argument.

As with other negative arguments, the disadvantage argument should follow the L-R-I-(P) model. In the *link,* the negative must identify specifically what portion of the affirmative plan initiates the chain of events that will then cause the negative consequences to occur. Here, the negative should point to the specific action in the affirmative plan that sets the disadvantage in motion. In the *rationale,* the negative details the chain of events that is produced by the plan link and ultimately yields the negative consequences. The negative needs to identify exactly what events—what responses, occurrences, or subsequent actions—will be set into motion if the plan is implemented. It is here and/or in the link component that the negative will establish the degree of probability that the disadvantage will occur. In the *impact* component the negative establishes the magnitude, the degree of severity, of the undesirable consequences. The negative should be prepared to assess the cost and significance of the effects they claim will result from the plan. Finally, the negative may choose to include a *preempt* component. If the negative side believes the affirmative is likely to argue that the studies supporting the impact statement are flawed, the negative might preempt that attack by arguing that the methodology used in the studies is the most appropriate for the risk analysis of this effect. The sequence of a sample disadvantage follows.

SAMPLE DISADVANTAGE
1. The Affirmative plan bans U.S. military support for allied nations. (Plan Link)
2. Allied nations will increase their own defense technologies. (Chain of Events)
   A. Perceived weakness of the United States will lead to increases of arms in other countries.
   B. Leaders will work to protect their power.
   C. Populace will call for increased internal security initiatives.
3. Nations will develop nuclear technologies. (Chain of Events)
   A. Leaders will favor the nuclear option.
   B. Populace will favor the nuclear option.
   C. U.S. shield currently keeps countries from pursuing the nuclear option.
4. Development of nuclear technologies will be disastrous. (Impact Statement)
   A. Proliferation will significantly increase the risk of regional conflict.
   B. Proliferation will significantly increase the risk of accidental global conflict.
   C. Proliferation will significantly increase international terrorism.
   D. Overall, proliferation will threaten world peace and cause a significant potential for massive conflict and loss of life.
5. Preemptions. (Preempt)
   A. U.N. measures will be ineffective in controlling proliferation.
   B. Proliferation scenarios are based on conservative estimates.
   C. Nations will easily be able to acquire technologies.

Policy debates typically occur in a cost-benefit paradigm, asking the question, "Will we be better off or worse off if we adopt this plan"? Because the world of human affairs is complex, arguing absolutes is often difficult: this plan won't work at all, or there is no harm now existing that the plan might eliminate, and so on. Within this framework, it isn't surprising that disadvantages are common and usually important elements of the negative's overall argument. Few negative teams will debate a round in which they do not introduce at least one plan disadvantage.

Disadvantages, like solvency arguments, will often be employed in nonpolicy debate when the affirmative has used specific policy changes as a means for supporting the adoption of the resolution. Negatives debating either kind of proposition, therefore, must be prepared to argue disadvantages well.

Principles for Constructing Disadvantages

Certain basic principles can be applied in constructing all arguments based on disadvantages. These principles are explained here.

1. *Clearly identify and be able to defend the plan link.* The only way the negative can establish a viable disadvantage is to be able to demonstrate how the affirmative plan will specifically set in motion the steps of action that will lead to the undesirable consequences. Clarity and believability of that link are crucial.

2. *Develop a reasonable chain of events.* The more complex and protracted the chain of events leading to the undesirable consequences, the easier it will be for the affirmative to demonstrate a break in the chain. Also, the more extended the chain, the more difficult it is to establish high probability. Even if every step in the chain *could* occur, it now becomes even less likely that it *would*. The negative is responsible for all assumptions that serve as the foundation for their chain of events and should be prepared to defend each step individually as well as the entire chain collectively.

3. *Know your impact.* The negative team must be able to specify and defend the accuracy of their impact projections. Look for realistic assessments and maximize their credibility. Explore relationships to determine the various dimensions and aspects of the impact and be able to explain exactly what you are claiming will result, how significant it will be (the magnitude), and why that particular cost is unacceptable.

4. *Be able to support the disadvantage.* A disadvantage is nothing more than a claim (or series of major and supporting claims). As such, the negative side assumes a *burden of proof* to demonstrate why their claims should be accepted. Disadvantage claims must be supported with evidence, just as the affirmative is required to support the claims in its case.

5. *Keep the disadvantage as simple and direct as possible.* Overly complex and drawn out disadvantages can be time-consuming to present and difficult to defend. Make certain to include each of the components in the disadvantage but do so in as simple and direct a manner as possible.

6. *Be reasonable with preempts.* It is easy for debaters to get carried away with preempts and attempt to argue against every conceivable response their opponents may make. Remember, your opponents do not have to respond to any preempt you make unless that preempt applies specifically to an objection a debater intends to raise. Use your time wisely and preempt only those potential objections that you feel are most likely to be raised, will be the most damaging if they are raised, and are capable of being legitimately preempted.

Counterplans

Solvency arguments and disadvantage arguments are common forms of plan attacks; counterplans are used far less frequently. Also, whereas most negative off-case arguments are presented by the second negative constructive speaker, a counterplan off-case should be advanced in the first negative constructive. In the counterplan, the negative accepts (or "grants") the rationale portion of the affirmative case. The negative says that it agrees with the significance, inherency, and harm that the affirmative has presented. The negative argues, however, that the counterplan is a *better* plan for removing or eliminating the harm.

In addition to being "better," the negative plan must differ from the affirmative's in that it must be *nonresolutional.* That is, the affirmative plan "embodies" or "fulfills" the resolution, and adopting the affirmative plan is equal to adopting the resolution. In contrast, the negative counterplan must be a vehicle for *rejecting* the resolution; it must, therefore be nonresolutional. In debating the proposition, "Resolved: that the federal government should adopt an energy policy that substantially reduces the nonmilitary consumption of fossil fuels in the United States," the affirmative might argue that the civilian sector's overreliance on fossil fuels endangers the military's ability to wage war, as the military is also a chief user of fossil fuels. The affirmative might then mandate a federal policy requiring utility companies to convert 60 percent of their power-producing plants to solar, hydroelectric, or nuclear power. The affirmative's plan is resolutional: it mandates a federal policy that substantially reduces the nonmilitary consumption of fossil fuels in the United States.

A negative team choosing to respond with a counterplan would agree with the affirmative's rationale: the military is indeed endangered by the civilian sector's overreliance on fossil fuels. The solution, the negative might argue, is to change the government's *military* policy and not its *civilian* policy. The negative might argue that the government should convert its military war machinery to exclusive use of solar and/or nuclear power. The advantages to this counterplan, the negative might argue, are that (1) converting specific military machinery rather than entire power plants reduces costs; (2) it avoids increasing power costs, which would incur tremendous economic disadvantages; and (3) the associated military spending on solar research and development would have significant nonmilitary economic and environmental advantages. Note that the negative counterplan is nonresolutional: it introduces no federal policy regarding nonmilitary consumption of fossil fuels.

A negative team introducing a counterplan must be ready to advance and defend four central arguments: the nature of the counterplan; that the counterplan is nonresolutional; that the counterplan corrects the harms identified by the affirmative side equally or better than the affirmative team's plan; and that the negative team's counterplan is more advantageous than the affirmative team's plan.

Like the affirmative side's presentation of its plan, the negative team must be specific as to the nature of their counterplan. In presenting a counterplan, the negative has taken on the same burden of proof that the affirmative has for its plan. Like the affirmative plan, then, a counterplan has four core elements: the agent of action, the action steps, the resource requirements, and the enforcement mechanism. The negative may also choose to include a clarification plank. Finally, again like the affirmative, the negative has the power of "fiating" its counterplan into existence.

The negative counterplan *must* be nonresolutional. Because the negative must support a position that *rejects* the resolution, the negative team's counterplan must differ from the action called for by the resolution in some significant way. Although this is an obvious point, it is occasionally overlooked; negatives sometimes make the mistake of advancing a counterplan that is different from the affirmative's plan but is itself still resolutional. A simple but crucial point is that the counterplan *must* be nonresolutional.

Next, the negative must *justify* the adoption of its plan over that of the affirmative. Remember that in advancing a counterplan, the negative team has accepted the affirmative side's rationale on the harm and the significance of that harm. As part of its justification, the negative must argue that its counterplan has solvency in regard to those harms. The negative's counterplan may have slightly less solvency than the affirmative plan, but only if the counterplan produces *significant* advantages over the affirmative plan. In general, however, the negative will need to argue equal or superior solvency even *in conjunction* with some additional advantages produced or disadvantages avoided.

Finally, the negative team must complete its justification of the counterplan by demonstrating its superiority to the affirmative plan. The negative may argue that its counterplan has superior solvency, creates additional advantages, avoids creating significant disadvantages that the affirmative plan would incur, or some combination of all three. In arguing for superior or additional advantages, the negative team constructs its argument in exactly the same fashion an affirmative team does for its plan: there should be significance, inherency, and solvency. Special attention needs to be paid to the inherency component, however, in order to differentiate the counterplan from the affirmative plan.

For any disadvantages the negative side claims will be produced by the affirmative plan but will not be caused by the counterplan, the negative constructs a standard disadvantage argument. Again, special attention needs to be paid to the link step of the argument if the negative is to argue convincingly that the disadvantage will be produced by the affirmative plan but *not* by the negative side's counterplan.[13]

A counterplan is often a risky strategy for the negative side to employ. In using a counterplan, the negative agrees to much of the affirmative case. Technically, by granting the affirmative's arguments of significance, inherency, and harm, the negative has indicted the status quo and has thus ceded most or all of its PRESUMPTION. The negative has acknowledged that significant change from the status quo is needed; now the debate has become, "Which change shall we incur?" Psychologically, too, for the negative side to argue a counterplan can be advantageous for the affirmative because it means that the negative accedes to many of the affirmative's case arguments as being correct. Also, because the affirmative plan is the first one introduced and is most directly tied to the now-accepted rationale, the affirmative plan often gains psychological presumption in the round.

Because of the risky nature of the strategy, many negatives employ **conditional counterplans.** Unlike the traditional counterplan, the first negative constructive speaker rejects the affirmative's rationale in the conditional counterplan strategy. However, the negative then argues, just in case the judge *does* agree with the affirmative's rationale, here's a counterplan that solves the problem but in a nonresolutional way.

The conditional counterplan is a *disjunctive* argument (see Chapter 6) and carries with it all the advantages and disadvantages of that kind of argument. It provides for the possibility that the primary argument ("the affirmative's rationale is wrong") may fail by providing a backup argument ("our counterplan will correct the harm identified by the affirmative"). By constructing two arguments instead of one, however, the negative team may stretch itself too thin. Also, conditional counterplans may be psychologically perceived as indicating indecision —an inability of the negative team to decide which argument they *really* want to pursue.

Conclusion

In this chapter, we have examined the form negative arguments should follow and the two major components of the negative case: on-case arguments and off-case arguments. Negative arguments are most effective when they follow the L-R-I-(P) structure: Link-Rationale-Impact-(Preemptive Argument). The L-R-I-(P) structure ensures that the negative argument will clearly respond to the affirmative case, present its supportive reasoning, and define the impact of the argument on the overall decision regarding the resolution. The preemptive component allows the negative team to anticipate and respond to probable affirmative refutation.

The negative on-case argument should directly address the definitions, rationale, and any preliminary or summary components included in the affirmative case. It is important for the negative to respond to all parts of the affirmative case, even when the negative is only signaling agreement with a particular part of the argument. It is also important for the negative to place jurisdictional and definition challenges at the head of its first negative constructive speech.

Off-case arguments are those that construct a competitive negative position but do not directly attack the affirmative's case. Off-case arguments differ depending on whether the resolution is nonpolicy or policy in orientation. Nonpolicy off-case arguments can include value objections, countercontentions, and/or counterexamples. Off-case arguments in policy debate may include solvency arguments, disadvantages, and/or counterplans.

Regardless of the particular arguments a negative team develops, they should avoid employing any arguments that would threaten the coherence of their overall position. The negative side should remember that, psychologically, the most effective argument is one that exhibits coherence. An important element of that coherence is the identification of key voting issues in the debate and the strategic refutation of the affirmative team's arguments on those issues.

Notes

1. The affirmative can win the round this way. If it presents a prima facie case and the negative attacks on it are completely ineffective, the affirmative could, technically, win the debate even if it did not respond to a single negative attack. This would not constitute good debating, of course; we point it out simply to illustrate the different roles assigned to these two argumentative positions.

2. The negative side could also advance the position that we should keep our commitments exactly as they are.

3. Sometimes a second negative constructive speaker will extend the first negative speaker's on-case rationale arguments. This is generally an inefficient use of time, however, because the first negative will be delivering his or her rebuttal immediately following the second negative's constructive speech.

4. The negative team may still call it an *underview* in order to maintain consistent labeling, even as they include it in the introduction of their constructive. Thus, the negative side may *begin* their constructive by saying, "Let's look first at the affirmative's underview, then at its definitions, and then at its rationale."

5. Negative teams often choose to frame topicality arguments *disjunctively*, however (see Chapter 7). They argue in an overview that a case or part of a case is not topical, but then they argue in the rationale portion that, just in case the judge does not accept the topicality argument, here is the reason the affirmative argument should not be accepted. Technically, a negative side need enter no other argument than "it's not topical" to win either that

point of the affirmative case or the entire debate. In practice, few negatives are willing or interested in gambling everything on a single jurisdictional argument.

6. *Quasi-policy* is a term not always accepted in the debate community and still in the process of being carefully defined. Typically, in a debate in which the proposition is defined as quasi-policy, the affirmative is expected to meet the burden of providing an "action step"; however, it has no burden of specifying the agent of action, enforcement, or resource requirements *unless* the action step requires an unusual commitment of agents, enforcement, or resources. For example, an action step that required every citizen to register and vote would probably need to specify the enforcement mechanism: How would the affirmative team force every citizen to comply? An action step that provided every citizen with a guaranteed minimum income would probably need to specify the resource mechanism: How could such an expensive program be funded?

7. As you consider voting issues and rebuttals, it may be useful to refer to the discussion of speaker responsibilities in Chapter 11.

8. The difference between the two types of debate and the resulting solvency arguments occurs because in policy debate the affirmative's plan *becomes* the "proposition"; that is, if the affirmative's plan is adopted, the proposition has been adopted. Thus, solvency is a plan attack. In nonpolicy debate, the affirmative is responsible for the general adoption of the proposition.

9. Some consider criteria arguments to be "off-case" arguments, especially when combined with countercontentions to create a competitive negative "case" that counters the proposition. Even if the argument is labeled off-case, however, countercriteria need to be introduced in the first negative constructive.

10. As discussed in Chapters 9 and 12, there are other ways of constructing a nonpolicy affirmative case. The majority, however, follow the model described here.

11. There are exceptions. The "Emory switch" is a negative strategy wherein the first negative constructive develops the off-case position and the second negative constructive argues the on-case position. By deferring on-case attacks until the second negative constructive, the negative gives itself more time to prepare its on-case attacks and provides the affirmative with less time to respond to those attacks. The strategy, however, is psychologically risky in two ways: (1) it allows the affirmative case to go unchallenged for two speeches, and (2) it violates the norms of speaker responsibilities. The Emory switch is probably best employed when the negative is developing its own unique approach to the resolution—for example, using countercontentions in nonpolicy debate or a counterplan in policy debate.

12. One approach to presenting an alternative perspective or competing interpretation of the resolution is to introduce an alternative paradigm and then construct countercontentions that present the resolution from that perspective (see Chapter 9).

13. Some theorists use **competitiveness** as the quality of the counterplan that justifies its adoption. Competitiveness is determined in reference to two standards. The first is that the affirmative's plan and the negative's counterplan cannot structurally coexist. That is, the policymaker is forced to choose one or the other but cannot opt to enact both. The second standard is that adoption of the counterplan produces a net benefit over the adoption of the plan. This net benefit can be derived from fewer disadvantages, greater solvency, more advantages, or any combination of the three.

Selected Bibliography

Bile, J. "When the Whole Is Greater than the Sum of the Parts: The Implications of Holistic Resolutional Focus." *CEDA Yearbook* 8 (1987): 8–15.

Branham, Robert. "Roads not Taken: Counterplans and Opportunity Costs." *Argumentation and Advocacy* 25 (1989): 246–55.

———. "The State of the Counterplan." *Argumentation and Advocacy* 25 (1989): 117–20.

Gass, R. H., Jr. "Resolutional Assumptions: Inviolable Argumentative Ground." *Argument and Critical Practices: Proceedings of the Fifth SCA/AFA Conference on Argumentation.* Ed. J. W. Wenzel. Annandale, VA: Speech Communication Association, 1987. 365–70.

Herbeck, Dale A., John P. Katsulas, and Karla K. Leeper. "The Locus of Debate Controversy Re-Examined: Implications for Counterplan Theory." *Argumentation and Advocacy* 25 (1989): 150–64.

Lane, Gina E. "The Justification of Counterplans in Nonpolicy Debate: A Skeptical View." *CEDA Yearbook* 15 (1994): 33–42.

Madsden, Arnie, and Robert C. Chandler. "When the Whole Becomes a Black Hole: Implications of the Holistic Perspective." *CEDA Yearbook* 9 (1988): 30–37.

Madsden, Arnie, and Alan Louden. "Jurisdiction and the Evaluation of Topicality." *Argumentation and Advocacy* 24 (1987): 73–83.

Panetta, Edward M., and Steven Dolley. "The Topical Counterplan: A Competitive Policy Alternative." *Argumentation and Advocacy* 25 (1989): 165–77.

Perkins, Dallas. "Counterplans and Paradigms." *Argumentation and Advocacy* 25 (1989): 140–49.

Sherwood, Ken. "Claim without Warrant: The Lack of Logical Support for Parametric Topicality." *CEDA Yearbook* 15 (1994): 10–19.

Solt, Roger. "Negative Fiat: Resolving the Ambiguities of 'Should.'" *Argumentation and Advocacy* 25 (1989): 121–39.

Walker, Gregg B. "The Counterplan as Argument in Non-Policy Debate." *Argumentation and Advocacy* 25 (1989): 178–91.

Ulrich, Walter R. "Counterplan Theory and the Power to Select Resolutions." *Argumentation and Advocacy* 26 (1990): 154–59.

Discussion Questions

1. What are the components of the L-R-I-(P) model?
2. What is the difference between a topicality argument and a justification argument?
3. Why are voting issues particularly important in rebuttal rounds?
4. How do counterexamples differ from countercontentions and value objections?
5. Why do reduced solvency arguments and disadvantages arguments complement each other well?

COMMUNICATING EFFECTIVELY AS A DEBATER

*I*n Chapter 1, we explained the importance of viewing debate as a communicative interaction. We also explained how the role of a student in a formal debate is similar to that of a source or receiver in a communicative interaction. In this chapter, we return to that basic notion and explain the particular ways students should prepare for debate as a communicative interaction. First, we discuss the importance of audience analysis—a fundamental principle of communication—and suggest ways that debaters can adapt to their audience. Second, we examine the critical role of credibility in debate. We explain some ways that credibility judgments are made in debates and suggest methods by which debaters can enhance their credibility. Third, we discuss the importance of listening in debate and suggest ways that debaters can enhance their listening skills. Finally, we turn our attention to one of the most challenging portions of a debate—cross-examination—and explain how debaters can communicate more effectively by enhancing their ability to ask and answer questions.

Audience Analysis

Beginning with Aristotle, who advised speakers that they must be able to discover the best available means of persuasion in each specific case, and continuing through modern social scientific research about the ways receivers process and respond to information contained in a message, one fundamental principle of communication has remained constant: to be successful, speakers must adapt their message to the audience receiving it. Without adapting the message and the way it is presented to the needs, values, and expectations of the audience, no speaker is likely to be successful.

History offers many notable examples of speakers who have ably adapted the message to the audience. In his speech to Congress asking for a declaration of war against Germany in 1917, Woodrow Wilson was concerned about the large number of recent German immigrants to America. To adapt the speech, he included an extended section that praised the German people and proclaimed that America had no quarrel with them. Rather, he said, the quarrel was between autocratic government, represented by the Kaiser, and democratic government, such as America's. In addition to this explicit argument separating the German people from their government, Wilson ended the speech by indirectly referencing the German Protestant reformer, Martin Luther, paraphrasing the famous phrase with which Luther had closed his defense before the Diet of Worms: "Here I stand. I can do no other. God help me. Amen." Wilson finished his speech by saying "the day has come when America is privileged to spend her blood and her might for the principles that gave her birth and happiness and the peace which she has treasured. God helping her, she can do no other."

Douglas Wilder, an African-American Democrat running for governor in Virginia in 1989, provides another significant example of audience analysis and adaptation. Wilder, a pro-choice advocate, defended his stance not on the basis of women's privacy rights but through a civil libertarian/antigovernment argument that said, "government has no business making that decision—let's keep government out of our lives." Although the privacy rights argument is favored by most women's rights groups, Wilder knew he had their votes already. His argument was targeted at Republican women, who would find the antigovernment argument more appealing. Election polls indicated that Wilder was indeed successful in attracting votes from Republican women, and he went on to win the election as well. As both Wilder's and Wilson's experiences demonstrate, speakers who adapt their message to the special needs and circumstances of their audience significantly increase their chances of being successful.

Debaters, like other communicators, must analyze and adapt their cases and presentations to the audience. The concept of psychological presumption is closely related to audience analysis. As we explained in Chapter 8, psychological presumption suggests that a judge's preferences will influence the way that judge processes, values, and weighs information presented in a debate. For example, if a judge has a preference for empirical examples over testimonial evidence, debaters who construct arguments with empirical examples as evidence are likely to have their arguments favored—granted a psychological presumption—during the debate. The judge in a debate—like any other receiver of a persuasive message—has needs, expectations, and values to which the debater must appeal.

Bases of Audience Analysis

Judges can bring many types of specific preferences to a debate—so many that it would be impossible for a debater to adapt to all of them. In most cases, however, debaters should be able to analyze and adapt to the general preferences the judge has regarding the basic **argument construction style, refutation style,** and **style of presentation.**

Debaters' argument construction style is determined by the way they fashion their cases (affirmative or negative). Numerous variables, such as the number of claims presented (few or many), the complexity of the claims (elaborate or simple substructure), the types of evidence used to support claims (testimony, statistics, studies, examples), the variety of evidence used (reliance on multiple or single types of evidence), and the amount of evidence used to support a claim (multiple or single pieces) affect the way a case is constructed.

Debaters' refutation style is determined primarily by the methods of refutation they employ and the components of the argument they attack. Debaters can use a number of different methods of refutation in a debate including direct refutation, counterclaims, cross-applications, and generic positions. Moreover, they can focus their refutation on various parts of their opponents' argument— evidence, warrants, claims, and so on. Debaters can use a fairly homogenous refutation style in which they rely almost exclusively on a single method of refutation consistently targeted to the same components of their opponents' argument (such as direct refutation of the evidence used to support claims), or they can use a heterogenous style that incorporates various methods of refutation targeted to a variety of components of their opponents' argument (such as direct refutation of some claims combined with generic positions that offer alternative scenarios or ways of understanding the issues in the debate).

Debaters' style of presentation is determined primarily by their delivery style and the way they advance and explain their cases. Speaking rate, volume, and vocal inflection are important components of a person's speaking style. In addition, the overall clarity of the oral presentation and use of nonverbal delivery systems such as eye contact and gestures help define a speaker's delivery style. Inclusion of repetition, restatement, and organizational devices such as signposts and transitions also help define a person's style of presentation. Debaters can vary their style of presentation by the way they introduce evidence —providing detailed citations and extensive application, or providing minimal citation with little or no application.

The Adaptation Process

For debaters, adapting their argument construction style, style of refutation, and style of presentation to the preferences and expectations of the judge is not always easy. The first obstacle they encounter is knowing what those preferences are. Debaters can acquire this information in several ways. One of the most useful is simply to ask judges about their preferences. For classroom debates, debaters might poll the other students in the class about their preferences if the students are assigned to judge the debate. In the classroom situation, your instructor should provide a clear statement about the type of debate performance he or she favors and expects. Debaters on the competitive circuit can also acquire information by asking. Many judges are more than willing to share their preferences if debaters pose specific questions and refrain from asking judges to justify these expectations.

On the competitive circuit, debate teams are likely to encounter the same judge a number of times throughout the season. Debaters can learn about their judge's preferences by reading ballots carefully and using the judge's ballot as a context for reconstructing and reflecting on what occurred in the debate. Some debate squads also maintain judging assessment booklets in which they catalog the tendencies and preferences of particular judges. Some national championship tournaments compile judging philosophy booklets that contain written philosophy statements by the tournament judges. Debaters can use the information contained in such booklets as a general guide to the preferences of the judges, although in any given debate the judge's decision may not be perfectly consistent with the preferences expressed in a written philosophy statement.

Once you understand the preferences of your judge, your second task is adapting to those preferences. Debaters can adapt their argument construction style to the judge's expectations in a number of ways. If the judge favors simple arguments, debaters should construct their cases with uncomplicated, direct claims, avoiding elaborate substructures. If the judge has a preference for corroborated evidence—evidence of various types that substantiate the same claim—debaters should reduce the number of claims they present and provide a variety of types of evidence to support each claim. Other judges may prefer that each argument reflect a detailed and multifaceted view of the issue. To adapt to this preference, debaters would construct their case with claims that are further developed with supporting claims. Such supporting claims should ideally address different dimensions of the issue embodied in the major claim and would likely also contain evidence drawn from a variety of sources.

Debaters can adapt their refutation style to the preferences of the judge in a number of ways. Some judges want debaters to engage in direct refutation of arguments; they expect debaters to take their opponents' arguments head-on, attempting to invalidate the arguments directly. For such judges, debaters should avoid presenting generic position statements and should limit the number of cross-applications they use; instead, they should concentrate on a straightforward, point-by-point response to the arguments their opponents present. Some judges prefer extensive assessment of the evidence used to support claims. For these judges, debaters would minimize the use of counterclaims in their refutation and would instead assess their opponents' evidence more extensively by applying a wider variety of tests to the evidence and, when possible, introducing evidence to contradict that presented by the opponents. Other judges prefer that debaters focus their refutation on a more global assessment of the issues involved in the debate. For these judges, debaters would resist the tendency to engage in a point-by-point refutation of their opponents' arguments and would construct broader position statements that subsumed or invalidated the overall thrust of the opponents' case. Other judges want debaters to key all their segments of refutation directly to the opponents' case by first identifying the argument they are attacking, explaining their attack, supporting the attack, and explaining the effect of that attack on their opponents' total case. For judges with such a preference, debaters should follow all the steps of the process to create the most favorable context for processing and evaluating their refutation.

Debaters can adapt their style of presentation to the preferences of the judge. Many judges prefer that debaters demonstrate sound public speaking skills in a debate. For judges with such a preference, debaters should speak slowly and liberally incorporate basic organizational and clarifying devices such as signposts, transitions, and repetition in their speeches. They should also use effective eye contact and nonverbal cues in their presentations. Some judges have a preference for detailed explanation of the debater's argument. To adapt to this preference, a debater would restate claims and follow each piece of evidence with a clear explanation of how that piece supports the debater's claim. Other judges have a preference for complete citations of evidence (source, date, publication, and so on) and tend to give serious consideration to completely cited evidence in their assessment of the debate.

For some debaters, adapting their argument construction, style of refutation, and style of presentation may seem tedious and unnecessary. After all, debaters can make choices and can present their cases in any manner they desire. As true as that basic principle is, it is equally true that judges can impose whatever preferences they choose on the decision-making process they use in the debate. Any debater who refuses to adapt to the preferences of the judge undermines his or her ability to be a successful advocate. The time and effort spent making even the simplest adaptations for the judge can reap a potentially significant payback by psychologically predisposing the judge to give your case a more favorable hearing than the case of your opponents. Below we have listed some of the key guidelines debaters should use when trying to adapt to their audience.

GUIDELINES FOR ADAPTING MESSAGE TO AUDIENCE
Actively seek out information about the judge.
Adapt to rather than criticize the judge's preferences.

Develop alternative approaches to case construction.
Be well versed in a variety of approaches to refutation.
Be able to use different delivery styles effectively.
Be flexible.

Establishing Credibility

Speakers with high credibility are more likely to be successful persuaders and advocates than speakers with low credibility. Speakers who project high credibility are more likely to capture and maintain the receivers' attention, more likely to have their message accepted, and less likely to be challenged or questioned by the receivers than speakers with less credibility. Because of the importance of credibility, serious speakers work actively to project this characteristic to their listeners. Debate is a communicative interaction and credibility is no less important to the success of a debater than to any other type of speaker.

The Credibility Judgment Process

Each receiver determines her or his own assessment of the speaker's credibility. Although receivers use individually constructed standards, there are broad generalized standards that receivers across most situations are likely to use in one form or another to assess the credibility of the speaker. Standards relating to the character and competence of a speaker, for example, are generally used by receivers to assess credibility.

In a debate, the judge will determine each debater's credibility and will likely do so on the basis of specific standards related to the character and competence of the debater. Judges will arrive at evaluations about character and competence by observing what debaters say and do before, during, and after the debate. Every verbal and nonverbal cue a debater transmits can potentially be used by the judge to assess credibility.

Judgments about character generally reflect the degree to which the debater is perceived to be an advocate who is respectful and worthy of trust. There are many specific indicators of character in a debate interaction. Judges, for example, can make inferences about a debater's character by observing the way she interacts with her opponents—whether she treats her opponents with respect and dignity or whether she is condescending, demeaning, or even abusive to them. Judges may also make inferences about a debater's character by observing how accurately she portrays her opponents' arguments and how accurately she represents her own case.

Judgments about competence will generally indicate the degree to which the debater is perceived to be a knowledgeable and informed advocate. Judges may make decisions about competence based on any number of specific behaviors. One important indicator of competence is the ability to explain your arguments clearly. Debaters who are unable to explain what their arguments mean, to identify the assumptions on which their arguments are based, or to explain how their arguments relate to each other as well as to their opponents' arguments will be perceived as not very competent.

Other indicators of competence a judge might assess are debaters' ability to use key terminology correctly and to organize their cases clearly. Most certainly, a judge will weigh debaters' use of evidence as an indicator of competence. How skillful a debater is in using a variety of approaches to refutation and in selecting the most appropriate approaches for the specific situation will also be important indicators of competence.

These are a few of the general indicators judges might use to determine a debater's character and competence. Ultimately, the indicators that any judge uses to assess the debater's character or competence will be individually selected, applied, and interpreted by that judge. It is impossible to compile an exhaustive list of every specific indicator of competence and character that might be used in a debate round. That does not mean that debaters should throw their hands in the air and take a passive approach to credibility. On the contrary, debaters can and should take an active role in promoting their credibility. In the next section we identify some of the more general ways debaters can attempt to enhance their credibility in a debate.

Approaches to Enhancing Credibility

Debaters can work actively to promote their credibility in four critical ways. First, they should avoid doing or saying anything that might undermine their credibility. Debaters can do much to enhance their credibility simply by carefully assessing their behavior and avoiding anything that might elicit negative credibility evaluations. The following guidelines caution debaters to avoid behaviors that typically reinforce negative credibility evaluations and can adversely affect their team in a debate.

> **GUIDELINES FOR AVOIDING NEGATIVE CREDIBILITY BEHAVIORS**
> Do not intentionally misstate or misrepresent your opponents' arguments.
> Do not claim that your evidence proves something that it does not.
> Do not use specious reasoning.
> Do not claim that you presented evidence or arguments that you did not.
> Do not act condescendingly to your opponents.
> Do not falsely accuse your opponents of misrepresenting their position.
> Do not attack your opponents' character.
> Do not use abusive or offensive language in a debate.

Do not claim that your opponents "dropped" an argument when they
   did not.

Do not present your case in a disorganized manner.

Do not present evidence and arguments that you cannot explain
   accurately.

Do not disrupt your opponents.

Do not use key terminology incorrectly.

Do not violate the norms of the process by disregarding time limits.

Second, debaters should actively seek to establish high credibility by the
way they use evidence in a debate. One primary way to do so is to provide sufficient preliminary information about the evidence. Debaters should introduce
evidence by completely identifying its source, the basic qualifications of the
source, and the date the evidence was published. When a debater introduces her
evidence by saying only, "According to Johnson . . . ," the judge has little information with which to make a positive initial credibility evaluation, and her
opponents are likely to challenge the evidence. However, if the same debater
introduced that evidence by saying, "According to Dr. Fred Johnson, professor
of political science and distinguished member of the Carnegie Foundation in
his 1993 report . . . ," the judge would be better able to ascribe a positive initial
evaluation to the evidence and the debater's credibility would also be enhanced.

Third, debaters should also work for high credibility in the cross-
examination period. They should always remember that their actions during
cross-examination have a direct effect on their credibility as advocates. Although
cross-examination is only one factor affecting credibility judgments, it can have
a critical effect on how others—particularly the judge—perceive you as an
advocate. During cross-examination, the judge gains a sense of your honesty,
your reasonableness, your intellectual capability, your ability to interact with
another advocate, and your effectiveness as a communicator. Debaters can
enhance their credibility during cross-examination by asking clearly worded and
relevant questions, maintaining a positive tone with their opponents, and providing direct and understandable answers.

Just as easily, debaters can undermine their credibility by attempting to
trick their opponents, intentionally misstating their opponents' answers, avoiding obvious answers, feigning a lack of understanding, or launching personal
attacks against their opponents. Debaters should think about how they look
and sound during cross-examination because everything they do in some way
ultimately affects others' judgments about their credibility.

Finally, debaters should carefully assess the image they are projecting. They
should attempt to look professional in both appearance and composure. Debate
is a formal process and debaters should attempt to dress appropriately for the
activity. Having their material organized can also help project a professional

image. File cases should be organized for easy retrieval of information. Judges, like any receiver, make inferences about debaters based on their composure. Debaters who want to project a professional image will try to remain calm and poised no matter how strenuously their opponents challenge their case. Moreover, debaters should try to exhibit a professional manner of interacting with their colleagues. Openly criticizing your colleagues can harm their credibility as well as your own. Treat your colleagues with respect and allow them to develop and present their own arguments in the debate.

Credibility is a fundamental component of the communication process. The receiver's judgment about the credibility of the source will always have a significant impact on how willing the receiver is to listen to, accept, or contest the source's claims and ideas. We chose to return to that fundamental concept in this chapter because as important and basic as it is, credibility is often neglected by debaters as they prepare to debate. To be a successful debater, you need to assess your own behaviors continuously in terms of their impact on your credibility as an advocate.

Listening During a Debate

Throughout this book, we have emphasized the importance of viewing debate as a communicative interaction. The natural inclination might be to think of debate primarily as an oral communication activity, thus placing emphasis on development of basic speaking skills; however, we should not ignore the importance of listening as a complementary skill to speaking. Successful debaters not only must have well-honed speaking skills but must also be good listeners. In this section of this chapter, we discuss the listening process in debate, barriers to effective listening, and suggestions for improving basic listening skills in a debate.

Listening Skills in Debate

Beginning debaters find out very early that mastering good listening is imperative. Good listening is necessary for understanding and evaluating your opponents' arguments and developing appropriate responses to them. Debaters use their listening skills during every phase of the debate process: listening is important before, during, and after the debate. Before the debate, listening is essential in all interactions with partners and coaches. During the debate, debaters listen to their opponents present constructive and rebuttal speeches and ask and answer questions during cross-examination; debaters listen as they themselves interact with their partners to plan strategy and responses for the debate. After the debate, debaters depend on their listening skills to process the feedback they receive about the debate. In addition, good listening directly complements the development of oral communication skills by helping debaters construct accurate models of appropriate and inappropriate speech practices. Despite the importance of good listening to debate, many debaters remain poor listeners because they do not understand the listening phenomenon or how to change poor listening habits.

To become better listeners, debaters must understand what listening involves. Listening is in itself a complex process. Many people assume that "hearing" and "listening" are synonymous. Although hearing is the first step in the listening process, hearing is simply the physical capability to receive sounds. Generally, hearing is a passive act that requires no more effort than to be within the range of noise. In any given situation, the human ear is bombarded with a variety of sounds yet only a portion of those sounds actually gain our attention, and an even smaller portion actually motivate us to listen. Researchers have estimated that the average person has only a 25 percent to 50 percent listening efficiency.

Unlike hearing, listening is an intentional, active process that requires both a physiological and psychological effort. Listening occurs when an individual attends and attaches meaning to aural stimuli. Such meaning is gained through interpreting, analyzing, evaluating, and retaining the received message. For example, while the negative debaters listen to the first affirmative constructive speech, they interpret the connotative and denotative meaning of the claims, analyze and evaluate the claims based on that interpretation, and retain that assessment in their memory. These steps must be achieved with remarkable speed because most of what the first affirmative speaker says is transitory; debaters rarely repeat themselves and there is not likely to be any official written or recorded transcript of a speech a debater can analyze while the debate is in progress.

Numerous factors influence people's capacity to listen. Their values, attitudes, needs, and expectations influence listening by determining what aural stimuli command attention, how those stimuli are interpreted, and how the debaters assess the stimuli. For example, a negative debater with a well-developed block of responses against a particular type of evidence will be likely to detect uses of that type of evidence by the affirmative, will interpret such evidence as the type in question, and will assess the evidence as faulty. People's physical and psychological conditions also influence their capacity to listen. Physical states such as level of energy, hunger, or tiredness and psychological states such as level of anxiety or happiness can influence listening by affecting the hearer's mental alertness and establishing a context for interpretation and assessment of aural stimuli. A debater who is sleepy and hungry will be less capable of processing her opponent's arguments than she otherwise would be. Similarly, a debater who is happy and relatively anxiety free might have a different interpretation and assessment of his opponent's arguments than he would if he were distraught or in a condition of high anxiety. The characteristics of the message also affect a person's capacity to listen. Characteristics such as the attractiveness of the message, the way it is presented, and how well organized it is can influence both attention level and interpretation. If a disadvantage is clearly structured, well organized, and presented by a debater who can effectively use signposts and incorporate appropriate vocal attributes into the delivery, others are more apt to attend to the arguments within the disadvantage and interpret them accurately. Conversely, poorly organized and presented disadvantages are likely to generate more selective attention and adversely affect the listener's interpretation of what the disadvantage actually means.

Types of Listening in Debate

Debaters are primarily engaged in two types of listening: discriminative and evaluative. Debaters use *discriminative listening* to learn. Through discriminative listening, debaters gather information and seek to understand their opponents' questions, answers, arguments, and refutation. Debaters also use *evaluative listening,* a type of listening that results in some judgment. Debaters use evaluative listening to judge the worth of a standard in a criterion, the soundness of a claim, the strength of a particular pattern of reasoning, or the comparative merit of an advantage versus a disadvantage, to name just a few. Debaters encounter many potential barriers to effective discriminative and evaluative listening. Three of the most common ones are selectivity, changing channels, and premature evaluation.

Selectivity is a variable inherent in all listening. For a variety of reasons including those we have already explained, individuals attend to only portions or bits and pieces they select out of the messages to which they are exposed. Through selectivity, individuals reconstruct the message—or at least what they have attended to within the message. Because people can understand and interpret only what they have attended to, selectivity directly affects their discriminative and evaluative listening capability. Debaters often use selectivity by focusing their attention on particular types of aural messages. For example, debaters use selectivity to listen for particular phrases, sources of evidence, claims, or components of a case. In some instances, selectivity can help debaters narrow down the focus of their listening to those critical issues within the debate. When used indiscriminately, however, selectivity can cause debaters to miss major ideas, misinterpret the opponents' case, or pursue an irrelevant line of questioning or refutation. In extreme cases, selectivity not only impairs effective listening but produces effects that damage credibility.

Good listening demands concentration. Consider the last time you tried simultaneously to have a telephone conversation and to watch a program on television. You probably were able to listen to only one message at a time, and you had to do that by blocking out the other message. When you switched from the telephone conversation to the television program, you changed channels. Changing channels can be a detriment to good listening because it blocks out—prevents attention to—potentially important messages. Because of the multiple demands placed on debaters and the limited time they have to execute those demands, debaters are prone to changing channels. When debaters shift their attention from an argument as it is being presented—the message—to what they will say in response to the argument, they have changed channels. When a debater shifts attention from evidence being read to support a claim to ask a partner who the source of the evidence is, that debater has changed channels. In both these examples, the debaters' attention to the message terminated at the point the channel was changed, and thus understanding and evaluation of the message would be limited to what had been processed before the channel change occurred. Because of the nature of the debate process, it is impossible to eliminate channel changes fully. However, debaters should be aware of this inevitable tendency and attempt to understand how it can adversely influence their listening effectiveness. Moreover, they should attempt, so far as possible, to avoid changing channels unless it is absolutely critical that they do so and they are reasonably certain that they have an adequate and accurate understanding of the message being presented.

Premature evaluation can be another major barrier to effective listening. In many ways, premature evaluation is simply a rush to judgment: the listener actively terminates message processing in favor of reaching some judgment or conclusion about the overall message before the complete message has been presented. Because debaters are informed advocates and they practice their advocacy in a highly competitive and often pressure-packed environment, they are naturally faced with the temptation to evaluate their opponents' message prematurely. Mere mention of a key term, the wording of a claim, citation of a particular source of evidence, or inclusion of a specific concept in a plan can trigger a premature evaluation. Premature evaluation limits discriminative listening because it terminates message reception; it results in poor evaluative listening because it can lead to incorrect judgments.

Understanding the potential barriers to effective discriminative and evaluative listening is an important first step in developing better listening skills as a debater. Debaters must work actively to enhance their listening skills and they must attempt to break the bad listening habits they may have nurtured for years. The following guidelines can be used to develop your listening skills.

GUIDELINES FOR IMPROVED LISTENING

Be physically prepared to listen. You will be a better listener if you are properly rested and nourished. Sit close enough to your opponents so that you can hear them adequately. Make certain, as far as possible, that your arrangement of chairs and desks is comfortable and provides usable and efficient work space.

Be mentally prepared to listen. You will be a better listener if you can focus all your attention on the task at hand—understanding and evaluating the opponents' case. Try to leave potential distractions such as what happened in the last debate or personal problems outside the setting for the debate in which you are engaged.

Listen for major ideas as well as facts. You will be a better listener if you focus attention on both the macroscopic and microscopic aspects of the message. Try to understand the context and major ideas as well as the specific claims and evidence.

Form a "buddy system" with your partner. You will be a better listener if you work actively with your partner to back up each other's discriminitive and evaluative listening. Check your understanding and evaluation of the message with your partner.

Judge the message as objectively as possible. You will be a better listener if you can judge the message apart from your needs and role as an adversary or opposing advocate. Try to place yourself in the role of the judge and understand what sort of discriminitive and evaluative listening he or she might be doing.

Keep your focus on the content of the message. You will be a better listener if you focus your efforts on understanding and evaluating the content of your opponents' message. Don't be sidetracked by personal feelings about your opponents or the topic area of their case. Do not let your attention wander because of the manner in which the message is being presented.

Cross-Examination

One of the most interesting aspects of any debate is the cross-examination phase. During this phase, debaters ask questions of their opponents and answer questions asked by their opponents. Debaters can use the opportunity to ask and answer questions to their advantage in a number of ways. In this section, we discuss the goals debaters can accomplish during cross-examination and then examine the various principles they should follow as they ask and answer questions.

Goals of Cross-Examination

Debaters can accomplish three primary goals during cross-examination. First, they can use the cross-examination period to clarify arguments or information presented in the debate. Cross-examination is the only phase in a debate when debaters have the opportunity to engage in a direct interaction with their opponents. It is important to use this opportunity to gather information about pertinent portions of your opponents' case or ideas. If you were unable to understand and/or record a major claim your opponents presented, cross-examination would be the appropriate place to ask them to provide whatever information you need to completely understand that portion of the case. If you did not understand how a piece of evidence your opponents used supports the particular claim they are putting forward, you can use the cross-examination period to gather information that will help you understand the relationship. These are only two examples of the many ways debaters can use cross-examination to gather information. Debaters need to be as informed as possible about their opponents' case, and cross-examination affords them the opportunity to gather critical pieces of the information they need to develop a complete understanding.

Second, debaters can use cross-examination to establish a foundation for their refutation, which must be both specific and relevant to be meaningful. Debaters can use the cross-examination period to identify specific weaknesses in their opponents' arguments. They could then target those weaknesses in their later refutation. Assume that your opponent read a piece of evidence from a "Dr. Smith" to support a claim about the effects of a new automobile technology designed to control emissions, and that your opponent introduced the source only as "Dr. Smith" without elaborating on the source's qualifications. You could use your cross-examination to determine whether an attack on the evidence would be warranted simply by asking your opponent to provide Dr. Smith's qualifications. If Dr. Smith was an eminent scientist who specialized in airborne pollutants, you would probably be able to determine that attacking the qualifications of the source would be ineffective. However, if you learned that Dr. Smith is an assistant professor of political science, you would not only know that an attack on Dr. Smith's qualifications is warranted, but you would also determine that your refutation should focus on forcing your opponent to explain why an assistant professor of political science should be considered an expert on automobile emissions technology. In either case, your refutation can be more reasonably and meaningfully focused because of the clarification you elicited during cross-examination.

Third, debaters can use cross-examination to expose weaknesses in their opponents' case or refutation. Debaters can use cross-examination to clarify refutation in two primary ways. In one sense, they can use it to identify key elements of their case or refutation to which their opponent did not respond. Suppose you included several pieces of evidence in your case to support a critical major claim and your opponent attacked one of those pieces of evidence but ignored the others. You could use the cross-examination period to indicate the lack of comprehensiveness in your opponent's refutation simply by asking him what his specific response to the other pieces of evidence was. In another sense, you can use cross-examination to clarify responses your opponent did make. Suppose you have a major claim that says "more severe punishment will deter serious crime," and your opponent responds to that claim by saying that "studies on deterrence are flawed." To support that claim, your opponent reads a general piece of evidence that talks about the theory of deterrence. In such a situation, you could use the cross-examination period to determine how your opponent's claim actually applies to your major claim. You could do so by asking your opponent whether her position accounts for the critical factor in your claim—*severity of punishment*—and if so, how that is the case. Obviously, knowing that information would be critical to the way you defend your major claim against your opponent's attack.

Whether you clarify ideas, establish a foundation for refutation, or expose weaknesses in your opponent's refutation, cross-examination can be vitally important to you as an advocate. In many instances, you will use the cross-examination period for two or even all three of these purposes. Knowing what you can accomplish in cross-examination and then implementing strategies to enable you to accomplish those goals can make you both a better informed and a more effective debater.

Principles of Cross-Examination

To make the best use of the cross-examination phase, debaters must understand basic principles about asking and answering questions. Debaters who are highly skilled in asking and answering questions can make productive use of the cross-examination phase of a debate; those who approach cross-examination without a firm understanding of key principles are likely to find this period to be frustrating and nonproductive.

The first key principle is that *debaters must prepare for the cross-examination period.* Debaters who enter the cross-examination period without some idea of what they hope to accomplish are not likely to make maximum use of the opportunity. Both affirmative and negative debaters need to determine what questions they might ask and how they will follow up with the answers they get. In addition, both affirmative and negative debaters should attempt to determine what questions they might be asked and how they can answer those questions. One way to help prepare for cross-examination is to conduct cross-examination drills with your partner or a classmate. Another way to prepare for cross-examination is to brainstorm a list of questions you might ask yourself about your case. If you choose the most difficult questions you could be asked and develop answers for those questions, you will be better prepared to deal with them if they are asked by your opponents. Certainly, debaters will have to adapt their questions and answers to the situation as it unfolds during cross-examination. However, debaters should always approach the cross-examination phase with a general idea of what they might do.

The second key principle is that *effective cross-examination requires effective listening skills.* Cross-examination does not occur in a vacuum; the only way to develop appropriate questions is to understand your opponents' case accurately, and the only way to provide effective answers is to understand the question being asked. Affirmative and negative debaters must listen to their opponents' arguments carefully and work diligently to understand what they are saying and not saying. Effective listening requires objectivity; although debaters are advocates of a position, they must attempt to understand their opponents' position *as it is actually presented.* If you do not listen carefully to what your opponents say, it will be difficult to develop relevant and appropriate questions. We discuss the listening process and how to develop better listening skills in the next section of this chapter.

Third, *debaters must utilize effective questioning and answering techniques.* As the questioner, you should always attempt to ask simple questions. The more complex the question, the longer it takes to ask, explain, and answer. In addition, debaters can easily undermine the significance of overly complex questions simply by dissecting them into seemingly unimportant or even trivial parts or by providing restrictive qualifiers to their answers.

As the questioner, you should also try to avoid "killer questions." Rarely will a debater get a fatal admission during cross-examination. Thus, asking your opponent questions such as "Your case really isn't topical, is it?" "Your source is not qualified, is he?" or "Your plan really has more disadvantages than advantages, doesn't it?" will rarely succeed in doing more than wasting your time.

As the questioner, you should also avoid repeatedly asking questions that are restricted to a yes or no answer. Certainly, some questions can be adequately answered with a yes or no, and requiring your opponent to do so can be an effective way to use your time more efficiently. However, framing most questions in a "yes-no" format may not be a reasonable approach to take during cross-examination. In many cases, the issues about which your questions deal are likely to be complex and require more than a simple yes or no to provide an accurate answer. Make certain that you give your opponent adequate opportunity to answer the question accurately; after all, if the question is important enough for you to ask, it should be important enough to be answered completely.

As the questioner, you should also make certain that your questions are as clear and straightforward as possible. Make certain that your question is framed in a manner that can be easily understood by your opponent and by the judge. Use terminology both the judge and opponent are likely to understand and be as precise in your language choice as possible. Remember, the less clarity your questions have, the greater responsibility you will have to provide further explanation and the fewer questions you will ultimately be able to ask your opponent.

Fourth, *debaters must formulate questions effectively.* As the debater answering questions, you should make certain you understand the question before attempting to answer it. There is absolutely nothing wrong with asking your opponent to restate or to further explain a question if you really do not understand what is being asked. On the other hand, there is much to lose by answering a question you thought you understood and then finding out that the question you answered wasn't the question that was asked.

As the debater answering questions, you also should use context qualifiers with your answers as appropriate. By context qualifiers we mean any explanation or clarification necessary for the listener to properly interpret or understand your answer. If your opponent asks you to answer a question with either a "yes" or a "no" and you believe that such a simple answer would not adequately reflect your position, you should provide the context qualifiers *before* answering with either a "yes" or a "no." Thus, if asked "Has the number of people without medical insurance coverage decreased, yes or no?" you might answer that question by stating "*If you look only at private medical insurance* (context qualifier), the answer would be no." Doing this enables you to provide a more complete answer and decreases the possibility that your opponent could use your answer against you in developing refutation.

Fifth, *debaters should use effective communicative practices and maintain appropriate tone during cross-examination.* Although cross-examination is a direct interaction between opponents, it should be conducted in a pleasant and friendly manner. Debaters should avoid issuing personal attacks during cross-examination, they should maintain their composure, and they should attempt to keep the questions and answers focused on the issues involved in the debate. In addition, debaters should always be conscious of their receivers during cross-examination—their opponents and the judge. As much as possible, debaters should establish and maintain direct eye contact with both the opponents and the judge, and they should indicate a direct awareness of both during the cross-examination phase. Finally, although we have emphasized the important role cross-examination can play in a debate, that does not mean that the cross-examination period has to be a stern test of wills between two highly competitive adversaries. Cross-examination can be fun, humor during cross-examination can be appropriate, and debaters can demonstrate respect for their opponent without jeopardizing their chance of success.

Next, it is important for *debaters to understand the role of time limits during the cross examination period.* As in every other phase in the debate, strict time limits govern the maximum length of time allocated to cross-examination. Debaters should follow those time limits closely. But more important, debaters must demonstrate a respect for the time allocation. By that we mean that both debaters have a responsibility to utilize the allocated time in the most productive manner possible. Debaters asking questions should use the allocated time to ask meaningful questions rather than questions designed only to consume time. Some debaters feel that because time spent in cross-examination is "free preparation time," there is a "strategic" advantage gained by using all the time allocated for cross-examination even if they have nothing important to ask. Technically they are correct. Pragmatically they may do themselves and the debate process more harm than good by wasting time on trivial, even irrelevant questions. We believe that the most useful approach to cross-examination is this: Ask as many questions as you choose, but make certain that each question you ask has some direct and meaningful connection to the key issues of the debate.

Similarly, debaters answering questions have a responsibility to utilize the time allocated to cross-examination in as productive a manner as possible. Debaters answering questions should always assume the time allocated for the cross-examination phase is actually allocated to their opponents—the debaters asking questions. As such, the debaters answering questions should assume the responsibility to provide the most direct and concise answers possible. This does not require sacrifice in the accuracy of answers; it simply means that the debaters answering questions have the responsibility to provide complete, accurate, and concise answers. They should not seek additional clarification for a question simply to avoid providing an answer, nor should they provide overly complex answers and unnecessary detail when simpler, more direct answers would be sufficient. Similarly, the debaters answering questions should avoid the tendency to try to seize control of the cross-examination period and start asking questions. Each debater has an opportunity to ask questions and debaters should avail themselves of that opportunity only when they are designated to fulfill that role.

Next, *debaters must remember that cross-examination is not a speech.* During the cross-examination phase, debaters should attempt to gather information, lay the foundation for refutation, or expose weaknesses in their opponents' case. They should not use the cross-examination phase as an extension of their speaking time. In cross-examination, debaters either ask or answer questions; they do not construct and advance arguments. The debater asking questions should be particularly careful to avoid long prefatory remarks to a question or pointed comments about the implications of an answer. The debater answering questions should also avoid the temptation to provide unnecessary detail and explanation and to make editorial comments about the nature of the question itself. For example, the debater answering questions gains little by taking issue with the importance of the question.

There is another implication of this principle: debaters must remember that they must use the information they gather during cross-examination for that information to have a direct effect on the outcome of the debate. Debaters must take the answers they get and use those answers in their subsequent speeches to construct arguments. Even when a critical piece of information is uncovered during cross-examination, that information is not necessarily considered part of the formal record of the debate. Debaters enter information from cross-examination onto the formal record by using that information during their constructive and rebuttal speeches. Debaters can use the information gained in cross-examination as evidence or warrants for their claims, but they should always reference the information to the cross-examination period in which it was collected.

Conclusion

Debate is a communicative interaction. To be successful, debaters must understand the basic elements of the communication process and be able to incorporate fundamentally sound communicative practices into their advocacy. Audience analysis is one such fundamental practice. Debaters should assess and adapt their speeches to the judge to enhance their effectiveness as communicators. Similarly, debaters should always be aware of the importance of credibility. Debaters should understand how credibility judgments can be made in a debate and they should work actively to enhance their credibility. Debaters cannot be effective communicators unless they have adequate listening skills. Listening is fundamental in any communicative interaction and it is no less important in a debate. Debaters should follow basic principles to enhance their listening skills. Finally, debaters must be able to ask and answer questions effectively if they are to be competent communicators. Cross-examination is a critical portion of a debate. Debaters can become more effective during cross-examination by following basic principles as they formulate questions and answer questions asked by their opponent.

Selected Bibliography

Brydon, Steven R., and Michael D. Scott. "Listening to the Rhetorical Situation." *Between One and Many.* Mountain View, CA: Mayfield, 1994. 140–55.

DeFleur, Melvin D., Patricia Kearney, and Timothy G. Plax. "Listening as Communication." *Fundamentals of Human Communication.* Mountain View, CA: Mayfield, 1993. 98–122.

Gill, Mary M. "Knowing the Judge: The Key to Successful Debate." *CEDA Yearbook* 9 (1988): 96–101.

Larson, Suzanne. "Cross-Examination in CEDA Debate: A Survey of Coaches." *CEDA Yearbook* 8 (1987): 33–41.

Miller, Thomas H., and Evan H. Caminker. "The Art of Cross-Examination." *CEDA Yearbook* 3 (1982): 4–15.

Discussion Questions

1. How might you have employed audience analysis more effectively in a recent everyday argumentative interaction?
2. What types of information about the judge are most critical for a debater to ascertain?
3. What credibility-building strategies do you plan to incorporate in your debates? How might you implement these strategies?
4. Do you have a potential credibility liability in debate? If so, how will you attempt to overcome that liability?
5. In what ways might you improve your listening skills in a debate?

GLOSSARY

absolute causality   A situation in which a cause invariably results in a particular effect. Also called *sufficient condition.*

action qualifier   The component of a policy proposition that describes or qualifies the basic nature of the policy directive. Action qualifiers may specify the magnitude, location, or basic nature of the policy directive.

ad hominem fallacy   A fallacy of reasoning that can occur when we use the messenger as a standard for evaluating the worth of the message.

ad populum fallacy   A fallacy of reasoning that can occur when we use the popularity of something as a standard for evaluating its quality or as a proof of its truth. Also known as *bandwagon appeal.*

agent of action   The person or persons charged with responsibility for implementing and or operating the policy directive in a policy proposition or in an affirmative plan. Also, the component of a policy proposition that specifies who is responsible for taking the prescribed action.

alternate causality   A situation in which two or more causes may result in a particular effect. Also called *necessary condition.*

analytical model   An organized way or procedure for analyzing, reasoning about, and debating about debate propositions. Analytical models prescribe the critical questions or stock issues of a debate proposition.

argumentative constructs   Basic assumptions on which the process of argumentation and debate are founded. Key constructs include the *burden of proof, presumption, the burden of rebuttal, prima facie evidence,* and *a burden of proof.*

argument construction style   The way in which debaters fashion their case. Variables associated with argument construction style include the number and complexity of claims and the types, amount, and variety of evidence used to construct their case.

argument field   Developed by Stephen Toulmin, an argument field describes the context or boundary in which an object of focus is thought to reside. The argument field determines how, or by what standards, an object of focus should be judged. Argument fields may be defined either broadly as relevant disciplines, or more narrowly according to a specific purpose or function of the object of focus.

association   A cognitive process by which we observe the similarities between objects.

audience analysis   The process of assessing the receiver's needs and expectations in order to adapt the way the message is constructed and presented.

Backing   In Toulmin's Model of Argumentation, the Backing is the reasoning or evidence that justifies the Warrant.

bandwagon appeal   A fallacy of reasoning that can occur when we use the popularity of something as a standard for evaluating its quality or as a proof of truth. Also known as the *fallacy of ad populum*.

being   A proposition of fact concerned with whether an object of focus exists or whether an action occurred. The proposition, "Resolved: that the United States has a comprehensive medical care delivery system for the elderly," deals with existence.

blame issue   Within the traditional needs approach, this stock issue focuses on assessment of the relationship between the problem and the status quo. In assessing the blame issue, debaters attempt to determine the degree to which the problem is caused by or inheres within the status quo. In debate, this issue is usually referred to as *inherency*.

brief   An outline that supports a particular claim by detailing and organizing the arguments and evidence in support of that claim.

burden of proof, a   One of the basic argumentative constructs. According to this construct, every advocate has the responsibility for providing adequate reasons to support the claims he or she asserts.

Burden of proof, the   The argumentative construct derived from presumption. The advocate who opposes the argumentative presumption in a dispute assumes the responsibility for proving why an alternative belief or policy should be adopted. The responsibility is called the burden of proof.

BURDEN OF PROOF, THE   The corollary of **PRESUMPTION**. The burden that the advocate who initiates the debate must fulfill in order to gain adherence for the proposition. In the Holistic Model, **THE BURDEN OF PROOF** is a stipulated concept and must be fulfilled by the affirmative debaters.

<burden of proof, the>　The corollary of <presumption>. The burden that the advocate who challenges the <presumption> must fulfill in order to gain adherence for her or his Claim. In the Holistic Model, <the burden of proof> is a psychological concept and may be accorded either to the affirmative or negative debaters.

burden of rebuttal　One of the basic argumentative constructs. According to this construct, each advocate has the responsibility for responding to the case and claims presented by his or her opponent.

case　1. The combination of arguments presented by the affirmative or negative in advocacy of their respective side of the proposition　2. When used to distinguish between "case" and "off-case," case arguments are generally regarded to be those presented by the first affirmative speaker exclusive of the affirmative plan when debating a policy proposition or the value implications launched by the negative when debating a nonpolicy proposition.

causal reasoning　The cognitive process of determining whether a cause-effect relationship exists between two phenomena.

causal-circumventing　The steps of action contained in an affirmative plan that minimize the effects produced by the problem rather than eliminating the direct causes of the problem.

Claim　In Toulmin's Model of Argumentation, the conclusion drawn from the other components of the argument.

clarification plank　A component of an affirmative plan that clarifies how the affirmative team intends for the plan to be implemented, to function, and to be enforced.

clash　To challenge directly some portion of your opponent's argument. Debaters must clash with their opponents' arguments to fulfill the burden of rebuttal.

common usage　A method used to define a term by identifying its generally recognized meaning across a variety of contexts.

comparative advantage model　An alternative method for analyzing a controversy in which the advocate assesses the advantages and disadvantages that are likely to result when a prescribed policy directive is implemented. Like the traditional needs approach, the comparative advantage approach can be used to develop and organize the major claims for the rational component of an affirmative case.

comparison of germane values with potential countervalues   Within the issue agenda model, a stock issue requiring debaters to assess the likely impact of adhering to the values implied in the prescribed judgment.

compelling reason   A necessary quality of a disadvantage. The disadvantage must be significant enough to provide a strong argument for rejecting the resolution.

competitive position   A refutative position in which the debater argues that there are competing truths that diminish the importance or validity of the opponent's argument.

competitiveness   A standard for evaluating a negative counterplan. It states (1) that the affirmative's plan and the negative's counterplan cannot structurally coexist, and (2) that adoption of the counterplan produces a net benefit over adoption of the plan.

composite evaluation   One form of judgment in a proposition of value. A composite judgment requires that the object of focus be compared/contrasted to an opposing object with which it conflicts. The proposition, "Resolved: that protection of the national environment is a more important goal than the satisfaction of American energy demands," requires a composite evaluation.

conclusionary testimony   A quotation that supplies the source's conclusion, or ultimate claim, but does not provide any of the reasoning or data used by the source to reach that claim.

conditional argument   A refutative strategy in which two arguments are made: a primary argument and a secondary, hypothetical argument that applies *if* the audience fails to accept the primary argument. Also called a *disjunctive* or *hypothetical argument.*

conditional counterplans   A counterplan that the negative argues should be considered only if the negative's on-case arguments are insufficient to defeat the affirmative rationale.

conjectural issues   Within the stasis system, issues that concern matters of fact. For example, has person Y been killed and do the available data demonstrate that person X is likely the one who killed person Y?

constructive phase   The portion of a debate composed of the first four formal speeches. During the constructive phase, debaters advance their respective cases as well as initiate attack upon their opponent's case.

context   A test of evidence that evaluates the evidence by the amount and appropriateness of the background (or context) from which the evidence was taken.

contextual definitions   A method used to define a term by denoting how experts within a relevant field actually use the term and what they intend for the term to mean.

contradictory position   A refutative position that denies the opponent's argument.

cost issue   Within the traditional needs approach, a stock issue that focuses on assessment of the likely cost and outcomes of implementing the proposed plan. In debate, this issue is usually referred to as *disadvantage.*

countercausal   Steps of action contained in an affirmative plan that directly eliminate the causes of the problem the plan is intended to address.

countercontentions   Major negative off-case claims that create a prima facie argument for rejecting the proposition.

countercriterion   An alternative criterion usually proposed by the negative team as a substitute for the criterion contained in the affirmative case.

counterdata   An evidentiary attack in which a debater uses new evidence to contradict or subvert the opponent's evidence.

counterexample   An argument describing an example that negates the resolution.

counterwarrant   An argument that negates the Warrant of an opponent's argument. Sometimes used incorrectly as a synonym for *counterexample.*

credibility   Judgments about the believability of a source. Credibility judgments can affect the degree to which the advocate is successful.

criteria   The yardstick by which we determine what judgments should be made and how they should be made.

criteria-application model   The most fundamental analytical model for nonpolicy propositions. The model consists of two basic stock issues: (1) How does one make the judgment prescribed in the proposition? (2) Using that method, do the available data demonstrate that such a judgment about the object of focus is warranted?

cross-examination phase   The portion of a debate in which debaters engage in direct question and answer. In most cases, the cross-examination phase proceeds as follows: the second negative cross-examines the first affirmative, the first affirmative cross-examines the first negative, the first negative cross-examines the second affirmative, and the second affirmative cross-examines the second negative.

cure issue   Within the traditional needs approach, the stock issue focusing on the degree to which the proposed plan is likely to solve the problem. In debate, this issue is usually referred to as *solvency.*

Data In Toulmin's Model of Argumentation, the Data consist of the facts or evidence from which the Claim is drawn.

deductive reasoning A method of interpretive reasoning in which a generalization is applied to a specific case.

de facto reasoning A fallacy of reasoning that can occur when we ascribe a positive value to something solely because it exists. Also called the *is/ought fallacy.*

definition of key terms Within the issue agenda model, a stock issue requiring that debaters clearly define the critical terms of the proposition.

definitional issues Within the stasis system, issues that speak to the relevant definitions of an issue. What, for example, are the technical differences between first and second degree murder?

definitive issue Within the criteria-application model, the stock issue that focuses on development of the standards that will be used to make the prescribed judgment. In debate, this issue is usually referred to as *criteria.*

democratic ethics An ethical approach that evaluates communication by how well (or how poorly) it helps achieve the goals of democracy—that is, full and informed participation by each citizen.

dependent contention A contention that must rely on one or more other contentions or supporting claims to prove that the resolution or ultimate claim is true.

dependent justification Condition in which two or more claims must be used in conjunction for a superseding claim to be justified.

designation A proposition of fact concerned with naming or classifying the object of focus. The proposition, "Resolved: that the United Nations is an obsolete organization," focuses on the classification of the United Nations.

designative issue Within the criteria-application model, a stock issue focusing on assessment of the degree to which data demonstrate that the standards established in the definitive issue are satisfied.

dialogical ethics An ethical approach that evaluates communication by how well (or how poorly) it helps achieve the purpose of dialogue—that is, reaching genuine, trusting exchange between or among the participants.

disadvantage Negative off-case argument holding that a certain harmful effect will occur if the affirmative plan is adopted.

discipline-based construction A method for defining the argument field of the object of focus according to either the academic discipline in which the object is most regularly studied or the discipline of the preponderance of experts who deal with the object of focus.

discriminative listening   Through discriminative listening, debaters gather information and seek to understand their opponents' questions, answers, arguments, and refutation.

disjunctive argument   A refutative strategy in which two arguments are made: a primary argument and a secondary, hypothetical argument that applies *if* the audience fails to accept the primary argument. Also called a *hypothetical* or *conditional argument.*

dissociation   The cognitive process by which we observe the differences between two objects.

enforcement provision   A component of an affirmative plan specifying the penalties and mechanisms to be used to ensure that the provisions of the plan are adhered to.

evaluative listening   Listening that results in some judgment. Debaters use evaluative listening to judge the worth or merit of portions of the messages they process.

evidence press   An evidentiary attack in which a debater questions the validity or appropriateness of the opponent's evidence.

examples   Evidence that uses either actual or hypothetical instances to illustrate a point.

exigence   Within the issue agenda model, a stock issue requiring debaters to determine why it is important to discuss the issue embodied in a nonpolicy proposition.

external consistency   A test of evidence that evaluates the evidence by whether it contradicts the receiver's (audience's) experience.

fallacy of ad novarrum   A fallacy of reasoning that can occur when we use the "newness" of something as a standard for evaluating its quality.

fallacy of ad verecundum   A fallacy of reasoning that can occur when we use the "oldness" of something as a standard for evaluating its quality.

fallacy of composition   A fallacy of reasoning that can occur when we believe that what is true of the part is necessarily true of the whole. Also called a *hasty generalization.*

fallacy of division   A fallacy of reasoning that can occur when we believe that what is true of the whole is necessarily true of the part.

fallacy of extension   A fallacy that can occur when we utilize an irrelevant standard of evaluation.

fallacy of false consolation   A fallacy that can occur when we use an inappropriate analogy as a standard of quality.

fallacy of indignant language   A fallacy of reasoning that can occur when we use inflamed language as a standard for evaluating the worth of a message.

false dilemma   A fallacy that can occur when we present a choice that is artificially restricted to only two options.

false standards   A fallacy that can occur when we utilize an irrelevant standard of evaluation. Also called the *fallacy of extension.*

field-dependent   As used by Stephen Toulmin, a term applied to the criteria used to make judgments. Criteria are said to vary from argument field to argument field. Thus, the criteria one uses to judge a president to be "great" and a car to be "great" will be different; they are field-dependent.

field-dependent standards   Standards identifying the specific basis to be used in making a judgment. They are roughly analogous to a test the object of focus must meet to satisfy the criteria.

field-invariant   As used by Stephen Toulmin, a term applied to the force of a judgment. Judgments such as "good" or "great" are said to carry the same force regardless of the field in which they are made; they are field-invariant.

flow   A method of note-taking during the debate.

hasty generalization   A fallacy of reasoning that can occur when we believe that what is true of the part is necessarily true of the whole. Also called the *fallacy of composition.*

hypothetical argument   A refutative strategy in which two arguments are made: a primary argument and a secondary, hypothetical argument that applies *if* the audience fails to accept the primary argument. Also called a *disjunctive* or *conditional argument.*

identification of audience-centered criteria   A stock issue within the issue agenda model requiring debaters to develop criteria that will likely be judged reasonable and appropriate by their audience.

ill issue   A stock issue within the traditional needs approach, focusing on assessment of the seriousness of a problem to determine whether taking action is justified. In debate, this issue is usually referred to as *significance.*

impact   The part of a refutative argument that points out the effect of the particular refutation on the debate as a whole.

independent contention   A contention that by itself is sufficient to prove the resolution or ultimate claim. Also called *independent justification.*

independent justification   Condition in which a claim can stand alone as sufficient justification for a superseding claim. For example, a major claim might offer justification for an ultimate claim, or a supporting claim might offer justification for a major claim.

inductive reasoning A method of interpretive reasoning in which we draw a generalization from a series of examples. Also called *reasoning by example*.

inherency See **blame issue**.

inherent The property of being an integral and inseparable characteristic of a phenomenon.

internal consistency A test of evidence that evaluates the evidence by whether it contradicts itself.

interpretive reasoning The cognitive process of drawing conclusions from a combination of our experiences and the phenomena we are currently observing.

is/ought fallacy A fallacy of reasoning that can occur when we ascribe a positive value to something solely because it exists. Also called *de facto reasoning*.

issue agenda model An analytical model developed for nonpolicy propositions. According to the model, issues emerge on public agendas when they are determined to be sufficiently important to warrant consideration, deliberation, and action.

judgmental qualifier The component of a nonpolicy proposition that clarifies the nature of the judgment to be made. In the proposition, "Resolved: that the United States Supreme Court, on balance, has granted excessive power to law enforcement agencies," the phrase "on-balance" is a judgmental qualifier.

judgmental term The component of a nonpolicy proposition that specifies the judgment or evaluation an advocate is required to make. In the proposition, "Resolved: that the American judicial system has overemphasized freedom of the press," the judgmental term is "overemphasized."

jurisdictional issues Within the stasis system, issues that address the question of "who decides?" For example, if X killed Y as part of an organized conspiracy, charges may be brought against X in federal court rather than at the state level.

justification A prima facie burden of the affirmative case to be sufficiently complete and important enough to justify adoption.

legal model A model drawn from the judicial system and used to assign presumption and the burden of proof in a dispute. According to this model, the accuser in a dispute—the affirmative—assumes the burden of proof and the accused—the negative—occupies presumptive argumentative ground.

legislative model A model drawn from the legislative process and used to assign presumption and the burden of proof in a dispute. According to this model, existing institutions or policies are said to occupy presumptive argumentative ground.

linear progression approach   Negative argument that a disadvantage occurs in a linear fashion; implementing the affirmative plan will exacerbate or magnify an already existing problem.

link   The part of a refutative argument that connects the response to the opponent's argument it is refuting.

logic of good reasons   One part of the critical core of the narrative paradigm, consisting of approaches to test the soundness of arguments.

major claim   Broad ideas or arguments used to justify acceptance of an advocate's position about the ultimate claim.

measurability   The question of whether the occurrence of a cause and effect can be adequately observed and recorded.

message   The idea that a source communicates to a receiver. Messages may be intended or unintended. In argumentation and debate messages, the message is generally assumed to be intended and composed of a series of claims or arguments.

narrative fidelity   Within the narrative paradigm, the stock issue that is concerned with the plausibility of a story, or how likely the various elements of the story are to be true.

narrative paradigm   Developed by Walter Fisher as an "alternative paradigm for human communication." In debate, the paradigm places debaters in the role of storytellers and requires them to construct plausible narratives or stories for their positions.

narrative probability   Within the narrative paradigm, the stock issue that refers to judgments about the structure of a story—whether the story considered as a story is coherent and free of internal contradiction.

narrative rationality   One part of the critical core of the narrative paradigm, consisting of narrative probability and narrative fidelity.

necessary condition   A question of whether a single cause is necessary for a particular result to occur. Also called *alternate causality.*

needs approach   A traditional method for analyzing the issues of a controversy. This approach includes four issues—significance, inherency, solvency, and disadvantage—that can be used to structure the major claims for the rationale component of an affirmative case.

negation   A method used to clarify the meaning of a term by explaining what the term does not mean.

nonpolicy proposition   A proposition formulated either as a question of fact or a question of value. Nonpolicy propositions focus on judgments of either accuracy or worth.

object of focus   The entity that is being evaluated or judged in a nonpolicy proposition. In the proposition, "Resolved: that violence is a justified response to political oppression," the object of focus is "violence."

off-case argumentation   Negative refutation that does not directly attack the affirmative's rationale. In policy debate, off-case argumentation typically consists of the plan attacks. In nonpolicy debate, off-case argumentation typically consists of value objections, countercontentions, or counterexamples.

on-case argumentation   Negative refutation of the rationale section of the affirmative's case.

on the brink approach   Argument in which the negative demonstrates that the status quo is "on the brink" of experiencing the disadvantage and that implementing the affirmative plan will provide the final impetus for the disadvantage to take effect.

operational definition   A method used to define a term by explaining exactly how it is intended to operate. Operational definitions are useful for defining the policy directive within the affirmative plan.

paradigm   An extensive analytical model that not only prescribes the critical questions of a debate proposition, but also identifies the procedure or process that should be used in decision making. Paradigms often prescribe metaphors for the debate process.

policy directive   The component of a policy proposition that specifies the action to be implemented.

policy proposition   A formally stated claim about a specified course of action. Policy propositions generally suggest that a particular course of action "should" be taken.

post hoc ergo propter hoc   From Latin, meaning "after the fact, therefore, because of the fact"; a fallacy of reasoning possible when we assume that, because one event followed another event, the first event was the cause of the second. Also known as *post hoc fallacies.*

post hoc fallacies   See the preceding entry.

precision   A test of evidence that evaluates the evidence by the amount of detail it contains.

preemptive argument   An argument that attempts to forestall later attack by providing a response to a hypothetical attack.

preliminary component   Introductory components of an affirmative case, usually consisting of an introduction and preview.

preparation phase   The portion of a debate in which debaters have the option of utilizing time to prepare for upcoming speeches.

presumption   The argumentative construct asserting that current beliefs or policies will remain in force until sufficient reason is shown to adopt alternative ones. The construct was derived from the writings of Archbishop Richard Whateley.

PRESUMPTION   The argumentative advantage accorded to the existing order. Within the Holistic Model, **PRESUMPTION** is a stipulated concept and the argumentative advantage of **PRESUMPTION** is accorded to the person, policy, or concept challenged by advancing the debate proposition. In formal debate, the negative debaters typically enjoy the argumentative advantage of **PRESUMPTION**.

<presumption>   The argumentative advantage associated with the preferences, biases, or predispositions of the auditors of an argument. In the Holistic Model, <presumption> is a psychological concept and may be accorded to either affirmative or negative advocates.

prima facie   An argumentative construct meaning "on its face," or on first glance. According to the construct, the advocate who initiates a dispute is required to present reasons of sufficient strength to force his opponent to defend the presumption of the challenged position.

primary testimony   A quotation from a source who has firsthand experience with the subject.

proposition   A formally stated claim identifying the central idea that is being contested in a debate. Debate propositions can be either policy or nonpolicy.

proposition of fact   A nonpolicy proposition that focuses on judgments of accuracy—what is or is not the case. Propositions of fact may deal with three primary types of issues: being, designation, or relationship.

proposition of value   A nonpolicy proposition that posits an evaluative judgment such as "good," or "more important" about the object of focus.

psychological dimension   The evaluative component of argumentation and debate in the Holistic Model of presumption. Within the psychological dimension, receivers accord presumptions and burdens of proof to the various arguments and components of argument presented in a dispute or debate.

purpose-based construction   A method for defining the argument field of the object of focus by determining the specific functions that object of focus performs.

Qualifier   In Toulmin's Model of Argumentation, the component indicating the degree to which the arguer believes that the Claim is probably true.

qualitative issues   Within the stasis system, issues that speak to how the events in a situation might influence our interpretation of the act. For example, we may agree that X killed Y but conclude that X did so because Y threatened X with a gun.

quasi-policy proposition   A resolution for which the affirmative is expected to propose the action step of a plan but is not expected to meet the other plan requirements unless the action step requires an unusual commitment of agents, enforcement, or resources.

question of consequence   In the narrative paradigm, one of the components of the logic of good reasons. This issue requires an advocate to assess probable outcomes of subscribing to a particular value.

question of consistency   In the narrative paradigm, one of the components of the logic of good reasons. This issue requires an advocate to compare the predicted consequences of adhering to a particular value with consequences that have actually been observed when that same value has been adhered to.

question of fact   In the narrative paradigm, one of the components of the logic of good reasons. This issue focuses on identification of the implicit and explicit values in an argument.

question of relevance   In the narrative paradigm, one of the components of the logic of good reasons. This issue requires an advocate to determine whether the identified value is the actual value assumed in an argument or if some other value is more relevant to the argument.

question of transcendence   In the narrative paradigm, one of the components of the logic of good reasons. This issue requires an advocate to determine whether outcomes validated by experience enhance the individual, group, or society to the fullest degree possible.

rationale   1. The part of a refutative argument that responds to the opponent's argument being refuted   2. The largest component of an affirmative case. The rationale contains the major claims and evidence the affirmative team proposes to support their advocacy of the debate proposition.

reasoning from analogy   A method of interpretive reasoning in which we either (a) interpret an unknown situation based on a known situation or (b) compare or contrast two known situations.

reasoning from sign   A method of interpretive reasoning in which we conclude that a certain situation exists because we see a physical characteristic, or sign, that we have come to associate with the occurrence of that situation.

Rebuttal   In Toulmin's Model of Argumentation, the reasoning that yields the Qualifier. The Rebuttal consists of those situations in which the Claim would not be true.

rebuttal phase   The final four speeches in a debate proceeding in this order: the first negative, the first affirmative, the second negative, the second affirmative. Debaters present final responses to their opponents' arguments, provide the final defense of their own arguments, and narrow their case to the most critical arguments during the rebuttal phase.

receiver   The person with whom the source attempts to communicate. In argumentation and debate, the receiver can be an opposing advocate, a designated judge, or a specified public.

redundancy rule   A rule debaters can use to distinguish between a proposition of fact and a proposition of value.

refutation style   The combination of methods of refutation debaters employ and the various components of argument that debaters attack.

relationship   A proposition of fact concerned with a cause-effect relationship. The proposition, "Resolved: that third parties increase political activism in the United States," posits a question of cause.

resource provisions   The basic inputs such as money or manpower that will be necessary to implement the affirmative plan.

responsive   The responsibility of the negative team to meet its burden of rejoinder by responding directly to the case the affirmative has presented.

screens   In the Holistic Model of Presumption, a preference, predisposition, understanding, or bias that the auditor has about the subject, the nature of the arguments being presented, or even the process of argumentation itself.

secondary testimony   A quotation from a source who is an expert on or has secondhand information about the subject.

selective refutative strategy   A refutative strategy that focuses on attacking the weakest or most important arguments an opponent has made.

significance   See ill issue.

singular evaluation   One form of judgment in a proposition of value that requires a judgment to be made about the object of focus proper. The proposition, "Resolved: that John Kennedy was a good president," requires a singular evaluation.

situational qualifier   The component of a nonpolicy proposition that specifies the context or situation in which the object of focus is to be judged. In the proposition, "Resolved: that significantly stronger third party participation in the United States presidential elections would benefit the political process," the phrase "the political process" is a situational qualifier.

shotgun attack   A refutative strategy that attacks every argument the opponent makes. Also called a *spread attack*.

spread attack   A refutative strategy that attacks every argument the opponent makes. Also called a *shotgun attack.*

solvency   The issue of whether the affirmative plan (or adoption of the resolution) will in fact eliminate or reduce the harms delineated in the affirmative's rationale. Also called the *cure issue.*

source   1. The person to whom a message is attributed. The source is generally assumed to be the person who constructed and transmitted the message. 2. A test of evidence that evaluates the evidence by the qualifications, experience, and possible bias of the source reporting the evidence.

specialized meaning   A method used to define a term by specifying the meaning of a term within a particular field or discipline.

standard   A standard identifies the specific tests or conditions an object of focus must meet in order to satisfy a criterion.

statistical evidence   Evidence that uses numerical data.

status quo   The current state of affairs.

stasis   Originally from the Greek meaning "standing" or "standstill." In English, the term means "a state of balance or motionlessness." In argumentation theory, stasis is achieved when two advocates are arguing the same kind of argument.

steps of action   The specific actions the affirmative proposes to take in their plan.

stipulated dimension   In the Holistic Model of Presumption, the structural component of argumentation that functions to provide form and order to the argumentation and debate process. The advocate who initiates the dispute—the affirmative—assumes the burden of proof and the advocate who defends the existing institution or beliefs—the negative—occupies presumptive argumentative ground.

style of presentation   The way in which debaters explain and present their case. A debater's style of presentation is determined by the nature of the verbal and nonverbal components of their delivery, clarity of their presentation, and the use of organizational devices.

stock issues   Fundamental and recurring questions that must be answered if the receiver is to accept or reject the debate proposition. Stock issues provide a framework for analyzing the debate proposition and can be used as an organizational structure for the affirmative or negative case.

sufficient condition   A situation in which a cause is sufficient, in and of itself, to result in a particular effect. Also called *absolute causality.*

summary component   The concluding component of an affirmative case, usually consisting of an underview.

supporting claims   Ideas or arguments used to justify acceptance of the major claims an advocate advances.

suppressed major premise   A fallacy of reasoning that can occur when we do not explicitly state a questionable generalization.

teleological ethics   An ethical approach in which behavior is judged by whether it aids or detracts from moving toward a telos, or goal.

telos   The goal or purpose of any particular activity or entity. A telos is usually unreachable but is still something to strive for.

testimony   Evidence that directly quotes an authority (either primary or secondary).

timeliness   A test of evidence that evaluates the evidence by when it was generated.

topicality   A prima facie burden on the affirmative case to stay within the boundaries prescribed by the wording of the resolution.

topoi   Lines of argument.

traditional needs model   The most widely used analytical model for debate. This model prescribes four critical questions or stock issues applicable to policy propositions.

turn   A refutative strategy in which the debater admits that some part of the opponent's reasoning or evidence is true but then uses that part to justify a completely opposite conclusion.

ultimate claim   The overall idea argued in a controversy. In formal debate, the debate proposition is the ultimate claim of the dispute.

value hierarchy   An ordering of values, usually constructed in descending order of importance.

value objection   Negative off-case refutation arguing that if the value contained within the resolution is adopted, certain disadvantages or objectionable effects will occur.

voting issues   Those arguments in a debate that are critical to deciding which side has won the debate.

Warrant   In Toulmin's Model of Argumentation, the generalization that, combined with the Data, allows one to arrive at the Claim.

weight   In the Holistic Model of Presumption, the element denoting the intensity of psychological presumption and the degree of influence arguments assigned a psychological presumption are likely to have.

whole resolution argument   A position claiming that the affirmative must adopt the entire resolution as a general principle and not just a single instantiation of it.

INDEX